The
Dull Knifes
of
Pine Ridge

A Lakota Odyssey

JOE STARITA

With a new afterword by the author

UNIVERSITY OF NEBRASKA PRESS
LINCOLN AND LONDON

First Bison Books printing: 2002

Library of Congress Cataloging-in-Publication Data
Starita, Joe.
The Dull Knifes of Pine Ridge: a Lakota odyssey / Joe Starita; with a new afterword
by the author.
p.   cm.
Originally published: New York: Putnam, c1995.
Includes bibliographical references and index.
ISBN 0-8032-9294-5 (pbk.: alk. paper)
1. Dull Knife family.   2. Oglala Indians—Biography.   I. Title.
E99.O3S82   2002
978.3'660049752—dc21
[B]
2002017985

For fathers and sons,

mothers and daughters,

and for Jesse

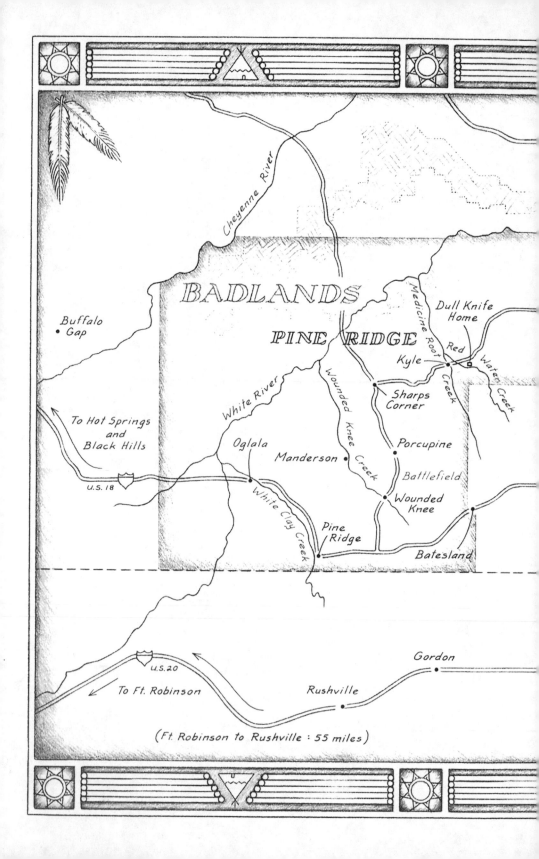

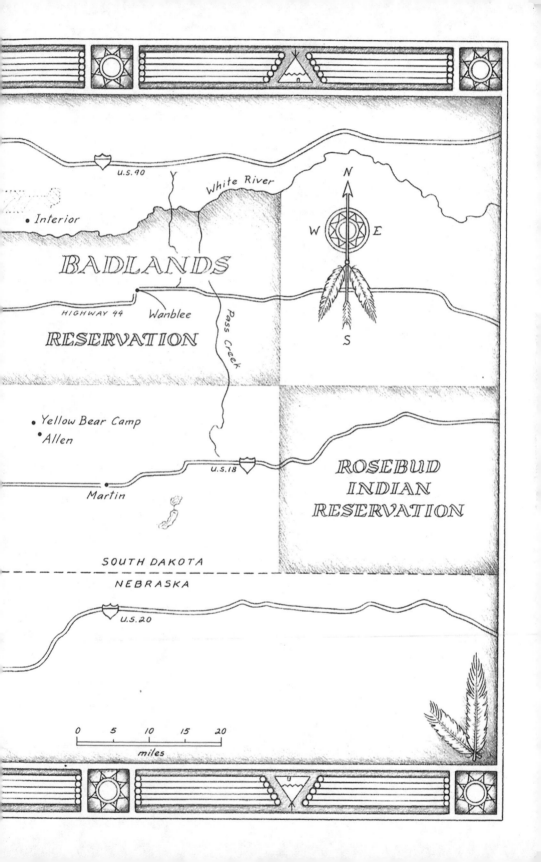

A people without a history

is like wind on the buffalo grass.

—CRAZY HORSE, OGLALA SIOUX

Acknowledgments

Many thanks are in order to the large numbers of people who contributed to this project. To Phil Krous, Judy Barker, Margaret Odgers, June Levine, Dan Ladely, Ben Gregory, Pat McLoughlin, Rich Lombardi, Bill and Kathy Steinke, Woody and Georgia Garnsey, Jim Starita, Judi Olivetti and Melissa Malkovich, whose friendship, good judgment and common sense helped keep the manuscript on course. To David Wishart, whose grasp of the subject matter and thorough reading of the text were invaluable. To Carl Hiaasen, Doug Clifton and Fred Grimm, friends and *Miami Herald* colleagues, who shared suggestions and encouragement from beginning to end. To Richard Ovelmen and Edward Soto, who provided documents and advice. To Jaime Obrecht and Bill Bowman, Vietnam veterans who knew the difference between a trenching tool and an entrenching tool, and a lot more. To photographers Ted Kirk and Bob Fader, whose technical skills spanned old photos and new and everything in between. To John Carter and the staff of the Nebraska State Historical Society, for their diligence in providing access to a vast array of photographs, microfilm, books and documents, frequently on short notice. To Tom Buecker, curator of the Fort Robinson Museum, for his superb knowledge of a place and time, and to the staff of the Sierra Vista Health Care Center, for their patience. To Ellen Allen, Custodian of Records at the Haskell Indian Junior College. To Will Norton and Michael Stricklin, at the University of Nebraska Graduate School of Journalism, for their support, and to

ACKNOWLEDGMENTS

the Hitchcock Center, for its generous Fellowship. To agents Steve Delsohn, Frank Weimann and Jessica Wainwright, who made things happen, and to editor Neil Nyren, at G. P. Putnam's Sons, whose steady hand kept it moving.

A special thanks for the two people whose importance to the project would be impossible to overstate: To Roger Holmes and Emily Levine, whose dedication, determination, and desire to get things right never wavered.

Finally, there is a heartfelt gratitude to the Lakota people. To Marcella Gilbert and her mother, Madonna, who was inside the village at Wounded Knee, and to Charles Trimble, whose brother, Al, spent a lifetime working for the best interests of the Oglala Sioux. To Charlotte Black Elk, Royal Bull Bear, Leonard Yellow Elk, Mel Lone Hill, Sam Loud Hawk and Richard Moves Camp, the people from the land who have endured forever and kept the traditions alive for the children.

And most of all, to the Dull Knifes of Pine Ridge, to the old man in the nursing home and his son and his son, to Nellie and Cora Yellow Elk, who for two years, graciously and patiently, answered questions and told the stories in tents and tipis, in cars and vans, at breakfast, lunch and dinner, in summer and winter, in the Black Hills and Rockies and on the shortgrass prairies of South Dakota, Nebraska, Wyoming and Colorado. *Mitakuya-owasin.*

The

Dull Knifes

of

Pine Ridge

Guy Dull Knife Sr.
(BOB FADER)

Chapter One

The Old Man in the Nursing Home

She doesn't quite know what to make of the old man sitting beside her.

Slowly and gently, he is speaking to her in the language of her people, but she is just learning English and so his words have no meaning for her.

"*Waste. Wicin'cala waste.*"

They are side by side, maybe a foot apart. Her tiny LA Gear sneakers barely creep over the edge of an olive army blanket spread across the nursing-home bed. She keeps looking at the old man and then over at the family across the room, her mouth wide open, her head shifting back and forth as if at a tennis match, her eyes searching for some sign that she is safe. She seems continually on the verge of rolling over on her stomach, sliding down the bed and running to the others, but right now she is too afraid to move, so she sits stockstill staring at the old man's face, at the black eyes, the high, flaring cheekbones, at the great hawk nose. Years ago, he stood six-feet-five and weighed three hundred pounds. Even now, she is dwarfed by his broad shoulders and thick chest. He is wearing a beige felt cowboy hat with an eagle feather stuck in the brim. His iron-gray hair, pulled neatly in a ponytail, hangs to the middle of his back.

Almost a century stands between his birth and hers and so he doesn't really know too much about the little great-granddaughter; knows nothing of her fascination with deep-dish pizza and Lego building blocks or the music videos she watched a few hours before the family arrived.

And she doesn't know much about the old man who is trying to make her smile with the funny-sounding words. She doesn't know of his old friend and neighbor, and the young lieutenant that friend saw coming through the dust and smoke on the east side of the Little Bighorn that afternoon. She knows nothing of his grandfather, the dignified chief and trusted statesman who had counseled peace, who cowered in the snow at the end, waiting for the soldiers, eating his moccasins to survive the last few nights.

She has yet to hear the stories the old man's father told him about the ride to the hill above Wounded Knee Creek after the shooting stopped; the lean years when he was a young boy in charge of feeding eleven brothers and sisters while his father was in Europe with Buffalo Bill.

Nor the stories of the mud and rain and mustard gas, of squatting in the trenches day after day, and how, when it was finally over, this old man, sitting now on the edge of the bed in a Colorado nursing home, couldn't vote in his homeland because the government that had sent him to the Great War did not consider him an American citizen.

There is a lot the little girl does not yet know about her family and her people.

For one thing, she doesn't know how happy he is to see her tonight. He takes her small brown hand and slowly draws it toward him, gently rubbing it against his face.

"Toksa. Le wicin'cala ni waste."

She hops down and runs across the room. The old man reaches into a drawer in the nightstand and offers her a stick of chewing gum. She runs back and grabs it, then quickly retreats to the other side. There is much laughter in the room. The old man removes the battered cowboy hat, smooths his ponytail and fingers a slender silver bracelet that his wife gave him fifty-three years ago. He looks up and smiles, satisfied that some progress has been made.

It is possible that Guy Dull Knife Sr. will live in three different centuries. Born February 17, 1899, on the Pine Ridge Reservation in South Dakota, he can see without glasses and hear without an aid. His hands are huge, his fingers fleshy. When he lowers himself into a wheelchair, the muscles in his arms are still firm and solid. His skin, a deep reddish brown, has the luster of a heart in good shape. And his appetite for meat, potatoes and sweets is the talk of the nursing home. The old man has the habit of crossing his legs, then folding his hands in his lap and rocking back and forth before he begins to smile. There are three teeth on the top row, five on the bottom. The staff that feeds him and makes his bed, that helps with speech lessons and an exercise program, likes to talk about the smile.

In his culture, the elderly are revered, and so Guy Dull Knife Sr. is a special case: He is among the oldest living Oglala Sioux and the sole surviving World War I veteran in the Lakota Nation.

A few months shy of ninety-five, he spends most days alone in his room at the Sierra Vista nursing home in Loveland, Colorado. There is plenty of time here to think back on the long life as a son, husband, father, grandfather and great-grandfather, soldier, broncorider, farmer, rancher, tribal councilman and respected elder, a life that has now consumed eighteen U.S. presidencies and five wars. There are the days when he is not quite sure what to make of it all. At one end are the friends and relatives who fought with Crazy Horse, Sitting Bull and Red Cloud in wars against the U.S. Army. At another end, friends and relatives who fought with the U.S. Army in wars against Germans, Japanese, Koreans, Vietnamese and Iraqis.

Inside Room 103—on the walls and in the nightstand, hidden in books and drawers and envelopes—he keeps the photographs of his family, of the five generations of Dull Knifes he has seen. A family that has gone from Custer to Hussein, from the Sun Dance to Holy Communion, from buffalo meat to pizza, from writing history on animal hides to programming computers. Sometimes, if he's in the mood, he will try and explain as best he can how it always seemed the same for each of the generations. Always the struggle. The sometimes desperate and despairing attempts to hold onto that part which made them Lakota, to somehow keep it alive, to keep it going in a century of massacres, disease, hunger, homelessness, poverty, alcohol, racism and corruption.

Yes, he will say, above all else, that is the thing that he remembers, the one that sticks out. Always the struggle to remain Lakota.

He was lucky, though, luckier than most of the people. His grandfather and father, his mother-in-law and wife did not believe they were a conquered people. They did not accept all the orders of the government agents and the preachings of the missionaries and the words of the boarding school teachers. Did not believe the Indian must die so the man could live.

When they cut off his hair the first time, he wept, then grew it back. When they outlawed his language, he spoke it anyway, in the old log house above Red Water Creek. When they forbade his sacred Sun Dance, he retreated to the far end of Yellow Bear Camp to fast for four days and nights, as his people had done for generations before him.

When the war came, he went to France with Black Jack Pershing, the sacred medicine bundle around his neck. A bundle like the one his brother would wear with Patton in World War II, his nephew with MacArthur in Korea, his son with Westmoreland in Vietnam, his grandnephew with Schwarzkopf in Desert Storm.

Even now, eighty-five years after the Sunday evening his father pulled out a knife and cut his hair so he could attend school the next morning, the old man will often introduce himself with a simple greeting: "My name is Guy Dull Knife Sr. I am Oglala Sioux."

His people, the Oglala, were once the largest and most powerful of the seven subtribes of Teton Sioux, prairie dwellers who lived farther west than the other tribes of the Great Sioux Nation. In their own language, Teton tribal members traditionally referred to themselves as *Lakota,* "alliance of friends." Over time, whites began referring to them as Sioux, the shortened version of *nadewisou,* an Ojibwa word meaning *treacherous snake.*

Pushed out by the Ojibwa from their ancestral woodlands home near the headwaters of the Mississippi in northern Minnesota, the displaced Lakota began migrating west and reached the heart of the

Great Plains about 1760. By the early years of the nineteenth century, they had become superior horsemen, skilled hunters and fierce warriors, commanding a huge section of the northern plains that at one time stretched from the Missouri River of South Dakota to Montana's Big Horn Mountains.

Among the seven subtribes of Lakota, where the warrior tradition had come to define their way of life, the Oglala counted many of the Sioux Nation's greatest chiefs. Red Cloud, whose raids had forced the U.S. Army to abandon a string of forts along the Bozeman Trail in 1868, was an Oglala. Crazy Horse, military strategist of the Little Bighorn, their greatest war chief, was Oglala. Little Wound, American Horse and Man Afraid of His Horses also were Oglala. So, too, was the Lakota holy man, Black Elk.

No matter how fast their ponies, how skilled their hunters, or how great their war chiefs, the eventual end was never in doubt. After a time, the bleached piles of buffalo bones lay white upon the shortgrass prairie. The Iron Horse cut through all their lands, and the sacred Black Hills, the place where the holy woman lived, gave way to the search for gold. Some of the people gave up and some fought on, but they were always hungry now and the soldiers kept coming, even in winter. The chiefs held out as long as they could. Then, one by one, they came in to the soldier forts scattered across the northern plains.

Of the 545 identifiable Indian tribes in North America, perhaps none was less suited to reservation life, to a sedentary farming existence, than the Lakota.

Room 103 is neat and clean, on the first floor, a large plate-glass window opening onto a sunlit courtyard. The door is open and in the hallway outside, a steady procession of the elderly drifts by in wheelchairs and walkers. Most mornings, Verna Ping drops by to see how the old man is doing. He still gets excited when he sees her coming through the door, the smile moving across his cheekbones, into the black eyes.

"Good morning, Mr. Dull Knife. And how are you doing today?"

"Fine, fine. How are you? How are you doing?"

She is the nursing home's speech therapist. They sit on his bed, side by side, chatting in the easy give-and-take of good friends. Most days, this is what he loves: to talk, to laugh, to joke, to tease, the contact of another in the often empty room. All the time she's there, he doesn't stop smiling, never takes his eyes off her. For a long time, the old man didn't know she was Chinese. He thought she was Sioux, or maybe Northern Cheyenne. Some anthropologists believe that there was once a land bridge across the Bering Strait, linking Asia and North America. They think the first Indian tribes migrated across this bridge about twenty thousand years ago. Sitting next to one another, back and forth with their joking and teasing, Verna Ping and Guy Dull Knife do not dispel the theory. The nonagenarian Sioux and the young Chinese speech therapist could pass for grandfather and granddaughter.

Last February, Verna and the others put together a birthday party for him. While he was taking his afternoon nap, they made a sign and hung it on the door outside Room 103:

Happy B-Day!
Guy Dull Knife
Congratulations on your 94th Birthday.
Best Wishes for a very special day.
With love, from the residents and employees of Sierra Vista.

They got three balloons—red, white and blue—and tied them to the arms of the wheelchair beside his bed. On the red one, they wrote HAPPY BIRTHDAY. On the white was a 9, on the blue, a 4.

When he woke up, he saw the balloons floating above the edge of his bed. For a while, he didn't seem to know where he was or what was happening. He had forgotten and didn't understand, until the staff came in and sang "Happy Birthday." While they sang, he sat still on the edge of his bed, staring at them, a little embarrassed, but smiling. After the singing stopped, Verna Ping walked over and hugged the old man. "Happy Birthday, Guy." When he started crying a little bit, she rubbed his back and stroked his head.

The staff here takes good care of Guy Dull Knife Sr. They have heard some of the stories and they have seen some of the paperwork and so they know the old man has had a life that is different from the other residents of the Sierra Vista nursing home.

On a beige wall above his bed hangs a Frederic Remington poster. It depicts a warrior, bare-chested, an eagle feather in the long black hair, sitting alone in the hills on a war pony. There is a braided rope of sweetgrass, its tip burned black, stuck behind a corner of the poster. Next to it is a small bundle of sage. For generations, his people have burned the sweetgrass to make an area spiritually pure. The sage, used in many religious ceremonies, is placed beside the sacred pipe. His people believe it will keep the bad spirits away.

Below the poster, lying on top of a nightstand, is the old man's Bible. It has a frayed reddish cover and the binding has come loose. "This Prayer Book given to Mr. Guy Dull Knife Sr. on Jan. 16, 1987," reads a notation on the inside cover. It is inscribed:

Father Bear's Heart
1969 to 1975
Priest-in-Charge
Standing Rock Mission, S. Dakota.

The Bible is opened to Psalm 24. "The earth is the Lord's, and the fullness thereof; the world, and they that dwell therein." One page is in English, the other is in Lakota.

On another wall, twelve color Polaroids of family and friends are carefully arranged in two neat rows. Below the color snapshots is a black-and-white Xerox of a photo. A caption is in the old man's wavering hand: "In Loving Memory of Bernard Moves Camp Sr."

Until his death on the Pine Ridge Reservation on June 21, 1991, Bernard Moves Camp was one of the old man's closest friends. He was a medicine man, as was his father before him. Bernard's grandfather, Chips, was among the most powerful of all Lakota medicine men. More than a hundred thirty years ago, a young Oglala warrior had a vision that he did not understand and so he came to Chips. The medicine man listened to the vision and, afterward, he told the warrior that in battle, he must always wear a whistle made of eagle bone and a middle plume from the sacred bird's tail feathers. He must also carry a certain stone with a hole in it around his left shoulder. It was this interpretation, according to the oral history of the Lakota, that gave the young Crazy Horse his great power.

It is said that Crazy Horse willed himself into a dreamlike trance before each battle, believed that no bullet could harm him, no pain was too great to endure. Four months after leading his starving people into Fort Robinson, Nebraska, he was bayonetted in the back while resisting confinement to an army jail. Mortally wounded, he refused a cot, choosing instead to bleed to death on the floor of an adjutant's office, on the land he could not live without.

To the end, he had preferred the Lakota way of life, its values, customs and religion. He was never defeated in battle and never signed a peace treaty. He never allowed himself to be photographed, sketched or painted. After he died, his parents took the body and rode north into the South Dakota hills.

The old man has heard the stories of the Oglala war chief since he was a young boy. His mother's people had lived in the village of Crazy Horse. His long-time neighbor, Dewey Beard, fought with Crazy Horse at the Little Bighorn. When the soldiers burned his grandfather's village to the ground one November, he found shelter, food and clothing in Crazy Horse's winter camp on the Powder River.

The old man pushes his wheelchair across the room and turns off a small black-and-white television by the bed.

"We Indians have no written records to speak of. The stories of our people are passed on from one generation to the next. Dewey Beard and my mother used to tell the stories. My grandfather told my father some of the stories and my father told me. Now I have told the stories to my son and he will tell his son. That is how it is done with the Lakota."

A nurse comes into the room and asks if Guy Dull Knife needs anything, some coffee, soda, some cookies maybe. She is young, early twenties, a bob of blond hair bouncing off the starched white shoulders of her uniform. A college student working part-time until school begins in the fall. He does not answer and she stands in the doorway, waiting for him to finish.

"My grandfather told my father that Crazy Horse always rode at the head of the war party. That he always rode out front and took the first volley of shots. This way, the warriors riding behind him could take good aim while the enemy was reloading. He had eight horses shot out from under him, but he was never wounded in a battle.

"He was a very modest man, a humble chief. Not the show-off kind like some of the others. He never wore a war bonnet. Always just a single eagle feather. A lot of the time, he was seen in the evenings sitting up in the hills or at the edge of camp. He was almost always by himself."

The young nurse repeats her question and the old man says no, he's O.K. right now. She bounces back out the door. His gaze is lost in the beige walls. After a while, he collects his thoughts and continues.

"One time, the white people wanted to buy our Black Hills. Some of the chiefs agreed and they signed the papers. But Crazy Horse did not want to. He would not agree to sell any part of the Black Hills. He said to tell the soldiers, 'You cannot sell the land upon which the people walk.'

"He was a great man, our greatest chief. More than anything, he loved his people and his homeland."

He is drifting off again. He does this a lot, mostly late afternoons. Too many thoughts, too many feelings sometimes. He will stop talking in the middle of a sentence. Or he begins a sentence about one thing and finishes it with another. Or he says nothing at all, instead staring at the wall, alone in the mind. Clips and fragments lost in this year or that. Lost in the hunger and cold. The tent out front. Buffalo Bill and the funny black horse. A bag full of silver dollars, a coin with the Eiffel Tower on the back. Grandfather eating his moccasins, hiding in the cave in the bluffs. The gas cloud rising up from the ground and then the smell. Of alfalfa, the second cutting, usually late July. The color of the *tinpsila*, purple tops on a hillside, the day he came walking home in his uniform. Sonny's best friend, bleeding to death on the roadside. The broncos at the Gordon Fair. Dewey's little girl, three bullets in her side, lying in the frozen creek bottom. His father's pipe, the red catlinite bowl blackened from kinnikinnick. Rose, beloved Rose, gone to the Spirit World so many years. Always there, sitting in back before the vote, nodding her head. Is Sonny coming? Will he come to see me tonight?

"More than anything, Crazy Horse loved his people and his homeland," the old man says again. "He was a great man, a great chief."

The staff at Sierra Vista, like many nursing homes, knows it is best not to leave the elderly alone too long. They drop in to see if there's anything they need and they try to promote a structured life, to give the residents something to look forward to each day.

MAY 28:
9:30–12—Petting Zoo.
2—Word Games
3—Manicure and Spelling Bee
4:30—"Primetimers" (Little Function Group)
7—Bible Study

May has been a busy month. There were spelling bees, exercise classes, bingo and word-power games, ice cream socials, a church brunch, a movie-and-popcorn night and several sing-alongs. They also went to a rodeo in Greeley, twenty miles to the east.

When the staff director first told the old man about the rodeo, he panicked. "No, no. No rodeo." He kept shaking his head. "I'm too old to ride. Too old now." The staff director laughed, and when they finally got it straight, the old man laughed, too. On a hot and muggy Sunday, he and about twenty others boarded a bus in front of the nursing home and went to watch the rodeo.

When he was a small boy, he had helped take care of the horses his father loved to race across the open prairie. When he entered World War I, he was assigned to the cavalry for a while. When he returned home, he rode broncos every chance he got. When he married, he tended cattle on horseback. After ninety-four years, his love of horses is undiminished, and the trip to Greeley was one of the better days he'd had in a while.

Some days he is talkative. Will talk all afternoon. It is hard for him to walk now, but he will put on a sweater and his battered beige cowboy hat, ease into his wheelchair and take the afternoon sun in the courtyard outside. He is comfortable here in the fresh air. He can see the Rockies looming to the west, and the sun seems to put him in a good mood. Like many elderly, he can recall in startling detail events that happened more than half a century ago, but struggles to remember if it was last week or last month that he went to the rodeo in Greeley. Some days, he will seize on a single thought and talk about it for several hours.

It is said that the Lakota medicine man Sitting Bull often walked around the village barefoot; that, in the mornings, he would remove his moccasins and walk in this way so that he could feel the earth, the soil, and the grass, beneath his feet. It was a ritual that gave him strength and comfort and one that continued to the end of his life. His people had never understood the *Wasichu* word for the lands where they lived. In Lakota, there is no word for *wilderness*.

The sun is warm, the sweater neatly folded across one arm of the wheelchair.

"I was born in 1899 in a log house, but my father was born in a tipi. His generation was the last one that lived in tipis. The tipi was in the shape of a circle and in the middle of the tipi there was always a campfire. This, too, was in the shape of a circle. In the summers, when the Sioux from all over the Dakotas, Nebraska, Wyoming and Montana would gather for the Sun Dance, the tipis in the villages would always be arranged in a circle.

"The circle was our symbol. It was a holy symbol that helped to remind us that we were connected to everything else. That if we were to live, so must the buffalo and the deer and the elk. Everything had to live. All the plants, the birds, the fish, everything. If something happened to any of them, then something would happen to the Indian, too. We would suffer. When we began to live in log houses, I think something bad happened to us and, in a way, we have never been the same since.

"When I was a small boy, you could go to No Flesh Creek and be sure that you would always catch a lot of fish. Now it is all dead. The fish are gone. Everything is different."

Sometimes he is not so talkative. His voice lacks the bitter edge that others have, but now and then, the words are blunt. Complex events reduced to simple language.

"First they killed our buffalo. Then they took our land. Then they outlawed our language and our religion. Then they took our culture and our way of life. Finally, all hope was gone and the dreams disappeared.

"After that, the only thing left for many was the whiskey."

Unlike some of his people this century, Guy Dull Knife Sr. did not lose his life in a bottle. As a young boy, he helped his father farm some of the poorest land in South Dakota. As a young man, he raised cattle and rode broncos in rodeos around the Pine Ridge Reservation. As a husband and father, he herded cattle, cut hay, raised chickens and helped make sure there were plenty of vegetables in the big garden outside the log house he built by hand in 1927. For thirty years, he served as a tribal councilman, lobbying for new schools, hospitals, police substations, sewer lines, roads and a center for the elderly. Tucked away in his nightstand are the letters from presidents Kennedy and Johnson recognizing his long commitment to the poorest community in the United States.

Then, too, his wife would never have put up with it.

The one time he and his friends came home with the whiskey all over them, she let him know it would be a bad thing to do again.

He met Rose Bull Bear at a dance near Kyle, South Dakota, in 1922. He was back from the war, somewhat shy and easy-going, a huge man who towered over the petite, proud, forceful young woman on the dance floor. She was a descendant of Chief Bull Bear, one of the Oglala's first great leaders, a strong-willed man who had been murdered by the young warrior Red Cloud in 1841.

In the years before the murder, the Oglala had enjoyed an idyllic life on the northern Great Plains of America. Their pony herds, swollen by repeated raids on the Crow, Arikara, Pawnee and Snake, were the envy of their enemies. Their lodges, reflecting an abundance of game, overflowed with buffalo, elk, deer and antelope. The Black Hills, rising high above the endless plains, had come to define the heart of their land. There were no forts and few whites to disturb the way of life. Many of the trappers and traders who journeyed into the land were considered friends.

During this time, the Oglala had divided into two main bands: the Bull Bear people, led by Chief Bull Bear, and the Smoke people, led by Chief Smoke, whose followers included Red Cloud.

In the early part of the 1840s, in another land more than five thousand miles away, a sudden fashion change set into motion a series of events that would have a profound effect upon the Lakota and the other Indian tribes living on the northern plains. The introduction of the European silk hat collapsed the North American beaver market overnight. With the demand for beaver pelts gone, the giant fur trading companies quickly shifted their attention to what would become the universal currency of the plains trade for much of the nineteenth century. Beginning in about 1840, and continuing for several years after, a bitter war developed among the fur trading companies for buffalo hides. The companies fought hard to keep their favored suppliers in line. Throughout, the weapon of choice was predominately whiskey.

Before 1840, it would have been unusual for one Oglala to murder another. During the early 1840s, it was not. Whiskey peddlers, aligned with one fur trading company or a rival, set up shop in

Indian encampments around the trading posts. For the Lakota, the results were disastrous. Like most tribes in the region during the early part of the nineteenth century, they had little tolerance for the white man's potent whiskey, and few weapons with which to fight it. Almost daily, suppliers with the American Fur Company or Pratte, Cabanne & Company made the rounds, handing out free bottles in the Indian camps.

By the fall of 1841, chiefs Bull Bear and Smoke were struggling for control of the Oglala. In November, Bull Bear and a few followers arrived at Smoke's camp along Chugwater Creek in what is now Wyoming. Liquor traders from the American Fur Company, headquartered in nearby Fort John, were already in camp. Before long, some of Smoke's warriors got Bull Bear's followers drunk, and a brawl began. When Bull Bear emerged from his lodge to stop the fight, Red Cloud shot him. A century and a half later, the murder still provokes tension among some descendants of Bull Bear and Red Cloud who live on the Pine Ridge Reservation.

The old man's wife was a fourth-generation descendant of the murdered chief. She was strong and passionate in what she valued, a stern woman with a firm grasp of right and wrong, who ran her household with a tight grip, believing that the day's work began when the sun rose and ended when it set. If Auntie Rose was coming to visit that day, the children made sure that the dishes were done, the toys put away, the floors swept, scrubbed and mopped.

He has not forgotten that unyielding belief in discipline and hard work, or her trust in the old ways. She maintained throughout that, although the people may have strayed in years past, there remained something pure at the center of Lakota life.

She knew the plants and herbs that for generations had taken care of snakebites and the flu, colds and fevers, indigestion and insomnia, knew about the small thistle plant that many now walked past, not knowing it would cure a bad toothache. And she never forgot what happened to her grandfather, Lone Bull, who was lured off the reservation and kept in a cage to show the people of Boston, New

York and Philadelphia what the savages who killed Custer looked like. It changed her, as it did her mother. Politically active when few women had the chance, the time or the energy, she wrote the speeches, stumped for the hospital, got out the vote, all the time, until diabetes made her too weak to continue. In truth, the old man will say, there was never any question. Through good times and bad, she was the one who kept things going, kept the family together.

Rose Bull Bear loathed alcohol. Had no use for it. Would not allow it inside the two-room log house where they lived together for forty-six years. This he remembers clearly.

"One time, this was back in the late Thirties, during the Depression, I was at a meeting and it went on pretty late. When it finally ended, me and several of my friends who were also at the meeting decided to have a few drinks."

The old man enjoys telling this story, his face and eyes brightening in the way that half a century of a good marriage can do.

"Well, one thing led to another, and before long the three of us, we were really drunk. We were having such a good time that we decided to take the party back to my house and finish off the bottle that one of the men had brought along with him in his truck.

"It was late and we figured that Rose was dead asleep. The three of us kind of stumbled through the front door and when I looked up, Rose had turned up a kerosene lantern that we had and was standing by the little wood-burning stove that we kept in the kitchen. Without saying a word, she reached down and grabbed a log and cracked me on top of my head.

"She knocked me out cold. I fell over and spent the night on the floor. The next day, she never said a word about what happened. She just went about her business and I went about mine. But that was the first, the last and the only time that me or anyone else ever came through the door carrying a bottle of whiskey."

When diabetes took her, the old man sat in the log house reading his Bible in Lakota at a kitchen table by the small wood-burning stove. He left their home a few months later and never returned.

. . .

Memorial Day dawns warm and cloudless.

Outside Room 103, the Rockies are hooded in caps of deep white powder. The light coming off the peaks of snow through the plate-glass window is different now. So is the air. Late spring turning the corner on early summer.

For weeks, in his mind and on a wall calendar above his bed, the old man has been working down the days. Usually, the room is still, the hum of the small black-and-white TV occasionally breaking up the long afternoons. Today, it is loud and boisterous, the long wait finally over. He is sitting on the edge of the bed, his head tilted downward, his chest and shoulders heaving with the force of his laughter. His son is sitting beside him, speaking to him in their language, and it is has reached the point where every time the son says something, the old man starts to laugh which, in turn, starts everyone else laughing. Desperate for some news from home, he keeps badgering his son, so the son tells him that all the husbands of his old girlfriends are dead now and that this would be a good time for him to return to Pine Ridge.

The old man lets out another roar and tries to catch his breath. After a while, he asks about Jake Little Thunder, an old friend from back home. He is fine, the son says. Then he asks about another old man, someone he has known for half a century, someone he never really cared for. The son leans over and tells him in a voice loud enough for everyone to hear that the old enemy has been made chief of all the Oglala Sioux. The old man starts in again, slapping his legs and pounding his son's back, his laugh filling the crowded room until a nurse arrives to see what all the commotion is about. She takes a quick look around, smiles and walks back out.

No matter how many spelling bees, how many rodeos, Guy Dull Knife Sr. is like most of the others at Sierra Vista. He misses his home. He misses his people. The longing to return to Pine Ridge, three hundred fifty miles to the north and east, is always there. Like most of the others, these are the days that keep him going.

He remembers the names of each of his six grandchildren and five great-grandchildren. He keeps meticulous track of their ages and birthdays. Keeps up-to-date on their health and how they're doing in school. He has known for weeks that there is no work or school today, and with a little luck four generations of Dull Knifes will be gathered inside his room.

The old man takes a sip of Sprite and reaches for the top drawer in the nightstand, pulling out a tin of sardines. He is addicted to sardines and crackers, and eats them almost every day, a habit that began during World War I.

Guy Dull Knife III loves his grandfather, will often ride his bike the three miles from home to spend an afternoon with him, but hates his sardines. Like his grandpa, he will be huge. Only 14, he already stands six feet tall and weighs 210 pounds. On weekends, when the family sometimes brings Guy Sr. home with them, his grandson will put a tape of the old man's favorite movie in the VCR, and the two of them will sit in the living room watching *Dances with Wolves.* The grandfather likes the movie because they sometimes speak his language. His grandson likes the buffalo hunt.

But the grandson cannot take the sardines. He is sitting in the old man's wheelchair, and when the first whiff arrives, he wrinkles his nose and begins to button his jacket, black and silver for his favorite football team, the Los Angeles Raiders. He walks toward the door, the POW-MIA — WE HAVE NOT FORGOTTEN visible across his back, then turns for a brief flurry of shadowboxing. "There he is," laughs the old man, "there goes the next Joe Louis."

Nellie, age ten, hasn't yet decided whether to join her older brother outside. She has the dark eyes, high smooth cheekbones and luxurious black hair of her people. Shy and reserved, she can disappear for hours, lost in the music of her Walkman. Mostly Billy Ray Cyrus and country-and-western. She doesn't like rap. "They use too many bad words."

Like her brother, she is no fan of the sardines, but she sits quietly, watching and listening to her father and grandfather carry on in the language that she understands but cannot speak.

Not yet two, Torrie Dull Knife seems oblivious to the smell, but can't quite take her eyes off the old man. She has a rubber pacifier in her mouth and every time she strays a little too close, the old man reaches out and playfully tries to take it from her. She stops for a moment and gives a sheepish smile, looking at each of the faces in the room. She has never seen anyone who looks like him and cannot decide if he is a kind man who will be her friend or someone who might invade her dreams at night. So she makes the circuit, scooting across the linoleum from grandpa to Nellie, from great-grandpa to grandpa, from Nellie back to Cora Yellow Elk.

Cora, the old man's daughter-in-law, speaks the language and, after great-grandpa, she laughs the hardest at the teasing and joking going on in the room. She got to know the old man in 1973, the year Rose died. He left their log house in the hills that year and moved to her home, to Wanblee, a traditional community on the reservation's eastern edge, to be with his son. She is the one who usually makes sure the old man is well stocked with sardines. Amid the laughter of the day, Torrie seems to favor Cora the most, hopping up on her lap at the first sign of trouble.

In February 1985, Cora and a friend were returning to Wanblee after work. It was dark and the friend hit a patch of ice and lost control of the car on a desolate stretch of reservation highway. Bleeding badly, Cora crawled out of the wreckage and lay on the frozen pavement for two hours until an ambulance arrived. When she awoke three days later at the Regional Hospital in Rapid City, doctors had removed both of her legs below the knee.

In the Dull Knife family home in Loveland, Colorado, her quill and beadwork fill the counters and shelves and table tops. Intricate and colorful patterns hand-stitched on deerhide dolls, knife sheaths, jackets, gloves and dream catchers. For beading, she uses the "lazy stitch" that her grandmother taught her mother and her mother passed on to her, and in the long months of rehabilitation, it was the beading and quilling that kept her mind off of what she had lost. That and her faith, a faith passed down from her great-great-grand-father, the Lakota medicine man, Chips.

She is fine now, bouncing Torrie quietly on one knee until the small girl is ready to move on.

"Is Sonny coming? Is Sonny coming today?"

It is a question the nursing home staff has gotten used to.

The old man cannot bear to be away from his son for very long.

Guy Dull Knife Jr. could have left his father with friends and relatives in South Dakota, back on the Pine Ridge Reservation, but in truth, he cannot bear it either, so when he moved to Loveland in 1989, he brought the aging father with him.

The son, an only child, is an artist, a painter and sculptor. For two years, he has been sculpting statues of the dances that once defined Lakota culture and tradition, statues depicting the Kettle, Horse and Rabbit dances; the traditional Eagle and War dances; the sacred Sun Dance. When he is finished, there will be eighteen in all, sixteen inches high, weighing fifteen pounds each.

After returning from the Vietnam war, Guy Dull Knife Jr. wanted to try and use his art to preserve the old Lakota ways, a way of life he was just beginning to understand. He wanted to sculpt the buffalo dance. But none of his friends could remember the clothing and movements.

"It was scary, worse than anything I had felt in Vietnam," he says now. "It seemed our entire culture had disappeared in a few generations."

In generations past, with their powerful ponies and portable tipis, the Lakota roamed far across the prairie in search of the animal whose migratory habits determined those of the tribe, an animal whose existence had become intertwined with their own.

Its hide provided shelter and clothing and the robes they could trade for knives, blankets, coffee, guns and ammunition. Its meat, lean and rich in protein, got them through harsh winters. The horns were used for ladles, brain grease for tanning hides, the hair for rope, tallow for candles, tendons for bow strings and its intestines for canteens. Boiled hooves became the glue for arrows, and sinew the thread for sewing. From its bones came needles, clubs, ornaments and scrapers. Dried or sliced, even the buffalo chips had a purpose. They became fuel on the treeless prairie, diapers for the children.

In the last quarter of the eighteenth century, when the British were losing the war far to the east, millions of buffalo covered the Great Plains, herds so vast they were often measured by area. It was not uncommon for a single herd to occupy a section of prairie forty-five miles long by thirty miles wide. Faster than a horse, weighing up to a ton, the animals were well suited to life on the flat, grassy plains. Where cattle were later found frozen on their feet, buffalo turned into the storm, facing the blizzard head on until it passed. A mature bull, six feet tall at the shoulder, produced enough meat to feed a family from late fall to early spring.

Each year, the most important business of the Indian camp was to follow the meat supply, and so when the buffalo moved from their winter resting grounds in the hills and mountains, out to the fresh spring grass of the prairie, the Lakota broke camp, too, following the herds across the plains, from the Bighorn Mountains in the west to the Missouri River in the east.

Along the way, whenever a kill was made, women butchered the animal and stored its meat in the earth. The hide and meat were best in autumn and it was then that many of the animals were killed. Camps were built along the river valleys, and women and children dug for wild turnips and picked the plums and chokecherries that blossomed in bushes and thickets beneath the cottonwood trees.

By late autumn, the Lakota began moving back to their winter camps in the mountains and picked up the meat they had stored along the way. They dried and pounded and mixed it with wild berries, then waited until spring, when the cycle would begin anew.

In the old days, before each hunt, the Lakota often held a dance to thank the buffalo that must die so they might live.

But by 1976, Guy Dull Knife Jr. and his young friends remembered little about the Buffalo Dance. Finally, he turned to the ones whose wisdom and knowledge are revered in his culture. The old people helped him. They told him how it used to be.

Today, the son feels pretty lucky. He never really figured he'd make it to forty-seven. In grade school, his own people used to tease and taunt him—"big, dumb Indian," "devil-worshipper"—when he spoke the only language he heard in the old log house in the hills. When he refused to go to religious instruction on Monday afternoons, they finally gave up and put him in a room by himself with his paints and brushes. He got in trouble, fought a lot and finally stopped going for a while, instead spending the day with his dog and fishing pole down on Red Water Creek.

In Vietnam, he arrived in the aftermath of the Tet Offensive. His army unit suffered heavy casualties, a lot of them going home in the black, zippered body bags. His first night back in the States, at the Seattle-Tacoma airport, the college kids threw eggs and tomatoes, so he changed his clothes for the flight back home. When he reached Pine Ridge, he put the uniform back on. His people slapped him on the back and stuffed his pockets with dollar bills.

Not long after Vietnam, a bloody civil war tore his people apart, traditional and nontraditional Lakota killing each other within the boundaries of the second largest reservation in the United States.

Outside the nursing home, the son almost always speaks in a low, gentle voice, so soft it is sometimes difficult to hear. Guy Dull Knife Jr. has the barrel chest and broad shoulders of his father, the same skin color and high wide cheekbones. His thick black ponytail is wrapped tightly and falls halfway down a black T-shirt, past a white POW-MIA insignia stitched across the back. Phosphorous bombs from the war have left a welter of bumps and red scars across his forearms. The eyes are dark and quiet. They miss nothing.

"After I got back from Vietnam, I had a lot of anger in me. A lot of the time, I felt I was ready to explode. I had been through a lot the last ten years and nothing seemed to make any sense to me anymore. Finally, I decided to try the one thing that seemed to make sense, the one thing I had any confidence in—my art."

Yes, the son will say, he feels pretty lucky to see six statues lining the shelf behind his workbench at a foundry on the edge of Loveland.

Each is cast in bronze and hand-painted—seventy-five to a hundred hours per statue—and each is dedicated to a special friend. One is for the old neighbor Dewey Beard, last survivor of both Custer and Wounded Knee. One will be for Eskra Fire Thunder, the hundred-year-old medicine man who helped him after Vietnam. One for Frank White Buffalo Man, who remembered what the eagle dancers used to wear. Another will be for Uncle Daniel, who went to Memphis one summer to sing for the King of rock and roll.

And one is for Byron DeSersa, Black Elk's great-grandson and his best friend, murdered at the edge of the Badlands.

The old man has stopped laughing now. There is something he wants to show his son, the thing that has him upset. He reaches into a drawer in the nightstand by his bed and pulls out a newspaper that his sister-in-law, Auntie Bessie, has recently sent from Rapid City.

On the front page, in the lower left-hand corner, is a large photograph of eight men dressed in war bonnets and buckskin. The photograph shows four Lakota warriors standing on one side and four Pawnee on the other. In the middle, wearing his trademark fringed jacket, deerhide gloves, and black leather boots, is Buffalo Bill Cody.

Standing in the back row, second from the left, is the tallest and youngest-looking warrior. He has two eagle feathers in the part behind his braided hair. There is a large silver medallion around his neck and an axe in one hand. A woolen blanket falls to the top of his moccasins.

The son and his wife and their children crowd around the old man sitting on the bed, the newspaper spread out on his lap. They study the face of George Dull Knife, the old man's father. The son goes out in the hallway and returns with young Torrie in his arms. He puts her on the bed next to the old man and points to the photograph, telling her in English and Lakota that the tall man with the feathers in his hair is her great-great-grandfather. She pays no attention, climbs down the bed and runs back into the hallway.

In the caption beneath the photograph, George Dull Knife has been misidentified, an error that Auntie Bessie has circled in red ink.

The old man is angry. He wants his son to call the newspaper and get it straightened out. The son says he will take care of it.

When the old man was a young boy, George Dull Knife taught him how to use the bow and arrow. He showed his son how to hunt deer and rabbit in the deep snow of the Yellow Bear Camp, a rugged section of the Pine Ridge Reservation where many traditional Lakota lived at the turn of the century. Back then, George Dull Knife was often away with Cody's Wild West Show, leaving his oldest boy to help with the feeding of the younger brothers and sisters. One winter they had to take the buffalo-bladder canteen and boil it in hot water for soup and broth, but they survived, and the rest of the winters weren't as bad.

For more than twenty years, after the trips to Europe ended, the old man's father worked as a tribal policeman and patrolled the eastern edge of the reservation on horseback. In the summer, his bosses on the western edge of the reservation would order him to report anyone he saw performing the Sun Dance. By then, Washington had officially outlawed the Lakota's most sacred religious rite. Its practitioners could be arrested and jailed, their family food supplies cut off for ten days.

For as long as any of the people could remember, the Sun Dance had been the most important event of Lakota life. In the summer months, tribes from throughout the northern plains would gather in large numbers for the annual ritual. It was a time of feasting and dancing, of renewing friendships and rejoicing in their customs and traditions. For the dancers, it was a time of sacrifice, a time when they offered their bodies to *Wi*, the sun, in the hope that their pain and suffering would make the people stronger.

Those who pledged the sacrifice danced and fasted for four days. At night, they went to the sweat lodge, a low dome of saplings covered in hides and heated with stones, to be purified. They laid out the holy sage, smoked with the red catlinite pipes and prayed for the welfare of loved ones. They wore ritual clothing and sacred ornaments, and on the final day, they faced the sun, straining against ropes of rawhide attached to wooden sticks skewed in their chests, pulling and straining until the skewers tore through the flesh and broke free.

Their sacrifice complete, their faith restored, the Lakota scattered back across the open plains, returning again during the moon when the turnips bloom, the moon when the cherries ripen.

It is said that when Bloody Knife and the other Indian scouts first saw the deserted Sun Dance grounds in the days before the battle, they became afraid. Sitting Bull had offered fifty pieces of flesh from each arm, and afterward, he had a dream of soldiers falling into camp. The scouts could see that a great number of Lakota and their allies had gathered on the Rosebud that summer and they could feel the power in the deserted grounds. They tried to warn Custer, but he was worried that if his soldiers didn't move fast enough, the people would escape. On the morning the cavalry moved down from the ridge toward the Little Bighorn, Bloody Knife wore his death clothes.

Throughout the long summer months on the eastern edge of the Pine Ridge Reservation, George Dull Knife heard the drumming in the hills and saw the cottonwood trees inside the sacred circle. He heard the eagle-bone whistles and saw the chest scars and he never told his son, or his friends, or any of his people, to stop. He made no arrests and never told his bosses. For twenty-three years, he turned his head and looked the other way.

At the top of the old Yellow Bear Camp, the high, flat prairie sweeps across the land for miles around. No one lives here anymore and, save for the bleating of a distant cow or a meadowlark's faraway call, there is no sound, only the wind rolling in gusts across the grasslands. In the middle of the vast knoll stands the old Episcopal church. Built in 1881, it lists badly to one side now and all the wood is streaked in slats of weathered gray.

Inside, rusted hooks where gas lanterns once hung jut down from the ceiling, sagging and buckling with age, a home to large flocks of pigeons, bats and swallows. The blue and white paint has long since faded.

From the doorway, extending a quarter mile to the west, two wagon wheel ruts cut through the tall grass, gradually climbing a small hill to the cemetery. When the wind blows hard enough, it flattens out the buffalo grass, and for a moment, a small white cross, its tip flecked with rust, pokes through the grass. The blue and white paint is mostly washed out.

George Dull Knife
Age 80
Died: Febr. 28, 1955

It has been almost five years since the old man last visited the top of Yellow Bear Camp. He can no longer make the climb and he is too old for the memories, but he has told his son that when it is time to go to the Spirit World, he wants to begin the journey beside his father.

The evening has turned pleasant, spring twilight on the eastern slope of the Rocky Mountains. The sun is an hour from dropping behind the peaks, its light turning pink above the tree line, across a jagged ridge of snow.

Outside the nursing home, a blue and white bus pulls up at the curb and deposits an elderly couple on the sidewalk. Several Jeeps with their tops rolled down cruise past, then a family station wagon and a red Ford pickup. Soon, there is the screaming whine of an ambulance and, not long afterward, a fire truck.

It has been a long day and Torrie is getting cranky. She circles Cora Yellow Elk like a pesky fly, tugging on Cora's blouse, throwing her pacifier to the ground. Nellie and Guy Dull Knife III miss their friends and want one last chance to make the rounds before it gets dark. They don't say anything, but they don't have to. They lean against the family's blue and white GMC van parked on the street, opening and closing the doors.

Nearby, the children of the neighborhood can feel the end of school in the warm breeze and there is a steady parade up and down West Eighth Street. A pack of them, teenage boys, pedals past the nursing home, turning on their bike seats to shout at a plump straggler who is running along the curb dribbling a basketball. He finally stops and flings the ball above their heads, the hooting and hollering echoing down the street. A pair of young boys, thirteen or fourteen, whirls around the corner on skateboards, clicking down the sidewalk, laughing and shouting in the gathering dusk, a few feet from the old Indian sitting alone on the bench.

The son knows how his father dreads these moments and he's trying to hold on as long as he can.

For the last hour, the old man has sat peacefully on the small concrete bench, his legs crossed, a blanket around his shoulders, his gaze drifting toward the darkening peaks to the west. In one hand he has kept a rolled-up magazine article that he occasionally uses to shoo away the bugs.

Anyone venturing into his room the last few weeks has been offered the article. "Here, here is a story about my grandfather. My grandfather was a chief." Someone, he doesn't remember who, sent it to him from back home and, like everything else he values, it is kept in a drawer of the nightstand by his bed. He has shown it to Stephanie, the nursing home's director of social services, and to Verna Ping, the speech therapist; to Dianne, the rehab aide, and to Kelli and Audrey, the nurse's aides.

It is a short article, three pages, and he has been trying to get his son to read it before the family leaves.

His son already knows the story, has heard it since he was a small boy. From his father and grandfather, his mother and grandmother. From aunts and uncles and the older cousins. A story that most of the people have heard many times. The story of a people who loved their home and their land, who missed the old way of life. Sick with the fever, freezing and starving, they followed their chief, walked back toward the place where their children were born and their ancestors buried. Many never saw the homeland again.

The son takes the article and sits down on the bench. When he finishes, he rolls it back up and slips it in the old man's hand. After a time, he stands up and moves around to the back of the bench, gathering the folds of the blanket and pulling it tighter around his father's chest.

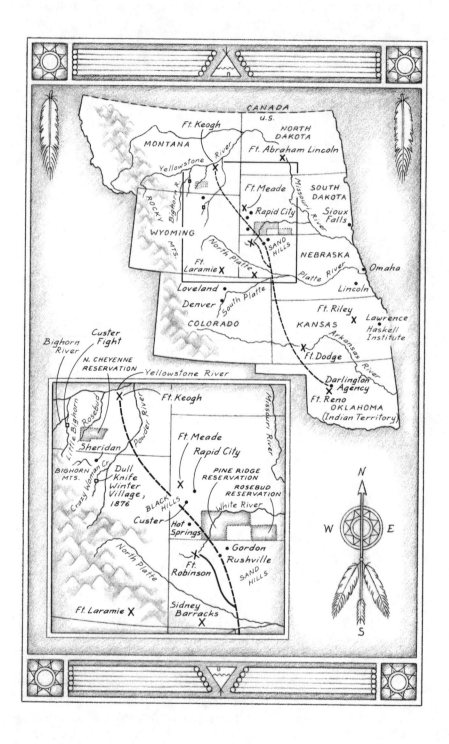

Chapter Two

A Chief Called
Dull Knife

On the morning of April 21, 1877, a long, winding column of Indian men, women and children began their slow descent from the rugged pine-covered buttes high above the Nebraska plains to the valley floor below, heading for the soldier fort along the banks of the White River.

Riding out front, at the head of the mile-long procession, was a man now more than sixty years old. He had the bearing of a leader, tall, dignified, square-jawed, thick through the shoulders and chest. In years gone by, he had been a great warrior, had devised military tactics and led the charge of the war parties. But for much of the last decade, it was usually his voice which counseled peace. Around the council campfires at night, he had said it was the only way they could survive. He spoke well, forcefully and eloquently, and he was often chosen to represent the people during discussions with other tribes, at peace parleys and in their meetings with whites. His wisdom and thoughtfulness, his courage and dignity, were greatly admired, and so he was made a head chief of the tribe and assumed the mantle of an elder statesman.

In the language of his people, the Northern Cheyenne, he was called *Wo'he Hiv'*, Morning Star. Among whites and the Lakota, with whom he had intermarried and lived for many years, he was called Dull Knife.

For the people in the village of Chief Dull Knife, the previous winter in the Big Horn Mountains had been the worst they had ever known. Everything had changed quickly after Custer. When news of the massacre reached the East, the people there could not believe it. Did not believe half-naked savages with bows and arrows could wipe out five companies of heavily armed U.S. soldiers. In its aftermath, the army began a final campaign against those bands that had not grown weary of the fight, that had not yet succumbed to the hunger and cold.

Throughout much of the 1870s, hunger and cold, deadlier than the Springfield rifles, Colt pistols and artillery fieldpieces, had become the weapons the Indian could no longer fight. The great herds of buffalo—slaughtered at first for traders, then by railroad mercenaries and finally as an instrument of government policy—had all but vanished, their numbers reduced from an estimated 50 million at the beginning of the century to less than five hundred by the end.

For the Indian, each winter had brought more hardship than the last. And each spring, more and more bands of plains tribes began drifting into the agencies near the soldier forts, where promises of fresh beef and clothing were held out as rewards for giving up the old ways. The Indian came to places like Fort Robinson, a soldier outpost on the White River.

Both Dull Knife and Little Wolf, another chief in the village and its most capable warrior, knew there would be trouble following the Custer fight. Some of their people had participated in the battle, and afterward, they moved deep into the Big Horn Mountains for safety and shelter from the winter storms.

That fall, Gen. George Crook, U.S. Army Commander of the Platte, had assembled a large fighting force to move against the remaining hostiles. He chose Gen. Ranald S. Mackenzie to lead the force. It consisted of eleven companies of cavalry, eleven companies of infantry, and four companies of artillery. A supply train of 168 wagons and 400 mules, attended by 285 drivers and assistants, followed the troops. Behind them were seven ambulances. In front, rode more than four hundred Indian scouts, mostly Pawnee, Shoshoni and Crow, men who now tracked their old enemies on behalf of the government that fed and clothed them. All told, more than two thousand men set out from Fort Fetterman, Wyoming Territory, in mid-November.

At dawn on the morning of November 25, 1876, five months after the Little Bighorn, General Mackenzie attacked Dull Knife's sleeping village near the head of Crazy Woman's Fork of the Powder River in what is now northern Wyoming. When the first volley was fired, the warriors quickly formed a skirmish line against the attackers, while Little Wolf led the evacuation of women and children through a driving snowstorm. Wounded seven times during the fight, Little Wolf held his position until the women and children reached the protective bluffs above their camp. The battle raged most of the day, but by nightfall the village was lost. From the bluffs overhead, the Indians watched as their lodges, clothing, cooking utensils and winter food supplies were piled high and set on fire. They had lost 25 dead, 173 tipis and more than 500 ponies. That night, Dull Knife and Little Wolf and the rest of the survivors fled to the north and east, deeper into the Bighorn Mountains.

Many had little clothing as they marched through the mountain snow drifts. Their first night out, the temperature dropped to 30 below, and eleven infants froze to death. On the second night, warriors shot several of the remaining horses and gutted them, then placed many of the smaller children inside the disembowled animals. · Some of the old people stuck their hands and feet beside the children to keep them from freezing. Several days later, the survivors found refuge in the winter camp of Crazy Horse's Oglala Sioux on the Powder River.

All his life, the Powder River country, the mountains of Wyoming and Montana, had been Dull Knife's home. He had been born there, in the Rosebud Valley, and for many years afterward, few whites had ever seen the rugged peaks, freshwater rivers and valleys of buffalo that defined his homeland.

While still a young boy, he had shown an uncommon bravery, and so his people believed the mark was there from an early age. Passed from generation to generation is the story of the nine-year-old who was playing in the river with his family one summer when a buffalo herd stampeded across. While his mother climbed a tree, the boy swam to his sister and pulled her to an abandoned beaver lodge, then stayed inside the shelter with her until the herd had safely passed. Years later, when his hungry people were caught in a winter storm, he helped organize a relief party that traveled a hundred fifty miles in search of wild game. The hunting party returned to camp with bales of fresh buffalo meat tied to their packhorses.

When the boy became a young man, he followed the warrior tradition of his people and joined the other young men in raids against the Crow, Arikara, Snake and Shoshoni, earning a reputation for fierceness and courage that the elders of his tribe began to notice.

Later, as more and more whites began pushing into their homeland, Dull Knife and his warriors joined the Sioux in wars against a string of forts cutting through the heart of their last great hunting ground. On December 21, 1866, he and Crazy Horse led a decoy party that lured Capt. William Fetterman away from Fort Phil Kearny. The pursuing troops followed the decoys into a trap and a larger war party lying in wait massacred Fetterman and all eighty-one of his men.

Although his warriors had won the battle, Dull Knife began to feel that winning a war against the whites was hopeless. Not long after the Fetterman fight, he, like many chiefs on the northern plains, found himself in a difficult position. If his people continued to fight, they would eventually be wiped out. If they surrendered, they would lose their homeland and their way of life. More and more, Dull Knife began to tell his people that the whites were too many and too powerful, that the only way they could survive was to try and live in peace. He was a gifted orator and a skillful negotiator, and so he began to visit the forts, talking to the soldiers, attending peace parleys, looking for a way out for his people.

In 1868, he was among the chiefs who signed the historic Fort Laramie Treaty, a treaty that set aside the sacred Black Hills and the western half of South Dakota for the Indian people in exchange for peace. At the signing ceremony, he agreed never again to "sharpen his knife" against the whites. Dull Knife kept his word. Eight years lager, while others of his tribe left for the great fight on the Little Bighorn, he and Little Wolf stayed in their camps a few miles southwest of the battle.

Col. George A. Woodward, a commander of Fort Fetterman, had met Dull Knife and Little Wolf when they visited his post in the spring of 1871. Years later, he remembered their meeting: "Of the three head-men of the Cheyennes, Dull Knife was, I think, greatly the superior. Tall and lithe in form, he had the face of a statesman or church dignitary of the grave and aesthetic type. His manner of speech was earnest and dignified, and his whole bearing was that of a leader with the cares of state. Little Wolf had a less imposing presence, but looked more the soldier than the statesman."

Now, on this early spring morning in late April of 1877, General Crook and General Mackenzie stood waiting for Dull Knife and his people as they rode down from the bluffs, into the fort along the White River. Riding behind their chief, the different warrior societies—Kit Fox, Crazy Dog, and the Elkhorn Scrapers—were aligned in tight formation, a white flag fluttering above the first company of warriors. Behind them came the women and children and the old people. Then the horse-drawn travoises carrying what was left of their belongings. They were followed by the pony herd. Bringing up the rear, as was their tradition, were the Dog Soldiers, the elite warrior corps who always served as the rear guard, as the first line of defense, men who were honored to die protecting their people.

As the Indians drew closer, soldiers who had fought them for years were sickened by what they saw. For weeks, the people had survived on horse meat and many were emaciated, their legs and arms mostly bone, gaunt faces hollowed out from the hunger. The ribs of the horses were flattened tight against thin hides. The riders wore little more than rags, and the flesh of many was blackened, eaten away by frostbite. Many arrived with knife and gunshot wounds that had never healed. Lt. John G. Bourke, the aide-de-camp for General Crook, later examined them and concluded that they had been wounded in "a horrible manner." Wounds that "would keep an American soldier in bed for months."

Chief Dull Knife brought the procession into the fort and stopped directly in front of General Crook. He and the other leaders stepped down from their horses, shook the general's hand, and then, one by one, they began to hand over their weapons. When they finished, 68 rifles, 34 pistols, and 14 bows lay on the ground. Several soldiers began a head count. According to the official log, 554 Indians came into the fort that day. By late afternoon, when they had turned over the last of their pony herd, the surrender was complete.

Dull Knife assumed his people would be allowed to stay on the northern plains, their homeland, with the Oglala Sioux at the nearby Red Cloud Agency. The Oglala were their friends, their relatives. For several generations, they had hunted the same lands, wintered in the same mountains, fought the same enemies, adopted many of the same customs, dress and rituals. Northern Cheyenne women had married Oglala men. Oglala women married Northern Cheyennes. Their relationship was a close one.

Almost ten years earlier, the powerful Oglala chief, Red Cloud, had also signed the Fort Laramie Treaty. Among other things, it provided Red Cloud and his followers with a place to live. It guaranteed each Indian over the age of four a pound of beef and a pound of flour a day, plus coffee, sugar, clothing, cooking utensils and canvas tipis for each Indian family. The treaty had created the Red Cloud Agency. And in turn, as was the custom then, the agency had created Camp Robinson, which was later changed to Fort Robinson. Like other agencies scattered across the Great Plains, this was the place where government annuities promised in the peace treaties would be dispensed: the seeds for the new reservation way of life.

But the late April arrival of Chief Dull Knife and his village had swollen the number of Lakota Sioux and Northern Cheyenne gathered at the Red Cloud Agency to more than five thousand.

Then, on May 6, 1877, riding at the head of a two-mile-long procession that stretched across the plains and into the valley, Crazy

Horse surrendered 899 of his Oglala Sioux at the fort. The presence of the Lakota's great war chief created a stir among Indian and soldier alike, and soon General Crook's orders arrived from Washington: Dull Knife's people were to be moved south, to the Indian Territory that would become Oklahoma. They were to join their cousins down there—the Southern Cheyenne—as soon as possible.

Dull Knife and Little Wolf could not believe what they heard. Four years earlier, in November 1873, they and other headmen of the tribe had agreed to board a Union Pacific train in Wyoming Territory and journey to Washington, D.C., to meet the president. When the topic came up, they had told President Grant and the secretary of the interior and the commissioner of Indian affairs that they could not imagine leaving the north country, could not imagine living away from their homeland. The Fort Laramie Treaty, they said, gave them the option of staying in the north with Red Cloud's Sioux. The president and his men said there was never any option. The translator must have misunderstood and given them bad information, they said. Dull Knife and Little Wolf walked out of the meeting, got back on the train and went home.

All of this they repeated again in the spring of 1877, but General Crook was insistent. He told Dull Knife and Little Wolf that it would be good for them to be reunited with the southern half of their tribe. That they could start a new life, become farmers and live in peace on their reservation in the south. There would be new wagons, horses and plows, and gifts for all the chiefs. Crook's superior, Lt. Gen. Philip H. Sheridan, told them that, unlike in the north, they would not have to worry about food. Down south, he said, there was more than enough food. The game was plentiful and they could hunt wild turkey and buffalo, as in the old days.

Despite the assurances, Dull Knife and Little Wolf told the soldiers that they did not want to go. Finally, government authorities told them that if they were still unhappy at the end of a year, they could return north. But for now, they had no choice. They had to go. Confused, afraid and dispirited, they agreed to the move.

· · ·

Early on the morning of May 28, 1877, Dull Knife, Little Wolf and 931 Northern Cheyenne began to fall in line for the long march south.

The military escort, led by Lt. Henry W. Lawton, U.S. Fourth Cavalry, moved to the front of the line. Behind them, Dull Knife and Little Wolf rode slowly until they reached the head of their people. Resting in the crook of their left forearms, signifying their role as chiefs, were the traditional long-stemmed pipes used to bless the people, to pray for a safe journey.

On Lieutenant Lawton's signal, the column began to move out to the open plains. There were wagons for the old and the sick and the poor. There was a supply train and a soldier detail to guard it. Bringing up the rear was a herd of cattle to be slaughtered en route, fresh meat that would keep the hunger at bay.

They were to head down the western rim of the Nebraska high plains, near the edge of the desolate Sandhills, then angle across the Kansas prairie and into Oklahoma.

The lands they passed through during the first few weeks were ones Dull Knife and his people had known all their lives. They knew the rivers and valleys and streams, the rock formations that had signaled a certain point on the journey. The old people had used the stars to move across these lands at night. They camped here, hunted here and fought here. The young were born here and it was where they had buried their dead. Although the land was still familiar, it had changed, it looked different.

After the Civil War, the Great Plains had been overrun with adventurers seeking their fortunes in gold, mining, ranching, farming and hunting. There were cattle now, and some barbed wire. A few villages and towns, ranches and farm homes. Part of the grasslands were plowed under, the crops an occasional checkerboard across the prairie. Telegraph lines sometimes crisscrossed the open spaces, while steel rails cut through the heart of the Platte River Valley. And the plains had been swept of the buffalo.

36

Not long into the journey, Dull Knife and Little Wolf had received permission to go on a buffalo hunt. As in the old days, the chiefs gathered the leaders of the warrior societies together and each selected ten men from his group. Lawton gave them rifles and ammunition and they rode out in search of the buffalo. As they pushed farther south, the buffalo disappeared.

For years, professional hunters had made a living wiping out the animal the Plains Indian needed to survive. Armed with newly developed heavy-caliber guns and repeating rifles, the hunters crept to the edge of a herd and shot thousands in a few hours, dousing their barrels with water when they overheated. Between 1872 and 1876, more than 6 million buffalo were killed on the Great Plains, a slaughter eventually encouraged by the military as the fastest and cheapest way of forcing the Indian off their sacred lands and onto reservations.

"The white hide hunters have done more in the last two years to settle the vexing Indian question than the entire regular army has done in the past thirty years," said Lieutenant General Sheridan. "They are destroying the Indians' commissary. For the sake of lasting peace, let them kill, skin and sell until the buffalo are exterminated. Then your prairies can be covered with speckled cattle and the festive cowboy."

On August 5, 1877, after a journey of seventy days, Dull Knife and Little Wolf led their people into the new homeland in the south, the Darlington Agency, Indian Territory, just outside of Fort Reno. The procession that came into the agency that day included 235 men, 312 women and 386 children.

At first, during the initial few weeks, the move did not seem so bad. It was good to have the long trek over. It was good to see long-lost relatives and renew old friendships and acquaintances. There was dancing and singing and some feasts for the new arrivals.

But it didn't last.

Before long, hostilities developed between the Northern and

Southern Cheyenne. The two groups had separated more than thirty years earlier and had little in common. The southern tribe, which had lived on the reservation for several years, felt threatened by the new arrivals. They called them "fools" and "Sioux" and asked them why they came. The northern tribe retreated to a hill twelve miles above the fort, near the Canadian River, and lived by themselves.

Alone in their camp, they felt that the change in climate was overwhelming.

Dull Knife and his people had never known the kind of heat and humidity that now rose like a cloud from the scorched Oklahoma prairie. They had never seen the swarms of flies and mosquitoes that covered the riverbottoms, nor the ticks that infested the trees and bushes. They had come from the north, lived there all their lives, and so they had become accustomed to the high, dry climate of their homeland.

Within weeks, many in the tribe became ill. The old people got fever and chills, the ague. Soon, some of the children began to break out in red rashes, their faces spotted, their noses bleeding. Not long afterward came the first cases of the disease that mosquitoes carried. In the north, measles and malaria had been unknown to them.

Chief Dull Knife visited the lodges of his people that summer. He saw the sickness and he heard their voices and he felt the same way.

On August 31, 1877, John D. Miles, United States Indian Agent at the Darlington Agency, filed a report to his superiors summing up his impression of the new arrivals:

"It is not singular that we should find among them a feeling of distrust, as it has been a very short time since they were in open hostility to the whites, and many of them are now mourning the loss of sons and brothers in battle, and others are suffering from wounds received in battle against the whites. It will require time, firm and just treatment, to win their confidence, and when this is gained, I shall expect progress."

In addition to his duties as agent, Miles maintained two other enterprises at Darlington: He was part-owner of the agency's only

Indian trading company, and he had a financial interest in a large cattle herd. The trading company charged Indians three times what they charged whites and did a brisk liquor business. He permitted the cattle herd to graze on reservation lands.

By the end of September, less than a month after his report, many of the women and children were suffering from a problem they had not expected when they arrived from the north. They were starving.

The food promised in the treaties did not arrive, or it was always short. The regular issue was three pounds of beef for each family member per week, but sometimes there were only two cows for sixty-eight people. Often, the cows were small and underweight and the meat was consumed in three days, leaving nothing to eat until the following week. Corn and flour did not arrive at all and neither did the hard bread, hominy, rice, beans or salt. Coffee and sugar came sporadically.

That same month, September, Agent Miles ordered the chiefs to start sending their children to the agency schools. At first, Dull Knife and Wild Hog, leader of the Elkhorn Scrapers warrior society, refused. After Miles threatened to withold their food rations, they relented, and their children began instruction in the white man's ways.

Some of the children had also begun religious instruction. Agent Miles was pleased. Of the Christian efforts, he wrote, ". . . and although we see but little fruit just now, yet I have faith to believe that 'bait' is now being scattered that will eventually attract many souls into the 'Gospel net.' "

As winter approached, the hunger became more acute, and to ease the food shortage, Miles permitted a number of Indians to leave the agency in search of wild game.

On November 15, a large Indian party rode out of Darlington to look for buffalo. While they were out hunting, many of their ponies were stolen by horse thieves. They found but a few buffalo, and it was only by shooting and eating some of their remaining ponies that they managed to survive until rescue parties from the fort were able to bring the hunters home. When they returned, the food rations they were due while out on the hunt had not arrived.

That year, fifty-eight who had come from the north died of starvation and disease. Some were young men and women and some were the old people. Most were children.

"They gave us corn meal ground with the cob such as a man feeds his mules, some salt and one beef for forty-six persons to last for seven days," Wild Hog said later. "We ate it in three and starve in four days. . . . A great many starved to death. We had goods and provisions in our commissary, but our agent used them. The grass was so poor, our horses died, and there was no wood."

In the spring of 1878, a measles epidemic swept through the Indian camps of the Darlington Agency. By early summer, Agent Miles estimated that at least 2,000 of the agency's 5,004 Indians were diseased. There was one physician, Dr. L. A. E. Hodge, and he had no medicine. Medical supplies had been requested on May 12, but did not arrive until January 17, 1879.

For Dull Knife's people, worse than the lack of food and medicine, the unfulfilled treaties and punishing climate, the death and disease, was another sickness.

The Northern Cheyenne leader Little Chief later spoke of the feeling that many shared after their forced removal to the Indian Territory.

"I have been sick a great deal of the time since I have been down here—homesick and heartsick, and sick in every way. I have been thinking of my native country and the good home I had up there, where I never was hungry, but when I wanted anything to eat could go out and hunt the buffalo. . . . It does not make me feel good to hang about an agency and have to ask a white man for something to eat when I get hungry."

Wild Hog, too, spoke of this feeling.

"We could not forget our native country anyway—where we grew up from childhood, and knew all the hills and valleys and creeks and places we had hunted over; where the climate was cooler, the air purer and healthier, the water sweeter . . . that instead of being better than the land we had left, everything was so much worse, we got homesick for our own country again."

Late that summer, Dull Knife and Little Wolf decided to leave, to take their people back to the north country, to the Powder River and Big Horn Mountains of Montana. To go home.

Ahead lay more than a thousand miles of open prairie. Cowboys and ranchers, farmers and homesteaders. Two railroads, a dozen forts and thousands of soldiers. Along the way, there would be no mountains to hide in, little wild game, few weapons and not enough horses. Some would have to walk and some were afraid.

"We are sickly and dying here," the chiefs told them, "and no one will remember our names when we are gone. We will go north at all hazards and if we die in battle, our names will be remembered and cherished by all our people."

They left late on the night of September 9, 1878.

Shortly before midnight, Dull Knife and Little Wolf gathered their people and led them on foot toward the pony herd grazing outside the village. The women had packed clothing and dried meat in parfleches. Some carried children, still feverish and sick, on their backs. While scouts fanned out far ahead, looking for safe campsites to the north, Tangle Hair, chief of the Dog Soldiers, moved his warriors to the rear, watching for troops, waiting for the old people and women and children to reach the horses. The main body stayed tightly together, moving forward through the dark, protected by the chiefs out front, warriors on both sides and the Dog Soldiers in back. There were some three hundred in all. Sixty adult men, thirty old men and young boys. The rest, about two hundred, were women and children.

They had left the tipis standing, their fires burning, to fool the soldiers camped nearby, and when they reached the pony herd, they rode hard, heading for the Cimarron River to the north.

For months, there had been a growing antagonism between the soldiers who had brought the people in and the government agencies which were to care for them. The military had warned of the risk, had said a people without food and medicine, without hope, would grow desperate. Now it had happened. When news of the escape reached Fort Reno the next day, September 10, the tension began to mount.

On September 15, 1878, Lt. Col. W. H. Lewis telegraphed his superiors from Fort Dodge, Kansas. He had recently spoken to Amos Chapman, an interpreter at the Darlington Agency, who had visited Dull Knife's people and knew them well. He told Lewis that in the final weeks before the escape, they "were down to eating horse flesh taken from horses that had died from disease or natural causes.

"In his opinion," continued Lewis, "there will be a larger outbreak by the coming Spring, unless something is done to improve their condition at the Agency."

E. A. Hayt, commissioner of Indian affairs, who had heard from Agent Miles at the Darlington Agency, eventually told a different story to his superiors in Washington. "[Miles] denies in toto the statements which have been made, that for lack of provisions they have been obliged to eat diseased meat, and affirms that there was really no good cause for dissatisfaction on their part," Hayt informed the secretary of the Interior.

"The truth is that Dull Knife's band contained the vilest and most dangerous element of their tribe. . . . No undue sentimentality should stand between them and a just punishment for their crimes."

Later, there would be a congressional investigation. During the hearings, Agent Miles admitted the Indians were starving at the time of the escape. For three years, he had let them go to hunt buffalo and each year, they had returned "worse than they went out." Each year, he testified, they had received only nine months' rations from the twelve months they were due.

"They have lived and that's about all," said Miles.

At the end of the third day, the scouts found a safe place to camp. It was behind a hill, in protective bluffs above the Little Medicine Lodge River, a tributary of the Cimarron. They were now fifty miles northwest of the Darlington Agency. Exhausted from the hard ride, the women unpacked some food and tended to their children. While the pony herd drank in the river, Dull Knife and Little Wolf discussed strategy. Their warriors headed for the high bluffs, looking for dust clouds to the south.

Gen. John Pope, commander of Fort Leavenworth, would coordinate the pursuit. He telegraphed his superior, Lt. Gen. Philip Sheridan, on September 12:

The following dispositions have been made to intercept the Northern Cheyennes: One hundred mounted infantry leave by special train tomorrow for Fort Wallace, to head off the Indians if they cross the railroad east or west of that post. Two companies of infantry leave Fort Hays this evening to take post at two noted crossings of Indians on the Kansas-Pacific railroad between hays and Wallace. One infantry company from Dodge is posted on the railroad west of that point. Two cavalry companies from Fort Reno are close on the Indians, and will be joined by the cavalry company from Camp Supply. Col. Lewis will assume command of them as soon as they reach the vicinity of Dodge. The troops at Fort Lyon are ordered out to watch the country east and west of that post, and are ordered to attack the Indians at once whenever found, unless they surrender, in which case they are to be dismounted and disarmed.

Farther north, in the Department of the Platte, General Crook ordered the Fourth, Ninth and Fourteenth Infantry under Major T. T. Thornburgh rushed to Sidney, Nebraska. There, a special train was cut loose along the Union Pacific Railroad to ferry troops east and west to blockade the way. Within a few days, more than two thousand troops were closing in.

Sheridan's orders to General Crook were blunt: He should "spare no measures . . . to kill or capture the band of Cheyennes on the way north."

Late in the afternoon of the third day, scouts in the bluffs above the Cimarron River saw the dust cloud on the plains below and they quickly relayed the information to Little Wolf. It was Dull Knife who had spoken in the councils and at the peace parleys and in the agency meetings, but now Little Wolf assumed command. He was the military tactician, perhaps the greatest warrior the tribe had ever known.

Shortly before they left, he had gone to the office at the Darlington Agency. "We have come to ask the agent that we be sent home to our own country in the mountains. My people were raised there, in a land of pines and clear, cold rivers," Little Wolf said. "I do not want to see blood spilled about this agency. If you are going to send soldiers after me, I wish that you would first let me get a little distance away from this agency. Then, if you want to fight, I will fight you, and we can make the ground bloody at that place."

Little Wolf told his warriors to get their guns and horses, to take defensive positions in the bluffs, in front of the women and children. He told no one to fire until he gave the command and then he got his horse and rode alone toward the column of soldiers moving across the plains.

Capt. Joseph Rendlebrock, Fourth Cavalry, had left Fort Reno soon after the escape. Riding with him were Southern Cheyenne Indian police and several Arapahoe scouts. He ordered his two cavalry companies to halt, and sent Ghost Man, one of the scouts, to meet with Little Wolf. The two men sat on their horses on the open plain, away from the troops, away from the Indians. The scout spoke first.

"The Arapahoe told our Indians that the troops had come after them to take them back to the agency," Old Crow, a subchief of the Dull Knife band, said later. "Little Wolf answered for our Indians that we did not want any trouble, but we did not want to go back to the agency; that we were willing to plow and work at farming, to give up our children to go to school, to do anything, but we wanted to do it in our own country. We told them that we were afraid to go back; we were afraid that if we went back we should all die of sickness; that we did not want any trouble with the soldiers; we wanted them to go back and leave us alone to go peaceably on our way to our northern home.

"The Arapahoe, who had been sent on ahead to talk with us, then went back to the soldiers. Then the troops fired on us."

The fighting began in late afternoon and lasted until dark and then began again in the morning, lasting most of the day. Late that afternoon, the soldiers unexpectedly retreated, the column moving back across the plains, back toward Fort Reno and the Darlington Agency. The younger warriors wanted to follow, but Little Wolf and Dull Knife said no, there wasn't enough ammunition.

After the battle, the bodies of two soldiers and Ghost Man lay on the plains. In the bluffs, there were no dead, but five seriously wounded, one a small girl whose ankle had been shattered by a bullet.

Some of the women moved down to skin and butcher the soldiers' dead horses—food and clothing for the days ahead. The next morning, they split up into smaller groups—harder to see, harder to find—and travelled only at night, everyone pushing north toward the flat Kansas prairie.

They traveled for two more nights, and on the next morning, scouts saw another column of soldiers coming at them on gray horses from the north. The warriors quickly formed a skirmish line, giving the women and children time to run, then they rode toward the moving column. Both sides charged, then retreated several times and, after a while, the soldiers turned around and rode back in the direction of Fort Dodge.

Anxious to get their people across an open prairie that afforded few hiding places, Little Wolf and Dull Knife broke camp shortly after dawn the next day and led the weary band steadily north. About noon, the scouts signaled that another soldier column was moving toward them from the Arkansas River, and this time, they saw cowboys, hunters and trappers riding alongside. When the troops saw the Indians, they attacked, but after only a few shots, the troops retreated back across a hill, camping there that night. Little Wolf and Dull Knife camped along a creek bottom not far away.

Early the next morning, scouts on top of the hill saw the soldiers advancing toward their camp and they rode hard to tell the chiefs

there were many more troops than the day before and they were followed by about forty wagons.

Little Wolf and Dull Knife shouted to the warriors to dig a row
of rifle pits and to move the women and children quickly behind a
line of breastworks. The soldiers were coming fast, moving closer
and closer, using the wagons as a protective shield. When they got
within a few hundred yards, the soldiers drew up their wagons and
got in formation, then advanced slowly and methodically on foot,
keeping up a steady barrage of fire into the Indian camp.

As the troops moved closer, a few of the younger warriors began
to panic. There were many soldiers now and they were almost on top
of them, and Little Wolf had ordered no one to fire until he gave the
command. Finally, he did and a soldier fell, and then the other soldiers quickly dropped to the ground, firing wildly toward the
Indians. Soon, about twenty soldiers jumped up and ran toward the
wagons, grabbed their horses and swung around to try and attack
the camp from behind. Little Wolf ordered a group of warriors to get
their horses and follow him. They circled back and charged the
twenty soldiers, killing one and forcing the others to retreat. When
Dull Knife saw the retreat, he ordered the rest of the warriors to
charge the wagon train. The soldiers ran to their horses, turned the
wagon teams around and fled back across the hill. As the younger
warriors gave chase, Little Wolf again ordered them to stop, telling
them that their horses were worn out and were needed to keep the
people pushing north.

The battle had lasted all day and the women had kept the campfires going, had cooked food and fed the warriors throughout the
fight. It was almost dark now and everyone was exhausted.

That night, Little Wolf told his people they had to keep moving,
there were too many soldiers around, and so they packed up after
dark and set out again, moving throughout the night, north toward
the Arkansas River.

The next morning, along a stream not far from the Arkansas,
they came upon a camp of hide hunters and Little Wolf ordered his
warriors not to shoot if the hunters surrendered. The hunters did

and, in their camp, the warriors found eighteen buffalo cows. They took the buffalo, their heavy caliber guns and the ammunition. After the much-needed meat and weapons were packed on horses, the warriors let the hunters go and rode back to camp.

It was the first good meal the people had eaten in the two weeks since leaving; soon the scouts also came back in and told the chiefs they had found a good place to cross the river and they'd seen no soldiers. That night, after everyone had eaten, they pushed on, crossing the Arkansas in the dark on September 24.

They traveled until midday and stopped along a stream in a canyon where high bluffs rose on each side. They were on the Punished Woman's Fork of Running Creek, in the Smoky Hill country, a place the people knew well, had been to many times in years past. Dull Knife and Little Wolf said it was a good place to camp— there was fresh water, firewood and protection in the bluffs—and so while some of the women began to build breastworks along the knolls above the creek, others scraped hides and pounded wild plums and chokecherries into the dried meat they would need when the weather turned colder.

And while a few of the men went out to hunt, others began to go off in different directions. Since the last few battles with troops, Little Wolf and Dull Knife had found it increasingly difficult to control some of the younger warriors. They had told them to kill no civilians, only the soldiers who were trying to kill them, but a number of them were going off in small groups anyway, raiding homesteads and farms, stealing horses and cattle, murdering the settlers and cowboys. They would slip back into camp after a few days, bringing fresh horses, fresh beef, blankets and bedspreads, and playthings for the children.

"We tried to avoid the settlements as much as possible," Little Wolf said. "We did not want to be seen or known of. I often harangued my young men, telling them not to kill citizens, but to let them alone. I told them that they should kill all the soldiers that they could, for these were trying to kill us, but not to trouble the citizens. I know they killed some citizens, but I think not many. They did not tell me much of what they did, because they knew I would not like it."

The settlers and cowboys retaliated whenever they could, forming posses, riding with the troops and, occasionally, riding on their own.

A. N. Keith, a cowboy hired to help drive two thousand head of cattle from Kansas City to Kearney, Nebraska, was part of a group patrolling the Beaver Creek area of northern Kansas in late September.

"On the divide north of Beaver, we found an old man that had been left behind. He was old and almost blind and toothless. Must have been a hundred years old. They were carrying him in a travois and it had broken down. One of the poles had broken and he had been left to die and the boys were discussing what to do with him when some one said to remember young Abbot [a settler killed by the Indians]. And then someone grabbed the end of the travois pole and the old warrior drew the blanket over his face and the cowboy hit him with the club and killed him."

Late on their second day in the canyon camp, the scouts came riding hard, rushing to Little Wolf with the news that they had found more soldiers, the most they had seen, camped only a few miles away. There were several companies, both cavalry and infantry, and they were supplied with many guns, artillery pieces and a long column of wagons.

The next afternoon, Col. W. H. Lewis, commander of Fort Dodge, marched his Nineteenth Infantry toward the canyon along the creek where the Indians were camped. Riding out front were Pawnee scouts, followed by the cavalry, then the infantry and finally the wagon train.

For years, Little Wolf had enjoyed a reputation among his people as a masterful tactician and military strategist. He made his plans carefully and he had employed them with great success in battles with enemy tribes and the U.S. Army across the high plains of his homeland.

Little Wolf ordered all the women, children and old people up into a high, rocky draw behind a line of thick boulders, the breastworks they had built two days earlier. He then ordered a small group of younger warriors to hide above a narrow point of the canyon trail. Farther down the trail, behind another wall of boulders, the main warrior party would lie in wait. The smaller group of young warriors were to allow the soldiers to come down the narrow trail, into the steep canyon. When the main body attacked, the young warriors were to close in from the rear, opening fire on the soldiers and stampeding their horses. Another small group—three or four—would hide in a nearby willow thicket and grab the rifles of the fallen soldiers, then set brushfires at the canyon entrance to cut off any retreat.

About four o'clock, Colonel Lewis led his cavalry troops into the canyon.

Before they were all the way in, one of the young warriors panicked and fired a shot that echoed through the canyon, spooking the soldiers, who quickly scattered and began to fire wildly toward the Indians. Soon, the wagons were rushed up from the rear, and while infantry poured out, one group of cavalry circled behind the camp, found the Indian pony herd and fired down on the horses until more than than a hundred fell to the ground.

After a few minutes, the main body of cavalry dismounted and ran their horses back to the wagons. There, both the horse and foot soldiers regrouped and began a slow advance toward the camp, marching closer and closer to the line of breastworks, firing all the while, until their bullets kicked dust across the warriors' faces and arms. Still, Little Wolf ordered no one to fire. Tangle Hair, the Dog Soldier chief, would later say that at this time Little Wolf "did not seem to be like a human being. He seemed to be like an animal, like a bear. He seemed without fear."

Finally, Little Wolf gave the order. The Indian rifles exploded and a number of soldiers collapsed. Their leader, Colonel Lewis, was hit in the leg in the first volley; his men grabbed him and retreated swiftly to the protection of the wagons. Soon, they were heading back in the direction they had come. Lewis bled to death before the soldiers reached Fort Wallace late that night.

A few days later, the Chicago *Tribune* ran a front-page story on the fight between the Indians and the cavalry: "Dirty Red Renegades Kill Another of Our Best Soldiers."

Little Wolf and Dull Knife lost two warriors in the hard fight. Many of their horses lay dead and about eighty others were captured, including the pack horses with the winter meat supply. Many would now have to walk, and food would be a problem.

Cold, tired and hungry, they left their canyon camp late that night, pushing north through the dark toward the Kansas Pacific Railroad. The next day, the scouts came in and told the chiefs what they had seen: The soldiers had stripped their captured ponies and shot them. Afterward, they stacked the meat and their possessions, salvaged from the Montana attack two winters earlier, into a pile and set it on fire.

Little Wolf and Dull Knife pushed their people harder, and they traveled almost nonstop for two days and nights.

At Fort Leavenworth, General Pope telegraphed his superiors:

"Every available man in the Department within two hundred miles of the scene of disturbance was sent forward in ample time, but it is not to be expected that Infantry can head off or overtake mounted Indians." He urgently requested that his troops be armed with Springfield rifles "so as at least to put them on an equality with the Indians."

The Indians crossed the Kansas Pacific Railroad on Sunday morning, September 29, and a few days later, some of the younger warriors again struck the farmhouses and ranches of western Kansas.

A dispatch from Fort Wallace reported:

When about 25 miles north of Buffalo Station they commenced killing settlers, and so far 17 dead bodies have been found along Sappa Creek. The Indians do not go out of their way at all to kill white peo-

ple, but if they meet a man on horseback they kill him and take his horse. They are now 80 or 100 miles north of the Kansas Pacific Railroad, with troops pressing them pretty hard. They have killed no women nor children and have not thus far mutilated the bodies of their victims.

In early October, the Northern Cheyenne reached southern Nebraska, crossing over the Frenchman fork of the Republican River where, just north of the crossing, scouts once again saw soldiers and civilians riding into the valley from the south.

Tangle Hair and his rear guard of mounted warriors, the Dog Soldiers, moved quickly to the back. While the elderly and the women and children, some of whom had been walking for days, ran ahead looking for a place to hide, the scouts and other warriors rode off in different directions, making it harder to pick up their trail. Throughout the day, the warriors and troops skirmished back and forth, and late that night, the confused and weary soldiers stopped and camped along a small stream north of what is now Indianola, Nebraska.

They had made it back to the familiar prairie, to the old buffalo country. For as long as any could remember, this had been a part of their ancestral hunting grounds. In years past, they had moved across these lands following the great herds, the horse-drawn travois carrying their tipis and clothing, pack horses laden with the winter meat supply. They were worn out now, hungry and cold, with few horses, little clothing and no tipis, but it was good to see this land again. In the morning, the scouts saw no soldiers, so Little Wolf and Dull Knife led their people across the South Platte River, about four miles west of Ogallala, Nebraska. It was Friday afternoon, October 4.

They moved swiftly, crossing the Union Pacific Railroad tracks and then the North Platte River, moving all the time, heading for the desolate Nebraska Sandhills.

At the army post in nearby Sidney, Major Thornburgh was notified by wire of the crossing. The special service train brought his troops to Ogallala on the Union Pacific line late Friday afternoon. They were to march north toward the Sandhills. At Fort Robinson, General Crook ordered five companies of the Third Cavalry under Maj. Caleb H. Carlton to move out. They were to march east toward the Sandhills. At Fort Meade, South Dakota, troops from the Seventh Cavalry, Custer's regiment, were ordered out. They were to move south toward the Sandhills.

In the Sandhills of western Nebraska, the winter of 1878 came early and it came hard. By mid-October, cold winds pushed from the north and morning frost covered the prairie. Most of the people were exhausted. They had come more than five hundred miles in five weeks, had fought soldiers in four major battles. They had lost their food, possessions and much of the pony herd. There was little ammunition and, for a while, they had been shooting their worn-out horses and eating the flesh to survive. Some of the old people, some of the women and children, were sick again with the fever and chills. One woman lost her horse early on and had walked most of the way, carrying her baby on her back. She and many others did not think they could go much farther.

Chief Dull Knife saw his weary people and he wanted to turn off course now, take them to Red Cloud and his Lakota camp near the fort on the White River. The Lakota, their relatives, would help them, he said, and the soldiers would treat them fairly, would let them stay in the north with the Red Cloud Sioux.

Little Wolf did not agree. It is said that he could run for hours without resting and he wanted to keep everyone together, to keep pushing north, five hundred more miles, until they reached the heart of their old homeland. He believed he could lead them back to the Montana mountains, could lead all of them home.

"You can go that way if you wish," he said to Dull Knife, "but I intend to work my way up to the Powder River country. I think it will be better for us all if the party is not divided."

They had been together for a long time, had come a long way, and it was hard for the people to watch as their two great chiefs disagreed on what was best for them. Dull Knife would not change his mind, though, and finally, in the country above the North Platte, they decided to divide into two groups. Those who wanted to keep moving toward Montana went with Little Wolf and those who wanted to turn toward Red Cloud's Oglala Sioux, mostly the women and children and old people, followed Dull Knife. On the morning they departed, the group heading toward Red Cloud left one of their few remaining buffalo robes on the prairie. Upon it, was a small pile of bullets and some gunpowder, a parting gift for the people going home.

The soldiers first saw them moving slowly across a ridge, through a blinding snowstorm, early on the afternoon of October 23. They were at the end of Chadron Creek, twenty-eight miles southeast of the fort on the White River. It was 1 p.m. Capt. J. B. Johnson, Third Cavalry, moved in with two companies, sending his Sioux scouts and an interpreter out to meet with the Indians.

When the scouts arrived, they saw their old Cheyenne friends, gaunt and weak, their moccasins worn out, clothes hanging in ragged tatters. Some of the women were using bedsheets for blankets, huddled with their children against the driving snow. Dull Knife, the scouts told the soldier chief, had agreed to surrender. His people could go no farther.

The soldiers marched them through the blizzard all day, up Chadron Creek, and arrived after dark at the camp of Major Carlton, commander of the Third Cavalry. En route, Dull Knife told the soldiers they had left the south because they were starving and dying of disease. They wanted to stay in their northern homeland, with Red Cloud's people, he said, and they hoped the Great Father in Washington would agree to this. But they would never return south, he told them. They would die first.

That night, the blizzard continued and Dull Knife and his people huddled in a thicket to escape the harsh wind and snow. Additional troops and heavy artillery arrived throughout the night and, by morning, there were several howitzers set up on the hills and troops surrounded the thicket.

Soon, the Sioux scouts rode in to tell Dull Knife that Major Carlton had decided he and his people must go to Fort Robinson. The chief believed this was the first step toward resettlement in the south, and his warriors began digging rifle pits in the snow and building a line of breastworks around the thicket.

Major Carlton explained the standoff in a telegram to superiors:

The position of the troops seemed to me a delicate one. An assault would probably have resulted in killing the majority of men and women. It might have been considered that after the Indians had surrendered and had given up their horses and arms, the troops then murdered them.

Instead, Carlton had the Sioux scouts and the interpreter tell Dull Knife he was surrounded by heavily armed troops and field artillery. He did not want to open fire, because many would die, many of them women and children. Finally, he told them they would get no food unless they surrendered. The Sioux scouts encouraged them to give up. The Red Cloud Agency had recently been moved across the Nebraska border, to Dakota Territory, and there was little food at the agency, the scouts said. Better to go to Fort Robinson. At least they would not starve there.

Dull Knife and two subchiefs, Wild Hog and Old Crow, agreed to lay down their arms: thirteen rifles, three revolvers, one pistol, and fifteen to twenty bows. The soldiers then took their stock—131 ponies and 9 mules—and began a head count. According to the official log, they had 149 prisoners: 46 men, 61 women, and 42 children.

After the captives were fed, the soldiers tied the arms of the Indian men behind their backs and loaded the prisoners into wagons. The warriors refused to ride, and walked beside the wagons that carried their families.

They marched through deep snow and bitter cold. Along the way, four horses froze to death and fourteen Indian ponies were shot when their legs gave out. Again, throughout the march, Dull Knife told the soldiers why they had left and why they would never return.

Shortly before 11 p.m. on the night of October 26, they arrived at the fort. The prisoners were escorted to an empty cavalry barracks near the parade ground. Constructed of ponderosa pine cut from the area, the dimly lit barracks had no windows on the south side and were ninety feet long and forty-five feet wide. The building opened onto the parade ground below a line of rugged buttes to the north and west, about five hundred yards from the White River.

General Crook commended his troops in a telegram to superiors:

The expeditions commanded by Majors Thornburgh and Carlton did faithful and arduous work and met with as much success as might be expected in the pursuit of savages resolved at all hazards to escape and thoroughly acquainted with every feature of the country.

In the country that fall, President Rutherford B. Hayes was nearing the end of his second year in the White House. A summer epidemic of yellow fever had killed more than fourteen thousand in the southern United States. Thomas Edison had played the first record on a phonograph, and A. A. Pope manufactured the first bicycle. In New York, Dr. W. F. Carver launched what would become the forerunner to Buffalo Bill Cody's Wild West Show, and a German-American physicist measured the speed of light at 186,508 miles per second.

In their barracks at Fort Robinson, Chief Dull Knife and his people were better off than they had been in a long time, since the destruction of their winter village in the Big Horn Mountains two years earlier.

For the first time in two winters, they were not starving. They were eating regularly, sleeping well and no longer worrying about a surprise attack. In the north country, the fever and chills and disease began to disappear, and two army doctors tended to the sick and injured. When they asked for help with clothing, their Oglala Sioux friends brought them 104 pairs of moccasins.

"For a good while we were well treated and very pleasantly situated there," Wild Hog said. "We were kept under guard, but had a large house to stay in; and we had plenty to eat."

After a time, the soldiers let some of the men go out and hunt, while others went down to the river to pick kinnikinnick and gather red willow bark for their pipes. The women, too, were allowed fresh air and exercise, unloading grain wagons when the weather was nice. Inside their barracks, the men sometimes sat in small groups, playing cards and smoking their pipes, while the women did beadwork and the children amused themselves with games.

"They were very contented and good natured," said the post commander, Capt. Henry W. Wessells.

On December 24, 1878, Captain Wessells received his orders from Washington: Dull Knife and his people were to be returned to the Indian Territory as soon as possible.

The decision had been made more than fifteen hundred miles away, by the war department and the secretary of the interior. At the time, the settlement of the West was still tenuous, the reservation system fragile. If Dull Knife and Little Wolf were allowed to stay, Washington officials believed, it could set a dangerous precedent.

The orders, General Crook told his superiors, would be difficult to carry out. He wasn't sure he or his men had the heart for it.

"Among these Cheyenne Indians," Crook later wrote, "were some of the bravest and most efficient of the auxiliaries who had acted under General Mackenzie and myself . . . and I still preserve a grateful rememberance of their distinguished services which the Government seems to have forgotten."

The Cheyenne, he added, had made it clear why they had left and why they would not return. To physically remove them from their barracks, he said, would be difficult.

"They repeated their expressions of desire to live at peace with our people, but said they would kill themselves sooner than be taken back to the Indian Territory. These statements were confirmed by Red Cloud and other friendly Sioux Chiefs, who assured us that the Cheyennes had left their Reservation in Indian Territory to avoid fever and starvation and that they would die to the last man, woman and child before they could be taken from the quarters in which they were confined."

Furthermore, wrote Crook in a summary report to superiors, there were a number of practical considerations: "At this time, the thermometer at Fort Robinson showed a range of from zero down to nearly 40 below, [the freezing point of mercury]. The captives were without adequate clothing, and no provisions had been made to supply it. . . ."

On Christmas Eve, Crook telegraphed Lieutenant General Sheridan. "It would be inhuman to move them as ordered," he said.

Sheridan replied that he would refer the issues of clothing and whatever other supplies were needed to Washington. But the orders stood. The Indians were to be moved south as soon as possible.

Dull Knife and his people did not know about the new orders. During the last week of December and the first few days of January, they remained in their barracks, wrapped in blankets, their stoves burning against the bitter cold. Outside, Captain Wessells began lining up the food, clothing, wagons and troops that would be needed for the journey. The people were to be marched from Fort Robinson south to Sidney barracks and from there, they would proceed to the Indian Territory.

On January 3, 1879, Dull Knife and four subchiefs were summoned to a noon meeting with the post commander. It was near the barracks, in the adjutant's office, the building where Crazy Horse had bled to death sixteen months earlier. After the five leaders arrived, Captain Wessells told them that the Great Father in Washington had made up his mind, that they must all go back to the reservation in the south as soon as possible.

It was the news they had feared for weeks, had tried not to think about.

Inside the adjutant's office, Dull Knife rose from his chair, facing the soldiers, facing Wessells.

"I am here on my own ground," he said, "and I will never go back. You may kill me here, but you cannot make me go back."

For the next two days, Wessells told the prisoners they had no choice. He continued to summon Dull Knife and the subchiefs Wild Hog, Old Crow, Tangle Hair and Left Hand to the adjutant's office, telling them they had to return to the south. Those were his orders. They came from the Great Father and he had to carry them out.

Each time, the chiefs said no, they would not leave the land where their children were born and their ancestors buried, would not return to the place where their children had died and the old people suffered.

"I said, 'Look at us; see how we are clothed.' There was nothing on us hardly; the snow was that deep [about two feet]," Wild Hog recalled later.

Wessells persisted. They would go south at all costs, he said.

"You can starve us if you like," Chief Dull Knife finally told him, "but you cannot make us go south."

On the morning of January 5, Wessells ordered all food and heating fuel withheld from the prisoners. On January 7, he ordered the water supply cut off, hoping this would "bring them to terms."

After three days without food and heat, two without water, the old people and the children began to weaken. Soldiers guarding the barracks sometimes saw the windows crack open, saw the Indian hands scooping snow from the ledges so the children would have some water. Still, no one surrendered. They had decided they would not be starved into returning to a place they had left because they were starving.

After four days, the soldiers asked that the women and children be released from the barracks to be fed, but the chiefs said no. If one died, they would all die.

On the evening of January 8, Capt. Joseph Lawton walked down to the barracks with his wife and daughter to visit Dull Knife and Wild Hog. The Indians seemed sad and sullen, he said.

"They always told me they would do anything they were ordered except to go south."

Shortly before noon the next morning, January 9, Captain

Wessells asked to see Wild Hog in the adjutant's office. Both Wild Hog and Old Crow soon arrived.

"I asked them if they were ready to go south," Wessells said. "They said no. I then had them seized and handcuffed and removed to the cavalry camp about one mile from the post." During the struggle to place him in irons, Wild Hog cried out for help, but the doors were closed and the people could not hear his screams. Afterward, a third subchief, Left Hand, also was placed in irons and led away to the cavalry camp.

Wessells hoped to get each of the leaders away from the barracks. Then the people would weaken. They would agree to go south.

That afternoon, the wives of the three men led away in irons were told to remove their possessions and their families from the barracks. Before she left, Wild Hog's wife told Dull Knife what had happened. A dozen family members and four elderly women then left to join the three subchiefs who had been taken to the cavalry camp. There were now a hundred thirty left in the barracks. Angry and frightened, they expected to hear the soldiers' guns at any moment.

Inside the barracks, the warriors took their blankets and began to cover each of the windows.

On the day they had been captured in the snowstorm, more than two months before, not all of the weapons had been surrendered. A few rifle stocks and barrels had been hidden in the women's clothing, and some of the pistols, broken down into smaller parts, had been disguised as jewelry on the children. One wore a trigger around her neck, one a hammer on her wrist, another a spring in her hair. A little ammunition had also been concealed.

Throughout the afternoon of January 9, 1879, the warriors pried open the floorboards in the barracks where they had hidden their weapons and began to reassemble them. There were about sixteen in all—five rifles and eleven pistols. They made war clubs from the floorboards and fashioned crude shields from the metal stoves.

Outside, soldiers in the guardhouse could hear a lot of noise, heard the floorboards tearing loose, and many voices speaking at once. They knew something was going on, but they couldn't see inside.

Three times that day, Captain Wessells tried to lure Dull Knife outside. Twice at the door, once through the chinks in the pine log walls, he told the chief he would be well fed and returned safely if he agreed to come out and talk. Dull Knife refused.

At 4 p.m., during a shift change, seven armed sentinels were ordered around the barracks: three at the west end, two at the east, one in front and one in back.

At 5 p.m., Wessells ordered a side door to the barracks nailed shut with three large planks.

At 8 p.m., he ordered the post blacksmith to place heavy chains across the side door and both of the front doors to the barracks.

Inside, Dull Knife and his people took the last of their possessions, saddles, leather parfleches and some blankets, and piled them in front of the windows. "It is true that we must die, but we will not die shut up here like dogs," the people said to one another. "We will die on the prairie; we will die fighting." They put on the best of their moccasins and their nicest clothes and after nightfall, they kissed each other good-bye.

At 9:50 p.m., the glass shattered in a window on the west end of the barracks and a single shot cracked through the frigid night.

Soon, there were a great many shots and two soldier guards dropped to the ground. Tangle Hair and his four men smashed the remaining glass with their rifle butts and burst through the windows. They raced to the fallen soldiers, grabbed their .45 Springfield carbines and ran between the stable and Company C headquarters, fanning out five abreast between the soldiers and their people.

"A rear guard seemed to keep back to cover the retreat of the squaws," Pvt. Julius Janzchin, F Company, noted later.

For five minutes, the five warriors kept up a steady fire of .50 carbine brass reloading shells at the first wave of troops, who were now moving toward the barracks in a loud mass of shouting and firing.

The Dog Soldiers wanted to buy as much time as they could.

"They were the first out and stopped, and after the others had passed them, they commenced jumping and yelling and firing and remained there until killed," said Sgt. John Mitchell.

After the Dog Soldiers, Dull Knife and his son were the first to climb the makeshift ramp below the window. They were unarmed as they dropped to the ground and ran for cover, their people streaming through the shattered windows close behind.

That night, it was bright and cloudless, a full moon. The temperature was below zero and half a foot of snow lay on the ground.

Old Sitting Man sat on the ground by the window. His leg had been fractured by a soldier's bullet on the long flight north and when he jumped from the window, the leg gave out and he could go no farther. A soldier ran up, put a rifle muzzle to his head and fired.

The people ran as hard as they could, fleeing across the fort grounds, out into the flat, open meadow, toward the Saw Mill and White River about five hundred yards away. They wanted to get to the river bottom, to the protective trees, then follow it until they reached the rugged bluffs to the north and west. Some of the women carried the babies on their backs. Some of the old people tried to run with the smaller children. They had not eaten in five days and they were weak from the hunger and cold. The snow was too deep and the troops were coming on horseback now and some did not make it very far.

Big Antelope and his wife were running across the open field, trying to make it to the safety of the river bottom. Before they reached it, a soldier's bullet caught Big Antelope in the leg and he could go no farther. His wife crawled across the snow, to where her husband lay, and then another bullet hit her in the leg. In the distance, they could see the horses coming, and Big Antelope said they should both die, here in their homeland. He drew his knife and stabbed her, then he stabbed himself in the heart.

The next day, January 10, a burial detail arrived back at the fort. The dead were stacked like logs inside the wagons and the soldiers grabbed the bodies by the hair and tossed the frozen corpses to the ground. The wounded were brought to the post hospital. According to the official log, they included:

> Baby girl: 1 yr. old, both legs broken. Died 1 hour after arrival at post.
>
> Baby girl: 6 months old, left leg fractured by bullet. Died on morning of Jan. 12, 1879.
>
> Young girl: 5 years old, shot through abdomen. Died 12 hours later.
>
> Yellow Woman: gunshot wound to upper thigh; ball penetrating right lung. Died.
>
> Short Woman: gunshot wounds to right hand, head and chest; back and thigh fractured.
>
> Red Woman: gunshot wound to left thigh, little finger fractured, scalp wound.
>
> Medicine Woman: gunshot wound to head, right eye shot out. Dangerous.
>
> Little Boy: 7 years old, gunshot wound to head. Serious.

Later that morning, Captain Wessells arrived at the makeshift hospital and said to the wounded, "Now, will you go south?"

A girl, badly wounded in the foot, used a wall for support and rose slowly from the floor. "No," she said. "We will not go back, we will die rather."

Wessells ordered his cavalry to pursue the escaped prisoners, to find their trail and kill or capture them in the surrounding bluffs, and for the next two days, the troops fanned out through the countryside. Several times, the bitter cold and deep snow forced them to return to the post for more food and clothing. Finally, supply trains, fresh troops and artillery pieces were sent out into the field.

"I found trails of two Indians. One led up to the ice," said Captain Lawton, commander of one of the companies in pursuit. "I sent in a soldier, who found a little girl seven or eight years old who had a pack of cards and was sitting in the snow playing with them."

On January 11, Captain Lawton's command discovered some of the Indians and there was a firefight in the bluffs, during which a cavalry horse was shot. "I was afraid the Indians might get the horse to eat, so I made a detail of two men and burned the horse to cinders," said Lawton. "This took about two hours." When it got dark, the soldiers returned to the fort.

The next day, January 12, General Crook telegraphed his superiors. He told them that Captain Wessells had reported the "Indians were as well armed and supplied with as much ammunition as any Indians that ever went on the war-path."

On January 13, the main Indian body was discovered hiding in a ravine. Four cavalry companies and a 12-pound Napoleon gun were moved within range, and that afternoon, army troops fired forty rounds of artillery shells and solid shot into the rifle pits where the Indians were holed up. The firing continued until it was too dark to see, and that night, the uninjured Indians escaped, moving higher into the bluffs.

General Crook telegraphed that his troops were worn out. Wessells, he said, would start again the next morning with two fresh companies.

But the next morning, the soldiers had lost the trail and now they turned to Red Cloud, asking that he provide Sioux scouts to help track their old friends in the high bluffs above the White River.

After a while, Sioux scouts picked up the trail about forty-five miles north and west of Fort Robinson. The Indians were trying to make it to Red Cloud's people, but they didn't know where the new agency was. In their search, they moved down from the bluffs, to the open plains near Hat Creek Road, where the scouts eventually found fresh moccasin tracks and the soldiers followed. It was January 22.

When they saw the soldiers coming, the Indians ran to a washout, an old buffalo wallow about fifty feet long, twelve feet wide and six feet deep.

Four companies of the Third Cavalry, 147 men and five officers, surrounded the washout, one company on each side. Hiding inside were seventeen Indian men, and fifteen women and children.

For more than thirty minutes, the four companies poured a steady fire into the open pit at point-blank range. Occasionally, an

Indian hand came up and fired a shot. One bullet grazed Captain Wessells in the head. After more than two hundred rounds, the shooting stopped and the soldiers moved forward.

Before they walked very far, three warriors sprang from the pit—one with an empty pistol and two with knives—and charged the troops. They were instantly cut down.

Captain Lawton was the first to reach the washout.

"I saw a little girl on the opposite side of the pit looking imploringly at us. I immediately gave the order to cease firing and, leaping in onto the dead bodies, took the child by the hand and helped her out."

When the soldiers laid out the dead on a field of snow that day, they counted the bodies of seventeen men and seven women and children. Inside the pit, the men had stayed on top of the twisted pile. They had saved eight women and children.

On January 23, two weeks after the escape, the shooting stopped. Of the 149 Indians who had been brought to the barracks, 78 were captured and 64 killed—39 men, and 25 women and children.

Seven were still missing

Before the burial detail arrived, while the bodies of the men, women and children still lay in the snow, the soldiers saw civilians riding through the battlefield. First Lt. James F. Simpson saw one group, a party of three, looting the dead. Two were in the field, a third in the buckboard.

"I saw them search the bodies of dead Indians in the bluffs and heard one man say, 'I've got a pipe—that's what I've been looking for.' . . . The man in the buckboard called to the others to bring him blankets from the dead Indians, he wanted them too."

Second Lt. J. F. Cummings, Third Cavalry, was in charge of the burial detail. On January 12, he had buried the first group of Indian dead: fourteen men, nine women and four children.

Of the twenty-seven Indians he buried that day, more than half had been scalped.

"From the appearances of the bodies, I don't think the scalps had been taken off only ten or fifteen minutes before," said Cummings. "I then collected the remainder of the bodies. The bodies of the women were exposed, their clothing being drawn up over their heads."

One woman, while recovering in the makeshift hospital, told interpreter James Rowland that "after she was wounded and down, the soldiers tried to shoot her in the head, but she dodged and they shot her fingers off."

Among the dead were Big Antelope and his wife. Lieutenant Cummings had heard the story, and before burying him, he examined the body of Big Antelope. "I found six stab wounds on his right breast, close together," he said. His wife bled to death an hour after she was brought to the fort.

In the confusion, the darkness and excitement of the pursuit, it had been impossible to distinguish between men and women, old people and children, the officers and troops told their superiors. The killing of women and children had been regrettable, but unavoidable.

After a time, it was decided that the widows and orphans would be allowed to go to the Red Cloud Agency, to live with the Oglala Sioux. In early February, the first wagons carrying some of the surviving women and children set out from Fort Robinson for the agency, about seventy miles to the north and east, just across the Nebraska border in Dakota Territory.

On February 4, Wild Hog tried to take his life. Still in handcuffs, he stabbed himself four times in the chest, hoping his death would allow his wife and children to be among the next group sent to the Red Cloud Agency, where friends and relatives could care for them. Wild Hog did not die from the stabbing.

A few weeks later, after recovering from his wounds, he and Old Crow and five other Northern Cheyenne were shipped to Kansas to stand trial for the murder of white settlers killed on the flight north. In late February 1879, they arrived at Fort Leavenworth, where a sheriff's posse led by W. B. "Bat" Masterson was waiting to escort them back to Dodge City. State prosecutors, however, could not prove that any of the Indian men had committed the murders, and in October, Judge N. T. Stephens dismissed all charges.

After their release from jail, the Cheyenne were taken back to the Darlington Agency, to the hated reservation they had fled thirteen months earlier.

"I did not feel like doing anything for a while, because I had no heart," Old Crow said after his return. "I did not want to be in this country; I was all the time wanting to get back to the better country where I was born, and where my father was born and is buried, and where my children are buried, and where my mother and my sister and other relatives yet live; so I have laid in my lodge the most of the time, with nothing to think about but that, and the affair up north, at Camp Robinson, and my relatives and friends who were killed there. But now I feel as though if I had a wagon and horse or two and some land I would try to work. If I had something, so that I could do something, I might not think so much about these other things. As it is now, I feel as though I would just as soon be asleep with the rest."

For a long while, it was thought that of the forty-six Indian men who had surrendered in the snowstorm in the Sandhills, only Old Crow and six others—the ones shipped to Kansas on murder charges—had survived the outbreak from the barracks.

That night, Henry Clifford had heard the shooting from Mrs. Dear's general store a few miles east of the fort. Clifford was a civilian who spoke the Sioux language, and the army sometimes used him as an interpreter. He lived between the fort and the old Red Cloud Agency, and he knew many of the Indians in the area. The day after he heard all the shooting, he went to the post office with a friend, picked up his mail and rode to the battlefield. When he arrived, he found an army detail sorting through a pile of bodies, trying to identify some of the dead.

"A sergeant asked me if Dull Knife was in that party," Clifford said. "I looked it over and said no."

After the Dog Soldiers had smashed the window and jumped out to form the protective rear guard, Chief Dull Knife and eight family members had been the first to reach the ground.

As they ran toward the White River, a bullet caught one of the chief's daughters and she dropped in the snow. Her husband stayed back with her, and before she died, the daughter pleaded with her father to keep the family moving, to get to the river and run for the bluffs.

After hesitating at first, the family decided to keep going and, north of the river, they turned away from the path most of the others had chosen, instead moving swiftly through a shallow gully until they reached the bluffs. Dull Knife and the six surviving members of his party stayed as close to the rockface as they could, so there would be no tracks in the snow. After a time that night, they found a large hole in the outcroppings, a cave, and for ten days they stayed there, watching for the soldiers, waiting until it was safe to try to walk the last sixty-three miles to Red Cloud's people.

On the tenth day, Dull Knife's son saw the long column of soldiers moving far to the west, toward the distant bluffs above Hat Creek Road.

They left that night, and for eighteen nights they moved steadily east, traveling only in the dark, hunched against the winter winds, careful to avoid leaving any tracks in the snow. They ate roseberries and some sinew that the women carried with them, and then they dug through the frozen ground for any roots they could find. Finally, they ate the soles of their moccasins, chewing the rawhide to make it through the last few nights.

It is early summer, 114 winters after his people broke out of the barracks at the soldier fort on the White River. In the kitchen of his trailer home on the edge of Loveland, Guy Dull Knife Jr. has put away his paints and brushes for the night. He has been working most of the day on a statue of the Eagle Dance and so one counter of the cramped kitchen is covered in clay, knives, sketches, drawings and droppings of paint.

He leaves the cluttered kitchen, moving past a bookcase to a couch in the living room.

On a wall above the living room couch hangs a small pen-and-ink drawing of Chief Dull Knife. Opposite it, on another wall, is the red and white flag of the Oglala Sioux Tribe. The flag belongs to his father, the old man in the nursing home. Not far from the couch, on the bookcase that separates the kitchen and living room, is a black and gold pair of binoculars that belonged to Buffalo Bill Cody. In 1896, Cody gave them as a gift to his grandfather, George Dull Knife.

From his grandfather and his father, Guy Dull Knife Jr. has heard the story since he was a small boy. He takes a seat on the couch, his voice characteristically low and soft:

"On the night Chief Dull Knife and the others came into the Red Cloud Agency, some of the people there began to cry when they saw them. They looked like dead people. They were nothing but skin and bone. Their faces were hollow and they were half-naked, wearing next to nothing. Some were barefoot and their hands and feet had frozen. Chief Dull Knife was then about seventy years old and at first some of the people did not recognize him. When they found out what had happened to them, the men and women in the camp were so sad they started to cry.

"The survivors said that in the days before the escape, a lot of the men wanted to give up, but it was the women who forced them to go on. They said if they were all going to die, they should die in their homeland, die fighting.

"The first few nights after they arrived, Chief Dull Knife was given a tipi above Wounded Knee Creek. They brought in warm clothes and built a big fire and gave everyone as much food as they could eat.

"After a while, he was moved around a lot. The soldiers were still looking for him and the Sioux at Pine Ridge kept taking him to different places so the soldiers couldn't find him. For a while, he was taken to Yellow Bear Camp, where all of the relatives helped to hide him from the cavalry.

"At that time, there were some Sioux living in Brainard, South

Dakota, near Hot Springs. After he had eaten well and slept and rested up, they took him to the Sioux at Brainard. He was very sick then. He had pneumonia and they took him to Brainard to try and make him better."

Throughout the winter and spring, as he slowly recovered under the watchful eye of friends and relatives, Dull Knife hoped there would come a time when he could rejoin his friend, Little Wolf, in the land where their ancestors were buried.

After they split up, Little Wolf and his party had wintered in the Lost Chokecherry Valley of the Nebraska Sandhills. In early spring, they started north once again, moving across the western corner of Nebraska, around the edge of the Black Hills and into Wyoming, heading for the Montana mountains. In late March, after a journey of seven months and more than a thousand miles, they reached the head of the Powder River in their old homeland. The soldiers were waiting.

Lt. William P. Clark, who had participated in the destruction of their winter village in the Big Horn Mountains, found their camp and asked them to surrender. On March 27, 1879, Little Wolf rode into Fort Keogh and gave his weapons and ponies to Gen. Nelson Miles.

Later that year, Dull Knife was given permission to leave the Pine Ridge Agency in Dakota Territory and return to Montana. A military detail escorted him back to the place of his birth, to the Rosebud Valley, and in late November, he rejoined Little Wolf and the others who had survived the journey from the south. He died there of natural causes in 1883.

A year after his death, on March 26, 1884, an executive order of the U.S. government officially set aside a tract of Montana land as the permanent home for the Northern Cheyenne.

State Highway 212 cuts through the deep valleys and pine-covered mountains of Montana, following the Rosebud across the rolling reservation lands. East of Lame Deer, a small community in the center of the reservation, the highway sweeps around a curve, to a large wooden sign erected on one shoulder:

> *After the Northern Cheyennes helped defeat Custer in 1876, their pursuit eventually caused them to be detained in Oklahoma Indian Territory. Despite promises they could later return to Montana, these promises were never kept. Sick and hungry, determined to return to their homeland, the Cheyennes under Dull Knife and Little Wolf escaped. Pursued in the rear, intercepted on their way, these heroic people fought, froze and starved to death to reach home.*

To the north of the sign, beneath a steep butte overlooking the mountains and valleys of eastern Montana, a cemetery extends for several hundred yards. In one corner, inside a faded white wooden fence, Dull Knife and Little Wolf lie side by side.

Planted in the middle of the simple dirt graves, their frayed tips snapping in the breeze, are two small American flags.

Chapter Three

End of the Old,
Beginning of the New

In the higher altitudes on the eastern slope of the Rocky Mountains, it has snowed almost every day now for several weeks, and the towering pines clustered along the tree line are dusted in thick coats of powder. On a clear day, the light coming off the peaks is blinding and the air has a sharper edge. Late fall turning the corner on early winter.

Inside Room 103, the old man in the nursing home has had a rough week. The cold air hurts his bones, inflames his arthritis and rheumatism, and so he is frequently in a cranky mood that not even his good friend Verna Ping, the Chinese speech therapist, can seem to soothe. One afternoon, in the midst of an aching spell, Kelli, the young nurse's aide, walked in with her new dog, a six-week-old Alaskan malamute. The old man loves dogs, has been around them all his life, and when she asked him to help her name the new puppy, the old smile returned for a while. Guy Dull Knife Sr. looked at the little dog racing across the linoleum, chasing a sock, jumping on the bed, licking his face, and after a time, he motioned for her to come closer. "Dakota," he said. "You should call this dog Dakota."

Kelli liked the idea, agreed that it would be a good name and thanked him for the suggestion. As Kelli and Dakota got ready to leave, the old man asked her if she had seen the article on his grandfather yet. "My grandfather was a chief," said the old man, reaching for the drawer in his nightstand. "A chief like in the old days."

Chief Dull Knife was the last of his family to live the old way of life. He had been born in a tipi, raised in a village and reared in the traditional ways of his people, growing up in a mountain homeland of unspoiled beauty and richness, a homeland unknown to settlers, soldiers and prospectors for many years. At his birth in the first quarter of the nineteenth century, the Cheyenne and Lakota were masters of the high plains and roamed freely across parts of five states—Montana, Wyoming, Nebraska and the Dakotas. During this time, his people were secure and content, members of a close-knit culture with carefully defined roles, a culture that provided for all their needs. The annual Sun Dance had become the spiritual focus of their lives. An abundance of wild game provided food, clothing and shelter. The horse gave them mobility; weapons, a sense of protection and power. Pride and dignity, an individual's self-worth, were measured in many ways: from the beadwork on a pair of moccasins to the amount of meat hanging in a lodge, from the quality of one's horses to the number of coup counted on the enemy.

As a warrior, Dull Knife had distinguished himself in fights against the Shoshoni, Crow, Pawnee and cavalry, had joined the annual buffalo hunts through the sacred valleys of the Powder River country. Later, when the forts and railroads and wagon trains began to change the old ways, he changed, too. The warrior gave way to the diplomat, the hunter to the peacekeeper, and so his people had brought the traditional long-stemmed pipe of the leader to his lodge.

At his death in 1883, Chief Dull Knife had lived long enough to see the end of the old way, the beginning of the new. Whites were now the masters of the high plains, of the old homeland, and the people who had roamed freely for generations were gradually herded into smaller and smaller pockets of arid land. Within these new boundaries, during a few short years, the circular tipi of animal hide changed to canvas and finally to a rectangular house of logs. By and by, the medicine man gave way to the physician, horses pulled the plow, and the thrill of the hunt was replaced by the tedium of standing in line at a government agency, waiting for wagons to deliver a side of beef and a sack of flour. In the northern part of the Dakota Territory, Sitting Bull, spiritual center of the Lakota Nation, had surrendered his starving, freezing band from Canada and was languishing in a military prison. In the south, the nation's warrior heart, Crazy Horse, was dead. The new reservation system had begun.

George Dull Knife would spend most of his life on the Pine Ridge Reservation of South Dakota, a life much different than his father, the chief, had known. He was the first of his family to have a Christian name, the first to wear short hair and a suit, the first to eat with a knife and fork, plant potatoes, wear a badge and drive a motorized vehicle, the only one to visit Paris and the last born in a tipi.

Born in 1875, a year before the Battle at the Little Bighorn, George Dull Knife's early life mirrored the chaos and confusion that marked the final turbulent years preceding the new reservation way of life. After the Custer fight in June 1876, the great encampment of Lakota, Northern Cheyenne and Arapahoe broke up into smaller tribes and bands, and scattered throughout the northern Great Plains. Like the others, Chief Dull Knife's band moved continually, desperately searching for vanishing herds of wild game, trying to avoid the increasing number of soldiers, looking for remote, safer havens from the winter storms.

Among the plains tribes at the time, it was not uncommon for a chief to have more than one wife. As leaders of their people, the chiefs were expected to host feasts, greet visitors, entertain guests, conduct councils and present gifts of beaded clothing, robes and horses, so it was accepted that they would need more than one wife to fulfill their many obligations. Chief Dull Knife had two wives. Pawnee Woman, whom he had captured years before in a raid on a Pawnee village, bore him four daughters and a son. With Slow Woman, also called the Short One, he had three daughters and three sons. Throughout the 1860s and '70s, many had been struck by the family's beauty. Army officers encountering the daughters at various forts and agencies occasionally tried to court them. After a time, some of the troops began calling the Dull Knife children the "Beautiful People."

The tumultuous period after Custer eventually took its toll on the family. One of the chief's sons had been killed by Mackenzie's troops in the attack on their winter camp. The long flight north from Indian Territory had claimed Short One, the chief's younger wife. A few weeks into the journey, a group of warriors returned to camp with a string of ponies stolen in the raids on white ranches. Trampled to death by one of the skittish horses, she was buried in a shallow grave by the side of the trail. During the escape from Fort Robinson, troops had shot and killed one of the chief's daughters and a son, Little Hump. By late January 1879, when he and the six starving members of his family finally reached Pine Ridge, Dull Knife had lost three children, a wife and almost half the people who had chosen to follow him out of the Nebraska Sandhills. It is said that he never recovered upon hearing the fate of the others, that guilt and anguish overwhelmed him until his death.

Slipped in among their Lakota friends and relatives on Pine Ridge, the surviving Dull Knife family was passed from place to place until it was no longer necessary for the army to find them. In the ensuing weeks and months, many of the survivors from Fort Robinson were allowed to come to Pine Ridge. Several years later, some of the people who had been left behind at the Darlington Agency in Indian Territory also were given permission to come north, to rejoin their families and friends at Pine Ridge.

George Dull Knife was three years old when his father and some of their people fled the Darlington Agency. His family does not know many of the details of his early life, the period between 1875 and 1886, when his name appears on the first official census taken at the Pine Ridge Agency. The youngest son, the last one born to the chief and Short One, George was among the six hundred who remained in the Indian Territory after the others went north. From what his descendants were later able to piece together from other relatives, they believe the small boy was considered too young for the rigorous journey and so he was left at the agency in the care of extended family members. They think young George came north in the summer of 1883, when more than three hundred Northern Cheyenne made the move, under military escort, from the Darlington Agency to Pine Ridge.

"For many of the families, ours included, it was a very difficult time, a very confusing time," said Guy Dull Knife Jr. "Between the fighting and the removal from one reservation to another, families were split up, broken up and torn apart. The army back then was in the final stages of ridding the frontier of the 'Indian Problem' and once one group had been forced to surrender and taken to a reservation, it was difficult to leave the reservation from that point on. Sometimes, families ended up being separated for years. Even before then, right after Custer, tribes and bands and families were breaking up into smaller and smaller groups to try and evade the soldiers. There was very little food anymore and everyone was on the run. It was a time of panic and chaos and no one really knew what to do.

"I don't think my grandfather ever really knew, ever really understood what had happened to him or the family during the years when he was a small boy. It was a confusing time for everyone. From what we have been told, he eventually left with a large group from the Indian Territory and was taken in by relatives at the Yellow Bear Camp."

By the time George Dull Knife arrived at Pine Ridge, Chief Dull Knife had moved yet again. Granted permission to return to his native homeland by General Miles, the elderly chief, his wife, Pawnee Woman, his eldest son, Buffalo Hump, several daughters and a few of the Outbreak survivors had rejoined Little Wolf at Fort Keogh, Montana Territory, in December 1879. Three years later, they were all allowed to return to the Rosebud Valley, to the old homeland, where Chief Dull Knife died in March 1883.

For a number of years after young George Dull Knife arrived at the Yellow Bear Camp, there was a good deal of travel back and forth between the Northern Cheyenne in Montana and the Oglala Sioux on Pine Ridge. Various members of the two groups that had intermarried for years would leave one place, stay for a while with friends and relatives, then return home. During his first four or five

years on Pine Ridge, young George was among those who frequently
journeyed to Montana and spent long stretches with extended family
members before returning to the Yellow Bear Camp. It was a pattern
that would continue well into the next century.

"A lot of my grandfather's descendants have lived on the
Northern Cheyenne Reservation at one time or another, including
my father, who lived there off and on for seven or eight years when
he was little," Guy Dull Knife Jr. said. "Some of my dad's brothers
and sisters also lived there for a while. Most of the relatives from
Montana have been to Pine Ridge and most of the ones on Pine
Ridge have been to Montana. Some of them speak both Cheyenne
and Lakota. Even though there has been a lot of movement back and
forth and a lot of the Sioux and Cheyenne intermarried down
through the years, we have always considered ourselves Lakota since
the time of my grandfather. He was raised a Lakota, married a
Lakota, spoke Lakota and grew up with all of the Lakota customs
and traditions. That's how he and my grandmother raised their children and that's how my parents raised me. Since his time, we have
always considered ourselves Oglala Sioux."

In George Dull Knife's youth, the large, extended reservation
families provided homes, food, clothing and shelter for the many who
had lost a husband, wife, father or mother to warfare and disease.
His mother dead and his father in Montana, the small boy was taken
in by the Poor Bear family after he arrived at Pine Ridge from the
Indian Territory. The Poor Bears had married into the Dull Knife
family years before, and George lived with them in the Yellow Bear
Camp for much of the next ten years. Eunice Poor Bear, an Oglala
Sioux, helped raise the young boy and, after a time, George came to
Think of her as his mother. At the Yellow Bear Camp, he attended
the Sun Dances and sweat lodge ceremonies and he began to learn
some of the Lakota songs and dances. From what he later told his
family, he had some schooling, but not much. What he loved more
than anything was hunting in the hills and ravines of Yellow Bear
and riding his horse. By 1886, the year his name first appears on the
Pine Ridge census, the journeys back and forth to Montana had

ended, his family believes. After that, he stayed put at Yellow Bear, hunting and riding as often as he could.

Like most of the others during the decade of the 1880s, George Dull Knife and the people of the Yellow Bear Camp, a remote area of the agency where many traditional Lakota lived, began to learn a different way of life.

Later, the old man in the nursing home would hear the stories about this new way of life. As a young boy, and for many years after, he heard them from his father, George Dull Knife. Stories about how it was growing up on the Pine Ridge Reservation in those early days, how the Oglala Sioux struggled to learn a new way of living in the final years of the nineteenth century.

"He always told me that the life was very hard back then," said the old man. "That it was a very hard time for all of our people. They missed the old ways and they didn't know how to live anymore, how to live like the white people wanted them to. Toward the end, a lot of them were confused and many were afraid."

Late in the fall of 1878, about the same time that Dull Knife and Little Wolf fled the Indian Territory for their northern homeland, a permanent agency for the Oglala Sioux was established north of the great ridge of pines that pushes across the Nebraska border into South Dakota. For most of a decade, ever since the Fort Laramie Treaty of 1868, the Oglala agency had wandered aimlessly from place to place: from Fort Laramie in Wyoming Territory to Fort Robinson in Nebraska to an ill-fated year along the banks of the Missouri River in Dakota Territory. Now the agency headquarters had come to rest on a plateau near White Clay Creek, just across the Nebraska line, and it would not be moved again.

Before long, in addition to the agency's new location, there were other changes, too. Fearful that the Oglala's principal chief already had too much clout and prestige, the government decided to abandon its previous practice of calling it the Red Cloud Agency. After much wrangling—no one seemed to know for sure how to spell Oglala—it was officially named the Pine Ridge Agency. The new agency occupied several million acres of rolling ranchland and wind-blown prairie stuck in the desolate southwest corner of what would become the state of South Dakota. It was here, a little more than two years after they had taken out Custer and five companies of U.S. cavalry, that six thousand Oglala Sioux were expected to begin the civilizing process, to give up the old ways and embrace the new. This was the place where the government hoped that a new order of Indian could be coaxed from the debris of their barbaric, nomadic warrior past to become peaceful, productive Christian farmers.

The United States had signaled its policy regarding the nation's original inhabitants almost a half-century earlier. On December 3, 1833, during his Fifth Annual Message to Congress, President Andrew Jackson made clear the government's solution to the Indian Problem. Said Jackson, an early and vocal proponent of the reservation system:

"My original convictions upon this subject have been confirmed by the course of events for several years, and experience is every day adding to their strength. That those tribes can not exist surrounded by our settlements and in continual contact with our citizens is certain. They have neither the intelligence, the industry, the moral habits, nor the desire of improvement which are essential to any favorable change in their conditions. Established in the midst of another and a superior race, and without appreciating the causes of their inferiority or seeking to control them, they must necessarily yield to the force of circumstances and ere long disappear. Such had been their fate heretofore, and if it is to be averted—and it is—it can only be done by a general removal beyond our boundary and by the reorganization of their political system upon principles adapted to the new reservations in which they will be placed. . . ."

Under this plan, the Indian would be forcibly removed to barren tracts of land, as far from white communities as possible, where the social experiments could begin. Congress would appropriate the money to furnish food, clothing, medicine, housing and equipment, and to hire government agents who would oversee the day-to-day process of civilizing the savage. The agents would be assisted by churches, missionaries and boarding schools.

According to Jackson, the goal of the new reservation system was uniformly simple: Take the inferior red man, isolate him from the general population and make him over in the white man's image. It was a philosophy that would dominate the rest of the nineteenth century and have far-reaching effects well into the twentieth.

By 1880, when the reservation system began in earnest on the northern plains of America, a number of potentially serious problems with such a philosophy had become clear. Perhaps chief among them was one expressed by Sitting Bull:

"What white man can say I ever stole his land or a penny of his money? Yet, they say I am a thief. What white woman, however lonely, was ever captive or insulted by me? Yet they say I am a bad Indian. What white man has ever seen me drunk? Who has ever come to me hungry and unfed? Who has ever seen me beat my wives or abuse my children? What law have I broken? Is it wrong for me to love my own? Is it wicked for me because my skin is red? Because I am a Sioux; because I was born where my father lived; because I would die for my people and my country?"

Like many of his countrymen, Sitting Bull did not share the government's view of himself or his people. He and many others preferred the old way of life, their own beliefs, values and customs. They did not want to become white, Christian or farmers. They wanted to remain Lakota.

On March 10, 1879, the first agent assigned to the new home of the Oglala Sioux arrived at the Pine Ridge Agency. His name was Valentine T. McGillycuddy. Stern, efficient, conscientious, bristling with energy and an iron will, McGillycuddy seemed an ideal choice to induce the Oglala down the white man's road. By agency standards, he was incorruptible and, equally important, he was no stranger to the Oglala. A contract army surgeon, he had accompanied Gen. George Crook on military expeditions against the northern plains tribes and treated wounded soldiers after several serious engagements with the Sioux and their allies. As the post surgeon at Fort Robinson, he had lived among the Oglala when their agency was located along the White River a few miles from the fort. On the night of September 5, 1877, Dr. McGillycuddy had been summoned to the adjutant's office to treat an Oglala wounded earlier that day in a scuffle at the guardhouse.

When he arrived, Crazy Horse lay on the floor in a corner of the darkened office, his elderly father and Touch the Cloud, a Miniconjou Sioux chief, kneeling at his side. Wrapped in a blanket, his kidney punctured by a bayonet, he was bleeding badly. Shortly after McGillycuddy entered the room, an army bugler sounded taps on the parade grounds outside. When the Lakota war chief heard the bugle, he "struggled to arise, and there came from his lips his old rallying cry, 'A good day to fight, a good day to die . . .' and his voice ceased. . . ." Touch the Cloud reached down and pulled the blanket over his friend's face. "The chief has gone above," he said.

"I could not but regard him as the greatest leader of his people in modern times," McGillycuddy said years later. "In him everything was made secondary to patriotism and love of his people. Modest, fearless, a mystic, a believer in destiny, and much of a recluse, he was held in veneration and admiration by the younger warriors, who would follow him anywhere."

It is said that Red Cloud became intensely jealous of Crazy Horse after the war chief surrendered. Afraid the government would make Crazy Horse chief of all the Oglala, Red Cloud was among a small group of agency Sioux who told General Crook that Crazy Horse was plotting to kill the officer and return to the war path. The stories eventually led to his arrest, the attempt to jail him and ultimately his death.

Eighteen months later, when McGillycuddy arrived at the Pine Ridge Agency to begin his new duties as government agent, he found Red Cloud firmly entrenched as chief of the six thousand Oglala scattered throughout their new homeland. Red Cloud was not a hereditary chief, but had earned the position through his skill and valor as a warrior. Among Indian leaders of the era, Red Cloud was without peer as a savvy diplomat, skilled infighter and political power-broker, and he clung tenaciously to the position. As the agent assigned to dismantle the Oglala's old way of life, to usher in the new civilizing era, McGillycuddy clung just as tenaciously to his. For the next seven years, McGillycuddy and Red Cloud were bitter antagonists in a power struggle that would shape the lives of George Dull Knife and his descendants, as it would all the Oglala families living on Pine Ridge for generations to come.

Shortly after assuming office, one of McGillycuddy's first orders of business was to establish a police force on the new agency. By August 1879, the force consisted of fifty men—all Indian, all ranked, all outfitted and equipped with new Springfield rifles or the Sharps army carbine, weapons personally given to the agency by Gen. Philip Sheridan. Led by Capt. George Sword, each member of the force earned five dollars a month to enforce all civil and criminal laws within agency boundaries, an arrangement that Red Cloud and other traditional headmen of the tribe vigorously opposed.

For as long as any of the people could remember, the Lakota had always policed themselves. Over time, an elaborate social system evolved in which numerous warrior societies competed for the honor of maintaining law and order within the tribe. The Akicitas, as the elite policing societies were known, were appointed by the chiefs, usually for one season, and it was always to them the people had turned when discipline, order and punishment were needed. The Akicitas kept order in camp movements and communal buffalo hunts, when the war parties were assembled and throughout the great feasts, during celebrations and in any time of crisis.

For Red Cloud and the other traditional leaders, it was unthinkable that Lakota warriors now wore government clothing, fired government weapons and drew a government salary to perform a job the Akicitas had always done for honor and the good of the tribe.

Agent McGillycuddy, however, believed stongly in the concept of an all-Indian police force. He saw it as an indispensable tool that would undermine Red Cloud and cripple his hold on the Oglala, that would break down the old ways and accelerate the new, and he gave high marks to his newly created police force. "Situated as the agency is, in close proximity to the ever-increasing white settlements," he wrote to his superiors, "it would be impracticable and almost impossible to conduct this agency without this organization. It represents law and order, and the members, uniformed and disciplined, and far advanced in civilization, offer the best and most practical example for the other Indians of the tribe to copy after, which they are rapidly doing in the way of adopting civilized clothing, etc. . . ."

The agent also saw another advantage in using an all-Indian police force. He saw it as a way to shed the trappings of paternalism, a way to nurture faith and trust among the Oglala Sioux. Wrote McGillycuddy: "Admit that the Indian is brutal in many ways and low in the evolutionary scale as a human being, but he is endowed with reasoning powers, and a conscience to a certain degree, and it would be strange indeed if he did not appreciate the trust and confidence that has been placed in him here, in placing the controlling and restraining power in the hands of the Indian police as Indians, and the entire removal from the vicinity of the agency of the white man's soldiers, whose presence appears to be a constant reminder that the Great Father, and the agent who represents him, are afraid to trust him."

For the civilizing process to reach full bloom, McGillycuddy passionately believed that all vestiges of the Indian past must be swiftly and decisively eliminated: the chief system dismantled, the hunting tendencies crushed, the nomadic urges curtailed, the language, customs, traditional clothing and religious practices banned, its practitioners jailed, their food rations cut off if necessary. To that end, he soon introduced 5,600 head of cattle, 300 mules and 200 swine and supervised the cultivation of 2,200 acres and the construction of 700 new log homes on the agency.

A prolific chronicler who combined a surgeon's eye for detail with an uncommon zeal for the job, McGillycuddy carefully noted in his annual report to Washington some of the problems he initially encountered at the Pine Ridge Agency. In 1879, he wrote:

"Locality and love of home is as strongly marked, if not more so, in the American savage as in the white man. . . . The old maxim that 'a rolling stone gathers no moss' was never more applicable. It is not at all remarkable that the 'untutored savage' who originally 'knew no guile,' has become distrustful, and at the present day he at first looks with distrust on all efforts of our government to assist him, his experience with the white man in the past being a sad teacher. . . .

"The housing of these people cannot be too strongly recommended, as their living in easily transported canvas teepees perpetuates their roving dispositions and will keep them more or less unsettled. . . .

"If we wish to continue them as savages and feed them until they finally die out, I would recommend the tribal system as the most feasible one. But . . . it becomes apparent to one who will inquire into the subject, that these chiefs in control of their tribes must soon outlive their usefulness."

And in later reports:

"It is a mere waste of time to attempt to teach the average adult Indian the ways of the white man. He can be tamed, and that is about all."

"With the American Indian, as with other savage nations, the native medicine-man combines the calling of physician, priest, and prophet. He is, above all others, barbarism personified, and is through his influence over a superstitious following, one of the principal obstacles in the way of civilization. Therefore no effort or means should be neglected to destroy his influence and himself in his peculiar capacity."

"The Indians generally are rapidly abandoning their peculiar customs. Dancing is diminishing, and the heathenish annual ceremony, termed the 'sun dance,' will, I trust, from the way it is losing ground, be soon a thing of the past. The increase in the number wearing civilized costumes is marked."

"They are rapidly adopting the white man's way of living, in the way of clothing, manner of preparing food, etc., and the expending of their earnings in more useful articles, such as spring wagons, furniture, etc., instead of beads and trinkets."

Toward the end of McGillycuddy's first year in office, in November 1879, Chief Dull Knife and 120 Northern Cheyenne were permitted to leave the agency for their Montana homeland. "These were part of the Cheyennes who had departed from the Indian Territory in the season of 1878, and had afterward escaped with Dull Knife from the so-called Fort Robinson massacre in January, 1879," wrote McGillycuddy. "These people were a constant source of trouble, as they were mourning continually for their relatives who were killed after their escape . . . and I was only too glad to accede to a request . . . to transfer the party to Fort Keogh, Montana."

The departure of the Cheyenne in late November, the agent believed, marked the end of a turbulent decade and the beginning of a promising new one. He saw fewer tipis now, more and more log homes. Creek bottoms nourished crops of corn and potatoes; boarding schools and missionaries nourished the hearts and minds of children. The savage dancing had faded away, as had much of the clothing, customs and rituals. All in all, he believed, a solid foundation had been laid, a critical corner turned. At year's end, the new agent for the Oglala Sioux was cheerful, upbeat and optimistic, confident that the reservation system was working, the seeds of change soon to bear fruit. The old Indian trapped in his old ways was dead and dying, far less likely than ever to go "back to the blanket," while a new one—hewn from the white man's image—was about to be reborn.

In his first annual report to the commissioner of Indian affairs, Agent McGillycuddy concluded: "The prospects of the Ogalallas under the system adopted by the present administration are very encouraging, and it is not exaggeration to say that these people have advanced more in the past year than in any previous ten years of their history."

The family of George Dull Knife and the people of the Yellow Bear Camp and many of the Lakota scattered throughout the barren

Dakota prairie in the 1880s did not share their agent's view of the Pine Ridge Agency. When the traditional Oglala journeyed forth across their new home, they saw an age-old way of life that was under siege from all quarters. For generations, they had been among the most self-sufficient people on earth, fashioning all their needs from land they were free to roam and the wild game that inhabited it. "I do not wish to be shut up in a corral," Sitting Bull had said. "It is bad for young men to be fed by an agent. It makes them lazy and drunken. All [reservation] agency Indians I have seen are worthless. They are neither red warriors nor white farmers."

But within a few short years, through a succession of complicated treaties and acts signed by some of their chiefs, men who often did not discover until much later what it was they had signed away, the Lakota found themselves almost entirely dependent upon government handouts—handouts needed to sustain a new way of life they neither understood nor had ever fully accepted. In effect, the treaties had bartered peace for dependence, had secured the West for settlement while creating a chain of reservations that became the nation's first welfare states.

Within these welfare states, many Lakota during the decade of the 1880s began to feel an overwhelming sense of despair, each year bringing a little more heartbreak, a little more futility, a little less hope than the last.

By 1881, they saw their children disappear inside six agency schools that now dotted the Dakota prairie. Here, instructors began to shear Indian boys of their long hair, the traditional symbol of Sioux manhood. When horrified parents pulled their distraught children from the schools, the threat of hunger forced them to relent. The treaties had required all Lakota children between the ages of six and fourteen to attend the schools regularly. Those who failed to do so were to have their food rations cut off. The first schools on Pine Ridge were not government schools, but parochial ones. Years earlier, President Ulysses Grant had directed American churches to educate the Indian, and he assigned different denominations to different reservations. Initially, the Episcopal church was in charge of educating most of the Lakota. Later, Catholics and Presbyterians joined in the task.

By 1882, the debilitating effect of bootleg liquor smuggled into the agency from nearby ranches had reached alarming proportions. Prohibited from bringing it onto Indian lands, whites established a free-for-all dance hall and whiskey ranch just across the Nebraska border, about two miles from the agency. The Lakota, having seen priests drinking wine during church services, called the potent alcohol *mini wakan*, holy water. To help stifle the abundance of liquor flowing into the agency, an executive order dated January 24, 1882, added a buffer strip of land five miles wide and ten miles long across the Nebraska border.

On April 10, 1883, the government enacted a Federal statute which prohibited the speaking of Lakota and the practice of Lakota culture and religion. That summer, about fifteen thousand Lakota attended the last open Sun Dance held on Pine Ridge. After that, it was officially banned for almost a century, its adherents forced to practice their most sacred religious rite underground, within the far-flung hills and valleys of the sprawling agency. Agent McGillycuddy noted the passing of the ritual in his annual report: "They have also made great progress in abandoning many of their old customs, noticeably that of the Sun Dance, which for the first time in the history of the Ogalalla Sioux and Northern Cheyenne was not held. The abandonment of such a barbarous and demoralizing ceremony, antagonistic to civilization and progress, as it has been proved, is a bright and promising event in the tribe's struggle toward advancement in the white man's ways. . . ."

In 1884, McGillycuddy helped install a Court of Indian Offenses to further ensure that the Sun Dance and other impediments to progress would be eliminated. The court was composed of three Indian judges, each of "good moral character, integrity and intelligence," handpicked by the agent. The three-member Indian tribunal sat in judgment on other Lakota accused of violating various rules that were designated as an "Indian offense." The rules, many of which remained on the books into the twentieth century, included:

No. 4: The "sun dance," and all other similar dances and so-called religious ceremonies, shall be considered "Indian offenses" and any Indian found guilty of being a participant in one or more of these offenses shall, for the first offense committed, be punished by withholding from him his rations for a period not exceeding ten days; and if found guilty of any subsequent offense under this rule, shall be punished by withholding his rations for a period of not less than fifteen days nor more than thirty days, or by incarceration in the agency prison for a period not exceeding thirty days.

No. 6: The usual practices of so-called "medicine men" shall be considered an "Indian offense" . . . and whenever it shall be proven to the satisfaction of the court that the influence of a so-called "medicine man" operates as a hindrance to civilization of a tribe, or that said "medicine man" resorts to any artifice or device . . . or shall use any of the arts of the conjurer to prevent the Indians from abandoning their heathenish rites and customs, he shall be adjudged guilty of an "Indian offense," and upon conviction of any one or more of these specified practices, or any other, in the opinion of the court, of an equally anti-progressive nature shall be confined in the agency guardhouse for a term not less than ten days. . . .

For a time, there were not enough funds to hire judges, so it fell to three senior members of the underpaid Indian police force to enforce the agency's new civil laws. Lt. Standing Soldier explained to Agent McGillycuddy the dilemma posed by such an arrangement:

"Father, we have served the Government and our people faithfully for five years. In protecting life and property and adopting the white man's ways we have risked our lives and incurred the enmity of many of our people, and for that service we, as commissioned officers of the police, receive but eight dollars per month and furnish our own horse, while the enlisted private white soldier is paid fifteen dollars per month and is supplied with a horse. Now, to act as judges over our people and condemn them to punishment when necessary will still further endanger our lives and increase their enmity, and we will be paid nothing in addition therefore, and we do not think that it is well to have the same man that acts as judge also act as policeman and perform the punishment. They tell me that is not the way the white man manages his own court. We are still willing to remain as policemen, hoping the Great Father will some time give us more pay for our service."

By the mid-1880s, even McGillycuddy's customary resilience and buoyant optimism began to wane, muted by a succession of crippling setbacks that made the last half of the decade far more distressing for his Lakota clients than the first half had been.

For a number of years, Pine Ridge had been a favorite hunting ground for circuses, Wild West exhibitions and quack-medicine shows seeking Indians as special attractions. By 1889, more than two hundred young Lakota men were missing. While some left with permission from the agent, others were lured off by quasi-bounty hunters or kidnapped by middlemen who often took them to the rail station in Rushville, Nebraska, and shipped them East, sold to the circuses at so much a head. This "recruiting" practice peaked at the end of the decade, creating a great deal of ill will and hardship among the Lakota. Families deprived of their able-bodied young men struggled to make ends meet and the men themselves often returned home demoralized and debilitated. When the Indians were no longer needed, they were frequently turned loose and forced to find their own way home. In the spring of 1889, seventy-two young Lakota men left for Europe with Cody's Wild West Show. "Five of these have died among strangers in a strange land while seven others have been sent home owing to their shattered health rendering them unfit for further service," the Pine Ridge agent reported at the time.

"One of these young men was taken from the cars at Rushville, Nebr., a few months ago, in a dying condition," wrote the agent. "The authorities of the town asked what should be done with him, as he had not a cent of money and could not be taken to the agency until his condition improved. I requested them to take the best possible care of him and I would contrive some means to pay whatever expense might be incurred. After remaining there several days the young man begged to be taken to his home to die. They started with him to the agency, but he died before half of the 25 miles had been traversed. The expense of caring for him while at Rushville, some $15, was paid by his friends. This is merely an isolated case, but the record of suffering, demoralization, and death among the Indians traveling with shows, for one year, would fill a volume."

For those who remained behind, agency life was often just as harsh. The forced transition from old to new had come quickly, the changes numerous, rapid and confusing. Raised on wild game, the Lakota could not adjust to eating beef. They were disgusted with the "spotted buffalo," finding its texture and smell repulsive, and there was seldom enough of it to go around. At first, Lakota women did not know what flour was or how to use it. Issued in 100-pound sacks to a family of six, the flour sometimes was dumped on the ground, the empty bags used for making children's clothing. Coffee arrived in the form of raw beans and there were no mills to grind it. Eventually, the women used rocks to pound the beans, creating a strong brew that the Lakota called *pejuta sapa*, "black medicine." Food was a constant problem. From the beginning, the great hope of the government had been to make the Lakota a self-sustaining people, primarily by teaching them how to become farmers, how to till the soil and grow crops on their own land. For a while, a number of Lakota men tried the new approach. In the end, their efforts failed, doomed by withering droughts, scorching summer winds and arid soil, lands that in the best of hands seemed incapable of yielding a minimal food base.

A disillusioned McGillycuddy summed up the problems in a report to superiors: "White men, well trained in farming, have tried to till the soil in northern Nebraska, and have lost all the money invested, and have not produced enough to pay for seed. I can confidently venture to state that if the experiment were tried of placing 7,000 white people on this land with seed, agricultural implements, and one year's subsistence, at the end of that time they would die of starvation, if they had to depend on their crops for their sustenance."

Although the land did not bear fruit easily, it had a considerable value in other ways that would have far-reaching consequences for the Lakota. The railroad, ranching and oil industries coveted Indian lands and, collectively, they began pressuring Congress in the last half of the 1880s to carve up the Great Sioux Reservation within Dakota Territory, to set aside smaller and smaller tracts for the Indian and sell off the surplus to white homesteaders and businesses. Squeezed by the land boomers and industrial magnates, Congress began looking toward the one tool that had been successfully employed for years to accomplish the task. It began looking at a new wave of documents, at a new set of laws, commissions and official government acts.

Beginning in 1851, the Lakota had signed a number of treaties with the government, and each time, they had lost more and more of their ancestral homeland. The Fort Laramie Treaty of 1868, signed by Chief Red Cloud and other headmen, had created the Great Sioux Reservation, an enormous land mass of 43,000 square miles exclusively set aside by law for the Indian. The reservation comprised all land west of the Missouri River, about half of present-day South Dakota, and included all of the Black Hills. The treaty forbade whites to enter the reservation without Indian permission and prohibited any sale of the land without the written consent of three-fourths of all adult Indian males.

In 1874, an army expedition led by Custer illegally entered the Black Hills and confirmed reports of large gold deposits within the Indian lands. Soon, mining companies were pressuring the government to open up the Lakota's sacred hills to prospectors. After a few feeble and unsuccessful attempts to get the required signatures, the government eventually declared that all Indians unwilling to sell the Black Hills would be considered "hostiles," enemies of the U.S. government. Those who did not surrender to the agencies by January 31, 1876, were to be hunted down by the army. After the Little Bighorn, and relentless political and military pressure and threats to withhold food rations, clothing and shelter, the army finally coerced Red Cloud and a small number of other chiefs into signing the necessary papers. On February 28, 1877, the government officially appropriated the Black Hills and 23 million surrounding acres. The illegal seizure had cost the Lakota their holiest site, a place the people called "the heart of everything that is." The loss of the Black Hills left a gaping hole in their physical, cultural and spiritual landscape and a bitter taste that would linger through the next seven generations.

Ten years later, in 1887, the government wanted to break up what remained of the Great Sioux Reservation into six smaller reservations and, in the process, reduce Lakota land holdings from 21,593,128 acres to 12,845,521 acres. The 8.7 million surplus acres would eventually be sold on the open market for $1.50 an acre, the proceeds going toward a general education fund for the Indian. Under this plan, the head of each Lakota family would be awarded 160 acres. He and his family would then become solely responsible for their own reservation land. Led by U.S. Senator Henry Dawes of Massachusetts, the government believed that crushing Lakota resistance to private ownership was the last great obstacle in the path to civilization. Among Indians, noted Dawes, "There is no selfishness, which is at the bottom of civilization."

But the Lakota steadfastly refused to go along with the plan. Between 1778 and 1871, the U.S. government signed and ratified 371 treaties with the American Indian. All were either broken or annulled. By 1887, chiefs Red Cloud, Little Wound, Young Man Afraid of His Horses and other Lakota headmen had lost all faith in negotiating with the government. They adamantly refused to sell any part of their remaining land and instructed their followers to do the same. As to the 160-acre plots, they could not conceive of an individual Lakota privately owning the land. It went against all their beliefs. Possession and ownership had always been the province of the tribe, not the individual.

To circumvent their resistance, government agents initially tried to gather the signatures of six- to fourteen-year-old boys, a ploy

Congress rejected. Finally, after several years of failed attempts and rancorous debate, the government turned to George Crook. It was left to the aging army general to convince the Lakota that it was now in their best interest to sell off some of their land in exchange for the security of long-term annuities, critical food supplies and a generous share of any proceeds from the surplus land sale. Throughout the long and heated discussions between Crook and the Sioux, food again surfaced as the one key issue. Lakota who had seen promise after promise dishonored in one way or another firmly believed their food rations would be greatly reduced once they signed away the land, and it took all of Crook's considerable skill as a diplomat, intimidator and Indian expert to convince them otherwise.

Eventually, after weeks of feasting, fierce debate and confusing legal jargon, weeks in which Lakota men were isolated from the chiefs and counseled in private, after the tribe had become bitterly divided along progressive and traditional lines, the Lakota's old military foe prevailed and secured the necessary number of signatures Congress needed to legally approve the sale of Lakota land.

Two weeks after Crook left with the signatures in hand, the government slashed the beef issue on Pine Ridge by 1 million pounds. On February 10, 1890, President Benjamin Harrison made it official: He formally announced acceptance of the land agreement and threw open the ceded territory to white settlers. On the Pine Ridge Reservation, the Oglala's aging chief, nearly seventy and half-blind, his health failing, spoke for many of his countrymen: "They made us many promises, more than I can remember," said Red Cloud, "but they never kept but one; they promised to take our land and they took it."

The 1880s had ended and, for the Lakota, the first decade of reservation life had brought unrelieved heartache and a festering resentment unknown to their forefathers, each year compounding the problems of the previous one, blunting hope at every turn. Some began to believe they were a cursed people, pointing to a succession of misfortune and disaster that had closed out their first decade on the Pine Ridge Reservation.

When the land set aside for them in Dakota Territory proved unsuitable for farming, many had turned to ranching. The new reservation offered good grazing, and for a while, some had prospered in their new roles as cattlemen. But in the spring of 1888, a disease called "black leg" swept through the herds, killing many of their cattle. When they tried a return to farming, two successive summers of record drought—in 1888 and 1889—wiped out the entire corn crop and most of the potato. Following both droughts, severe winter epidemics of *la grippe*, measles and whooping cough struck most of Pine Ridge. There was but one physician to care for the sick, who were scattered across a reservation 110 miles long by 60 miles wide, and so disease and death had visited many of the Lakota families in their new log homes and old tipis. By winter's end, in March of 1890, many were starving and reduced to a near-total dependence on government rations for survival. And now the rations had been slashed, a large part of their lands taken from them.

About this time, the Lakota holy man, Black Elk, returned to Pine Ridge. He had been gone for three years, touring the East Coast and Europe with Cody's Wild West Show. "My people looked pitiful," he said many years later. "There was a big drouth, and the rivers and creeks seemed to be dying. Nothing would grow that the people had planted, and the Wasichus had been sending less cattle and other food than ever before. . . . It looked as though we might all starve to death. We could not eat lies, and there was nothing we could do."

By now, the collective gloom that had settled over Pine Ridge was evident to the government as well.

In a lengthy report to the secretary of the interior, Commissioner of Indian Affairs T. J. Morgan later summed up his portrait of Pine Ridge from the Lakota vantage point:

"It is hard to overstate the magnitude of the calamity as they viewed it, which happened to these people by the sudden disappearance of the buffalo and the large diminution in the numbers of deer and other wild animals. Suddenly, almost without warning, they were expected at once and without previous training to settle down to the pursuits of agriculture in a land largely unfitted for such use. The freedom of the chase was to be exchanged for the idleness of the camp. The boundless range was to be abandoned for the circumscribed reservation, and abundance of plenty to be supplanted by limited and decreasing Government subsistence and supplies. Under these circumstances, it is not in human nature not to be discontented and restless, even turbulent and violent."

As the decade drew to a close, both government bureaucrat and Indian holy man looked across the Pine Ridge Reservation and reached the same conclusion. In a few short years, the Lakota had been reduced from a powerful, independent, self-sustaining nation to a weak, splintered, wholly dependent people. They had lost their Sun Dance, many of their rituals and much of their traditional clothing. The schools and churches had taken their children, cut their hair and begun teaching them a new language and way of life. Despite strict laws and a land buffer, bootleg liquor flowed throughout the reservation, and their own people now wore the uniform of the government policeman and sat in judgment on those who would act in the old ways.

More than a century later, on an early winter afternoon in the bright light of his Colorado nursing home, the old man spoke of the life his father had known in the early days of the Pine Ridge Reservation. George Dull Knife had been a young boy then, staying close to his family and the other traditional Lakota living in the rugged hills of the remote Yellow Bear Camp.

"He had a favorite way of explaining how it was back then, the same story that he used to tell me and my brothers and sisters when he thought we were old enough to understand," said the old man. "My father used to tell us that it was like all of our people had gone to sleep one night and when they woke up the next morning, everything had changed. They didn't recognize things anymore and they didn't understand where they were or what they were supposed to be doing. Some people tried the new ways and then they gave up and some did not try at all. They got confused and then they got afraid.

The thing he said he always remembered the most was that almost everyone was hungry and everyone was afraid.

"After a time, after they had lived like this a while, that's when all the dancing began. They were afraid and so they thought the dancing would make the Great Spirit take pity on them and that He would somehow make a better life for all our people."

Chapter Four

On the Hill above
Wounded Knee Creek

In the early spring of 1890, after the long summers of drought and the winters of disease, after the land sale had been approved and the beef issue slashed, a small party of Oglala Sioux returned from a journey across the western mountains and deserts of the United States to their home on the Pine Ridge Reservation.

They brought with them a wondrous story, a story about an Indian messiah who foretold a promising new world, a world in which all the white people would soon disappear and the buffalo would return and all the dead Indian ancestors of long ago would rejoin the living in a new way of life. A way that was much like the old, a way that had been lost in the spiraling gloom and hopelessness of the last decade. It was a story that soon found its way to George Dull Knife and the people of the Yellow Bear Camp, to Red Cloud and his Oglala band in the west, to chiefs Sitting Bull and Big Foot in the north, to Crow Dog and Two Strike in the east, a story that quickly swept through all the Lakota tribes that were now scattered across six reservations within the new state of South Dakota.

The miraculous story of a new world order had been told to the Oglala by the messiah himself, a full-blooded Paiute shepherd named Wovoka. The son of a medicine man, he had been raised by white Christian ranchers and lived in the Walker Lake region of western Nevada. On January 1, 1889, during a full eclipse of the sun, Wovoka had had a dream, a vision in which he died and journeyed to heaven. He saw God there and conversed with many of the long-ago dead. He also saw a new world, one exclusively set aside for the Indian people. Great herds of buffalo, elk and deer were everywhere. The dead were living and they were blessed with eternal happiness. No one suffered, no one starved. The people were without disease, strife or material want. God spoke to him and provided a set of commandments, and if they were obeyed, they would bring about the salvation of his people. When Wovoka returned to earth, he came as the Indian messiah.

News of an Indian messiah had spread quickly among the western tribes and reached the Pine Ridge Reservation in the summer of 1889, about the same time General Crook was trying to convince the Lakota to part with more of their lands. That fall, as the rumors continued to circulate, the Lakota held a council. Chiefs Red Cloud, Little Wound, American Horse and Young Man Afraid of His Horses selected eight Oglala Sioux from Pine Ridge to journey west to get to the bottom of the messiah stories. Three others—Kicking Bear, Short Bull and Mash the Kettle—were chosen to represent the nearby Rosebud and Cheyenne River reservations. So that fall, a party of eleven Lakota set out for Nevada to find the truth.

They found Wovoka and they spoke with him at length and when some of them returned to Pine Ridge in March of 1890, they told their chiefs that the stories were true, that a new messiah was in the land, that there was now hope and the promise of a new life for their demoralized people. Wovoka had given them a letter. It detailed what they must do to help bring about the new world. Heavily cloaked in the trappings of Christianity, the messiah's teachings stressed pacifism, honesty and goodwill toward whites, whom he would soon sweep from the earth. Wrote Wovoka:

When you get home, you must make a dance to continue five days. Dance four nights and the last night keep up the dance until the morning of the fifth day when all must bathe in the river and then disperse to their homes. You must all do it in the same way. I, Wovoka, love you with all my heart and am full of gladness for the gifts which you have brought me. When you get home, I shall give you a good cloud which will make you feel good. I give you a good spirit and give you all good things. I want you to come again in three months; some from each tribe. There will be a good deal of snow this year and some rain. In the fall there will be such a rain as I have never given you before. When your friends die, you must not cry; you must not hurt anybody or do harm to any one. You must not fight. Do right always. It will give you satisfaction in life. Do not tell white people about this. Jesus is now upon earth. He appears like a cloud. The dead are all alive again. I do not know when they will be here; maybe this fall or in the spring. When the time comes, there will be no more sickness and everyone will be young again. Do not refuse to work for the whites and do not make any trouble with them, until you leave. When the earth shakes at the coming of the new world, do not be afraid; it will not hurt you. I want you to dance every six weeks. Make a feast at the dance and have food that everyone may eat, then bathe in the water. That is all. You will receive good words from me sometime. Do not tell lies.

The dance that would help usher in the new world became known as the Ghost Dance. Its practitioners frequently painted their faces red, in honor of *Wi*, the sun. The women wore dresses, the men shirts of white cloth or muslin over buckskin leggings. Their necks often slashed in a V and colored a deep blue, the shirts were passed through the smoke of the holy cedar and sage. They were festooned with symbols of the sun and moon and stars and sometimes trimmed in eagle feathers, and they became known as ghost shirts. Like most of the western tribes, the Lakota soon began shaping the Ghost Dance to conform with many of their own traditional rituals, and before long, it had come to resemble the forbidden Sun Dance.

After the Civil War, the army had discovered that many of the native tribes west of the Mississippi were much different than the eastern ones. Western tribes often fought fiercely for their way of life, bitterly resisting the incursion of whites into their lands and the attempts to herd them onto reservations. For the Lakota, fighting had long been a way of life. They loved warfare. It had been in their blood and in their culture for generations. With the closing of the forts along the Bozeman Trail and the signing of the Treaty of 1868, the Lakota became the only North American tribe that had ever forced the army to capitulate.

During the summer and fall of 1890, unlike the other western tribes, the Lakota began to imbue their version of the Ghost Dance with an additional feature: They gave it militaristic overtones. Short Bull and Kicking Bear, the most vocal believers of the new religion, told their followers that ghost shirts would make them immune to soldier guns, would make their bullets fall harmlessly on the prairie.

For as long as any could remember, the Lakota had also been a deeply religious people, their spiritual beliefs rooted in the lands where they lived, where their ancestors lay buried. Upon these lands, the rocks and plants and animals were considered sacred, and throughout, they had maintained a profound and unwavering faith in *Wakan Tanka*, the Great Mystery. It was a belief that had shaped their view of the world and dominated daily life, from morning prayers and purification rites, to dancing and healing rituals, to warrior visions and burial ceremonies. For much of the past decade, their innate spiritual longings had collapsed beneath an avalanche of tumultuous change, gradually giving way to a sullen despair that *Wakan Tanka* had forsaken them. Throughout their long history, the Lakota were never more apt to embrace a religious overture than in the spring of 1890. For many, the bitter taste left by a decade of unfulfilled treaties, land theft, starvation, emasculation, disease, misery and hopelessness began to fade away inside a circle of colorful cotton shirts.

At the height of the Ghost Dance religion, James Mooney, an ethnologist with the Smithsonian Institution, traveled throughout the American West. He studied the tenets of the religion and interviewed Wovoka and many of his disciples. "Hope becomes a faith," Mooney later observed, "and the faith becomes the creed of priests and prophets, until the hero is a god and the dream a religion, looking to some great miracle of nature for its culmination and accomplishment. The doctrines of the Hindu avatar, the Hebrew Messiah, the Christian millennium, and the Hesunnin of the Indian Ghost Dance are essentially the same, and have their origin in a hope and longing common to all humanity."

By August 1890, another summer of dry, scorching winds had decimated Indian food crops throughout the reservations of western South Dakota. The land deal was official and white settlers began to move in, picking off the choicest lands. The government, meanwhile, gave no sign that beef reductions would be restored. Short Bull and Kicking Bear had told the people that the messiah would now appear in the spring of 1891, and faced with the prospect of another winter of starvation and disease, many Lakota increasingly turned to the one place where hope existed. Late that summer, across

Sitting Bull
(D.F. BARRY, COURTESY
NEBRASKA STATE HISTORICAL
SOCIETY)

the reservations of Pine Ridge and Rosebud, Standing Rock and Cheyenne River, more and more ghost dancers purified themselves, held hands and moved slowly around the cottonwood tree, singing and dancing, praying for the messiah to save them, to return them to the old way of life. As the movement gained momentum, families began to abandon their log homes and pull their children from the boarding schools. Villages of canvas tipis sprang up along the creek bottoms, and entire days were given to feverish dancing. Inside the holy circle, some fainted, fell down in swoons. They said they had seen dead relatives and glimpsed a new world, a world in which the Indian no longer suffered.

In the beginning, government agents assigned to the reservations thought little would come of the dancing. Bewildered by the strange phenomenon, some chose to ignore it. The momentary craze would soon run its course, they believed, and if nothing else, the approaching winter winds, deep snow and numbing temperatures would outright kill it. In short order, their initial passivity gave way to concern, their concern to fear and fear to alarm. Soon, a panic had set in.

By mid-August, hundreds of Lakota ghost dancers had gathered along White Clay Creek, eighteen miles north of agency headquarters in the village of Pine Ridge. On August 22, alarmed at the size of the gathering, Agent H. D. Gallagher ordered the Pine Ridge Indian police to ride in and break it up. His police returned the next morning and told him they had been ignored. On Sunday, August 24, Gallagher, an interpreter and the police again set out for the Indian camp. They arrived to find the dance circle empty, the dancers hiding in a nearby grove of cottonwoods. When Gallagher stepped inside the dance circle, several Lakota came out from the cover, loaded Winchesters leveled at the agent. A furious Gallagher ordered his police to arrest the armed dancers. As they moved forward, more Lakota emerged from the woods, brandishing loaded rifles and prompting Indian police to draw their revolvers.

Chief Young Man Afraid of His Horses quickly rode into the circle and eventually got both sides to put away their weapons and agree to a council. The dance leaders were angry. It was Sunday, they said, and they demanded to know why religious services were being held throughout the reservations, throughout the land, yet when they wanted to hold theirs, they were ordered not to, at gunpoint, by their own Indian police. The Ghost Dance was not bad, was not harmful, they said, and so they invited Gallagher to sit and see for himself. He agreed to watch, and soon the people emerged from the sheltering trees and began to dance.

Perhaps the first white to view the Ghost Dance, Gallagher was horrified at the spectacle. He quickly urged his superiors to put an end to it, warning that permissiveness now could spell disaster later. Before long, other agents were filing similar reports. As late summer turned to early fall, as more and more reports reached Washington, a consensus slowly began to build among the architects of the reservation system. Where the Indian now saw relief from misery and despair, their caretakers saw something else: a regression, an ominous backsliding from a decade of civilizing influence. By the fall of 1890, while the Lakota viewed it as the harbinger of a hopeful future, the government saw the Ghost Dance as a return to the barbarous past.

Soon, much as the words of Wovoka had swept the Indian lands, news of the Ghost Dance craze spread quickly through the communities of white settlers ringing the reservations. The strange doings at Pine Ridge and elsewhere triggered immediate fear among nearby settlements that a general uprising was in the works, that a bloody return to Sioux wars of the past was about to begin. As a result, citizens and townfolk began bombarding the governors of South Dakota and Nebraska with urgent pleas to protect their farms and ranches, their families and communities. Newspapers quickly jumped in, fueling the mounting hysteria with inflamed stories of impending mayhem if troops were not rushed to the borders to teach the Indian a lesson.

On October 9, Pine Ridge Agent Gallagher, a Democrat, gave way to his Republican successor. The new man's name was Daniel F. Royer. A physician by training, he had also been a banker, druggist and newspaperman, and found time to serve two terms in the territorial Dakota legislature as well. During the turbulent fall of 1890, few men were less equipped to serve as Pine Ridge agent than Dan Royer. A political appointee, he knew nothing about Indians in general, nor the Lakota specifically, nothing of their history, habits, temperament, customs or rituals, and he was instantly overwhelmed by what he found on the prairies of western Dakota that October. It wasn't long before some of the Lakota began calling him "Young Man Afraid of the Sioux."

At the end of his third day in office, Agent Royer cabled his superiors that fully one half the reservation had now embraced the Ghost Dance, were refusing all orders to stop and were ready to fight if confronted. His police force had lost control and if he failed in getting the chiefs to stop the dancing, he warned, military force would be needed.

At one point, Royer imported a baseball-loving nephew to the Pine Ridge Reservation. He asked the teenage farm boy, Lewis McIlvaine, a pitcher from nearby Huron, South Dakota, to teach the Sioux how to throw and hit a baseball. The American national pastime, Royer reasoned, might get their minds off the Ghost Dance and improve their generally belligerent attitude. His uncle, McIlvaine later recalled, understood nothing of the dance or the Sioux. He longed to return to medicine and was terrified of life as the Pine Ridge agent. Some evenings that fall, McIlvaine rode the reservation roads in a buggy with his uncle, a loaded rifle at the ready. One evening, Royer aimed the rifle at a small group of dancers and ordered them to stop. A Lakota man approached the buggy and opened his shirt, revealing a chestful of Sun Dance scars to the startled agent. When they were out on their evening rounds, it was not unusual for Royer to open fire on a tumbleweed blowing across the darkened road. The baseball experiment a failure, McIlvaine returned to the farm and Royer was again engulfed in a panic, frantically appealing to the commissioner of Indian affairs for military troops to quell his restless clients.

As November approached, Royer was not alone in his problems with the Oglala Sioux on Pine Ridge. To the east, the Brulé Sioux under Short Bull were ghost dancing on the Rosebud Reservation. To the north, many of Chief Big Foot's band of Miniconjou Sioux at Cheyenne River had embraced the dance, and on the Standing Rock Reservation, some of Sitting Bull's Hunkpapa Sioux also were dancing. By early November, a succession of field reports specified that an increasingly dangerous situation existed on all the reservations, none more so than at Pine Ridge. On November 18, Agent Royer again telegraphed the commissioner of Indian affairs:

"Indians are dancing in the snow and are wild and crazy. I have fully informed you that employees and government property at this agency have no protection and are at the mercy of these dancers.

Why delay by further investigation? We need protection, and we need it now. The leaders should be arrested and confined in some military post until the matter is quieted, and this should be done at once."

Several months earlier, the supervisor of education in the Dakotas had journeyed through the area on a tour of Indian schools. Her name was Elaine Goodale, and along the way, she also observed the condition of the Lakota on their reservations in the summer of 1890. "The pitiful little gardens curled up and died in the persistent hot winds," she wrote. "Even young men displayed gaunt limbs and lack-luster faces. Old folks lost their hold on life, and heart-broken mothers mourned the last of a series of dead babies." Three months later, in the pages of the Chadron *Democrat,* a newspaper in one of the communities gripped by fear of Indian hostilities, an article appeared summarizing the situation on Pine Ridge. "From the best information obtainable, it appears that the religious craze is not wholly the cause of the general uprising," the Nebraska paper reported. "Bad faith on the part of the government, bad rations and not enough of them, have been the principal causes. . . . It will be found that the Indians sadly need a Messiah, or some other superhuman instrument to ameliorate their miserable condition brought about by the dishonesty and neglect of the Republican administration."

During the months'-long buildup of tension and unrest, it did not occur to the government that a restoration of treaty rights and an increase in food and medical supplies could dismantle what pleading, threats and armed police had so far failed to do. And it did not occur to the government again in late November, when, in a few short weeks, the conditions on the reservations had begun to spin out of control. Military might had settled the West, had created the network of farms and ranches, communities and churches, the railroads, shipping and telegraph lines, had made civilization possible, and now military might would solve this problem, too.

On the morning of November 20, two days after Agent Royer's plea, the Lakota camped near Red Cloud awoke to see five companies of infantry and three cavalry troops under Brig. Gen. John Brooke marching into the Pine Ridge Reservation. Bringing up the rear, after the 370 soldiers who filed into the agency that morning were the army's new Hotchkiss cannon and a Gatling gun. The three cavalry troops were part of an all-black unit that had arrived from Fort Robinson. Former slaves and sons of slaves conscripted into the U.S. Army, they had been sent west to fight Indians and clear the frontier for white settlement, and they occupied the same barracks that Chief Dull Knife and his people had broken out of eleven winters earlier. It is said the Lakota thought the hair of the black soldiers was like that of the buffalo; that the men who arrived on Pine Ridge that late November morning were bundled in thick coats made of bison robes. The Lakota soon began referring to them as *akicita tatanka,* the "buffalo soldiers."

That same morning, November 20, six infantry companies and two cavalry troops arrived on the nearby Rosebud Reservation. Six days later, after a long trek by rail from Fort Riley, Kansas, the Seventh Cavalry under Col. James Forsyth rode into the Pine Ridge Reservation. Fourteen years earlier, at the Little Bighorn, the Lakota and their allies had wiped out half of the regiment, including its famed commander.

For several weeks, the military buildup intensified as troops from throughout the West were summoned to seize control of Indian lands from the Ghost Dance leaders and their followers. The troops came from South Dakota, Nebraska, Kansas, Colorado, Montana and as far as New Mexico. By month's end, one half of the U.S. Army had made its way to the reservations of western South Dakota, ultimately gathering within its folds a group of men whose energy, ambition and philosophies threatened to overwhelm a small corner of the barren Dakota prairie.

Upon the Lakota reservations that winter lived their last two great leaders, the half-blind Red Cloud, a warrior-chief-turned-diplomat who still held powerful sway, and the aging Sitting Bull, a medicine man of unrivaled stature who adamantly refused to give up the old ways. "I don't want to have anything to do with people who make one carry water on the shoulders and haul manure," he had once said. "The whites may get me at last, but I will have good times till then. You are fools to make yourselves slaves to a piece of fat bacon, some hardtack, and a little sugar and coffee."

In Chicago, Maj. Gen. Nelson Miles, the division's new commander and a man rumored to have presidential ambitions, had cut a deal with Buffalo Bill Cody. The general, who had little faith in the agents' ability to control Indian leaders, thought Cody an ideal choice for the job of arresting Sitting Bull. If things went according to plan, the obstinate medicine man would soon be in exile, languishing in a Florida prison two thousand miles from the nearest Ghost Dance. In late November, Cody boarded a train and left immediately for the reservation, intent on hunting down his old friend, the former star attraction of his Wild West Show. About the same time, Valentine McGillycuddy, the flamboyant ex-army surgeon and former Pine Ridge agent, rode into his old reservation as a special emissary of the governor of South Dakota. Not long after, the Sixth Cavalry's A Troop was ordered to the southern perimeter of the Dakota reservation from its headquarters in Albuquerque, New Mexico. One of the unit's officers, Lt. John J. Pershing, was soon placed in charge of a company of friendly Sioux scouts. To the west, a troop of Northern Cheyenne scouts under the command of Lt. E. W. Casey set out from Fort Keogh, Montana, ordered to Pine Ridge to help subdue their old Lakota friends and allies. Eventually, Frederic Remington, on assignment for *Harper's Weekly,* arrived on Pine Ridge, as did the Baron Erwin von Luittwitz, a young Red Cross private who would later become a general and Germany's minister of defense. Years later, the German general and his troops would be defeated in the Great War by allied troops under the command of an American general, John "Black Jack" Pershing. On Pine Ridge, meanwhile, former slaves and the descendants of Custer's Seventh mingled among the Lakota of Red Cloud and Sitting Bull, the people who had fought them in the great battle in Montana.

On December 1, 1890, once the troops were in place, the commissioner of Indian affairs ordered all agents to submit to military rule on their reservations. Among the Lakota, little could arouse the kind of fear and panic created by the presence of hundreds of well-armed soldiers equipped with the latest field artillery. The growing soldier hordes sharply divided the Lakota into two camps: those who believed in the coming messiah and those who did not. The nonbelievers headed west, pitching their camps near Red Cloud on the far edge of the Pine Ridge Reservation. Angry, confused and afraid, many of the believers began to scatter wildly in all directions. About eighteen hundred Brulé Sioux stampeded through the snow from the Rosebud Reservation to Pine Ridge. They didn't know what was going on, what was happening upon the lands they had been given. Some were afraid they would be slaughtered; others feared their weapons would be confiscated. Many believed in the messiah's promise, that he would appear in the spring, and they desperately sought to continue the dancing until then. More and more, they began to congregate deep in the Dakota Badlands, in the northwest corner of the Pine Ridge Reservation, within a walled, natural fortress called the Stronghold. Inside the near-impregnable rock formation, Short Bull and Kicking Bear were the leaders, and here the panicked believers resumed the Ghost Dance with a fury.

For weeks, there had also been a steady influx of reporters streaming into the area. When the troop buildup began, editors from throughout the country had dispatched reporters to the scene, hoping to give their readers dramatic updates from the battlefield. However, for weeks, no shots had been fired and desperate editors, spoiling for a good fight and some good copy, demanded action from their own troops. A number of reporters eagerly complied, fanning the tense environment with wholesale fabrications and lurid reports, tales of massacres, outrages and atrocities committed, sensational stories of how the savage had already turned from the path of civilization to war.

Nothing in the history of the Lakota gave rise to any reasonable belief that they were about to embark on the warpath. Already there had been some snow and freezing winds and soon it would be the dead of winter. Many were starving and some were diseased. They had meager belongings, few tipis and nowhere to go. They had their women and children and old people and, by early December, half of the U.S. Army stood poised at their borders.

In mid-December, General Brooke invited Chief Little Wound into his office at agency headquarters in Pine Ridge. He asked the chief, an early adherent of the Ghost Dance, to explain the meaning of the dance and why the Lakota embraced it.

"Your white missionaries have told us of the white Messiah who came a long time ago to save the white people," said Little Wound. "They have told us how your people refused to believe on Him, and how in order to prove that He was all that was claimed He was put on a wooden cross and tortured to death, but that before He died He promised that He would come again. More than a month ago, Porcupine [an Indian who had traveled to Nevada] came down from the north and told us that he had come from a tribe that lived many moons away in the north to tell us that the Messiah of which the white man had told us had come and was an Indian. He said the Messiah had told his people that they must learn a certain dance and then go and teach it to other tribes, for when the green grass comes again He will travel far to the south to visit all the tribes, and that He would restore them to their freedom and hunting grounds and give them plenty to eat.

"But when He comes, Porcupine told us, he will stop only with the tribe that He finds dancing the Messiah dance and ready to receive Him; and if they are not dancing, He will pass them by and go to other tribes who believe and follow the teaching. I asked my people, and one of the chiefs said that if it were true we must dance the Messiah dance until the green grass comes again; and if it were not true we would know it then and go back to our way of living. So we started the dance, but not to go on the war path. The Indian does not go on the war path in the winter time. Then, general, the white

Red Cloud
(NEBRASKA STATE
HISTORICAL SOCIETY)

man comes with his soldiers and our young men were very angry, for they say that the soldiers were sent to keep our Messiah from coming to us. We have not had enough to eat for many moons, and that makes our young men hope for and believe in the Messiah."

Early on the morning of December 15, in the half-dawn of a gray drizzle, an Indian police force commanded by Lt. Henry Bull Head arrived at a modest log cabin along the banks of the Grand River on the Standing Rock Reservation. The police were sad, empty inside. They were frequently in a tough spot, as they did their jobs, and they had dreaded this one for a long time. Now it had come. Bull Head knocked on the door, and a muffled voice told him to enter. Inside, the Lakota police lieutenant informed a sleepy Sitting Bull that he was under arrest.

Three weeks earlier, the frantic appeals of Standing Rock Agent James McLaughlin had convinced President Harrison to cancel Buffalo Bill Cody's arrest orders for the Lakota medicine man. The agent believed it was his job to decide when and where the arrest would take place. It wasn't yet cold enough and to do it then, he argued, might backfire. It might drive more Lakota into Sitting Bull's camp and needlessly escalate the crisis. By now, the government's plan had taken shape. It intended to crush the Ghost Dance by identifying its most prominent leaders, arresting and then removing them to regions far from their disciples. A "hit list" had been compiled and the army would lead the roundup. That Sitting Bull's name belonged high on the list of agitators, no one doubted, least of all McLaughlin. He saw the Ghost Dance as a barbaric ritual and Sitting Bull as an unyielding, irritating regressive.

"Sitting Bull is high priest and leading apostle of this latest Indian absurdity; in a word he is the chief mischief-maker at this agency, and if he were not here, this craze, so general among the Sioux, would never have gotten a foothold at this agency," McLaughlin had written to superiors in mid-October. He described the Lakota leader as a "man of low cunning, devoid of a single manly principle. . . . He is a coward and lacks moral courage." The Ghost Dance, concluded McLaughlin, "is demoralizing, indecent, and disgusting." That fall, when Sitting Bull invited Kicking Bear to teach the Ghost Dance to his followers, Agent McLaughlin angrily threw him out. But Kicking Bear's message of the coming messiah survived. With Sitting Bull presiding, the new converts had been dancing in his camp on the Grand River ever since. Then, toward mid-December, as army units and cannons closed in, Kicking Bear and Short Bull invited Sitting Bull to join them in the Stronghold. Agent McLaughlin got wind of the invitation. The thought of the Lakota Nation's most powerful religious presence joining several thousand religious zealots inside a near-impregnable fortress put McLaughlin in a cold sweat. Now there could be no delay.

When Lieutenant Bull Head came through the door with his prisoner, he found an angry mob waiting outside. The sight of Indian police arresting their revered chief on orders from a white agent who did not approve of their religious ceremonies sent the crowd into a frenzy. Within minutes, a shot rang out and Bull Head reeled backward, a Winchester slug ripping through his right side. On his way down, Bull Head withdrew his service revolver and shot Sitting Bull in the chest. At the same moment, Sergeant Red Tomahawk grabbed his revolver and fired a single shot into the back of Sitting Bull's head. The Lakota holy man collapsed in a heap beside his cabin door. The shootings set off a murderous melee. When it ended, fourteen

Lakota lay dead or dying: Sitting Bull and seven followers, and six Indian police, including Lieutenant Bull Head.

Directly south of Sitting Bull's camp, on the Cheyenne River Reservation, lived the Miniconjou Sioux. The chief of one of their bands was a man his people called Spotted Elk. Years earlier, Spotted Elk had received a pair of oversized moccasins and, ever since, he was more commonly known as *Si Tanka*, Big Foot. His father had been a chief, and upon his death in 1874, Big Foot assumed leadership of the band. The Sioux Wars of 1876 severely crippled his people, and Big Foot surrendered in 1877, leading the survivors to their new agency home. On Cheyenne River, he was one of the first Sioux leaders to grow corn successfully. He helped build new schools and journeyed to Washington as a tribal delegate. Earnest and soft-spoken, he was now an elderly man, about sixty-five, a chief who had fashioned his reputation through diplomatic rather than military skills. Among the Lakota, Big Foot had long been regarded as the great compromiser, a consummate negotiator who was frequently summoned to mediate intertribal disputes and settle squabbles within various factions of the Great Sioux Nation. To the Miniconjou, he was also known as a soft touch, the chief who could always find a place for the growing number of widows, orphans, homeless, sick, wounded and hungry. It endeared him to his people.

In the fall of 1890, Chief Big Foot was among the Indian leaders who initially embraced the Ghost Dance, and so his name appeared on the list of agitators to be rounded up by the army. His band numbered about 350—230 women and children and 120 men. Many of the women were widows, had lost their men in battle, and they danced in the belief they might soon rejoin their husbands in the new world to come. By early December, Big Foot had personally disavowed the Ghost Dance, but many of his followers had not. They continued to dance and their chief's name remained high on the list of troublemakers. A nearby military unit, under strict orders to prevent marauding bands of Lakota from leaving their assigned reservations, was now keeping a close eye on the Miniconjou village. The unit's commander, Lt. Col. Edwin Sumner, had met frequently with the chief and was convinced "that Big Foot was making an extraordinary effort to keep his followers quiet."

About this time, in early December, several runners arrived in Big Foot's camp. They brought word from Red Cloud that the Oglala chiefs wanted him to journey south. If he succeeded in patching up a number of disputes on Pine Ridge, they would give him a hundred ponies. On December 16, Lt. Colonel Sumner received orders for Big Foot's arrest. He was to be sent west, taken to Fort Meade and jailed as a military prisoner of war. Two days later, several exhausted warriors, one of whom carried a bullet in his leg, straggled into the Miniconjou camp. They were among four hundred Hunkpapa Sioux who had stampeded from Standing Rock after the Grand River shootout, and they brought word that Sitting Bull was dead. In the next few days, more and more of the dead chief's frightened followers sought refuge in Big Foot's camp. He gave them food and shelter, and then his scouts brought more bad news: Soldiers were advancing from the east. The old chief did not know what to do. His people were cold and hungry and in a panic. He was frightened, too, and before any decisions were made, Lt. Colonel Sumner and his troops rode into their makeshift village.

Sumner immediately ordered all of them to return to their permanent cluster of cabins along the Cheyenne River. Big Foot agreed and, under military escort, the group arrived at their cabin homes a few days later. Before leaving, Sumner ordered the chief to report the next day to his army camp a few miles away. That night, a white rancher named John Dunn came to Big Foot's village. Dunn had just left the nearby military camp and he told the frail chief that Big Foot and his people were to be taken to Fort Bennett the following day. If they didn't go voluntarily, Dunn said, the soldiers might start shooting. Many might die, he said.

Once again, Big Foot found himself in a quandary. It had all happened so fast and now he didn't know whom to trust, where to turn. He could stay put, take his chances and see what happened. He could also keep his appointment with Sumner the next morning. Or he could move out that night and head south to Pine Ridge, as Red Cloud had requested. He had not been feeling well lately and he didn't know if he could make the long ride. His people were frightened, that much he knew. After consulting his headmen, a decision was reached. They quickly packed their few belongings, gathered the horses and wagons and broke camp, heading south, toward the Oglala Sioux and Pine Ridge about a hundred fifty miles away. Within a day's ride of reaching Red Cloud, near their sacred Porcupine Butte, the Seventh Cavalry caught up with them. It was late in the Moon of Popping Trees, December 28, 1890.

That December, George Dull Knife was fifteen years old. He was a big kid, tall and thick through the shoulders and chest. It had been a rough winter in the Yellow Bear Camp, and he had frequently taken his bow and arrows and disappeared into the rugged, pine-covered hills, searching for the deer and wild turkey that would help fill his family's empty stomachs. Chiefs Little Wound and Yellow Bear, the leaders of his Oglala band, had encouraged the Ghost Dance, and so the camp had done their share of dancing as autumn turned to winter.

One morning in late December, George Dull Knife and his people awoke to the sound of muffled gunfire far to the west. Soon, there came the distant sound of the big guns, weapons the Lakota feared above all else, and a kind of dread and nervous excitement swept Yellow Bear. Some of the young men grabbed their horses and set off toward the west. George Dull Knife had a fast horse and he could borrow a .12-gauge shotgun that belonged to a friend. He got his horse and was walking to the friend's house when his mother caught up with him. She grabbed him and held him and wouldn't let him go. Over and over, he persisted, but his mother would not relent. Finally, she hid his horse in a place where he could not find it. Many years later, in the middle of the next century, George Dull Knife told his young grandson about the day the people of the Yellow Bear

Camp heard the cannons and how his mother had conspired to keep him home.

Guy Dull Knife Jr., the artist and sculptor, remembers it well. It was 1954 and he was seven years old. That fall, Gen. Dwight D. Eisenhower, passionate golfer and World War II hero, was finishing up a second year as president. Abroad, North Korea had gone Communist and at home, Senator Joe McCarthy was looking for sympathizers. In New York, the Yankees found a muscular young replacement for DiMaggio, and down in Tupelo, a skinny white kid had started a fever singing the black man's music. Suburbs and care-free vacations, the family station wagon and two-car garages were coming into view. Abundance, hope and prosperity seemed every-where. It was a good time.

Guy Dull Knife Jr. and his grandfather were walking through a field of buffalo grass on the Pine Ridge Reservation. They were look-ing for native plants, herbs to stockpile for the winter season of colds and flu. George Dull Knife was seventy-nine that fall, and he loved walking the autumn prairie with his grandchildren. When they came to a rise above Medicine Root Creek that morning, the old man stopped for a while. Pointing to the west, he began to tell a story the small boy had not heard before.

"One of the things Grandpa said he had always remembered about that day was how warm and sunny it was. He said it seemed almost like a spring day, even though it was the end of December," recalled the grandson. "The gunfire continued for quite a while and he was really mad at his mother. There was a lot of commotion in the camp and many had ridden off to see what was going on and he couldn't find his horse anywhere. Late that afternoon, one of the young men came riding back into the Yellow Bear Camp. All the people started running toward him. From what Grandpa said, I guess he was really exhausted and really afraid. He told the people that something terrible had happened at a place the Lakota call *Cankpe Opi Wakpala*."

. . .

Maj. Samuel M. Whitside, Seventh Cavalry, sent his scouts fanning out ahead to find Chief Big Foot.

The army was in a panic, haunted and overwhelmed by the many possibilities for catastrophe. The Brulé Sioux had already stampeded from their Rosebud Reservation to Pine Ridge. Many Hunkpapa Sioux had done the same, fleeing wildly from Standing Rock to Cheyenne River. Inside the Stronghold, a large throng under the militant Short Bull and Kicking Bear danced with increasing fervor, many convinced they were now impervious to soldier bullets. The army feared that roving bands of hostile Lakota might soon strike the white settlements. That Sitting Bull's enraged followers would slaughter innocent ranchers. That Big Foot was making a last desperate flight to the Badlands. That he would soon reach Short Bull and Kicking Bear, emboldening them in a final rampage. General Miles desperately wanted him captured, his followers disarmed, arrested and shipped by rail hundreds of miles from the Dakota reservations. On Pine Ridge, army officers had offered twenty-five dollars to the first scout who found the Miniconjou chief. A bored pool of reporters soon bumped the ante to fifty dollars. In late December, an army dispatch to field commanders flashed across the frozen prairie: "If he fights, destroy him."

Big Foot lay in the back of a wooden wagon, huddled beneath blankets, coughing up blood. He had come down with pneumonia and he knew nothing of the rewards and messages, the hysteria and panic, as he and his people struggled across the winter prairie. They had never intended to go to the Stronghold and now, twenty-three miles from Red Cloud's camp, the caravan slowed to a crawl. To the rear, cold and hunger consumed his people. They had little warm clothing and had been shooting some of their horses the last few days. In the age-old custom of mourning, some of the women had cut their hair and slashed their arms, signs of grief for the passing of Sitting Bull. Many were sick and worn out, afraid, and they desperately wanted to reach Red Cloud, the last great leader they had. With him, they would be safe, would have food and shelter, some warmer clothes. In the front of the procession, the old man chief lay in the bed of a rickety wooden wagon, riding at the head of his people as chiefs had always done.

Bat Garnier, a half-breed scout, was one of the first to make contact. He told Big Foot that the panicky soldiers were everywhere, the Seventh Cavalry camped but a few miles away. Exhausted and near death, Big Foot said he wanted no trouble and so he told the scouts to send word that he would go directly to the army camp. After the scouts had left, a white cloth flag fluttering from a pole above the old man's wagon, he and his people began moving once again across the prairie. Major Whitside and the cavalry soon appeared on a distant rise. After a few anxious moments, the officer advanced to the chief's wagon. He told Big Foot they must all proceed to the army camp and the chief agreed, saying that was where he was going all along. Whitside signaled for an ambulance to come forward, and when it arrived, several soldiers carefully removed the old man from his wagon bed. He was bleeding badly from the nose and now they lifted him by the blankets and eased him into the ambulance. Late that afternoon, the Seventh Cavalry and the Miniconjou arrived at the army camp on *Cankpe Opi Wakpala,* on Wounded Knee Creek.

The soldiers directed the Indians to pitch their tipis in a dry ravine near the road that led to agency headquarters in Pine Ridge, sixteen miles away. Major Whitside ordered an army tent, equipped with a stove heater, set up for Chief Big Foot, and an army doctor soon arrived to tend to him. Atop a long, flat hill overlooking the Indian encampment, Whitside also ordered his troops to set up two Hotchkiss guns, breech-loading cannons that weighed 337 pounds apiece. The cannons were capable of firing fifty shells per minute. Upon impact, each 2 1/2-pound shell would explode, shredding everything within a wide radius. Throughout the late afternoon and evening, additional troops and artillery under Colonel Forsyth arrived from Pine Ridge. Before leaving, the officers had been furnished a keg of whiskey. Long into the night, down in their village in the ravine, Big Foot's people heard the distant wagons, horses, marching, some merriment and the sound of metal clicking into place. All along, they had assumed they would eat breakfast the next morning, then head to Pine Ridge—that by next evening, they would be camped in the safety of Red Cloud's village.

When the 230 Miniconjou women and children and 120 men awoke on December 29, an unseasonably warm and sunny day, they found themselves surrounded by more than five hundred soldiers, the barrels of four Hotchkiss cannons trained on their village from the hill overhead. The overwhelming show of force initiated an instant fear. They weren't sure what to do, what all the guns and soldiers meant. Unknown to them, the army's orders were clear. The Miniconjou weren't going west to Pine Ridge, to Red Cloud. They were to be marched thirty miles south, to a rail depot in Gordon, Nebraska, and then shipped by train to Omaha, more than four hundred miles to the east. Before leaving, they were to be disarmed.

For years, disarming Indians had been a delicate matter, fraught with complications, and for the Lakota, weapons had long been among their most cherished possessions. They were sometimes acquired at great cost, bartered for numerous goods and services. They were the means to hunt, defend and achieve honor in battle. Lately, the new Winchester and Springfield rifles had found an additional use: to help ensure that the Ghost Dance ceremonies would continue. On the morning of December 29, the army assumed such a show of force would make the disarming of Big Foot's people a simple matter. To be both surrounded and disarmed, believed some Lakota, would now make a bad situation worse.

About 8 a.m., after everyone had eaten, the commander of the Seventh Cavalry, Colonel Forsyth, called for a council in front of Big Foot's tent. The ailing chief was carried outside and he sat on the ground, swathed in blankets and a head scarf. Through an interpreter, Forsyth then directed the Miniconjou to surrender their weapons and place them in a pile near their chief. Afterward, they would all leave for a new camp. A circle of soldiers ringed the council grounds, and on the hill above, battery officers stood by the cannons. Out of earshot, in the Indian camp nearby, some of the women were dismantling tipis and packing wagons for the trip to Pine Ridge. Dogs chased after the children, and the children after one another. Inside the council grounds, the Miniconjou men began to mill nervously about, tense and confused. After a time, they returned with a few broken-down weapons. Irritated at the meager pile, Colonel Forsyth ordered a tipi-by-tipi search. His men went to the lodges and wagons, ransacking piles of clothing, bundles, personal possessions and household goods, and soon they came back with many more guns, bows, knives, axes and hatchets. Forsyth then directed his soldiers to begin frisking each of the men, to search their clothing and blankets for any concealed weapons. The older men complied, but many of the younger ones did not. They began to move away, pacing back and forth, panicky, not knowing what to do.

For several minutes, a Miniconjou medicine man had been circling the council grounds. His name was Yellow Bird and he was painted in fantastic colors. He wore a Ghost Dance shirt and a tail of eagle feathers, and he was singing and chanting, tossing dirt in the air, telling the warriors they had nothing to fear, the bullets of the soldiers would fall to the prairie. As he continued to sing and dance, inexperienced soldiers and young warriors began to fidget and Colonel Forsyth directed the medicine man to stop, to sit down and be quiet. For a while, Yellow Bird did as he was told. When the body searches began, he again resumed the chant of the Ghost Dance, circling along the council perimeter, exhorting the young men to take courage, to believe in the prophecies of the messiah, in the new world to come. Soon, a young Indian held his rifle aloft. Black Coyote was deaf. He began to shout that he had earned the rifle, it was his, that he would not give it up without compensation. Two soldiers approached and grabbed him from behind. During the struggle, his rifle accidentally discharged and a single shot echoed through the camp.

The soldier guns exploded, a withering barrage of gunfire pouring into the council grounds. In moments, hundreds of rounds kicked up a thick blanket of swirling dust and gunpowder, making it impossible to see more than a few feet. As the soldier circle burst forward,

Miniconjou men swarmed over the pile of discarded weapons, grabbing whatever they could, and for ten minutes, the two groups bitterly fought hand-to-hand with guns, knives, clubs, axes and hatchets. A knife sliced off most of interpreter Philip Wells's nose. Capt. George Wallace dropped in his tracks, a bullet tearing off the top of his head. Along one edge, a group of eight to ten Lakota boys, dressed in matching gray school uniforms, lay piled in a twisted heap. Bleeding badly from head wounds, his body riddled with bullets, Chief Big Foot slumped to the ground, a white flag flying above the door of his tent. Outside the council grounds, atop the long, flat hill overhead, a battery sergeant now ordered the Hotchkiss cannons turned toward the ravine. Chunks of earth exploded, tipis burst into flame and the bodies of mangled women and children fell across the village grounds. Hysterical relatives, screaming and crying, joined the surviving men, running down the ravine toward Wounded Knee Creek. From the rear, mounted troops and Hotchkiss guns pursued them into the sheltering cutbanks. The shooting continued throughout the afternoon.

Early on the morning of the first day of 1891, George Dull Knife convinced his mother that he would be careful, that he would return at the first sign of trouble, and so she allowed him to get his horse and ride out of the Yellow Bear Camp. For three days, the camp had been paralyzed with fear. When the rider returned with the news, his people had hurriedly packed their belongings, preparing to flee. A rumor had consumed the camp—that the soldiers would soon go door to door, killing as many Lakota on Pine Ridge as they could find, the Seventh's revenge for Custer. He and his family, like many of the others, had stayed up all night packing, ready to leave at first light. For several days, however, a severe blizzard had moved across the prairie, bringing snow and freezing cold. Although a few had slipped away, many at Yellow Bear had nowhere to go. They did not know what to do now. George Dull Knife got his horse, picked up a friend and rode out of the camp, heading west.

Late that afternoon, the two boys reined in their horses, pulling up on a hill that overlooked Wounded Knee Creek. It was a cold day and a bitter winter wind made their eyes tear when they stopped on the hill and looked down. In the distant ravine, strips of canvas flapped from the few lodgepoles still standing. Below the blackened poles, scraps of clothing, pieces of blanket, shredded dresses and shawls blew across the deserted village grounds. Near the road to Pine Ridge, they saw splintered wagons clustered in heaps, the dead dogs and horses scattered between them. Opposite the village, strung out along a field of snow, lay the bodies of Chief Big Foot and his followers. Some were in heaps and some were alone, many now frozen in grotesque shapes. The two boys did not speak, and when they saw a few soldiers and some wagons far across the way, they silently turned their horses and started for home, riding back to their people in the Yellow Bear Camp.

"It was a sight that my grandfather never forgot," said Guy Dull Knife Jr. As a small boy, he had heard the stories of Wounded Knee from his grandfather and his father and he had heard them, too, from the family's longtime neighbor, Dewey Beard.

For almost half a century, Dewey Beard lived in a dugout about a mile from the Dull Knife family home near Kyle, a community in the middle of the Pine Ridge Reservation. The coffeepot was always on in their home and Beard was a frequent guest. One bitterly cold winter day, the Dull Knifes were gathered in their tiny kitchen, clustered in blankets and coats around the wood-burning stove, when there was a knock on the door. For a while, no one moved, no one wanted to leave the stove's warmth. Finally, Rose Bull Bear got up and went to the door. "It was well below zero that day," said Guy Jr., "and when my mother opened the door, Dewey was standing there in a light jacket, a head scarf, overalls and a pair of moccasins. He had no socks and no gloves. He was probably about ninety-seven at the time and he had ridden over to our house bareback. Dewey was raised in the old ways and the cold didn't seem to bother him the way it did the rest of us."

At eighteen, Beard had been among a group of warriors who

crossed the Little Bighorn in the final moments of the battle. At thirty-three, he and his family were camped in Big Foot's village. Years later, the last Lakota survivor of both Custer and Wounded Knee talked at length about the fight inside the council grounds, about the flight from the Miniconjou village into the ravine. Beard spoke through an interpreter, who both summarized and quoted him directly:

"The struggle for the gun was short, the muzzle pointed upward toward the east and the gun discharged. In an instant a volley followed as one shot, and the people began falling. He saw everybody was rolling and kicking on the ground. He looked southeastward and he did not know what he was going to do. He had only one knife. He looked eastward and saw the soldiers were firing on Indians and stepping backwards and firing. His thought was to rush on the soldiers and take a gun from one of them. He rushed toward them on the west to get a gun. While he was running, he could see nothing for the smoke; through the rifts he could see the brass buttons of the uniforms; he rushed up to a soldier whose gun rested over Dewey's shoulder and was discharged when the muzzle was near his ear, and it deafened him for a while. Then he grabbed the gun and wrenched it away from the soldier. When he got the gun, he drew his knife and stabbed the soldier in the breast. . . . While Dewey was on this soldier, some other soldiers were shooting at him, but missed him and killed soldiers on the other side. When he got up he ran right through the soldiers toward the ravine, and he was the last Indian to go into the ravine. The soldiers were shooting at him from nearly all directions, and they shot him down. . . . Dewey tried to get to the ravine and succeeded in getting on his feet. . . . Right on the edge of the ravine on the south side were soldiers shooting at the Indians who were running down into the ravine, the soldiers' shots sounded like fire crackers and hail in a storm; a great many Indians were killed and wounded down in there. . . .

"When he went to the bottom of the ravine, he saw many little children lying dead in the ravine. He was now pretty weak from his wounds. Now when he saw all those little infants lying there dead in their blood, his feeling was that even if he ate one of the soldiers, it would not appease his anger. . . . The Indians all knew that Dewey was wounded, but those in the ravine wanted him to help them. So he fought with his life to defend his own people. He took his courage to do that—'I was pretty weak and now fell down.' A man with a gunshot wound through the lower jaw had a belt of cartridges, which he offered Beard and asked him to try to help them again.

" 'When he gave me the cartridges, I told him I was badly wounded and pretty weak, too. While I was lying on my back, I looked down the ravine and saw a lot of women coming up and crying. When I saw these women, girls and little girls and boys coming up, I saw soldiers on both sides of the ravine shoot at them until they had killed every one of them.'

"He saw a young woman among them coming and crying and calling, 'Mother! Mother!' She was wounded under her chin, close to her throat, and the bullet had passed through a braid of her hair

Body of Chief Big Foot
(SMITHSONIAN INSTITUTION)

and carried some of it into the wound, and then the bullet had entered the front side of the shoulder and passed out the back side. Her mother had been shot behind her. Dewey was sitting up and he called to her to come to him. When she came close to him, she fell to the ground. He caught her by the dress and drew her to him across his legs. When the women who the soldiers were shooting at got a little past him, he told this girl to follow them on the run, and she went up the ravine.

"He got himself up and followed up the ravine. He saw many dead men, women, and children lying in the ravine. When he went a little way up, he heard singing; going a little farther, he came upon his mother who was moving slowly, being very badly wounded. She had a soldier's revolver in her hand, swinging it as she went. Dewey does not know how she got it. When he caught up to her she said, 'My son, pass by me; I am going to fall down now.' As she went up, soldiers on both sides of the ravine shot at her and killed her. 'I returned fire upon them, defending my mother. When I shot at the soldiers in a northern direction, I looked back at my mother and she had already fallen down. I passed right on from my dead mother and met a man coming down the ravine who was wounded in the knee. . . .'

"Dewey was wounded so that his right arm was disabled; he placed the thumb of his right hand between his teeth and carried his Winchester on his left shoulder, and then he ran towards where he had heard that White Lance [his brother] was killed. As he ran, he saw lots of women and children lying along the ravine, some alive and some dead. He saw some young men just above, and these he addressed, saying to them to take courage and do all they could to defend the women. 'I have,' he said, 'a bad wound and am not able to defend them; I could not aim the gun,' and so he told the young men this way. It was now in the ravine just like a prairie fire when it reaches brush and tall grass . . . ; it was like hail coming down; an awful fire was concentrated on them now and nothing could be seen for the smoke. In the bottom of the ravine, the bullets raised more dust than there was smoke, so that they could not see one another.

"When Dewey came up into the 'pit,' he saw White Lance upon top of the bank, and was rolling on down towards the brink to get down into the ravine. He was badly wounded and at first was half dead, but later revived from his injuries. When Dewey went into the 'pit,' he found his brother William Horn Cloud lying or sitting against the bank shot through the breast, but yet alive; but he died that night. 'Just when I saw my wounded brother William, I saw White Lance slide down the bank and stand by William. Then William said to White Lance, "Shake hands with me, I am dizzy now." ' While they had this conversation, Dewey said, 'My dear brothers, be men and take courage. A few minutes ago, our father told us this way, and you heard it. Our father told us that all people of the world born of the same father and mother, when any great tragedy comes, it is better that all of them should die together than that they should die separately at different times, one by one. . . .'

"White Lance and William shook hands. Then White Lance and Dewey lifted their brother up and stood him on his feet; then they placed him on White Lance's shoulder. White Lance was wounded in several places and weak from loss of blood, but he succeeded in bearing William to the bottom of the ravine. . . . Dewey said they now heard the Hotchkiss or Gatling guns shooting at them along the bank. Now there went up from these dying people a medley of death songs. . . . Each one sings a different death song if he chooses. The death song is expressive of their wish to die. It is also a requiem for the dead. . . . 'At this time, I was unable to do anything more and I took a rest, telling my brothers to keep up courage.' The cannon were pouring in their shots and breaking down the banks which were giving protection to the fighting Indians. . . . The Hotchkiss had been shooting rapidly and one Indian had gotten killed by it. His body was penetrated in the pit of the stomach by a Hotchkiss shell, which tore a hole through his body six inches in diameter. The man was insensible, but breathed for an hour before he died. . . .

"In this same place there was a young woman with a pole in hand and a black blanket on it. When she would raise it up, the soldiers would whistle and yell and pour volleys into it. One woman here spoke to Beard and told him to come in among them and help them. He answered that he would stay where he was and make a fight for them; and that he did not care if he got killed, for the infants were all dead now, and he would like to die among the infants. When he was saying this, the soldiers were all shooting furiously. . . .

Dewey Beard (right) and his brothers,
White Lance and Joseph Horn Cloud, 1907.
(NEBRASKA STATE HISTORICAL SOCIETY)

"Dewey laid down again in the same little hollow and reloaded his gun. The soldiers across from him were shooting at him while he was reloading. While he was loading, he heard a horseman coming along the brink of the ravine—could hear the foot falls. This man as he came along gave orders to the men which he supposed were to fire on the women in the pit for a fusillade was instantly opened on them. . . .

"The sun was going down; it was pretty near sundown. . . . He saw five Oglala Sioux on horseback. He called them, but they were afraid and ran away, but he kept on calling and going till they all stood still and he came upon them. He went on with them a little way and soon he met his brother Joseph coming toward them on horseback. Dewey asked, 'Where are you going?' Joe answered, 'All my brothers and parents are dead and I have to go in and be killed, too; therefore I have come back.' Dewey said, 'You better come with us; don't go there; they are all killed there,' and the five Oglalas joined with Beard in the same appeal. Now the Oglalas left these two brothers. Then Joe got off his horse and told Dewey to get on. Dewey was covered with blood. He mounted the horse and Joe walked along slowly. After a little, a mounted Indian relation came up behind them. The three went together over to White Clay Creek. . . .

"Dewey's little infant, Wet Feet, died afterwards in the next March. This child was nursing its dead mother who was shot in the breast. It swallowed blood and from this vomited and was never well, was always sick till it died."

On October 21, 1913, Dewey Beard received a commendation from the U.S. government. The official document read in full: "This is to certify that twenty-two years ago I gave Dewey Beard a certificate of good character and am much gratified to learn that he has maintained that character ever since. He is one of the survivors of the Wounded Knee Massacre, in which he was twice seriously wounded and lost his father, mother, two brothers, sister, wife and child killed. Nelson A. Miles, Lieutenant General U.S. Army."

. . .

The Reverend Charles Cook hastily removed all the pews and then he covered the floor of the Holy Cross Episcopal Church with a bedding of straw and quilts. The Christmas season was upon Pine Ridge. Garlands and wreaths decked the walls and a homemade sign— PEACE ON EARTH, GOODWILL TO MEN—still hung above the altar of his church. Shortly after 9:30 p.m., the first wagons arrived carrying survivors from the Miniconjou village. When Dr. Charles Eastman, a Santee Sioux in charge of treating the wounded, and the Reverend Cook and his church staff first saw the men, women and children carried in from the wagons, they cried out in anguish. "All of this," said Eastman later, "was a severe ordeal for one who had so lately put all his faith in the Christian love and lofty ideals of the white man."

Steals a Running Horse, age five, was among thirty-eight survivors laid out in rows on the church floor that night. Bullets had torn apart the small boy's throat, and when doctors tried to feed him, the food and water came out the side of his neck. Blue Whirlwind had been wounded fourteen times. Her two small sons were shot up, but still alive. Her husband, Spotted Thunder, was dead. Louise Weasel Bear had been one of the first to flee the village for the ravine. "We tried to run but they shot us like we were a buffalo. I know there are some good white people, but the soldiers must be mean to shoot children and women. Indian soldiers would not do that to white children." Bertha Kills Close to Lodge, seventeen, ran with her relatives through the ravine, stopping when she heard a burst of gunfire behind her. "I went over there and it was my sister and her mother was pregnant at that time. I found she was killed. I was wounded but was able to go to where they were. My sister was near death and I stayed with her. When she died I straightened her out, laid her out the best way I could." Alice Dog Arm saw a soldier on a bay horse riding toward her family. "I ran and hid in a ditch with my mother and two brothers. My father came and took my older brother to care for him. Soon he came back and said that they had killed my brother. Then my mother cried and as she wanted us all to be together and die together so my father took us to a safer hiding place and then he left us and soon a man named Air Pipe came and told us that my father was killed." Afraid of Enemy, thirty-six, said she saw an officer on a sorrel horse swing around the left end of the camp. "I heard him give some command and right after the command it sounded like a lightning crash. That is about all I know. When I became conscious I was lying down. As I rose and started to go I began to get unconscious again. For that reason I do not know a great deal of what took place after this. I have my old cloak and it has nine bullet holes in it." After the initial cannon salvo, Rough Feather and her family fled toward the ravine under heavy fire. "My father, my mother, my grandmother, my older brother and my younger brother were all killed. My son who was two years old was shot in the mouth that later caused his death."

On New Year's Day, 1891, a burial detail rode out of the agency headquarters in Pine Ridge with an army escort. Under contract at two dollars per body, the civilian detail of thirty men spent two days combing the snow-covered battlefield, tossing frozen bodies in the back of wagons drawn by mule teams. They found Chief Big Foot, wrapped in a thick coat and head scarf, propped up beside the blown-out remains of his army tent, his body frozen in a half-sitting position. Not far away, inside the council circle, was the charred remains of the medicine man, Yellow Bird. Strewn along a trail more than three miles long, they found the remains of three pregnant women riddled with bullets, another with her abdomen blown away and a young boy whose upper body had been torn apart by a cannon shell.

They also found a baby girl, covered in snow, huddled beside her dead mother. She was wrapped in a shawl, her head, hands and feet severely frostbitten, but still alive. On her head, the eight-month-old infant wore a tiny buckskin cap with a needlepoint design in the shape of an American flag. When news of her discovery reached the Lakota, they began to call her *Zintka Lanuni*, Lost Bird. She was eventually adopted by Brig. Gen. Leonard Colby, commander of the Nebraska National Guard, and raised in his home in Beatrice, Nebraska. In the end, the burial detail found seven adults and two children still alive. They had survived two days of blizzards, four days without food.

On the hill where the Hotchkiss cannons once stood, the burial party dug a large rectangular pit eighty feet long, six feet wide and six feet deep. After all the bodies had been collected, they were unloaded from the wagons and stacked like wood near the open grave. There were 146 in all: 102 adult men and women, 31 elderly, 6 boys ages five to eight and 7 babies. Without a funeral service, religious ceremony or last rites, after some had been stripped of Ghost shirts, ceremonial objects and other souvenirs, the frozen corpses were dumped in the mass grave. "It was a thing to melt the heart of

The burial detail at Wounded Knee.
(NEBRASKA STATE HISTORICAL SOCIETY)

a man, if it was stone," one observer remarked, "to see those little children, with their bodies shot to pieces, thrown naked into the pit." Before covering it with dirt, the burial detail posed for photographers, then set off for Pine Ridge. After the battle, surviving friends and relatives had already removed many more bodies from the battlefield. The official army report eventually placed the number of Indian dead at 290—90 warriors and 200 women and children. Thirty-three soldiers had also died, many of them killed in the cross fire from their own troops.

In the weeks leading up to Wounded Knee, the friendly chiefs on Pine Ridge had encouraged the Ghost Dancers under Kicking Bear and Short Bull to give up the fight, to come into the agency and make a peace. For a short while, after hearing of Wounded Knee, the hardcore believers mounted an offensive, firing on the Pine Ridge Agency, attacking an army supply train and engaging troops in a battle near the agency's Catholic mission. Soon, the skirmishes ended and peace talks were under way, and on January 7, Chief Big Road led his followers into the agency. The tension that had begun in late summer, that had gathered momentum in the fall and led to Wounded Knee by winter, ended on January 16, when Kicking Bear surrendered his rifle to General Miles. Eventually, Kicking Bear, Short Bull and others whom the army deemed troublemakers were shipped to a military camp at Fort Sheridan, Illinois.

Later, in a confidential letter to a friend, Miles harshly criticized the military conduct at Big Foot's camp and deplored the number of dead.

"Wholesale massacre occurred and I have never heard of a more brutal, cold-blooded massacre than that at Wounded Knee," wrote Miles. "About two hundred women and children were killed and wounded; women with little children on their backs, and small children powder-burned by the men who killed them being so near as to burn the flesh and clothing with the powder of their guns, and nursing babes with five bullet holes through them. . . . Col. Forsyth is responsible for allowing the command to remain where it was stationed after he assumed command, and in allowing his troops to be in

Ghost Dance leaders who survived the massacre.
Kicking Bear is number 4, Short Bull is 5, Lone Bull is 12.
(GEORGE SPENCER, COURTESY NEBRASKA STATE HISTORICAL SOCIETY)

such a position that the line of fire of every troop was in direct line of their own comrades or their camp."

The army eventually conducted an official investigation of Wounded Knee, initiated at the behest of Congress. Written by Gen. E. D. Scott, the report concluded: "There is nothing to conceal or apologize for in the Wounded Knee Battle—beyond the killing of a wounded buck by a hysterical recruit. The firing was begun by the Indians and continued until they stopped—with the one exception noted above.

"That women and children were casualties was unfortunate but unavoidable, and most must have [been killed] from Indian bullets. . . . The Indians at Wounded Knee brought their own destruction as surely as any people ever did. Their attack on the troops was as treacherous as any in the history of Indian warfare, and that they were under a strange religious hallucination is only an explanation, not an excuse."

The U.S. government later awarded twenty Medals of Honor to soldiers who had fought at Wounded Knee. One of the honorees was Corp. Paul H. Weinert. He was part of the artillery detail manning the Hotchkiss guns atop the hill. When the Miniconjou began to flee their devastated village, Corporal Weinert had rolled his cannon down the hill, following them into the ravine. "I kept going in farther, and pretty soon," said Weinert, "everything was quiet at the other end of the line."

The stillness of the Wounded Knee battlefield marked the end of an era. Lakota resistance to reservation life had been crushed, the desperate hope for a return to the old ways forever silenced. After December 29, 1890, the West would be wild no more. It would linger on only as romantic illusion, the province of entertainers and showmen.

On March 14, 1891, a small item appeared in the *Chadron Democrat*. Datelined Chicago, it read: "Buffalo Bill has secured the consent of the government and will within a few days start for Europe with the hostile Sioux now held at Fort Sheridan. They are to be a part of his Wild West show."

Chapter Five

From Pine Ridge
to Paris

Freshwater streams spill through deep ravines, creek bottoms lay-
ered in groves of cottonwood, elm, ash and oak. Thickets of plum
and chokecherry fan out from the banks, packed tightly against a
rutted dirt road. High above, the dense green forest fades to steep
cliffs ringed in ponderosa pine. Beyond the canyon walls, in rolling
swells of native grass and pine, a succession of sloping hills are pock-
marked with old log cabins, windmills, rusty pumps and broken-
down corrals. The hills gradually climb all the way to the top, past an
occasional tipi or a sweat lodge draped in canvas, until they reach the
immense, flat plateau overlooking miles of unbroken prairie.
Halfway across the plateau, wagon ruts cut through knee-high grass
to the wooden church and loop west toward a small cemetery on the
hill.

Rugged, remote, isolated, the Yellow Bear Camp was home to
traditional Lakota who did not know how to give up the old ways. It
is where the people had hidden Chief Dull Knife after the escape
from Fort Robinson in 1879, and where George Dull Knife heard the
big guns firing along Wounded Knee Creek eleven years later.
During much of the decade of the 1890s, the Pine Ridge Reservation
became a cultural, emotional and psychological wasteland, a place
where the dead Ghost Dancers symbolized the end of the Lakota's
world. Traditional families who survived, who had endured years of
fighting, fleeing, forced removal and a desultory succession of reservation homes, eventually found their way to Yellow Bear. After wild

game gave way to sacks of flour and sides of beef elsewhere, Yellow Bear families still hunted deer, rabbit and wild turkey and fished the streams for trout. Throughout its harsh terrain, canvas tipis took longer to become log walls, and schools were slower to gain a foothold. At close-knit family gatherings, children and adults spoke Lakota. Horses were valued more than cattle, the medicine men more than priests. In summer, back in the hills, it was not unusual to hear the eagle-bone whistles of the forbidden Sun Dance.

For the families who lived here, who had made their homes in the tangle of the hill country, there remained a lifelong attachment to its powerful landscape, to the memories of what life had been like when they were trying to make the transition from one century to the next. Many were related, had lived in the old communal way, in the tightly woven extended families of the tribe. At the top, in the small cemetery on the plateau, lies Chief Yellow Bear. And the army scout, Joshua Wolf Soldier. Albert Has No Horse and Albert Trouble in Front. William Plenty Arrows and Abraham Conquering Bear. George and Mary Dull Knife.

Between the winter of 1879 and the summer of 1973, four generations of Dull Knifes came to Yellow Bear. The old man chief had come to hide, to heal after the escape from the barracks. His son, George Dull Knife, returned to rest up between Wild West Shows. Guy Dull Knife Sr. was born and raised in the camp, and came home to it from the trenches of World War I. A fourth later found comfort in the solitude of the pines after Vietnam.

In the early photographs taken in the years after Wounded Knee, George Dull Knife appears as a man of striking features. He is tall with broad shoulders and thick chest, coal-black hair framing a finely chiseled face: high, wide cheekbones, intense dark eyes and a set jaw. In one, there is the long, neatly parted hair, an eagle feather, a blanket and moccasins. In another, short-cropped hair, a buffalo robe coat, trousers and leather shoes.

"My grandfather lived until 1955," said Guy Dull Knife Jr. "He

Buffalo Bill Cody
(NEBRASKA STATE HISTORICAL SOCIETY)

was born the year before the Custer fight and died two years after the Korean War. So he had seen a lot during his eighty years. He was fifteen at the time of the massacre and for a long time afterward, he said a lot of the people on Pine Ridge didn't really care what happened to them anymore. A lot of them gave up. They didn't want to really do anything. Especially the men. They didn't care about farming or ranching or working or doing anything. There was a lot of drinking and just sitting around.

"During this time, my grandfather said it was the women who really kept things going, who kept the families together and just kind of took over. They were the strong ones while a lot of the men were weak, had more or less given up. They couldn't find anything to do that made sense to them anymore, so they quit. For a lot of the people, the years following Wounded Knee were the worst they had ever known.

"I think he was always kind of glad that the Wild West Show came along when it did. It was a hard life in many ways and after he got married and had a family, it was very hard on them, but at least it gave him something to do at a time when there wasn't a lot of options. It gave him something to do and it brought in some money that helped his family survive until things got better."

Through friends at the Yellow Bear Camp, George Dull Knife first met recruiters with Buffalo Bill Cody's Wild West Show in 1892. Off and on for the next fifteen years, he was a part of the large troupe of entertainers who reenacted the buffalo hunt, dramatic battles and heroic rescues in arenas throughout the eastern United States and Europe. For many Lakota who went on Wild West tours, the show life was often harsh. They were afraid and homesick and sick in other ways. Some died en route during the long Atlantic crossings; others died in Europe, buried in foreign soil far removed from their native lands. A few became addicted to alcohol and had to be sent back. George Dull Knife was seventeen when he went away for the first time. He was tall, sturdy, healthy and he was lucky. Over the years, he stayed healthy, earned some money and sent much of it home to help his people in the Yellow Bear Camp. Eventually, he became an interpreter for Cody, and for the rest of his life, like many other Lakota, he spoke well of the unusual man whose relationship with the Indian had always been a complicated one.

By the time he died in 1917, William F. Cody, as much as anyone, had come to define the American West. Born in Iowa and raised in

Kansas, he had scouted in Oklahoma and Montana, hunted in the Dakotas, ranched in Nebraska and retired to Wyoming, living out his last days in Colorado. Along the way, his numerous avocations mirrored a time and place, a way of life, that embodied many of the romantic myths and legends of an era. As a teenager, he had gone on a gold rush to Pike's Peak, ferried messages from a freighting company to Fort Leavenworth and ridden for the Pony Express. As a young man, he got in on the tail end of the Civil War, worked as a contract hunter for the Union Pacific Railroad and served as army chief of scouts in warfare against the plains tribes. At his death a few weeks before his seventy-first birthday, Cody could include among his friends and acquaintances Custer, Sitting Bull, Red Cloud, Wild Bill Hickcok, Calamity Jane, Annie Oakley, Frederic Remington, Charles Russell, generals Sherman, Sheridan, Crook and Miles, governors, presidents, counts and countesses, the Prince of Wales and Queen Victoria of England.

The transformation from frontiersman to showman had begun years earlier. While serving as chief of scouts for Gen. Philip Sheridan's Fifth U.S. Cavalry in 1869, the twenty-three-year-old Cody met a young writer, Edward Zane Carroll Judson, who was fascinated by the roving hunter and army scout. Writing under the name Ned Buntline, Judson began to churn out a succession of dime novels, each casting Cody as the stuff of legend—bold, fearless, flamboyant, a prolific killer of buffalo and Indians, the rugged new hero of the American West. The dime novels became enormously popular among East Coast readers starved for western adventure, a readership that soon began to link Cody's name to its romantic image of what life was like in the great lands west of the Mississippi.

In 1872, Cody cashed in on his newfound fame and starred with Wild Bill Hickok in a Buntline play—*The Scouts of the Plains*—that opened in Chicago to good reviews. Off and on for the next eleven years, he toured with the play throughout the eastern United States, returning frequently to the West between engagements. By 1882, Cody had settled on a four-thousand-acre ranch in North Platte, Nebraska, and in response to the pleas of townfolk that year, he agreed to stage a Fourth of July celebration. Credited by some as the beginning of the modern American rodeo, the Fourth of July bash was a huge success, and it gave Cody an idea.

On May 17, 1883, what would become known as Buffalo Bill's Wild West Show officially opened in Omaha. More than eight thousand spectators watched that afternoon as Cody, dressed in embroidered buckskin and gleaming black boots, rode into the packed arena on a white stallion. Behind him followed a procession of painted Indian chiefs, mounted warriors, a buffalo herd, horses, cowboys, trick-shooting specialists and a shining coach from the old Deadwood Stage Line. Entering to the music of a twenty-piece band, the troupe soon launched into a series of well-rehearsed performances: a Pony Express ride, an assault on the Deadwood stagecoach, an Indian attack on a settler's cabin and the finale—a boisterous, thundering buffalo chase around the sold-out arena. The crowd loved it. The next day, an enthusiastic press corps gave the performance rave reviews, and for the next thirty years, it would become the staple for a succession of American and European Wild West Shows.

To make good on a promise that his show was the genuine article, Cody needed real Indians, and for three decades, he found them on Pine Ridge and nearby reservations. For the first seven years, the show included Indian performers recruited from tribes of Pawnee, Arapahoe, Cheyenne, Crow and Sioux. However, age-old rivalries among the tribes eventually created too many problems, and by 1891, Cody decided to draw exclusively from the Sioux, primarily the Oglala. Among his troupe that year were Short Bull and Kicking Bear, the Ghost Dance leaders, and Corp. Paul Weinert, the Seventh Cavalry gunner who had manned the Hotchkiss cannon at Wounded Knee. Each Indian performer received a contract, guaranteeing that he would be well treated, fully supported while away and returned home in good health. The contracts also stated that a portion of each Indian's monthly salary, usually twenty-five dollars, would be sent back to the reservation.

In Wild West Shows at home and abroad, the Sioux became

crowd favorites. Cody, with his fringed buckskin, black boots, white stallion, trademark goatee and flowing locks, had long symbolized the American West, and now his Indian performers did, too. They had been the classic plains Indian. In the cities of the United States and Europe, it was their culture—feathered, nomadic warriors living in tipis, hunting the buffalo, fighting settlers and the cavalry—that was represented on thousands of colorful posters, flyers and hand-bills promoting the arrival of Buffalo Bill's Wild West Show. Eventually, the image of the Sioux Indian would find its way onto stamps and coins, calendars, dolls, coffee mugs and plates, an image that twentieth century western novelists and Hollywood filmmakers incorporated into scores of books and movies, until for many, it was the Sioux who had come to symbolize all Indians. Cody's Wild West Show had set it in motion, had initiated the creation, marketing and distribution of a powerful American subculture, a genre steeped in

General Miles and Buffalo Bill Cody view hostile Indian camp near Pine Ridge, January 16, 1891.
(Nebraska State Historical Society)

romantic stereotypes and mythic heroes. What began in Omaha soon spread east, then overseas—and it never really stopped.

In the beginning, Cody had earned a name for his proficiency at killing the animal the Lakota needed to survive. As a contract hunter for the Union Pacific Railroad, he claimed to have shot and killed more than four thousand buffalo in less than nine months, sixty-nine in one eight-hour stretch. Later, he had served as a scout in the army's campaign to rid the plains of hostile Indian bands. On July 17, 1876, three weeks after the Little Bighorn, his cavalry command intercepted a band of Cheyenne at War Bonnet Creek, Nebraska. During the battle, Cody is said to have killed Chief Yellow Hand, a deed later reenacted in many Wild West performances. When the Ghost Dance troubles began, it was Cody whom General Miles had chosen to arrest Sitting Bull. A few weeks later, he rode with the army during the days of unrest following Wounded Knee.

George Dull Knife liked Buffalo Bill Cody. When the Lakota were strangers in foreign lands across the water, homesick and out of sorts, Cody did not forget his Indian guests. He took good care of them, often leaving his comfortable hotel to sleep in their camps. He made sure they had enough to eat, took them on sight-seeing tours throughout Europe and gave them parting gifts, small things that the others had forgotten, that George Dull Knife would remember. Over time, the young Lakota and the middle-aged showman became friends. It was a friendship that lasted until Cody's death in 1917, the year before George's oldest boy went off to war in the white man's army.

In a large black trunk at the family home in Loveland, Colorado, are some of the mementos of the Wild West days. On top, there is the faded pair of black binoculars, scratched and dented, and the inscription *La Dauphine—Paris*, a gift from Cody to George Dull Knife.

Of the many stories Guy Dull Knife Jr. heard as a small boy growing up on the Pine Ridge Reservation in the early 1950s, some of the ones he remembered best were the stories his grandfather used to tell about the years he traveled with the Wild West Show. The boy was fascinated by the large black trunk and he spent hours rummaging through its contents, looking at the mementos and keepsakes the family had gathered from one generation to the next. Inside, he found the binoculars and an old dusty pistol, nickel-plated, with a pearl handle and leather holster. After the last show of the season one year, Cody had given the pistol to his grandfather, and the boy used to take an oily rag and buff it and polish it until he could see his face on the barrel. At the bottom of the trunk, he found a bundle of photographs tied together with a rawhide thong and he saw that there were a few very old ones of his grandfather and the showman. In one, Cody wore fringed buckskin and his grandfather had an eagle feather in his hair. Another was taken in Paris, in front of the Eiffel Tower. His grandfather and the other Indians were wrapped in blankets, huddled together, looking at the camera with blank expressions.

Later, long after George Dull Knife had died, when the grandson was in Vietnam, sitting by his father's bed in the nursing home or driving alone through the Dakota Badlands, he would think back on the photographs and the stories he had heard and he would try to imagine what it must have been like to be a young Lakota from the Yellow Bear Camp walking the streets of Paris and London at the turn of the century. During the years that his grandfather was away, it was forbidden to talk like an Indian, dance like an Indian and worship like an Indian on the Pine Ridge Reservation. But off the reservation, in foreign lands five thousand miles from the Yellow Bear Camp, European royalty and commoners paid good money to sit in the stands and watch the American natives, to see the dances, war bonnets and fast ponies, to hear their singing, chanting and battle cries.

Of all the things he found in the trunk as a small boy, Guy Jr. had liked the photographs best, was fascinated by them, and so he would ask his grandfather a lot of questions. In the early years of the 1950s, he and his parents would occasionally drive to the Yellow

Bear Camp to visit his grandparents in their old log home. During the winter months sometimes, George Dull Knife would put on a heavy coat, wrap himself in a blanket and sit in the kitchen by the wood-burning stove, his grandson on his lap, telling stories that made the boy laugh out loud.

"One year when they were in England, they had the day off and so Cody decided to take some of the Indians to a kind of fair or circus that was playing in the same general area where the Wild West Show was. All the Indians were dressed up in their native clothing and they were walking around, and pretty soon, they came to a part of the fair that had some rides. They didn't know what they were and Cody asked if they'd like to try one. They said sure, so they got their tickets and they entered it one by one.

"Inside, the ride was completely covered with mirrors—on the ceiling, on the floor, on all of the walls. My grandfather said they had never seen anything like this, and before long, they were all doing their war dances and watching themselves in the mirrors and laughing out loud at the strange box, when the room suddenly started to move. It moved slowly at first, but after a while, it began to spin faster and faster, until they weren't sure what was going on or what they should do about it. One of the men started to move around the room to try and find the door, but nobody could stand up and pretty soon, the room really began to spin and then everyone started to panic. Some of them began to get sick and a few others started to sing their death songs. Finally, the room began to slow down and then it stopped. When they got outside, everyone was sick. Grandpa said it was the last time any of the Sioux ever went on a carnival ride.

"Another time, they were at a different fair or carnival, and when they passed by a tent, a man ran up to them and began talking real fast and pointing to the tent behind him. There was a picture of a giant ape on a board outside the tent and one of the Indians asked Cody what the man was saying. He told the interpreter and the interpreter told the Indians that the man was offering twenty dollars to anyone who could wrestle his ape to the ground. The Indians got together and talked it over and one of them told Cody he wanted to try it. Grandpa said Buffalo Bill got really upset. He told the interpreter to tell the man that the ape was called an orangutan and that it was really strong and he might end up getting hurt. But the man would not change his mind, so Buffalo Bill gave up and everyone walked inside the tent.

"The man told the Indian to step into a ring where the ape was sitting down. All the other Indians formed a circle around the ape, and before he stepped forward, the man did a little war dance and sang his battle songs. When he stepped to the center of the ring, the ape suddenly jumped up and sprang on him and threw him to the ground like he was a toy. Well, the Indian was really afraid then, and when the ape started to try and rip off his breechcloth, the man jumped into the ring and broke it up. By now, all the Sioux were laughing really hard at their friend. Grandpa said they teased him for the rest of the trip. When they got back to Yellow Bear, they told him they were going to tell everybody on Pine Ridge about the ape who counted coup on the great Sioux warrior."

For many Lakota, a tour with the Wild West Show lasted a long time, from a year or eighteen months to as long as two or three years. When they left the rough hill country of Yellow Bear, some did not know they would cross an ocean, heading for distant lands they had never heard of. They were usually paid monthly, the amount depending on their status in the tribe, their job description and previous show experience. One year, when 125 Indians traveled with the show, 72 were Pine Ridge Lakota. Their monthly salaries ranged from $75 for Rocky Bear, an early and long-time favorite of Cody's, to $60 for the interpreter John Shangreau, $35 for Bear Foot and Sam Last Horse, $25 for Thomas Kills in Winter and William Feather on Head to $10 for Her Holy Blanket, Good Dog and Looks Back. From Yellow Bear, George Dull Knife and the other Lakota from Pine Ridge often rode horses or buckboards to the rail station in Gordon, Nebraska. From Gordon, they took a train east to New York, where they were transported by ship across the Atlantic, two-week journeys that many of the Indians never forgot.

"Grandpa always said that the ocean crossings were the worst part of the Wild West Show," said Guy Dull Knife Jr. "The Indians had lived on the plains and they had never seen anything like the ocean. It terrified them. Some of the Indians aboard the ship never made it across. Some of them were in bad shape before they left New York. They were depressed and lonely and the shock of crossing the ocean was more than their systems could take. Their nerves went bad. Some of them had diseases and they got seasick and they couldn't stop vomiting. They had always been on land and they couldn't adapt to the water. Some of them died and so there were some burials at sea. Others got sick and died overseas and they were buried in many different places, in England, France, Holland and Belgium."

On March 31, 1887, the first Wild West Show to play overseas left New York for London. Aboard the *State of Nebraska* that day were 138 soldiers and cowboys, 97 Indians, 180 horses, 18 buffalo, 10 elk, 10 mules, 5 Texas steers, 4 donkeys and 2 deer. Annie Oakley was a featured attraction, and Red Shirt, an Oglala subchief from Pine Ridge, led the contingent of Lakota, Cheyenne, Kiowa and Pawnee. A week out to sea, an intense storm battered the ship for forty-eight hours, pitching it between huge swells and setting off a fear and panic among many of the crew. Many became violently sick and some of the Indians began to sing their death songs. Badly stricken himself, Cody went from cabin to cabin, talking to the Indians, asking them to stay calm, saying the storm would pass. It eventually did and the ship arrived safely in London on April 14.

It was not unusual, the grandfather had said, for Cody to do whatever he could to help them when they were alone and afraid. The Indians did not forget, and told their friends and families back home; and over time, they came to trust him. One spring, after the show had closed out a long European run, the troupe set sail for New York from Hull, England. The day before, the Oglala holy man Black Elk and three Lakota friends, all members of the show, had gotten lost and so they missed the boat. Stranded and homesick, they eventually signed on with a smaller, rival wild west show and traveled through England, Germany, Italy and France, trying to save enough money to get back to Pine Ridge. In France, Black Elk became ill and was cared for by a French family in Paris. A year later, Cody returned to France and Black Elk rejoined the show. When Cody asked if he wanted to stay or return home, Black Elk said he had been away for more than two years, that he missed his people and he wished to go back. A few nights later, Cody held a large feast in Black Elk's honor. Afterward, he gave him ninety dollars cash and a ticket for a ship sailing to New York the next morning.

In another year, in the summer, Sitting Bull traveled with the show for four months, sharing top billing with Annie Oakley. Throughout the tour, Cody let him sit out the mock battles between cowboys and Indians. Instead, the Hunkpapa holy man was introduced individually, a spotlight following him into the arena. That year, the tour played before packed houses in more than forty U.S. and Canadian cities. When Sitting Bull was introduced, the American crowds frequently booed. In Canada, they cheered. By the end, he was astonished at the number of whites he saw in the East and the poverty he found there, often giving away his show money to the ragged horde of children who followed him around. "The white man knows how to make everything," he told Oakley, "but he does not know how to distribute it." Sitting Bull and Cody became friends, and when the tour ended, the showman gave the Lakota leader two gifts. One was a white sombrero, the other a gray horse trained to dance at the sound of gunfire. On the morning Sitting Bull died, during the first burst of gunfire outside his cabin along the Grand River, the horse sat down and pawed the ground. It is said that some of the dead chief's shaken followers believed it was doing the Ghost Dance.

When the Lakota first arrived in England, George Dull Knife told his grandson, many could not adjust to British food. Hearty meat-eaters all their lives, they found it difficult to get by on plates filled with a lot of vegetables and little meat, meat they had never eaten before. One year, shortly after checking into an expensive London hotel, a large group of hungry Lakota were summoned to the dining room. Many of the younger men arrived at the table in native dress, painted faces and feathered hair. Soon, white-gloved waiters brought in platters of mutton and vegetables for their American Indian guests. "The meat was cut into small pieces and served with potatoes and other vegetables and some greens," Luther Standing Bear, an Oglala from Pine Ridge, later recalled. "We cared nothing for the greens. All we wanted was meat, and plenty of it. So we would take the meat off the platter and hand the platter back to the waiter with the potatoes and other things still on it."

On one occasion, Cody tried to bridge the cultural distance between host and guest. "Buffalo Bill apparently took a group of Sioux to some kind of a polishing class in London. My grandfather said there was an instructor at the class who was trying to teach the Indians which forks they should use while eating and how to properly pull back a chair at the dinner table for a woman to sit on. Some of the Indians at that time had never eaten with a fork and they thought the whole thing was pretty funny. For a while, after they got back to Pine Ridge, they used to tease each other. They would say they saw so-and-so eating with his meat fork when he should have been using his salad fork.

"Another time, I don't know exactly how this happened, but they all ended up going to see the Pope. When they got there, the Pope wouldn't see them. Grandpa said he told the Sioux to come back again when they had found a different way of communicating with the Great Spirit."

Of the many Wild West performances abroad, the highlight of each season often became the shows that were staged for royalty. On May 9, 1887, more than 28,000 came to London's Earl's Court to witness Cody's first European show. Fascinated by what had happened in their former colonies, London newspapers primed the event for weeks in advance. On April 25, while British and American workers readied the large stage grounds, William Gladstone, Britain's most powerful politician, visited the Wild West campground and met Cody, who introduced him to Chief Red Shirt. Not long afterward, the Prince of Wales, his wife, their three children and a small group of French and German aristocrats arrived at the cold and rainy camp. The prince asked Red Shirt if the persistent cold bothered him. It was nothing, Red Shirt assured him, compared to the cold of his Dakota homeland. Before leaving, the prince gave the Lakota a box of his favorite cigars. A few nights later, the actor, Sir Henry Irving, invited Red Shirt and a group of Lakota to see his production of Goethe's *Faust* at the Lyceum Theater. Seated in private boxes at the posh theater, the Indians watched the performance, with Irving playing Mephistopheles. A newspaper review said the Lakota seemed "greatly scared at its horror." Afterward, Red Shirt said it had all seemed like a big dream.

On June 20, the day before Queen Victoria's Golden Jubilee, celebrating her fifty years on the throne, the Wild West troupe gave a special command performance. Before the show, Cody had worked out some changes for the Deadwood stage rescue scene. Inside the coach were the kings of Belgium, Denmark, Greece and Saxony and the Prince of Wales. As Queen Victoria and the crown heads of Europe looked on, the Cody-driven stage survived an Indian attack, its royal guests eventually making it back to the safety of their private boxes.

George Dull Knife often told his grandson the story of another performance before European royalty. It was the small boy's favorite and he had asked to hear it again and again. After their first trip abroad, Cody knew the Lakota did not like the taste of beef, pork and mutton. In later years, before leaving for Europe, he arranged to bring along a few extra head of buffalo so the Indians would have a fresh supply of the meat they craved. The rest were used for the chase scene, which became the crowd favorite for many Europeans.

"When they were preparing for a show in Spain one time, a member of the Spanish royalty came to the camp to look at the buffalo," said the grandson. "He had heard of the buffalo, but he had never actually seen one and he kept coming to the campgrounds every day to look at them. Finally, after a week or so, he came up to Cody and challenged him to a special match between his prized bull and one of Cody's buffalo. He told Cody that these strange, hairy creatures he had brought from America were no match for his Spanish bull. Cody tried to explain to him that he was sure he had a fine bull, but that it was a domestic bull. The buffalo, Cody told him, were wild animals and they would tear his bull to pieces. But the Spanish man paid no attention to Cody and he kept bugging him about it until finally, my grandfather said, Cody came to the Indians one day and asked them what he should do. The Indians all said, 'Hao, Hao, Hao—do it,' and so a match was set up between the bull and the buffalo.

"On the day of the match, there was a lot of people in the stadium and the Spanish bull, a large white bull, was all decked out in colorful flags and pennants. Cody had brought several big buffalo bulls with him, but he and the Indians chose a younger, smaller and faster one for the match. When the match began, the Spanish bull charged and hit the buffalo flush on the side, rolling him across the stadium floor. After a while, the buffalo got up and when he did, he went wild. He was a lot faster and he charged the bull furiously, over and over, until he finally got the exhausted bull down on the ground and then ripped him open with his horns.

"The bull did not live very long and after it was all over, the Spanish man came down from the stands. He was really mad. He told Cody that the bull was very expensive, that he had spent a lot of money feeding and grooming and caring for the bull and that he had come from a long line of champion bulls. Cody let him talk and then he told him that he had tried to warn him, but that he hadn't listened and so it was more his fault than Cody's. In the end, the Spanish man gave the dead bull to Cody and Cody gave it to the Indians. That night, they butchered it in the camp and had a big feast."

When they traveled overseas, the Indians all lived together. Shortly after arriving in England, France, Germany, Italy or Spain, their camps soon began to resemble the camps they had always lived in on the plains. A village of tipis clustered in traditional fashion emerged near the show grounds. Inside the tipis, animal hide parfleches contained native clothing, and many had packed their favorite catlinite pipes in beaded deerskin bags. Sometimes, Indian men were allowed to bring their families, and children ran through the villages abroad as they had always done. There were usually a number of campfires burning and in the close-knit Indian village, the occasional smell of fresh buffalo roasting on a spit drew the people together. While women tended the fire and beaded inside the tipis, the men sat in small groups smoking and talking, relaxing between shows. The Lakota were introduced to dominos during the trips abroad and many became fascinated with the new game. Clustered on the ground, whooping and hollering, occasionally making wagers on the outcome, they would sit in circles and play the game for hours.

Despite royal visits, frequent dinner invitations and the general social swirl of European cities, Cody often preferred life in the Indian camp. He liked the nightlife, liked to drink and liked the parties, but after a while, George Dull Knife said, Cody wanted to be with his own kind of people, people who had lived in the American West. "One afternoon, Grandpa said, they all went to a fancy bar in Paris. By the end of the day, Cody was really loaded. He had his six-shooter on, and at one point, he pulled out his gun and emptied it in the ceiling. The French people in the bar dove under the tables and everyone started to panic. When the gun was empty, he put it away, finished his drink and they all left. That night, instead of sleeping in a nice hotel where some of the others were staying, Cody slept with the Indians in a tent back at their campgrounds. My grandfather said it was something that he often did. He would spend a night or two in the hotel and then show up with his bedroll back in the Sioux camp.

"In one of those years when my grandfather was with the show, they had all been gone a long time, about a year and a half, and all the Indians were really homesick. They got back to New York and then they took a long train ride, three or four days, before they arrived in Gordon. Some of their relatives were waiting for them at the train station and there was a lot of crying and hugging, but instead of everyone breaking up and going home right away, Buffalo Bill insisted on throwing a big party for all the Sioux. He wanted to thank them for their work in the show, so he had some of his people slaughter eight or ten head of cattle and there was a couple of barrels of cognac and I guess they had quite a going-away party. My grandmother had come in with some of the others from the Yellow Bear Camp to meet the train. She had never heard of cognac before and I guess she got pretty drunk that night. From what I heard, she never touched the stuff again.

"When the tours ended, the Indians were always happy. They missed their home and their people and they couldn't wait to get back. But Grandpa said Cody always seemed a little sad. He would talk about resting up for a little while and then he would see them again in the spring or the fall or whenever they would be leaving Pine Ridge to start another season."

For years, Washington bureaucrats entrusted with carrying out reservation policy had bitterly opposed the Wild West shows. They disliked the underlying principles associated with them and they had fought hard to end the use of Indians in the shows. In 1889, Commissioner of Indian Affairs John Oberley summed up the government's view:

"The effect of traveling all over the country among, and associated with, the class of people usually accompanying Shows, Circuses and Exhibitions, attended by all the immoral and unchristianizing surroundings incident to such a life, is not only most demoralizing to the present and future welfare of the Indian, but it creates a roaming and unsettled disposition entirely foreign and antagonistic to that which has been and is now the policy of the Government."

George Dull Knife would spend much of the decade of the 1890s traveling with the Wild West Show. He was among the few who left, who were frequently gone for long stretches. Most who stayed behind lived amid changes and conditions that had made George Dull Knife feel lucky that he had something to do, something that brought in a little money and made life easier. Between shows, when he returned home to the Pine Ridge Reservation, he saw the many changes, the condition of his people, and in later years, he would tell his son and then his grandson about the life of the Oglala Sioux in the last decade of that century.

During the 1890s, in the aftermath of Wounded Knee, the demoralization of the Lakota was complete. In a last desperate attempt to bring back the old ways, many had fervently put all faith in the dance that promised salvation, that promoted a belief in better days to come. A crude mass grave filled with the butchered bodies of 146 Lakota now stood in mute testimony to the failure of the Ghost Dance. For many, it also symbolized something else, what they came to accept as a harsh and immutable truth: The gap between white and red culture could never be bridged. The distance was too great, the resentment too high.

For the Lakota, the emptiness and despair was marked by a withdrawal from all religious beliefs, Indian and Christian. In short order, church membership fell from more than twenty-five hundred before Wounded Knee to less than five hundred afterward. On September 13, 1892, John P. Williamson, minister of the Pine Ridge Presbyterian Church, noted in his annual report, "The effect of the ghost dances in the former years was very deleterious to Christianity, and is still felt among the Ogalallas. The excitement of a false religion has left a dead, indifferent feeling about religion. We look for a reaction and a brighter day in the near future."

Throughout the decade, government agents and church missionaries continued the process of making over the Pine Ridge Reservation in the white man's image. The American flag now flew from the top of all government buildings, schools, libraries and two new homes for elderly women, a symbol the agents hoped would promote "an active, ever-living civilizing influence upon the camp Indian."

To hasten assimilation into the dominant culture, agents began to isolate each segment of Lakota society, assigning specialists to break it down and then rebuild along "progressive" lines.

Indian women, the government believed, had long been neglected in a headlong rush to make Christian farmers of Lakota men. To correct the imbalance, field matrons were introduced into the distant camps. Called "instructors in domestic economy," the field matrons were to civilize and educate Lakota women, to teach them how to become better wives, mothers and homemakers. Using Christian wives as models, the matrons stressed neatness and cleanliness over "greasy paint and barbaric ornaments."

Government-appointed farmers, meanwhile, began teaching Lakota men the techniques of modern ranching. For a time, some Oglala did well in their new roles as cattlemen. They enjoyed the spring roundups and branding season. By 1898, their herds had grown to nearly 40,000, including 8,000 calves, the largest ever. That year, the Lakota sold more than 2 million pounds of beef raised and brought to market on their own lands. For some years, neighboring white ranchers had indiscrimately used private Indian lands as personal pastures, and there was some talk of fencing off part of the reservation and patrolling its perimeter.

To assist Lakota children, day schools increased from fifteen to thirty-five. Agents wanted the schools closer to distant camps, closer to the traditional Lakota families. This, they believed, would cut down on the long commute, boost attendance and—by getting the children early, by helping erode their instinctive suspicion of whites—give the Lakota their best hope of traveling the civilized path. Some schools proved moderately successful, some did not. Frequently, the day schools were dilapidated one-room shacks with packed dirt floors, boiling in summer, freezing in winter, a large supply of dogs usually in attendance. Lunch often consisted of bean soup and bread. Two boarding schools also operated on Pine Ridge—the Ogalalla Boarding School and the Holy Rosary Mission. While day-school children commuted from their camps, boarding school students moved in for the academic year and lived in segregated dormitories where alcohol and tobacco were banned. For many, the long separation from family became unbearable, and truancy was a chronic problem. In the boarding schools, half a day was given to academics, the other half to vocational training and fieldwork. Boys were taught how to farm and raise stock, instructed in the ways of the blacksmith, tinsmith, butcher, carpenter, painter and cobbler. They drew water, cut wood, planted and cultivated gardens of onions, potatoes and pumpkins and learned how to milk cows. Young girls were taught sewing, cooking, washing and cleaning, how to become a good and useful wife.

By 1895, the government was spending $51,701 to educate 773 Lakota children, about one tenth of the Pine Ridge population. In the schools, both boarding and day, white teachers were deemed superior role models for the students. It was thought that Indian and mixed-blood teachers could not command the same respect, were neither thrifty enough nor equipped with the proper Christian values and work habits. In the schools, speaking Lakota was expressly forbidden.

In the years after Wounded Knee, while various institutions sought to make over the individual men, women and children of the Pine Ridge Reservation, there also began an aggressive campaign to dismantle the full sweep of Lakota society. The campaign's target, believed to be the last great roadblock in the civilizing process, was the people's age-old social bonds and their sacred tie to the lands where they lived. Of the many changes George Dull Knife noticed when he returned from the Wild West Shows, none was greater than the pressure to wrest control of reservation lands from the tribe and place it in the hands of individual Lakota families.

For as long as any could remember, Lakota society had been rooted in the *tiospayes* — "those who live together." The *tiospayes* were an extended family, a close-knit group of husbands and wives, sons and daughters, grandparents, in-laws, cousins, aunts and uncles and close friends. It is how the Dull Knifes had lived, how many of the plains tribes had survived for generations. The origins of the *tiospaye* lay in the tribe's early need for a cohesive hunting unit capable of providing food and protection for all its members. In the last half of the eighteenth century, when the Lakota first arrived on the Great Plains from the Minnesota woodlands, hunting in one place could sustain only a small number of people. To survive, the tribe needed to follow wild game across vast areas. To provide enough food for everyone, single families had to merge into larger hunting groups. Eventually, these extended hunting groups, the *tiospayes*, became the fundamental social unit of Lakota society. For generations, the strength of an individual family had increased with its bond to the larger *tiospaye*. The *tiospayes*, by creating a larger pool of hunters and warriors to draw on in emergencies, further enhanced the overall strength of the tribe.

The lifestyle of the seven tribes of the Lakota Nation, of the individual families and the larger *tiospayes*, fostered a deep attachment to the lands they traveled. Over time, from countless journeys back and forth across the plains, they began to divine meaning from the rivers, mountains and valleys, from a particular butte or stone formation, a different rock or tree and from the wide variety of wildlife that inhabited the lands. Gradually, the Lakota came to accept that each living thing, like themselves, was endowed with its own spirit. They believed that the trees and plants, the fish, birds and four-legged animals, all had the same right to live as they, and this knowledge was shared and passed down to the people, from one generation to the next.

To avoid offending these spirits, the Lakota developed a complex web of cultural and religious beliefs—embodied in ceremonial songs, dances, rituals and sacred objects—that celebrated and nourished the life forces they encountered. The buffalo, they believed, had come from the earth's center, where there lived an inexhaustible supply of the great herds. After a time, the buffalo had disappeared from the plains and returned home, not because they had been hunted to the brink of extinction, believed the Lakota, but because the slaughter had dishonored their spirit. During the Ghost Dance years, they sought to invite the buffalo back. If the sacred rituals were renewed, if the animal's spirit were celebrated properly, then large herds would once again return to the plains from their home in the earth's center.

In the Lakota view of the world, the eagle, *wanbli*, flew closest to the Great Spirit, and so it was thought to be a messenger of the gods.

The feathers of the eagle became sacred, its spirit presiding over councils, hunters, war parties and battles. The spirit of *capa*, the beaver, became the patron of work, provision and fidelity. *Mato*, the bear, was celebrated for his help in love, bravery, wounds and in the use of different medicines. He also became the patron of mischief and fun. Because of its endurance and longevity, the spirit of *keya*, the turtle, was honored as the guardian of life. To promote health and a long life, Lakota mothers often placed the umbilical cord of their newborns in turtle-shaped amulets.

Like most of the Native American tribes, the Lakota revered their children. Births were sometimes spaced several years apart so parents could devote as much time and energy as possible to their care and upbringing. Rarely left alone, children were usually surrounded by a large and doting group of friends and relatives, the *tiospaye*. Punishment never included physical abuse. When the first contacts were made with the families of soldiers and settlers gathered at the forts, the Lakota were horrified at the beating of small children.

For generations, the spiritual and physical center of their world had been concentrated along the western edge of South Dakota, in the swell of pine-studded canyons, sharp peaks and rugged buttes of the *Paha Sapa*. The Black Hills, they believed, was where their ancestors had come from, where the Lakota Nation had been born. It was where the life-giving buffalo returned to wait out the winter storms, where the people had come for vision quests and the Sun Dance, to pray and bury their dead in sacred bluffs closer to the Spirit World. In 1875, when the government offered to buy it, the concept of selling the Black Hills escaped many Lakota.

"A long time ago," said Guy Dull Knife Jr., "when my grandfather was a very young boy, he and another boy about the same age were with a small party of men who had gone to hunt near the Black Hills. There were three men and the two boys and they were riding along a stream when they came upon a miner. He had a big, bushy beard and when he saw the Indians, he pulled out his rifle and shot the boy my grandfather was with in the leg. The Indian men shot the miner dead. Then they walked up to his horse and opened the saddle bags. Inside they found some leather pouches and they knew right away what it was. They took the pouches and dumped all the gold that was inside back into the stream and then they rode away. My grandfather told me this story many times before he died."

In 1874, the discovery of gold had brought intense pressure from mining companies, and the government soon offered to buy the Black Hills. When some Lakota agreed to listen to a government commission, a council was convened to discuss the sale. Crazy Horse refused to attend. Instead, he chose a subchief, Little Big Man, to convey his sentiments. The day of the meeting, Little Big Man rode up to the council tent, grabbed his rifle and strode into the talking circle. He said he would shoot the first Sioux who voted to sell the sacred hills. Sitting Bull, too, refused to attend. "Possession and greed," he said, "is a disease with the white man."

By the 1890s, the Oglala Sioux had seen their native landbase shrink dramatically for the fifth successive decade. With each contraction came not only a significant land loss, but a corresponding erosion of the old ways.

In the 1850s, they had roamed at will across an immense, five-state expanse of the northern plains. The Fort Laramie Treaty of 1868 reduced their lands to 43,000 square miles, most of it within the western half of South Dakota, lands the treaty called the Great Sioux Reservation. By the spring of 1879, the Lakota had lost the Black Hills and the Oglala were herded onto an agency occupying a small corner of the Great Sioux Reservation. A decade later, the Dawes Act of 1887 and the Sioux Act of 1889 reduced the large reservation by almost half, carving it up into six smaller ones and throwing open the surplus land to white settlement. The Oglala were left with 5,000 square miles in their new homeland, the Pine Ridge Reservation. Now, in the 1890s, the push for a final reduction began: The government wanted each individual Oglala family to live on privately owned, 160-acre plots. This had been the essence of the Dawes Act.

As outlined in the act, each family head would be awarded 160 acres. The family would privately own the land and the government would hold it in trust for twenty-five years. During this time, individual families would learn the value of private ownership, how to nurture and take care of their own land, how to make a profit from it. In effect, it would force them to become self-sufficient farmers and ranchers, motivated by the principles of a competitive, free-market economy. Ultimately, a taste for money and possessions would take hold among the Oglala, allowing them to achieve the same status as the white ranchers crowding their lands.

Despite their advanced years, Red Cloud, Little Wound and other traditional headmen of the Oglala vigorously resisted all attempts to carve the reservation into a checkerboard of single-family homes on 160-acre plots. It was against everything the tribe had traditionally stood for, they told the people. In the end, it would tear apart the Lakota's age-old cultural fabric, supplanting the collective good of all for the individual welfare of a few. Most fearful of all, believed Red Cloud, was the threat of hungry, desperate families initially leasing their land to white ranchers, then selling it outright at the end of twenty-five years. Eventually, he believed, the land, the people and their customs would disappear. There would be nothing left. The fear of the chiefs was shared by Charles Penney, an army captain who temporarily served as Pine Ridge agent. "The allotments of their lands in severalty," Penney wrote in his 1894 annual report, "will result in the degradation of this people and their speedy extinction."

Throughout the decade, the Oglala continued to resist each attempt to further reduce their lands. By 1898, not a single family had agreed to accept a 160-acre allotment. On no other reservation, a succession of frustrated agents noted, was the concept of private ownership more difficult to sell than among the Oglala of Pine Ridge. The Indians fear "that if allotments are made white settlers will be permitted to come upon the reservation and monopolize the grazing," said acting agent Maj. W. H. Clapp.

By now, the Pine Ridge Reservation had been divided into eight administrative districts. It was hoped that the districts, centered along the more fertile creek bottoms, would help break up the tribal village, paving the way for a rapid transition to farming and ranching on the privately held, 160-acre plots. Once the tribal village, the *tiospayes* and communal life disintegrated, believed the government, individual Oglala families would learn to sustain themselves instead of relying on the tribe. By the end of the decade, however, the great hope of making the Oglala a self-sufficient people had not worked.

Even by Dakota standards, the summer of 1893 proved unusually dry, and by fall, persistent droughts had destroyed the spring crops. That summer, the parched prairie grasses caught fire and burned over four fifths of the reservation, wiping out the season's hay crop. As a result, there was little winter food left for the livestock. "The general outlook for the winter is not cheerful," reported Agent Penney, "but with the return of spring, and the growing of another crop of grass, affairs will improve and a single good year will bring much material benefit. It is hoped that the chastening incident to a bad season will be conducive to great moral improvement."

But the spring and summer droughts of 1894 were worse than the year before, and critical hay crops were again wiped out. With two successive years of crop failures, the diminishing food base left both the Oglala and their livestock with little to eat. Hunger began to stalk the reservation. During the 1880s, their first decade of reservation life, the Oglala had enjoyed some success in providing for themselves. In 1882, they supplied half of their own food—25 percent from farming and 25 percent from hunting. Between 1886 and 1890, they met one third of their food needs by farming and hunting. Between 1891 and 1894, hunting and farming declined significantly. By 1895, unable to till the arid soil, the wild game extinct, their livestock crippled by crop failure, the Oglala had become totally dependent on government aid for their survival. That year, federal agencies provided 100 percent of the reservation food supply, a condition that would prevail for the rest of the decade.

Stripped of their ability to hunt and achieve honor in battle, their culture, religion and language outlawed, many Lakota spent much of the decade in a lingering depression, unable to find any meaning in the new way of life. On Pine Ridge, there were now four full-time judges sitting on the Court of Indian Offenses, meting out punishment to those who persisted in clinging to the old ways. The reservation's most serious criminal offenses, meanwhile, had come under U.S. jurisdiction. A federal court in nearby Deadwood, South Dakota, had the power to hang an Oglala convicted of a major crime, and the Indians, noted one agent, were greatly afraid of "going over the road to Deadwood."

Once a strong and robust people, they began to weaken under the multitude of forced changes. As their diet, exercise level and way of life were altered, so too was their physical health. In 1894, there were 285 deaths on a reservation of 8,000. Many succumbed to tuberculosis. Lakota children shipped to boarding schools in the East became sickly, the change in climate promoting a variety of diseases they had never known. On Pine Ridge, two agency doctors were assigned to treat a population scattered over 5,000 square miles. Extreme distances left many untreated, forcing some to embrace the native medicine men.

Agents who traveled across the Oglala lands saw a wretched, hopeless people. "The besetting sin of the Indians," concluded Captain Penney, "is idleness. I have spared no means at my command to induce them to work. They are, as is to be expected, incapable of sustained effort. They are shiftless, lazy and impossible."

As the old century ended and a new one began, most of the traditional adults had not succeeded in walking the white man's road. Frustrated at their resistance to Christianity, their inability to become self-sufficient farmers, their reluctance to embrace the value of private ownership, government agents came to believe that the Lakota's best hope lay elsewhere. It resided in their children, and within a growing population of mixed-bloods—the "half-breeds" frequently born of white fathers and Indian mothers who were clustered in the community of Pine Ridge. None of the half-breeds had been killed at Wounded Knee, noted Captain Penney, "because they were more intelligent."

In the schools, there was talk of expanding the educational system, of requiring all Lakota children between the ages of six and eighteen to attend the network of reservation day schools. Emphasizing education now, the government believed, would pay valuable dividends down the road. It would promote discipline, self-worth, hope and, most important, an appreciation for a new set of values among the younger Lakota. "He can see something in the future better than the war path, and will consider the white man's silver dollars more to be sought after than the scalps of enemies," wrote W. B. Dew, the Pine Ridge inspector of day schools.

As a young man in his late teens and early twenties, George Dull Knife had spent much of the decade far removed from the problems that plagued his people. Between shows, when he returned home, he saw the poverty, the idleness, the lack of promise and purpose, and he would later tell his son how it was on the Pine Ridge Reservation and about the life in Paris and London. When he came back, he was more fortunate than most, fortunate to have enough left over sometimes to buy a horse, a saddle, a new wagon, some food and clothing for his family and friends in the Yellow Bear Camp.

In the beginning, when he was frequently away for long periods, he had missed a lot of school. He could neither read nor write and he knew only a few words of the new language. On the long Atlantic crossings, Cody had sometimes sought out a quiet corner of the ship. He would gather a stack of newspapers, magazines and dime novels and read aloud to George Dull Knife. Starting with simple words and simple sentences, he would make the Lakota read them back, over and over. It was something they continued on the voyages home and on the long train ride to Gordon. Over time, after he returned to the reservation schools, George Dull Knife eventually learned English well enough to become one of Cody's interpreters.

Every once in a while, between Wild West Shows, George Dull Knife would throw his saddle in the back of a buckboard and set out from the Yellow Bear Camp for the train station in Gordon. From there, he would grab his saddle and take a train down the western edge of Nebraska, then east to North Platte, where Cody had a large ranch. "My grandfather loved horses and he always said that Cody had the best around," said Guy Jr. "So he would go to North Platte and visit him, and after a few days, Cody would end up giving him a couple of horses as a gift."

George would saddle the lead horse, then head back to Yellow Bear, riding alone with his horses through the Nebraska Sandhills, camping along the way. A generation earlier, Chief Dull Knife had come through the same area. He had been looking for the home of the Oglala when the cavalry caught him and his people, and took them to the barracks at Fort Robinson. In the summer of 1883, George Dull Knife had come north through the Sandhills in a wagon from the Indian Territory, heading for Pine Ridge and the relatives at Yellow Bear.

When he got back home, George Dull Knife liked to show off his string of new ponies. His people in the camp were curious about the man who gave him the horses and the time he had spent away in the world across the water. When the weather turned cold, they built a fire in the stove of their log house and he would sometimes pass the evenings telling them stories about the funny ride with mirrors and the buffalo that killed the bull.

In 1898, George Dull Knife married Mary Red Rabbit, a traditional full-blood Lakota from the Yellow Bear Camp. He was twenty-three and she was eighteen. In the last year of the last century, they became the parents of an infant son. Born on February 17, 1899, the boy was big and healthy, and throughout their fifty-seven-year marriage, the parents often remembered how he ate all the time. He was called Guy Dull Knife.

Chapter Six

When the Old Man
Was a Boy

Shortly after noon, the first plates are laid out on a half-dozen or so tables scattered about the dining room. In the back, a sliding glass door opens onto a quadrangle, a neatly kept courtyard of grass and trees, and today a strong mountain wind whips drifting snow across the bottom of the door, its glass steamed over from kitchen heat and February cold. Plates of mashed potatoes and gravy, string beans, raspberry Jell-O and a small bowl of pears occupy the tables. As usual, the old man has rolled his wheelchair out of Room 103, down a hallway of thin gray carpet and across the dining room's yellow linoleum floor, one of the first to arrive at a circular table near the sliding glass door in the nursing home. He is wearing a dark blue workshirt stuffed into baggy gray sweatpants. His long silver hair, wrapped neatly in a ponytail, tumbles from beneath the old beige cowboy hat. When he scoots up to the table, he crosses his legs, the sweatpants creeping above his shins until large block letters written in black Magic Marker appear at the top of the white socks: DULL KNIFE.

Before some of the others have been helped from their beds, before the nurses have fastened bibs on Adams, Harris, Baker, Roberts, Patterson, Ross and Brown, Guy Dull Knife Sr. has swept his plate clean. Hunched over the table, he eats with a kind of steam-shovel precision, his hand frequently shaking but not missing the mark. At ninety-four, he still amazes the staff with his appetite. Dianne, a rehab aide, puts it bluntly: "He eats like a horse. Usually double portions. He doesn't like pasta, but he wolfs down just about everything else. Getting the elderly to eat is one of our biggest problems here. The doctor said if we could bottle Guy's appetite, we'd never have to worry about the others getting sick all the time. I think he spent so much of his early life being hungry that he's still worried about the food running out. So eating is what he enjoys the most. That and getting his feet tickled. Between the two, it's probably a toss-up."

A broken ankle at ninety-two has slowed him down some. Three times a week, Dianne leads him through a range of motion exercises and walks him along a 90-foot course to keep the leg muscles active. Before his vision slipped, says Audrey, a nurse's aide in the east wing, he'd read his Bible in Lakota every night. "He's still extremely independent. He does as much for himself as he can. We make his bed for him and that's about it. But the days can be long and he gets lonely."

It doesn't take long for the big lunch to have an effect. A few minutes after eating, he has turned his chair around and wheeled back across the linoleum, down the carpeted hallway and into his room. He eases up alongside the bed and unties a pair of black and white tennis shoes, then slides across the olive army blanket, curling up on one side for his customary afternoon nap. When he awakes a few hours later, he likes to talk, to spend the remaining time until dinner telling stories—about the early years at Yellow Bear, the strange little school, the horses and the medicine man. Stories about his family. His speech is simple and direct. "I was always afraid when my father would leave with Buffalo Bill Cody to go across the water. I was very young at the time, but I was still the oldest child and that meant I had to help provide for the family. My sister Sara and I, we used to walk to school together. Later, she studied shorthand and she got pretty good at it. She died a long time ago. There were six boys and six girls. They're all dead now. I'm the only one left."

Sonny arrives before the old man wakes up. He has been working most of the day at the foundry in Loveland, working on the statues of the Eagle Dance, the Fancy Dance and the War Dance, and he stops in to check on his father before driving home. He brings eight fresh packs of Big Red chewing gum, the old man's favorite. When he walks in, the father is still sound asleep, curled up on his left side, one stockinged foot tapping involuntarily against the army blanket. He puts the sack of chewing gum on the nightstand and quietly pulls up a chair beside the bed. Outside, the wind has come up again. It sweeps gusts of afternoon snow hard through the streets, occasionally rattling a plate-glass window at the far end of the room.

"Dad had to take on a lot of responsibility at an early age," the son says after a while. "Back then, there were a lot of mouths to feed and he had to look for food all the time. When he was young, there was also a lot of sickness in the Yellow Bear Camp. Two of his brothers died before they were five. They are both buried with his father and mother. About four years ago, before he broke his leg and could still walk O.K., we took him back to Yellow Bear for the first time in a long while. When he saw all the graves, he started crying, so we haven't been back since.

"He has seen a lot and been through a lot, but no matter how rough it was, I don't think he ever really lost his sense of humor. I think it's why he has lived so long. Even though times were hard, he could almost always find some humor in it, something to laugh about, and he would just keep going. I think I'm much the same way. When I first came back from Vietnam, it was really rough, but he used to tease me all the time about how easy I had it. He'd say that if you got wounded in Vietnam, they'd fly in a helicopter and have you in a good hospital with good doctors and nurses inside an hour. But back in his day, when they were stuck in the trenches, it might take two or three days to get a wounded soldier back to some broken-down field hospital that was covered with mud and germs. Half the time, the soldier would be dead before a doctor even saw him."

He stops for a moment and starts to chuckle. "Of all the people I've known, Dad is the only one who ever told me Vietnam was a cakewalk. If he's in the mood, if you get him talking, he will go on and on about the old days. He has a lot of good memories about growing up in Yellow Bear."

. . .

The old log house is still standing. There is a sloping hill of pine and at the bottom, in a small clearing covered in sunlight and knee-high grass, his old home. The roof is long gone, but the foundation remains. Parts of some walls have tumbled down, parts of others are still erect. In the beginning, floors were hard-packed dirt covering two rooms. One room to prepare the food, eat it and get warmth from a wood-burning stove. The other is where they slept. Kerosene lamps provided light, and Yellow Bear Creek the water for cooking, drinking and washing. They went to the bathroom outside. It was a crude house, dark and dank, built of pine cut from the surrounding hills. The old man was born on its dirt floors, the first of his family to enter the world inside four walls, and it is clear how fond he is of the old home, of the area where he grew up on the Pine Ridge Reservation.

"Back in those years, when I was a boy, spring always seemed like a small miracle to everyone who lived at the Yellow Bear Camp," the old man said one afternoon. "The winters were very hard. They had much snow and cold and there was a lot of hunger and sickness. Sometimes, the people did not know if they would survive until the spring. It did not seem possible that anything could live beneath all the snow and cold. But each year, the snows would melt. Then you could walk the hills one day and see for yourself that the animals were back again and all the wildflowers and berry bushes and it always made the people feel better."

When he was a small boy, Guy Dull Knife Sr. traveled back and forth between the Pine Ridge Reservation and Montana, where he and his family sometimes lived with their Northern Cheyenne relatives. By the time he was eight, after his father had left the Wild West Show, the Yellow Bear Camp became their permanent home. In the early years of the twentieth century, George Dull Knife often felt bad about the long months he spent away from his family, the winters most of all. The father loved his young son and he taught him how to help the family make it through while he was away. He showed the small boy how to use the bow and arrow, how to move through the deep snow of Yellow Bear, how to identify and track the wild game. In the mornings, they sometimes walked the land together, his father pointing out where animals were likely to seek shelter from the winter storms. He showed the boy how to stay downwind, how to move quietly through the pines. The old man remembers a lot about his hunting days, still likes to talk about them.

"When I was five or six, my father got his bow and ten arrows and we went to a spot in the woods where he made a target on a tree with his knife. Then he showed me how to notch the arrow. Next, he told me how to aim it and how to release it. He said it was important that I become a good hunter and he made me stay there most of the day. I ended up losing most of the arrows, but toward the end, I was getting pretty good. After that, about all I wanted to do it seemed, was go out and shoot the bow and arrow."

When he got a little older, the boy was good enough that he started bringing home rabbits, squirrels, wild turkey and an occasional deer for the growing family. One winter, the one he remembers best, the snow and cold was too much.

"It was a winter no one who lived through it ever forgot. I had three younger brothers and sisters then and they depended on me to get them food, but I could not hunt. The snow had drifted above my head, and every day there was a bad wind and a temperature below zero degrees. After a while, my mother did not know what to do. She was afraid because we had nothing to eat and she thought the younger ones might starve. After a time like this, she gathered up all the parfleches in our house. These were bags made out of animal hides that the Indian used to store food and clothing in. My mother gathered all of them together and dumped everything out of them and then she boiled the parfleches in a kettle of water on the stove. After they had boiled for a while, she made us drink the water. It was like a kind of soup or broth and we drank it for a long time. We survived, drinking the broth that way, until the blizzards stopped and I could go back out and hunt again.

"When the spring finally came, we were all still hungry all the

time. That year, I went into the hills, up into the cliffs above the creeks, and I searched in the caves up there looking for coyote puppies. When I would find them, I would have to kill them. So I would kill them and bring them back to our house and then my mother would make soup and stew from the coyote puppies. It was the hardest time I can remember and we were all happy to see my father when he came home that year."

More and more, in the Yellow Bear Camp and throughout the Pine Ridge Reservation, it was the women who kept things going. They struggled to keep food on the table, make clothing from

Guy, with bow and arrow, and his father, George Dull Knife, about 1905.

whatever they could find, get their children to the small day schools and keep their families together.

Mary Dull Knife was tall and dark, like her son. Born in 1880, she had heard the stories of the old way of life from her parents. They had been among the great encampment at the Little Bighorn. During the battle, her mother and the other women hid with the children in a ravine near the village. When a warrior rode up and said the fighting had ended, the women went to the battlefield and began to strip the bodies. Guns and ammunition were taken first, her mother said, then the saddles and cavalry boots. One pair of good leather boots could be cut into soles for several moccasins. Her parents had also gotten a sergeant's shirt and a rifle that day and they remained in the family for years afterward.

Between 1899 and 1921, the old man's mother had twelve children. She was quiet and resourceful, seldom venturing far from her home and children. In Lakota, she was called Her Pipe Is Holy, and it wasn't until well past middle-age that she allowed a photograph to be taken. Like other elderly traditionalists, she believed the camera would steal her shadow, take her soul and spirit from her. Years before, Dr. Valentine McGillycuddy had repeatedly asked Crazy Horse to pose for a photograph after he surrendered at Fort Robinson. The Oglala war chief always refused. "My friend," he told the post physician after one request, "why should you wish to shorten my life by taking from me my shadow?" The old man's mother felt the same way.

As a young mother at the Yellow Bear Camp, Mary Dull Knife was luckier than most. Sometimes, when her husband was away in Europe or on the East Coast, an envelope would arrive on the Pine Ridge Reservation. George Dull Knife could not write very well, so he would ask Cody to help him address the envelope and send it to Allen, South Dakota, a small community about ten miles southeast of

Mary Dull Knife (right) with friends.

Yellow Bear. When a friend or neighbor who had been to town told Mary Dull Knife that she had some mail, her son hitched up the buckboard, and the mother and her children would ride down a winding trail through the pine-covered hills, out along Yellow Bear Creek and over the rutted road to Allen. The family used the money to buy food and clothes and kerosene.

"My mother died in 1961," said Guy Dull Knife Sr. "She was eighty-one years old. All of her life, she knew only two words of English: yes and no. She used to carry around a little ink pad and any time she needed to sign anything, she would take out the ink pad and make a thumb print. She did this all of her life."

His mother loved to bead and she beaded traditional Lakota designs on clothing and covers most every day of her life. In the winter sometimes, she would teach her oldest son how to bead and, later, he would teach his son. In the early years of the century, while the father was away, the mother and her son took care of their log home in the Yellow Bear Camp. They spent a lot of time together, working as a team to make sure the younger children were provided for.

"One time," the old man said, "word came to the Yellow Bear Camp that there had been a big train wreck back east, back in Pennsylvania or New Jersey, I can't remember where, and that a lot of the Yellow Bear Indians were dead. We were told that they were bringing all of the dead back to Gordon by train. At that time, nobody knew who was dead and who was alive. They told us we would have to go to Gordon to see if my father was one of the dead or not. I was only in about third or fourth grade at the time, but I got the wagon and hitched it up and I drove with my mother all night to Gordon. We got there and the train with the dead had already arrived and so we had to look at all the bodies to see if my father was one of them.

"My mother and I looked at all of them and when we came to the end, we hadn't seen my father, so we were very relieved. One of the injured Indians who came back on the train told my mother that Dad was all right and he had continued on to New York. We were very happy to hear this, but on the ride home, we began to think of all the bodies we had seen and how we knew these people who had lived with us, and then we were sad for all our friends."

Late one spring, when the old man was a young boy, he was chopping wood in the front yard when he heard the sound of horses coming up the hill. He put down his axe and waited to see who it was. At first, he could not make out the figure riding through the pine. Then he began to run as hard as he could until the rider pulled up in front of him. His father jumped down and hugged the boy for a long time, then they walked over to where the others had stopped. George Dull Knife introduced his son to Buffalo Bill Cody and told him that Cody and some of their friends from the Wild West Show were going to spend a few days at the Yellow Bear Camp. Late that afternoon, Cody pitched a tent in the front yard, and in the evening, they held a feast to welcome him and the Lakota who had returned home from the end of a long season.

"That night, we built a big fire in our front yard. After everyone had eaten, my father, me, my brothers and sisters and the little kids from Yellow Bear started to dance Indian for Buffalo Bill Cody. We danced for a long time and when we were finished, he walked around the circle and gave every kid a nickel. They had never seen anyone who looked like him and some of the kids were afraid. But the next morning, they all came back over and Buffalo Bill showed us this special horse that he had brought with him. Whenever there was a loud noise, the horse fell down and played like he was dead. Pretty soon, all of the kids started standing next to the horse and clapping their hands as loud as they could. The horse would fall down and then everyone would really laugh and so we did this for a long time. It was about the best time we ever had."

One year, his father returned home from the Wild West Show with a bag of silver dollars. The boy was fascinated by the strange coins, so his mother gave him one. He put it in his pocket and rode to the house of his best friend, Archie Good Voice Elk. The two boys got on their horses and rode bareback a long way, to the big general store in Martin, about twenty-five miles from home. When they got to the store, they were thirsty, so Guy Dull Knife took out his silver dollar. The two boys knew some English from school and they could make out the word *beer* on some of the labels. They ordered three apiece and all the way back to Yellow Bear they drank from the bottles.

"By the time we got home, we figured we must be pretty drunk. Good Voice Elk fell off his horse, he thought he was so drunk. But when we got there, some of the adults looked at our bottles and told us it was only root beer. We were pretty embarrassed. My mother told me later that it's a good thing it was only the soda. She said if it had been real beer, the whipping I'd have gotten would have been more embarrassing."

In the summers, he and Good Voice Elk rode their horses all over the Pine Ridge Reservation, from Yellow Bear to Manderson, Porcupine and Martin. Often, they rode down to Yellow Bear Creek with their quivers and bows. They attached a piece of string to the arrows and patrolled along the banks of the clear water until they saw some trout. Then they would notch the arrows and shoot, pulling up trout with the string. Sometimes they made a net of chicken wire and spread it across the creek. They would grab a few sticks and wade in, furiously shouting and beating the water, driving the trout into the net. They'd pull up the net, dump the trout in canvas bags and bring them home. Later in the summer, the chokecherry bushes and plum thickets were heavy with fruit. The two boys filled wooden buckets with the ripe berries and brought them to their mothers, who used them for a pudding, *wojapi,* and the juice to sweeten a variety of foods. For more than seventy years, the old man and Good Voice Elk were close friends.

He is still sound asleep, curled on top of the worn army blanket. On the walls above the bed are the color Polaroids of his grandchildren, great-grandchildren and the old friends. On the nightstand, beneath a small jumble of medicine bottles and the sack of Big Red chewing gum, lies his Bible. The son is rummaging through a top drawer, making sure his father still has his wristwatch and some good batteries for the new hearing aid so he can hear the news if he wants, without turning up the TV too loud. He will stay a few more minutes before heading home to Cora Yellow Elk and the children.

"My grandfather retired from the Wild West Show in about 1907. For the next twenty-five or thirty years, he worked as a tribal policeman and a rancher. He eventually ended up taking his hundred and sixty acres and he raised some cattle and did a little farming. But he never really liked farming or cattle ranching. What he loved more than anything was the horses. In the end, I think if the government had allowed us to raise horses instead of cattle, everyone would have been better off.

"For years and years, the Lakota had always had their horses. They couldn't do without them. We used to use them for everything. To hunt the buffalo, to move camp, for the war parties, to trade for food and clothing, for guns, even in courtship. If a man wanted a woman to be his wife, the first thing he did was give her father a string of good ponies. They said Crazy Horse had a favorite war pony that no one was ever allowed to ride, that no one even dared to go near.

"The horse was prized so much by the Lakota that we had a dance, the Horse Dance, to honor it. But cattle had no value for my people. They had only one use. To be fattened and slaughtered, and this was something that my grandfather, and many other Lakota, never quite took to. Even today, if you go out in the districts where the full-bloods live, you will see the young boys on horseback. They ride without saddles, bareback, and some of them can really fly. They still love the horse."

He finds the wristwatch under a stack of letters, and then the batteries, still in the hard plastic pack. He peels off the cardboard backing and pops the batteries out of the pack, fitting them snugly into the new hearing aid. "Almost as soon as my father could walk, Grandpa had him on a horse. He taught Dad how to ride and, before long, he had turned Dad into a little jockey, riding all of my grandfather's fastest horses. Every summer, there was a lot of fairs and rodeos on the reservation and in a lot of the towns, like Chadron and

Gordon, that were near the reservation. Most of these fairs and rodeos had horse races and people from all over would come and bet on them.

"My grandfather's favorite horse was called Red Wing. The horse had no papers, it was just a reservation scrag horse, but he was really fast. Grandpa loved the horse so much that he ended up naming one of his sons after it. Everyone had to have a Christian name back then and so in school, his son was called Daniel Dull Knife, but in the Yellow Bear Camp, he was known by his Lakota name *Hupahu Luta*, Red Wing.

"For a while, my father rode Red Wing at all the races in the summer. But before long, Dad got too big, so then his younger brothers took over and they became the family jockeys. Over the years, Dad said that Red Wing won a lot of money for my grandfather.

"Grandpa kept a big field of alfalfa on his land that he used to feed his horses with, and after Dad got too big to be the jockey, it was his job to take care of the horses. Every day, he had to feed them and water them and groom them. He has always said that one of his strongest memories from childhood is the way the alfalfa smelled after it was cut. Up until a few years ago, if we were driving around in the summer and he got a whiff of alfalfa coming through the window, he would want to pull over and just sit there for a while."

In 1831, Chief Justice John Marshall defined the relationship between the American Indian and the government of the United States in paternalistic terms. "They [the Indians] look to our government for protection; rely upon its kindness and its power; appeal to it for relief to their wants, and address the president as their Great Father," wrote Marshall.

It was a philosophy that had dominated much of the nineteenth century. Conquered one at a time, the Indian tribes were herded onto reservations where they soon became wards of the federal government, looking to the Great Father for protection, kindness and relief, for food, clothing and a future. But paternalism soon created a problem. The Indian became *too* reliant upon the government.

For a while, it was thought that assimilation—converting Indians into Christian farmers and replacing tribal lands with the privately owned 160-acre plots—would solve the problem. The Indian "must be imbued with the exalting egotism of American civilization," the commissioner of Indian affairs had said in 1886, "so that he will say 'I' instead of 'We,' and 'This is mine' instead of 'This is ours.' " Once the Indian had blended into the dominant culture, paternalism would end, and so would the "Indian Problem."

But throughout the 1890s, assimilation had not worked and the problem did not disappear. At the end of the century, after two decades of prolonged effort, the Oglala Sioux and many other tribes had become more dependent on the Great Father than ever before.

By the early years of the twentieth century, the political winds in Washington had shifted. Assimilation was still the goal, but a succession of well-intentioned Indian commissioners now embraced a different approach. The Indian must become self-reliant. He must learn how to support his family and rid himself of government dependence.

In 1901, Commissioner of Indian Affairs William A. Jones ordered all able-bodied men who could support themselves and their families through work removed from the ration rolls. On the Pine Ridge Reservation, Agent John R. Brennan cut 857 Indians from the food rolls and offered jobs instead. He would pay them $1.25 a day to build dams and roads, construct new bridges and fence off part of the reservation. The policy switch created havoc. On Pine Ridge, many Lakota had settled into a life of ranching, farming and growing vegetables to supplement their food rations. The new edict forced them to leave their homes and families, travel to distant work sites and camp there for weeks at a time. Far from home, they were unable to tend their stock or vegetable crops. Many used most of the money they earned to buy food and support themselves while away. When the weather turned cold, they often returned home to find their stock missing, their vegetable gardens wiped out. With winter

setting in, many now found themselves with fewer cattle, no vegetables, no money and no ration day.

In early 1902, Commissioner Jones issued another order to
reservation agents. Jones admired much about the Indian. He
respected their devotion to children, their love of freedom and their
fierce ancestral pride. "Such a race," he said, "is worthy of all the
time, money, and labor expended on it by a generous Congress and
people." But the commissioner also believed that the Indian must
shed much of his past if he were to join whites on civilization's path.
Traditional Indian feasts and dances, the painting of their faces, were
"simply subterfuges to cover degrading acts and to disguise immoral
purposes." The long hair of Indian men, he believed, was a particular problem. In January 1902, he decreed that all Indian men working for the Indian Service or drawing rations must cut their hair. Any
who refused should be fired or have his supplies withheld. If he
became abusive, "a short confinement in the guard-house, with shorn
locks, should furnish a cure," said Jones. On February 22, Pine
Ridge Agent Brennan ordered all able-bodied Lakota men employed
by the government to cut their hair or lose their rations and their
jobs.

Brennan also sent word to the schools, instructing teachers to
make sure that Lakota boys complied with the short-hair edict. Like
others before them, the agent and the commissioner believed that the
education of children would create a new generation of Indian, a generation that would soon forget the old ways and embrace the new.

In a small clearing across the road from Yellow Bear Creek, where
deep-rutted trails wind down from the hills, little remains of the old
school. Weeds poke up from concrete slabs covering what was once
a dirt floor, and the log walls and roof are long gone. It was a small
building, flanked by steep cliffs in front and back. The full-blood
children used to come here from their log homes scattered across the
camp, the first full generation of Lakota born in houses, raised on
reservations and schooled in the ways of the dominant culture.

Weekdays, when the old man was a small boy, he set out from his home, took the trail down through the pines and out along the dirt road, about a mile and a half, until he reached the little school about nine-thirty each morning. For him and most of the others, it was their first contact with the other world.

"The day before we started school for the first time," the old man said, "my mother washed all of our clothes. She washed everything and it took all day. That night, she got water from the creek and she gave all of us children who were going to school the next day a bath. My sister, Sara, put on her nightgown and we all went to sleep. When we woke up the next morning, we were all afraid. We didn't want to go. But my mother said we had to. So she gave us our break-fast and then she walked us to the trail. Sara took a few steps and then she started crying and ran back to my mother. My mother told me to hold her hand and walk her down. When we got to the school, there was a doctor there and he tested all of the Indians to see if they had any diseases. Toward the end of the day, the teacher told an interpreter to tell all of the Indians that from now on, we could not speak our language in the school. We must start to learn English and that is the only language that we could use. Then the teacher told all of the Indian boys that they could not come to school anymore with long hair. When I got back home, I told my mother and father what they said and I cried and cried."

George Dull Knife waited a week and then he got out his hunt-ing knife and cut off his son's long braid. It had been the symbol of Lakota manhood for as long as anyone could remember, a symbol that embodied a spiritual connection and helped promote a long life, and the old man has never forgotten the shame and humiliation of the long-ago Sunday night. Eventually, after his marriage, after he became a Pine Ridge councilman, he grew it back, has worn it in a ponytail for more than thirty years.

In 1906, in the small Yellow Bear School, Guy Dull Knife Sr. began to learn English and some American history. He says he was luckier than most. From the Wild West Show earnings, his mother could usually buy him leather shoes and a good coat from the store in

Allen. Many of the other kids wore moccasins or went barefoot and they didn't have enough to keep them warm. The older kids rode horses, the younger ones came in buckboards or walked, often with their dogs. Inside the small log building, his teachers told him and the others the first stories they had ever heard about the white God.

By the early 1900s, the Pine Ridge Reservation had long been carved up into districts where different denominations and the government worked hand-in-hand. In the old man's youth, Episcopalians controlled the eastern half of the reservation, Catholics the west. If Lakota children were to attend government-financed schools staffed by churches and missionaries, the children were to have short hair, learn English and become baptized in the Christian faith. They also were to have new names.

"The church people would come into the Indian camps and ask the people what they would like to be called," said Guy Jr. "They would give them a choice of names. Most of the Yellow Bear families had no real idea what they were talking about. They'd say they didn't know, so an interpreter would pick out a name for them. He'd say, 'O.K., you'll be George and you'll be Guy and you'll be somebody else.' Then that would be the name they eventually entered on the census rolls. That's how my father got his name. An interpreter picked it out at random for him when he was a small boy.

"My father told me a story one time about an old man in the Yellow Bear Camp. When the interpreter asked him what he wanted to be called, he said, 'Jesus.' The interpreter asked him why and he said because that was a name he had heard a lot and it was the only English name he knew. The interpreter got kind of mad, Dad said, and told the old man he couldn't be called Jesus. He said if he couldn't think of anything else, he'd pick one out for him, so the old man became Elmer.

"The problems that came about after Wounded Knee, and for many years after," Guy Jr. said, "were very complicated in some ways and very simple in other ways. What whites did not understand then, and have never really understood, is that there is no such thing as an Indian religion. They thought they could simply Christianize us, give us new names and a better religion, and everything would be fine. But it was our way of life that was missing, a way of life that included our religion and this was something that went very deep into my people. It was something that could never be replaced by becoming a Catholic or an Episcopalian or by getting a new name."

After finishing third grade, Guy Dull Knife and the other Lakota children began traveling nine miles down the road to the new No. 20 Day School built in Allen. Near the new school was a slaughterhouse, where area ranchers under contract to the government drove their herds. As ration day neared, Sioux families camped out near the slaughterhouse, waiting for the government-issue beef. Afterward, there were parties and feasts. Not far from the slaughterhouse were the offices of the district farmer, a general store and a small, one-cell police station. Behind the police station was the one-room log school.

At first, he and the others rode to school in the back of buckboard wagons. In winter, their parents spread hay in the wagon box and the children huddled together to keep warm during the long ride. Some days it was too cold to go and some of the kids stopped going during the winter months. Later, when he was older, he rode his horse to school. His first year there, teachers passed out uniforms for each of the boys to wear, short pants that hit them just above the knee and dark blue cotton shirts. For part of each day, they listened to Bible stories and practiced their English.

The commissioner of Indian affairs had forbidden the use of native languages in all Indian schools in 1887, and more than twenty years later, when the old man was a boy of ten, speaking Lakota was still forbidden in the Allen Day School and on the grounds outside. Children caught speaking their language were forced to sit in a corner or not allowed to eat lunch. Some were spanked.

Away from school, in his log home in the Yellow Bear hills, Guy Dull Knife had always heard Lakota, the language his parents spoke and the only language his mother knew. By then, his father had made additions to the home to accommodate his growing family. As more children arrived, the house grew in length until it was known as *Ti Hanska*, the long house. His father also added a barn and a set of corrals for his prized horses. Each day, his eldest son took the horses down to the creek to water them. He also had to fetch water for the family and gather wood. The boy would load the wagon with empty wooden barrels and an axe, drive it to the creekbed and return with the water for cooking and cleaning and wood for the stove.

For as long as the boy could remember, there had been a sweat lodge in the front yard. George Dull Knife had built it of saplings and covered the dome frame with canvas and blankets. In the center, his father had dug a pit for the heated stones, and almost every day of his life, he had gone to the sweat lodge in the evenings. The boy often saw his father and the other men of the camp bundle the holy sage and smoke their pipes and he had been to many of the traditional Lakota ceremonies, had seen the dances and heard the songs. Some were held at the family home. For a long time, he had enjoyed the evenings when the old people would stop by and he could listen to the elders talk about the old days.

"This was a good time in my life," the old man said. "I loved to hear these stories, especially my father's stories. He was a good storyteller and he had a lot to tell me. Even though I had never lived it, I began to miss our old way of life, the life my father told me about. It always sounded like a better life to me."

George Dull Knife wanted his eldest child to know the history and tradition of their people. So he told him the stories and, in the evenings, he began to take him to the sweat lodge and teach him the traditional songs the Lakota had always sung in the purification ceremony. After a time, the boy began to have problems at the Allen day school. He was ten years old and it was harder to reconcile the two different worlds. By day, he was taught one way of looking at the world: To succeed, to have a future, he must wear short hair, dress like white people, learn their language, adopt their customs and accept Jesus. At night, back in the hills, he saw the braided sweetgrass and went to the sweat lodge. He learned the ways of *Wakan Tanka* and heard the stories of his people, always in the other language, a language that meant isolation, hunger or worse if he spoke it during the day. The conflict, which began in the early years of the century, had not yet been resolved by the end. On the nightstand, as he tells the stories, there is still the Good Book, Jesus speaking to him in Lakota.

One day, when the old man was about twelve, a stranger arrived at their home in the Yellow Bear Camp. He had long gray hair and wore a full-length overcoat, two pistols stuck in the waistband. "He was," the old man says, "the scariest-looking person I ever saw." His name was George Poor Thunder. A powerful, old-style medicine man, Poor Thunder was revered among traditional Lakota during the old man's youth. He arrived at their home with his wife and children in a buckboard wagon, leading two hundred head of horses he had driven from the nearby Rosebud Reservation. George Dull Knife admired many of the good-looking thoroughbreds, and after Poor Thunder settled in at the Yellow Bear Camp, the two men became friends.

Soon, Poor Thunder began to take charge of the religious ceremonies held in the camp and, after a time, he asked George's oldest boy if he would like to help him sing some of the traditional Lakota songs. "I told him I did not know all of the songs and I had never sung them in the ceremonies before," said the old man. "He said he would teach me." The medicine man began to teach him, and that summer, 1911, the twelve-year-old boy sang at his first Sun Dance back in the hills of the Yellow Bear Camp. Off and on for the next seventy summers, he would sing the Sun Dance songs throughout the Pine Ridge Reservation. Eventually, Guy Dull Knife Sr. taught his son the sacred songs he had learned from the medicine man, and Guy Jr. would teach them to his son, Guy Dull Knife III.

The last public Sun Dance on the Pine Ridge Reservation had been held in 1883. When the old man sang for the first time, the ceremony had been outlawed for almost thirty years. His father also became a Sun Dance singer, and in the summers at the beginning of the century, back in the Yellow Bear hills, the boy and his father sometimes joined the sacred circle gathered around the drums by the cottonwood tree. They sang together, as the singers had always done, giving the dancers the courage to sacrifice for the good of their people. For the father, it was a conflict not unlike what his son encountered at the No. 20 Day School in Allen.

George Dull Knife, his Wild West Show days over, now worked for the U.S. government. For more than twenty-five years, from 1910 until the Great Depression years, he served as a tribal policeman. The Indian Service provided a gun, a uniform and a badge and, for $48 a month, he patrolled between Kyle and Allen on horseback, looking for those who violated the reservation's civil and criminal laws. It was a difficult job. The area was large and rugged and there were frequent squabbles. Often, he became the cop, judge and jury in the remote hill country where ranchers sometimes hid their stills, selling and trading moonshine to the Indians. Taking prisoners to the town of Pine Ridge usually meant a two-day trip, one there and one back, and so he was frequently away from home. He disliked the work, but with a large family to support, it was one of the few paying jobs he could get.

Summers were the worst. He knew of the Sun Dances and sometimes went into the hills and joined them himself. George Poor Thunder often presided at the ceremonies and they were attended by many friends and relatives, and now his son. He was proud of the boy, proud that he had learned the songs and sang them to help the others. It was against the law, but he could make no arrests. "He told my father and later he told me that it was the one thing we could not lose," said Guy Jr. "If we lost the Sun Dance, he believed, then we would no longer be a people. We would be something else, but we would no longer be Lakota."

In later life, George Dull Knife would always say that the years between 1905 and 1920 were the hardest. "My grandfather and the others could not come to grips with the whole allotment process," said Guy Jr. "They never really understood that the land you walked on could be owned by one individual. They had always believed the land was there for everyone to use."

For most of two decades, the Lakota had listened to the old chiefs, resisting each attempt at carving their tribal lands into individual family plots. But in the new century, poverty and pressure

Lawman George Dull Knife, with Guy (left) and his brother Gordon.

began to erode the resistance and most of the old chiefs were dead or
dying. On the Fourth of July, 1903, when Guy Dull Knife was a boy
of four, the Lakota's last great chief gave his farewell address to the
Oglala of Pine Ridge.

"My sun is set. My day is done," said Red Cloud. "Darkness is
stealing over me. Before I lie down to rise no more, I will speak to my
people.

"Hear me, my friends, for it is not the time for me to tell you a lie.
The Great Spirit made us, the Indians, and gave us this land we live
in. He gave us the buffalo, the antelope, and the deer for food and
clothing. We moved on our hunting grounds from the Minnesota to
the Platte and from the Mississippi to the great mountains. No one
put bounds about us. We were free as the winds and like the eagle,
heard no man's commands. . . . Where the tipi was, there we stayed
and no house imprisoned us. No one said, 'To this line is my land, to
that is yours. . . .'

"I was born a Lakota and I have lived a Lakota and I shall die a
Lakota. Before the white man came to our country, the Lakotas were
a free people. They made their own laws and governed themselves as
it seemed good to them. . . .

"Our children cannot forget their own people, and when the
older people tell them of the time when the Lakotas moved across the
land as free as the winds and no one could say to them 'go here or
stay there'; of the time when men did not labor and sweat to stay in
one place; of the time when to hunt the buffalo and keep the tipi was
all the care there was; of the time when brave men could win respect
and renown on the warpath—then they sing the Indian songs and
would be as the Lakotas were. . . .

"The priests and the ministers tell us that we have lived wickedly
when we lived before the white man came among us. Whose fault
was this? We lived right as we were taught it was right. Shall we be
punished for this? . . .

"This was taught me by the wise men and the shamans. They
taught me that I could gain their favor by being kind to my people

and brave before my enemies; by telling the truth and living straight; by fighting for my people and their hunting grounds. . . .

"When the Lakotas believed these things, they lived happy and they died satisfied. What more than this can that which the white man offers us give . . . ?

"Shadows are long and dark before me. I shall soon lie down to rise no more. While my spirit is with my body, the smoke of my breath shall be towards the Sun, for he knows all things and knows that I am still true to him."

A year later, in 1904, the first lands on the Pine Ridge Reservation passed into the hands of private owners. In the next five years, 2,604 Lakota received allotments in parcels of 80, 160 and 640 acres. By 1916, of 2.5 million acres the tribe had once owned, only 150,000 acres remained. The rest had either been assigned to individual Indians and their families or sold as surplus to whites.

During this time, as whites and Indians found themselves ranching adjacent lands, cattle-rustling became a problem. Indian men sometimes slipped away to white ranches, stole a cow, butchered it and brought the meat home to hungry families. If caught, they could be "taken over the road" to the federal courthouse in Deadwood, convicted and hanged. George Dull Knife knew about the rustlers. One was a relative, who admitted stealing cattle to feed his family. Like most of the Indian police, George Dull Knife looked the other way. After a while, U.S. marshals moved in, offering reward money to anyone who provided names. A few of the Indians obliged and some of the rustlers were caught and hanged.

George Dull Knife and his son knew many of the white ranchers in the area. For a number of years, in summer and on weekends, they traveled the countryside together, felling cedar trees and loading them in the back of their buckboard wagon. At home, the father and son stripped the trees and cut them into posts. Then they would load them back in the wagon and ride out to the different ranches, selling the posts for a penny apiece. One of their best customers was a family of German farmers. Drawn from their homeland by handbills,

Guy (right) and Enos Poor Bear, a cousin.

brochures and newspaper ads promoting cheap land and a new life in the American West, they had settled on property not far from the Yellow Bear Camp. The immigrant family was poor and they knew no English, so a kind of sign language developed between the Germans and the Lakota. "They wanted our cedar posts for fencing," the old man said, "but they couldn't pay us. They gave us food instead. We gave them the posts and they gave us sausages from their smokehouse and a big wooden barrel of sauerkraut. My dad and me did not care for the sauerkraut, but sometimes we had gone through a lot of the sausage before we got home."

In the fall, the father and son usually had good luck hunting deer. They would take two of the deer and put them in the wagon, then ride to the German home. The Germans dressed the deer and put them in the smokehouse, and later, they would give one back to the Dull Knifes, keeping the other as a gift from their Lakota friends.

Throughout his childhood, the old man in the nursing home had found ways to help his large family. He had hunted with the bow and arrow, baled alfalfa, chopped wood, carried water, helped cut and sell the cedar posts, laid fence line and taken care of his father's horses. When he was fourteen, Guy Dull Knife started riding broncos. On a hill above the Allen day school, about a mile away, was a racetrack, and in the summer, he rode broncos at the track's annual fair and rodeo. If it had been a difficult bronco, he would pass the hat around and make a little money. Later, at a rodeo in Gordon one time, he remembers winning twenty-five dollars. At a rodeo in Chadron, he won thirty dollars.

Occasionally, people who lived in the area started asking him to break in some of their horses. One was a man who lived near Kyle, not far from the Yellow Bear Camp. In the 1860s, the mother of Chief Little Wound had found a small black child crying in a ravine on the Nebraska plains. She took him home and the chief adopted the boy, raising him as a son in the Sioux village. After the Oglala were settled on the Pine Ridge Reservation, Little Wound gave him some land and the orphan lived as a Sioux on Pine Ridge for the rest of his life. His name was Alec Baxter. Later, he told his Indian family that he had been with a party of former slaves heading west to start a new life. He wandered off, got lost and was left behind. The Lakota called him *Ha Sapa*, Black Skin, and he eventually came to speak their language and live as they did. On Pine Ridge, he was known for having the best vegetable garden and some of the finest horses around.

In his early teens, Guy Dull Knife used to break horses for *Ha Sapa*. "For every five horses I broke, he would give me one as a gift and I would bring it home to my father. When he died, they buried him in the same cemetery as Chief Little Wound. It is the same cemetery my wife, Rose, is buried in."

In the beginning of the summer of 1915, George Dull Knife told his son that he would not be returning to the Allen day school come fall. Down the road, the father believed, his son would be better off attending one of the federal boarding schools off the reservation. He would need the education to care for himself and his family, to make a better life than the one the father had known. The boy had never heard of the new place and he didn't want to go. He had never been away from his family and, over and over that summer, he told his mother and father that he did not want to go to Pennsylvania.

Chapter Seven

The Schoolboy Soldier
from Yellow Bear

"When it was time to go that year, my mother's heart was broken in two. We packed my things in a leather bag my father had used when he traveled with Buffalo Bill and we put them in the buckboard and then my father drove me from the Yellow Bear Camp to Pine Ridge. My mother stood by the trail and she cried and cried. When some of us came back home in the summer, all the mothers would be waiting at the train station and then everyone would start crying all over again."

Late in the summer of 1915, Guy Dull Knife arrived with his father at the office of the reservation agent. From Pine Ridge, Agent John R. Brennan drove him in a buggy to the train station in Rushville, Nebraska, twenty-four miles south. All along, the boy had thought he was going to Pennsylvania, to the same boarding school where a relative and other Lakota had gone in years past. But when they arrived at the station, he found out that he wasn't going to Pennsylvania after all. He was going, instead, to the Haskell Institute in Lawrence, Kansas.

For months after Guy Dull Knife arrived in Kansas, he could not adjust to the new surroundings. His sense of who and where he was had been lost during the long train ride across the flat, open prairie. At Haskell, he was alone, confused and frightened. "All my life, I had been used to seeing the sun come up at certain places in the hills at the Yellow Bear Camp and going down at certain places and then I could not make it out anymore. I wasn't sure where things were. I didn't know where my home was anymore and it scared me and the other boys."

Throughout the latter part of the nineteenth century, eastern reformers strongly believed in the concept of education and separation, of killing the Indian to save the man. Thirty-six years before Guy Dull Knife arrived in Kansas, a school that had pioneered this philosophy opened at an abandoned military barracks in Carlisle, Pennsylvania. Founded by Army Capt. Richard Pratt in 1879, the Carlisle Indian School was the first federally financed Indian boarding school in the nation that did not reside within reservation boundaries. Superintendent Pratt believed that reservation life retarded the growth of Indian students. It bound them to the old ways, blunting their assimilation into white culture, and so he had strongly urged that the schools be built away from reservations.

At Carlisle, Pratt's students participated in an "outing" system: They were sent away from school to live and work with white families, who were paid a government fee. For many, the changes were overwhelming. Indian youth had seldom been away from their families, and the long separation proved wrenching. Many had never been around whites and it heightened their sense of isolation and depression. Besides homesickness, they found it difficult to adjust to the new foods, clothing and climate, to a way of life they had never lived. A number of students came down with diseases they had never encountered. A few died and others were sent home. At home, some began to experience a different problem. For a long time, the story of Plenty Horses came to symbolize the dilemma of young Indians suddenly caught between two different worlds.

A Lakota from the Rosebud Reservation, Plenty Horses was a graduate of the Carlisle School. When he returned home from Pennsylvania, his people no longer accepted him because of his white ways. In the East, whites had rejected him because he was Indian. On January 7, 1891, in the turbulent aftermath of Wounded Knee, Plenty Horses shot and killed Lt. Edward W. Casey, commander of the Northern Cheyenne scout troop summoned to Pine Ridge to help subdue the Lakota Ghost Dancers. By killing the soldier, Plenty

Horses hoped that his people would again embrace him as one of their own. He was arrested and brought before a federal grand jury in Deadwood. "I am an Indian," he testified at a hearing that March. "Five years I attended Carlisle and was educated in the ways of the white man. I was lonely. I shot the lieutenant so I might make a place for myself among my people. Now I am one of them. I shall be hung and the Indian will bury me as a warrior. They will be proud of me. I am satisfied."

In June, however, a trial judge ruled that Plenty Horses could not be convicted of murder because the killing had occurred during a state of war. If he were tried and convicted, then the courts would be obliged to do likewise with soldiers who had killed Indians during Wounded Knee. After the judge's ruling, jurors returned a not-guilty verdict and Plenty Horses was set free.

Over time, the Carlisle Indian School became the model for other federal boarding schools that opened in Nebraska, Oklahoma, New Mexico, Oregon, Arizona and in Lawrence, Kansas.

The Haskell Institute opened its doors on September 1, 1884, despite a warning from the superintendent of Indian schools that it lacked sufficient heat and fresh water, the necessary buildings and medical supplies to help acclimate Indian students arriving from distant reservations, diverse climates and different cultures. Five years later, in the fall of 1889, the bodies of forty-nine Indian children lay in simple graves at the Haskell cemetery, a small plot on a hillside near the railroad tracks known as "God's Acre." Some of the children had died of diphtheria, many more of pneumonia and other lung ailments. By 1913, there were 102 graves.

After a government investigation, conditions began to improve. More money arrived and a hospital was erected with a larger staff of doctors and nurses. Heated buildings, fresh water and improved sanitation gradually contributed to the school's overall goal: to serve as an educational and vocational training center for thousands of Indian boys and girls drawn from tribes across the country. Some Haskell students stayed a few years, graduated and returned home. Others, orphaned on the reservation, arrived as youngsters and stayed for eight or ten years. Like Carlisle, the school was run in strict military fashion. Girls were segregated in one set of brick dormitories, boys in another, and all were expected to participate in a variety of industrial duties and chores.

Guy Dull Knife arrived at Haskell on the morning of September 3, 1915. He was escorted to a second-floor room in the boys' dorm. His home for much of the next three years, the room was freshly painted, with brick walls, wood floors and blanketed army cots, one for each of the three students sharing the room. Afterward, the students were given haircuts, weighed and measured and outfitted for clothing. They each got a pair of black shoes, blue cotton work shirts, overalls and a small round cap. Personal identification numbers were printed on all socks, shirts, pants and underwear.

The next day, he was given a physical. The school doctor noted in his report that Guy Dull Knife was free of tuberculosis, apparently in good health, but "considerably under weight." The boy was sixteen years old, six feet tall and weighed 116 pounds. A few days later, he was tested and placed in Mrs. Stanley's third-grade class.

Back at the Yellow Bear Camp, the boy's parents, torn between the desire to improve his life through education and the guilt of sending him so far from home, worried constantly about their son. Not long after the boy arrived at Haskell, his father sent a letter to the school superintendent. He wanted him to know how important an education was to the family. He could not write very well and his letter to Superintendent J. R. Wise was filled with misspellings and grammatical errors. It was dated September 15, 1915:

Dear, Sir.

I am Respectfully to say a few lines to you this morning. and tell you about my son Guy Dull Knife. this boy he never go school nonreservation—ownly go school in Day school. But he likes to go school in Haskel so I send him. I want you help him and make learn good, studie for any school job. I am working in

Indian service . . . and I am Corpel. I help U.S., all I can. . . . We want you help us and make this boy learn how. any thing.

That is all
You'r Respectfully
Geo Dull Knife
Allen, S Dak.

For months, the boy was so homesick he could not work or study or learn the things his father believed would help him in later life. Shortly after Christmas 1915, he was hospitalized for the third time since his arrival at Haskell. There had been tonsillitis, an abscessed knee and now the flu. In a letter dated January 7, 1916, the school physician, Dr. Charles Ensign, noted that he also "has been on the Trachoma list since his arrival and is likely to stay there for some time as his eyes are very slow in yielding, tho they are much improved." The doctor saw encouragement in a five-pound weight gain—from 116 to 121—but cautioned: "Guy's family history shows a great deal of Tuberculosis so the boy will need to be under obser-vation frequently, at present tho I see no need of his returning home, should such a need be evident, notice will be given at once."

By early spring, the boy's health and spirits had improved and he began to adjust to the daily routine, counting down the days until he could return to his home and his family for summer vacation.

Most days were the same at Haskell and the old man can recall them in detail, from beginning to end. At 6 a.m., a bugle sounded reveille and the Indian students awoke, washed, got dressed in their government-issue clothing and quickly gathered in an assembly hall downstairs for morning roll call. If the weather was good, they marched to the parade ground, drilled in formation for fifteen min-utes, then marched back to the dorm to wash up and eat breakfast. After eating, they made the beds and cleaned their rooms, and at 8 a.m., another bugle announced the start of morning classes. In the mornings, he and the others studied English, American history, geography and a variety of trade skills. At 11:30, a bugle signaled the end of classes and the students marched back to the dorm for lunch, girls at one end of the dining room, boys at the other. After lunch each afternoon, students disbanded to their respective trade stations or to the agricultural fields, where they worked until about 4:30. At 5 p.m., another bugle sounded retreat and they marched to the parade ground, took down the American flag, then marched back to the dorms for dinner. After dinner, there was some free time to study, relax and talk. At 9 p.m., the last bugle of the day sounded taps, the lights went off and bed checks began.

"On weekends, the girls got to go to town one Saturday and the boys went on the next one. On Sundays, there was usually a dress parade and we would line up on the parade grounds and march in the formation they had taught us to. Fort Riley was about a hundred miles west and sometimes the army people and the town people would come to see the Indians marching. There were Indians from all over back then. They had Cherokees from Oklahoma, some Sioux and Kiowa, Cheyenne, Arapahoe, Apaches and some Navajo. Afterwards, when we got back from marching, sometimes there was a social hour and they would let the boys and the girls mix for a while. That was usually the best part of the week."

Haskell students were expected to learn English, discipline and a vocation. In exchange for free room and board and their training, they worked while learning how to become carpenters, cobblers, tailors, painters, masons, mechanics and blacksmiths. There was also a large bakery, a dairy barn, orchards, gardens and farm fields scattered across the sprawling school grounds. Girls did some of the cooking and cleaning at the school, and in summer they were sometimes sent into the homes of nearby white families, where they learned to prepare food, set the table and be a good wife and homemaker. Haskell strove to be self-supporting and grew its own food to feed the students, so boys often worked the fields.

"For a while, I worked in a popcorn field," the old man said. "Each boy was responsible for his own little plot. They were very strict at the school and you had to make sure there was no weeds or anything growing in that part of the field that you were responsible for. There was a man called the chief advisor there, and he ran the boys' part of the school just like it was a military camp. If he or the other supervisors found weeds or anything else that wasn't supposed to be growing in your part of the field, they could take your privileges away from you. They could put you on restriction. So me and the other boys, we would get down on our hands and knees looking for any weeds growing in our plots.

"One time, I took some of the popcorn from the field and brought it back to the dorm. Then I cooked it up and sold bags of popcorn to the other boys for a penny a bag. I made a pretty nice little bunch of money doing that and when we went to town the next time, I bought all of my friends from Pine Ridge some sodas. I would have been in some big trouble if they caught me because, like I said, it was a strict place. They didn't tolerate too much nonsense there. It was a good training for army life."

For a while, he also worked in the large dairy barn. Dairy workers arose at 4 a.m., walked to the barn and milked cows until 6 a.m. The bakery was not far from the barn, and he and the others often grabbed a loaf of bread and washed it down with the fresh, rich milk. During his weeks at the dairy barn, he remembered putting on a lot of weight.

At Haskell, the old man studied carpentry and boxing. He loved to box and has been an avid fight man most of his life. One year, at a train station in Topeka, he and some classmates saw a large crowd milling about the station entrance. When they went to investigate, he found Jess Willard standing in the middle. He waited his turn and shook hands with the world heavyweight champion, a meeting that can still get him going most afternoons. Indian students were encouraged to participate in Haskell's numerous sports programs, and during his three years there, Guy Dull Knife played basketball and threw the javelin on the track team. He had grown bigger and stronger than many of the others, and one year he broke the school record in the javelin throw. With some of the money his father had sent, he bought a sweater trimmed in purple and gold, the school's colors. A girl he knew from school sewed an "H," his track letter, on the sweater and he wore it around the school as often as he could.

From the beginning, Indian students were forbidden to worship in their traditional ways. Bible classes were sometimes held in the evenings, and church attendance was required on Sundays. The students also could not speak their native languages. "They told us that right from the start. They said we were there to learn English and so that was what we must do. The English language was our language now." Sometimes, in small groups at the workshops, out in the fields or alone in their dorms, they spoke them anyway. Lakota, Cheyenne, Apache, Choctaw, Navajo. It was a confusing jumble. Students from the southern tribes could not understand the old man's Lakota, and their languages were incomprehensible to him. Now and then, they relied on the age-old sign language: Kiowas signing a quick message to the Lakota, an Arapahoe joking in sign with a Cheyenne. When they were alone in the evenings, those who knew how wrote letters home in the language of their people.

"At this time, I could read and speak some English, but I did not know how to write Lakota or in the English. So I could not write to my family and they could not write to me. A boy or girl from Pine Ridge would arrive at the school sometimes and that is how I would learn the news from home. I would talk to them until they had told me everything they knew and this would have to last me until I got back home in the summer.

"When some of the boys got letters from home, it made the rest of us sad. Everyone got lonely there and we were missing our homes all the time."

In January 1917, a package for Guy Dull Knife arrived from Allen, South Dakota. Inside was a Sioux dictionary that the father had sent his son. He hoped the boy could use it to write a few letters home, so he wouldn't feel so bad when he saw the others getting their mail.

By summer, he could not wait to return home, to his family and the Yellow Bear Camp. His father could not wait either. The work had always piled up by early summer, and George Dull Knife desperately needed his son to help with the haying, with harvesting the potato crop and running the saw mill he had built on their property.

On June 21, 1917, he wrote the Haskell superintendent:

My Dear sir

I am Respectfully to say a few words to you this after-noon. Please send my boy home at once as I need him there is saw mill run in our place & I cut logs for Guy D Knife for make a house for him so I want him help me. at once. the saw mill is running now. I can not work this summer . . . I have ownly that boy me & Mr. Ducan. we made a promise . . . the boy has some horse so he always put up hay to & I am working in Indian service long time as I am Indian police so Please help us let the boy come home at once as I need him. Hoping to hear of you at once.

your Respy,
U.S. Indian Police
Geo Dull Knife.

On June 26, 1917, the Haskell superintendent wrote George Dull Knife, explaining that the boy could not return home for another month, until July 25.

"We cannot allow him to go sooner as we have a great deal of work at Haskell this year that must be done before September first and we need the help of as many boys as we can get," said H. B. Peairs. "I regret that it is impossible to grant the entire vacation period to all boys desiring it, but the situation has been explained to the boys and they are responding splendidly for the most part. I trust you will be able to make other arrangements for your work between now and the time Guy will be permitted to come home."

By the following year, in the early summer of 1918, the boy's three-year enrollment at Haskell had been completed. He left Lawrence, Kansas, by train on June 14 and arrived at the station in

Gordon, Nebraska, shortly before 11 p.m. the next night. His parents were waiting in a horse-drawn wagon and the three of them rode home to the Pine Ridge Reservation.

He had been back in the Yellow Bear Camp only a few weeks when his friend, Archie Good Voice Elk, got an army draft notice.

They should go together, his friend said, go overseas and help fight in the war against the Germans. The people would be proud and there would be feasts and ceremonies to honor them when they returned home wearing the uniform of a soldier. Throughout their childhood, the two boys had heard the stories of Lakota warriors whose exceptional battle skills had once been turned against Indians and whites alike. They had heard their fathers and the elders talk of the old days when their people had swept the plains of enemy tribes and taken the prime hunting grounds for themselves, and, against Fetterman and Custer, had handed the army two of its most disastrous defeats. From an early age, the two boys often heard that bravery and honor in battle had been a young man's highest calling.

Guy Dull Knife had been thinking about it for a while. During his final year at Haskell, updates on the war in Europe had spread quickly through the school. After President Woodrow Wilson declared war against Germany on April 6, 1917, there was a growing excitement among the soldiers at Fort Riley. The excitement spread to the townspeople in Lawrence, to the students at the boarding school and, before long, it had come to the reservation. When he said he had thought about joining the army, his father was angry. "He didn't understand what the fighting was about," the son said, "and he was afraid for me. He said I should stay on the reservation and help him with the work."

Good Voice Elk persisted, then others he knew from Pine Ridge said they were signing up, too. In the early summer of 1918, Guy Dull Knife decided he would go against his father's wishes. The nineteen-year-old Lakota from Yellow Bear rode to Martin, South Dakota, and enlisted in the U.S. Army. A few weeks later, during their physical examinations, doctors discovered a spot on Good Voice Elk's lung. Tuberculosis disqualified him from military duty and he was sent home. The old man passed his exam and he, too, returned home, where he waited for orders to begin his basic training.

In every war since the birth of the Republic, America had used Indian warriors to advance its cause. Oneida and Tuscarora served as adjutants with Gen. George Washington's Continental Army in the War of Independence. In the War of 1812, Choctaws helped Gen. Andrew Jackson fight the Creeks and British. During the Civil War, Indian units served both Union and Confederate forces in campaigns throughout Arkansas, Missouri, Texas and the Indian Territory. Later, when Indian lands were needed to sustain the nation's growth, frontier cavalry units relied on a diverse group of Indian scouts to help defeat the Lakota and other tribes. Between 1866 and 1891, sixteen Indian scouts who had served the army in campaigns against the western tribes were awarded Medals of Honor. After Wounded Knee, the American Indian was invited into the U.S. Army for the first time as regular soldiers. Many white soldiers refused to cooperate. The possibility of one day taking orders from an Indian superior angered many. They fought hard to sabotage the plan, and by 1897, the six-year effort to invite Indians into the army on an equal footing was abandoned. A year later, Indian soldiers again found their way to the front lines, as scouts and auxiliaries in the Spanish-American War. Recruited by Theodore Roosevelt from the Indian Territory, some served as Rough Riders, mostly in Troop L, while others went on to China and the Philippines. When the war ended in 1898, the long history of Indian military service to the country was largely ignored or forgotten for the next two decades.

Entry into World War I exposed the nation's precarious position. Committed to war, it did not have a standing army. Gen. John J. Pershing, commander of the American Expeditionary Force, would have to build an army of 2 million from scratch, and he had little time to do it. As the military buildup intensified during spring and summer of 1917, the government found it again needed the resources and services of the Indian people. Ever since the failed experiment of the 1890s, there had been a good deal of debate about what form this service might take, heated disputes over how and if Indians should be used in the military. The coming of a world war brought the debate to a head.

Commissioner of Indian Affairs Cato Sells endorsed the idea of including Indian soldiers in the war effort, but strongly opposed placing them in segregated units, as some military and political officials had urged. Captain Pratt, founder of the Carlisle Indian School, also opposed the concept. Segregated units, he believed, reinforced racial prejudice and Indian stereotypes. It would further delay their assimilation into white society, said Pratt, who encouraged his Indian students to enlist only in integrated units. Many Indians, however, did not want to join integrated military units. They wanted to live and fight together, much as they had always done. Indian advocacy groups in the East, meanwhile, opposed any attempt to include Indian soldiers in the war. Most Indians had not been granted U.S. citizenship, they argued, and it was wrong to ask them to fight for a country in which they could not vote. Still others believed that the Indian could never be transformed into a disciplined American soldier and no effort should be made to try.

Gen. Hugh Scott, the army chief of staff who had commanded the last Indian unit at Fort Sill, strongly disagreed. By February 1917, Scott was already promoting the enlistment of large numbers of Indians for the imminent war. "The idea that an American cannot make a good soldier of an Indian is preposterous," said the general. "The people of Egypt were made into good soldiers by the English, although the Egyptian had been in slavery for three thousand years; whereas the Indian has been the best light horseman the world has ever seen. They have fought us for three hundred years, and frequently gotten the better of us."

Scott and others pointed to an incident that had occurred the year before as proof that Indian soldiers could be invaluable in wartime. On March 15, 1916, after Pancho Villa attacked the community of Columbus, New Mexico, General Pershing led a punitive expedition across the border in search of the Mexican revolutionary. Knowing his men would find the harsh terrain difficult, Pershing asked for an elite troop of Apache and Sioux trackers. The war department attached seventy-five Indian scouts to the 11,000-man force, and on the morning of May 5, about twenty Apache scouts located a heavily armed Villista ranch deep in the Mexican mountains. After cavalry reinforcements arrived and fighting began, the Apache scouts quickly abandoned a formal charge. Employing their traditional battle skills, using camouflage, ambush and skirmish tactics, they cut off the retreat and helped force a surrender. Some of the seventy captured Mexicans later said they had surrendered rather than engage the long-feared Apache enemy. Afterward, Pershing made note of the Indian unit's role in the Villa campaign and commended the scouts for their bravery and skill. The incident made the newspapers and magazines and, a year later, it helped erode some of the debate over what to do with native soldiers.

By summer 1917, the government openly encouraged its Indian wards to assist in the national war effort. In previous American wars, Indian participation in military campaigns had been limited to small groups within a narrow spectrum of tribes. It now cut across all tribes from throughout the country. Beginning with World War I, Indian contributions in manpower, resources and money were substantially greater than its population warranted.

Based on war department estimates, more than seventeen thousand Indians registered for the draft in World War I. Of the nine thousand who eventually served, more than half had volunteered and an estimated three quarters were not U.S. citizens. By war's end, between 20 and 30 percent of all adult Indian men had served, compared to about 15 percent of all adult American men.

Throughout the nation's reservations, superintendents were encouraged to enlist Indian support for stamps and war bonds. By February 1918, the reservations had contributed $9 million. By the end of the war, the bond drive had grown to $25 million, or about $100 per Indian. Indian Commissioner Sells often used the outpouring from impoverished Indian communities to promote greater contributions nationwide. He also saw it as a sign of their continuing progress along civilization's path. "I have been almost amazed by the wonderful and spontaneous fidelity of the Indian to the highest welfare of the nation," said Sells, "as well as his ready appreciation of a desirable investment. The promise of thrift and the saving habit as a coordinate feature of his response to our present colossal needs is a most encouraging evidence of growth toward the principle of self-support, so essential to his stability and progress as a citizen."

While men signed up for war, Indian women tended to the reservations' farms and cattle. Many also joined women's clubs and Red Cross groups, knitting socks, sweaters and caps, wrapping bandages and rounding up spare clothing for shipment to soldiers and civilians on the western front. Others used beadwork, basketmaking and weaving to produce goods that were then sold, the money reinvested in war bonds.

In the federal boarding schools, the war all but emptied classrooms and vocational workshops. Carlisle eventually sent 161 students and graduates overseas, including Marine Corps Pvt. Joseph Oldshield, a grandson of Chief Red Cloud. In Phoenix, Arizona, a small Indian school provided sixty-two volunteers for military service and raised $27,000 in war bonds. At Haskell, students raised a service flag of 150 stars. At a Ford Motor Company plant in Detroit, Indian secondary students were recruited to help assemble military vehicles. Nationwide, an estimated thirty thousand Indian students and five thousand adults enrolled in Red Cross organizations geared to the war effort.

Throughout the war, Indian motivation to serve was varied. While the military, Congress and Indian commissioners all encouraged their participation, so too did a variety of Indian publications. The *American Indian Magazine*, founded in 1911 by Indian intellectuals, stressed the patriotic nature of many Indians and their inherent ability as warriors and soldiers. Months before America entered the war, one issue noted, some Indians had already crossed the Canadian border so they could join the fight overseas. After America entered the war, the magazine's editorials became more passionate. Said one: "Stand by the flag, red men; it is your flag. Under it there is the only hope you may ever expect for yourself and your race."

Asked his reason for enlisting, Joseph Cloud, a Lakota from Sisseton, South Dakota, summed up the feelings of many Indian soldiers. Said Cloud: "The men wanted to go; the women ordered us to go. No good Indian would run away from a fight. We knew that the life of America depended on its men, and we are Americans." For others, the war offered an alternative to the idleness of reservation life. Young men with nothing to do signed up to escape the daily monotony of life at home. Still others were motivated by the pull of the old ways. The war was an opportunity to exhibit battle skills and bravery their people had long revered.

With few exceptions, Indian soldiers who arrived for basic training were assimilated into white military units. They eventually were found in every branch of World War I service, from tactical air squadrons and the engineering and medical corps to military intelligence. Sometimes, the military placed its Indian recruits in units suited to their tradition and culture. By war's end, one third of the Oglala Sioux inducted into the military had served in the U.S. cavalry.

He remembers riding in the buckboard with his father and mother, down through the pines of Yellow Bear and out on the road to Allen. His father was still angry with him, his mother too distraught to speak. When they got to Allen, it was late afternoon. Some of the other boys from the eastern edge of Pine Ridge had already arrived, and they all stood around with their families waiting for the bus that would take them to Fort Meade. When the bus arrived, the mother hugged her son and began to sob. George Dull Knife carried his bag and walked him to the door. When they got there, his father reached in his pants and pulled out a small bundle from his trouser pocket. He gave it to the boy and told him the medicine man, Poor Thunder, said he should wear it around his neck until he got back home. George Dull Knife shook his son's hand and told him to take good care of himself.

As the bus, filled with Indian soldiers, rolled out of Allen and began to move across the reservation lands, the old man remembers how his stomach was balled up and it was hard to think straight for a while. He thought about his mother, riding back into the hills in the wagon, and it bothered him how upset she had been. There were a lot of other kids to take care of and she would probably get over it in a few days. He wondered what Good Voice Elk was doing then. When they found the spot, his friend had been more upset at missing the war than at the discovery of an illness.

His father, he knew, didn't understand any of it and he wasn't sure he did, either. He knew nothing about Germany or Germans. The only ones he'd met had given him smoked sausage and deer meat, and he was fond of them. But for years, he had heard the talk of war, about going into battle, and it had sounded good to him. In Gordon recently, he had seen all the troop trains going by filled with soldiers waving and shouting, and it had seemed exciting, what they were doing, where they were going. In the end, he decided he had made the right choice. "It was my country and if the country was at war," he said years later, "it was my duty to go and fight."

The bus passed through Kyle, headed toward Porcupine and Wounded Knee, and while it was still light, he took the leather thongs and tied the medicine bundle securely around his neck. Before long, he and the others were playing games, laughing and hollering in Lakota, and his stomach started to feel better. They arrived at the edge of the Black Hills late at night, late in July 1918.

Built in 1878, Fort Meade had been used to protect mining camps in the sacred *Paha Sapa*. That fall, General Crook had sent troops south from the fort toward the Nebraska Sandhills, looking for Chief Dull Knife. Twelve years later, Fort Meade cavalry units were used to help crush the Ghost Dance. In the summer of 1918, the post was readying cavalry units to fight Germans.

"Before daylight the next morning," said the old man, "this big sergeant went through all the barracks and he started flipping the beds over while everyone was still sleeping in them. He ordered all of us to get dressed and then he marched us to breakfast. After we all ate, he told us to come outside and line up. He started laughing when he saw how we were dressed."

It was a hot day, their first day at Fort Meade as World War I soldiers, and as he stood stiffly in line, waiting for the sergeant to pass by, everything went black. "I was very afraid that morning, and in the commotion in the barracks, I wrapped my leggings too tight and they cut off the circulation in my legs. I was too scared to move or say anything and so I fought it as long as I could. The sun was really beating down, and after a while, I started to get light-headed and then I passed out."

In the weeks that followed, Guy Dull Knife and the other Oglala soldiers began to adjust to army life. Throughout basic training, the young Indian recruits were taught how to shoe horses and instructed in their proper care and grooming, instructions Guy Dull Knife quickly absorbed. For three or four days at a time, they bivouacked in the Black Hills, sleeping in Sibley tents, eating by campfire, learning how to function with discipline and precision, as a military unit. Back at the fort, they practiced shooting.

"I was wishing the people back home could see me that first day on the firing range. I had my new uniform on and a shiny new rifle and I was really hitting the targets. When a cannon exploded behind us, we all jumped and hit the ground. The sergeant laughed at us and told us to get up. He passed out a knife to everyone and then they brought in bags of potatoes and we peeled them the rest of the day."

After basics, Guy Dull Knife was shipped south to Fort Riley, the Kansas post that had been among the first on the frontier. Troops from the fort had pursued his grandfather and Little Wolf on the flight from Indian Territory and, for a time, it had served as headquarters for Custer's old regiment, the Seventh Cavalry. In 1890, the Seventh had come north from Fort Riley to Wounded Knee. It was about 150 miles west of the Haskell Institute. The trip from Fort Meade to Kansas was long and tedious. By then, numerous troop trains were crisscrossing the country, and a logjam sometimes developed on the rail lines. For two days in eastern Nebraska, he sat on a train unable to move.

At Fort Riley, they received "combat issue" clothing, equipment and weapons. He was assigned to a U.S. Army cavalry unit called the Rainbow Division, one of the first World War I units, the old man said, that accepted black soldiers. Eventually, he was put in charge of a group of blacks at the fort. For a while, one of his jobs was supervising KP duty, and so he had the black soldiers peel potatoes. "I had grown to about six-feet-five and weighed over two hundred pounds then. A lot of the black soldiers there had never seen an Indian before and they were afraid of me. After a while, they started calling me chief."

Later, he was assigned to help break in new horses at the fort. "Some of them were really wild and they were hard to break in. A lot of the saddles didn't have horns on them and there were mornings when I would get bucked off ten or fifteen times. When I'd finally get one broken, the commander would stop and put a new saddle with a big horn on it and then he would ride off. The next morning, I'd have to start all over again with the wild ones.

"At Fort Riley, I was trained to be with the cavalry," the old man said, "but when I got to the front, there was no riding. Only the officers rode horses. Everybody else went to the trenches."

At home and abroad, the wartime press was fascinated with the image of Indian warriors fighting foreign tyranny. Soon, qualities once regarded as savage vices were transformed into virtues. In news stories, editorials and photographs, Indians became heroic fighters, racially and culturally predisposed to excel in combat. "They are perfect specimens of manhood and if their fighting ability is on a par with their forefathers, it is to be regretted there are not thousands of them where there are hundreds," said the *Baltimore Star*. The *New York Evening World* stated that the Indian was "none the less courageous for the absence of feathers and war paint." President Wilson added to the wealth of romantic imagery, frequently repeating the story of the Indian doughboy who complained to his boot camp officers, "Too much salute, not enough shoot."

As the fighting dragged on, the government and press sought to use the myth of the American savage, portrayed in numerous dime novels, the Wild West Shows and early films, to wartime advantage. "War," observed the *New York Evening World*, "seems to be the natural business of the Indian" and it is hoped they "do as much killing in khaki as their fathers did in blankets and war paint." On patrol, the Indian stalked noiselessly through the forest and could endure far greater pain than whites. They had keener eyes and were better shots, were valorous, brave and stoic.

A July 23, 1918, edition of the *New York Mail* ran a photo of Pershing's Apache scouts. Below the photo was the caption: "Yes, von Hind, the N.A. Indian is really on your trail. Here's the truth of it, too: a bunch of real Apaches who are serving Pershing's Army as scouts. Whoop! Maybe this is what made the boches 'turn tail and run like hell' the other day. These redskins (real dyed-in-the-flesh Indians!) served with Pershing in Mexico, and he knows what they can do—and are doing—in stalking the savage Hun."

For a time, the press had speculated on how Indian soldiers would fare in the disciplined military arena of World War I. It was thought the highly mechanized German troops could pose problems for a people used to individual combat and skirmish fighting. "There was some question as to whether the Indian would take kindly to trench warfare," the *Literary Digest* reported, "but he loves it."

"We'd sit there for two or three days," said the old man, "and then someone would give the orders to charge and we'd all jump out, go a few yards, and then just sit there again for two or three more days. Most of the time, you could hear the German shells hit. Then there would be a fog about four feet high and you could see it coming in across the ground toward you. I got a good whiff of it one time. My body went numb and I started shaking all over."

The war had not been what he thought it would be. For six weeks, he sat in the trenches in France, cold, wet, miserable and hungry, wanting it to end, wanting to go back home.

Assigned to the U.S. Army's First Infantry Division, nicknamed Big Red One, Guy Dull Knife had left Fort Riley in the early fall of 1918 and arrived in New York by troop train. A few days later, he was aboard a troop ship bound for Europe. The crossing took about two weeks. Like his father before him, he remembered the voyage as a difficult time. "Most of the soldiers on the ship were from the Midwest and they had never seen the ocean before. The bunks were six-high to a room and before we had gone very far, a lot of us started to get sick. About everyone smoked in the room and after a while, even those who weren't sick from the waves started getting sick from the smell of the smoke and the vomit. The refrigeration wasn't too good on the ship, and in a few days, a lot of the food started to spoil and there wasn't much to eat. Most of us were too sick to eat by then, anyway. When we finally reached land, a lot of the men said a prayer of some kind."

En route to the western front, he remembered thinking how small the French farms seemed, compared to those in his Great Plains homeland. By late September 1918, he was in the trenches. "We would sit in them day after day. Sometimes, we could look out and see the Germans sitting in their trenches across a small patch of ground called the no-man's-land. We looked back and forth at each other across this small piece of ground all day, then everyone would go to sleep and the same thing would happen all over again in the morning.

"It rained a lot of the days and it was cold. You had to have your gas mask ready to go at any time in the trenches, but if they got wet, they didn't work too well. We spent a lot of our time trying to keep our things dry. After a while, we ran out of gun oil and so we started using axle grease. We used it to keep our weapons clean and to smear it on our boots to try and make them waterproof. It seemed like it rained every day I was there."

He came down with pneumonia once and "they sent me to this old blown-up building connected to a hospital at the back of the line.

I was pretty sick at the time, but I preferred going back to the front because the smell in the hospital was worse than being in the trenches." Later, he preferred being in the rear. "In this war, if someone got shot, even a small flesh wound, they could die on account of the gangrene. This happened to quite a few of the people in my unit. For a time, I was put on the stretcher detail and so I had to haul the wounded from the front lines to the back. After I had done this for a while, I started volunteering for the stretcher duty, because when you got all the way to the back, where they had the doctors and nurses, the food was a lot better. They kept the cooks way at the back and by the time the food got all the way up to the trenches, it was cold and the meat was sometimes rotten. The only thing that stayed the same was the stuff like bread called hardtack."

In France, he met another soldier who spoke the language he had not heard in a while. His name was Medicine Blanket, a Sioux from the Rosebud Reservation. The two men spoke Lakota in the trenches and discovered they had been to some of the same places — the general store in Martin and the summer rodeos in Gordon. They knew some of the same people and, on the western front, they talked about their home and how much they missed their families. Often, they passed the time talking of what they would do when they returned. "We became friends in the trenches," the old man said, "and we visited one another up until the late 1960s, when he died."

On November 11, 1918, the armistice was declared, bringing an end to World War I. Indian soldiers had suffered casualty rates five times greater than the American Expeditionary Force as a whole. An estimated 5 percent of all Indians who served died in action. Among some Oklahoma and South Dakota tribes, the casualty rate was twice as high. Epidemics of influenza and other diseases claimed many more lives. Throughout the war, Indians had often been assigned the most hazardous duties. Field commanders believed they were innately superior combat soldiers and so preferred them for the dangerous scouting work and behind-the-lines maneuvers.

Sgt. Otis Leader, a Choctaw machine gunner from Oklahoma, had been with the Sixteenth Infantry at Cantigny, Saint-Mihiel and the Argonne. Cited for his bravery during intense fighting, Leader was selected by the French government to serve as the "model original American soldier" in a painting later displayed at the War Museum in Paris.

Francis Lequier, an Ojibwa, attacked a German machine-gun nest with three comrades who were killed in the fight. Shot eleven times, Lequier managed to overpower the Germans by himself,

Guy, World War I.

killing several and capturing the rest. In November 1918, another Ojibwa, Corp. Walter Sevalia, swam the Meuse River near Brieulles, France, with a heavy steel cable needed for a pontoon bridge, despite a steady volley of German gunfire. While patrolling on the Soissons front, Joe Young Hawk, the son of one of Custer's trusted Arikara scouts, was surrounded and captured by five Germans. A short time later, he turned on the Germans, killed three with his hands and captured the two others. Shot in both legs during the fight, Young Hawk marched the two German prisoners back to the Allied camp. He died on July 15, 1923, in Bismarck, North Dakota, from wounds and gas attacks suffered during the war.

Of the many Indians cited for World War I valor, Pvt. Joseph Oklahombi received the highest honors. A full-blood Choctaw with the 141st Infantry, Oklahombi ran through 210 yards of barbed-wire entanglements under intense gunfire, overpowered a German machine-gun nest and captured 171 prisoners with the enemy machine gun. Despite a barrage of mortars and exploding gas shells, Oklahombi held the position alone for four days. Later, French Field Marshal Henri-Philippe Pétain pinned the Croix de Guerre on Oklahombi's uniform.

Perhaps the most enduring legacy left by World War I Indian soldiers belonged to the "code talkers." In October 1918, German intelligence tapped into the phone lines of the 142nd Infantry near St. Etienne. The regimental commander sent two Choctaw to different communication posts and instructed them to speak their native language over the radios. The experiment proved successful, and soon the 142nd established a separate unit of code talkers who spoke twenty-six different Indian languages. German intelligence was unable to decipher the coded messages for the remainder of the war.

When the war ended, Indian servicemen returned home to a country in which many still could not vote. A year later, after pressure from advocacy groups and the media, a congressional act of November 6, 1919, granted citizenship to all Indian servicemen who had been honorably discharged, but only if they requested it through the courts. Upon the nation's reservations, there was a newfound

pride among the people and they held "honoring" ceremonies to welcome the soldiers home. The soldiers themselves were often thankful
for the opportunity to serve. Louis Atkins, a Potawatomi from
Oklahoma, told the *New York Evening Sun* that "war is a terrible thing,
but I'm glad I was in it. I feel I can look the whole world in the face
now that I went and have come back."

Military service, noted government and Indian office officials,
had been a powerful tool in the assimilation process. In the end, the
trench warfare of World War I had had a civilizing effect upon
Indian soldiers. They came back from the front, government handouts and press releases proclaimed, with a better grasp of English,
respect, discipline, self-confidence and an appreciation for their role
in helping break the back of German tyranny. Now they would
return home to the reservation as useful citizens and role models for
their people. Not long after the war, the agent on an Oklahoma
reservation filed a report to the commissioner of Indian affairs. "One
Cheyenne, typical, no-account, reservation Indian with long hair,
went to France, was wounded, gassed, and shell-shocked. Was
returned, honorably discharged. He reported to the agency office
square-shouldered, level-eyed, courteous, self-reliant, and talked
intelligently. A wonderful transformation, and caused by conduct
with the outside world. He is at work."

Often, prolonged contact with white soldiers was credited with
the transformation. "They were in practically all cases the sole Indian
in a company and therefore compelled to take up in every way the
life and manners of the white man," stated a 1919 interior department release. The Indian had "learned to mix and mingle with white
people and to appreciate the good there is in them," said another.

On Pine Ridge, Lakota soldiers returning home found a reservation much different from the one they had left. After the declaration
of war in April 1917, the government demanded greater production
from the nation's unused reservation lands. Using national security
as his justification, the Pine Ridge agent began selling off Oglala cattle herds and leasing Indian-owned lands. Often without the Oglala's

consent, the lands were leased to white ranchers who were driving herds up from the south and needed the land for grazing. When the war ended, the cattle market went bust and the Oglala were frozen out of the once-lucrative cattle business.

Afterward, as large corporate farms began to move into western South Dakota, the government forced the Oglala to carve up their remaining tribal lands into allotments. Once the land had been alloted, a federal commission arrived on Pine Ridge to determine the number of "competent" Oglala landowners. Originally, the Dawes Act of 1887 had specified that alloted land was to remain in federal trust for twenty-five years. This had been done to prevent desperate Lakota from selling their lands outright, thus earning some quick money at the expense of the tribal land base. But intense pressure from agribusiness and the railroads soon led Congress to weaken legislation protecting Indian lands. Ranchers and farmers wanted the lands for production. To ensure profits, the railroads needed rights-of-way linking the two coasts. They also needed agricultural communities along the rail lines that would use their trains to ship produce east and west. The reservation communities fulfilled neither objective, so European immigrants were recruited to come West and settle along the railroad lines.

In 1891, Congress amended the Dawes Act and allowed Indians for the first time to lease their lands. Fifteen years later, the Burke Act gutted the provision that had kept the individual allotments in trust for twenty-five years. Beginning in 1906, the secretary of the interior could now issue "certificates of competency" to any Indian he deemed capable of handling his own affairs. Those found competent were then allowed to have their land removed from the federal trust, at which point it could be legally sold. As the years went by, destitute Oglala sold or leased more and more of their land to white ranchers and farmers, until control of most of the reservation land had passed from red to white hands. Those who sold out, who had no land left, were often the mixed bloods and they increasingly began to congregate in the village of Pine Ridge. In the outlying districts, in the remote areas of the reservation, the traditional Oglala Sioux maintained their old ways and held onto the land as long as they could.

In April of 1919, Guy Dull Knife stepped off the train in Gordon, Nebraska. It was a warm spring day, clear and sunny. He crossed the tracks, passed through the small train station and began to walk toward the north and east, the medicine bundle still around his neck. He had brought some of the hardtack and sardines, and the streams he crossed that afternoon provided fresh water. The new grass was soft and green, hitting his boots above the ankle, and it made a good bed. Late on the afternoon of the second day, he reached the small town of Batesland, South Dakota, where a white man in a buggy saw a large Indian walking down the road in his army uniform. "He drove up and asked me where I was going and I said I was going home. He asked me where that was and I told him. The man asked if I wanted a ride and I said no, thanks. I told him that I wanted to keep walking. We shook hands and then he left."

Toward the end of the next afternoon, he could see the distant outline of the Yellow Bear hills, and he began to run. He ran for a while, then walked, then started running again, until he reached the creek where he and Good Voice Elk had caught the trout. Crossing the creek, he took the trail up through the pines, until finally he reached the old log house.

He had covered the forty-five miles in three days, and the old man has always said they were among the three best days of his life.

Chapter Eight

Mothers and Daughters

In a long-ago winter, shortly after the Lakota arrived on the Great Plains, the people were starving. One day, two scouts were sent from camp to look for buffalo, and as they searched the plains from the top of a hill, they saw a figure approaching from the west. At first, they thought it was a buffalo, but as the figure got closer, they saw that it was a woman. She wore nothing at all, only the long black hair that fell across her body like a robe. The woman walked up the hill and when she got close to the men, she put a small bundle on the ground and covered it with sage. One of the men told his companion he would go to meet the woman and embrace her, and if she was good, he would take her to his tipi. The other man warned him not to do so. "This is a sacred woman," he said. "Throw all bad thoughts aside." His friend paid no attention, and when he got close and tried to embrace her, a cloud came up and covered the two of them. Soon, the beautiful woman walked out of the cloud and stood before the other man. The cloud blew away and he could see there was nothing left of his companion but a skeleton with worms eating it.

The woman said to the man, "You shall go home and tell your nation that I am coming. Therefore in the center of your nation, they shall build a big tipi and there I will come." Greatly frightened, the man ran back to camp and told the people what he had seen. They were all excited and they quickly began to erect a large tipi in the center of the village. The following day, lightning flashed on a hill above the village and she came into their camp, walking slowly toward the large lodge. Inside, the men and women were dressed in their finest clothing. They sat in a circle, the men looking at the ground, their heads bowed. The woman was now dressed in a beautiful fringed dress of soft white buckskin.

In her arms, she carried a large pipe, the bowl in her left hand, the stem in her right. As she entered the tipi, the woman began to sing:

> *With a visible breath I am walking;*
> *I am walking toward a Buffalo Nation,*
> *And my voice is loud.*
> *With a visible breath I am walking;*
> *I am walking toward this sacred object.*

She came inside and began to walk in a circle, as the sun moves across the sky. After a time, she stopped and held up the sacred pipe. The woman faced the people and said to them:

"With this sacred pipe you will walk upon the Earth: for the Earth is your Grandmother and Mother, and She is sacred. Every step that is taken upon her should be as a prayer. The bowl of this pipe is of red stone; it is the Earth. Carved in the stone and facing the center is this buffalo calf who represents the four-leggeds who live upon your mother. The stem of the pipe is of wood, and this represents all that grows upon the Earth. And these twelve feathers that hang where the stem fits into the bowl are from Wanbli Gleska, *the Spotted Eagle, and they represent the eagle and all the wingeds of the air. All these peoples, and all the things of the universe, are joined to you who smoke the pipe — all send their voices to* Wakan Tanka.*"*

Before leaving, she told the people they could learn many things from the Sacred Calf pipe. When the buffalo were scarce and there was no food, they must offer it to the Great Spirit. When the pipe grew long, the times would be difficult. When it grew short, they would be good. She sang another song and then she left. When the people raised their eyes, they saw a white buffalo calf kicking up its hind legs, leaving the village in a cloud, heading west.

The old man's wife had heard the story of White Buffalo Calf Woman ever since she was a small girl. She had heard it from her mother, frequently in the form of bedtime stories in the years before the Great War. Her mother told her that White Buffalo Calf Woman had saved their people from starving and had given them the sacred pipe, and through the years it had become their most venerated object. The holy woman had told them how they must live, had introduced their four great virtues—courage, wisdom, generosity and fortitude—and she had also given them the Seven Sacred Rites of the Lakota people. Before leaving on that long-ago day, her mother had told the small girl, she had taught them the spirit-keeping ritual, the female puberty ceremony, the ceremony for the making of relatives and *tapa wankaiyeya,* their sacred ball game. And she had showed them how to use the sacred pipe in their three oldest ceremonies: the vision quest, the sweat lodge and their most important, *wiwanyang wacipi,* the Sun Dance. The pipe, the holy woman told them, should remain in one family, passed down from generation to generation. On the Cheyenne River Reservation, the Miniconjou Sioux family of Arvol Looking Horse has been the keeper of the Sacred Calf pipe for nineteen generations.

In the years after she had saved them, women and the buffalo became the most powerful figures in Lakota rituals and mythology. Within the seven council fires of the Lakota Nation, the people grew to see them as interchangeable symbols for fertility and nurturing. Women and buffalo came to represent life itself.

While women often dominated their mythology, Lakota men had long dominated their history. The Lakota called the place where they lived *Maka Ina,* Mother Earth, and it was here that men became the chiefs and headmen of the tribe, leading the war parties, organizing buffalo hunts and deciding when to break camp. It was they who controlled the valuable pony herds, became the powerful medicine men and signed the historic peace treaties.

Yet throughout the many generations preceding the reservation years, neither men nor women dominated daily life in the Lakota villages. To survive on the often-forbidding plains, a complicated social structure evolved in which everyone—men, women and children— had specific roles and duties. Each was expected to do his and her job for the collective good of all, to ensure the tribe's survival. Within the camp's division of day-to-day labor, the groups complemented one another. Men and women alike had a voice in most matters concerning the people's welfare, and all were respected members of the tribe.

In the traditional villages of the Lakota, women bore the children, prepared the meals and tanned hides for clothing and tipis. When it was time to move on, it was they who packed the family belongings, broke camp and set it up again. They maintained the family lodge and did the beading and quilling. They were also the tribe's harvesters and gatherers. While men hunted, women and children dug for wild turnips and picked chokecherries, blackberries and wild plums. From the meat and fruits, they made *wasna*, the dried pemmican pounded into a powder that got them through winter and long treks, and they were the ones who gathered the many native plants used to cure a variety of ailments. Lakota women frequently maintained their own medicine bags and were known to have great powers. Before the war parties left, before important battles, it was the women who often gave men the courage to fight. They had told Chief Dull Knife it was better to die quickly as warriors in the homeland than slowly as farmers in the hated south. In time, many of the northern plains tribes had come to accept an old proverb of the Cheyenne: "A nation is not conquered until the hearts of its women are on the ground."

Between the last quarter of the nineteenth century and the first quarter of the twentieth, the lives of Lakota women became much different than the one their mothers had known.

Guy Dull Knife met Rose Bull Bear in the summer of 1922.

Back from the war, he had returned to the Yellow Bear Camp and lived with his family in their log home in the hills. There were ten children now—two younger brothers had died at an early age—and he had to do a lot of the work while his father, the policeman, was away on patrol. As the eldest son, he took care of the cattle and horses, mended old fences and put up new ones, chopped wood and hauled water. As often as possible, he took off a few days to ride the broncos at summer fairs and rodeos.

Indian dances were common throughout the Pine Ridge Reservation of his youth, and one evening when he was twenty-three, Guy Dull Knife stopped in at a traditional Rabbit Dance. It was along No Flesh Creek, in the rugged hill country between Kyle and Allen. Before long, he found he couldn't take his eyes off a young woman standing alone at the edge of the dance grounds. She was small and dark, with long hair and intense black eyes. He asked a friend who she was and he said her name was Rose Bull Bear.

A descendant of Chief Little Wound, Rose Bull Bear was fifteen the summer of the Rabbit Dance on No Flesh Creek. Little Wound's band of Oglala Sioux had settled in the Kyle area of the reservation in the late 1870s and the chief's large extended family had lived there ever since. Born in 1907, Rose was the eldest of Peter and Edith Bull Bear's five children. Her father had been sent to a church school in Pennsylvania as a young man, and when he returned home years later, he had lost much of his culture and forgotten how to speak Lakota. He was a stern father who believed that education would provide a better future for his children, and so each day Rose and her younger brother, Royal Bull Bear, walked a mile and a half to the Kyle Day School, where she finished the ninth grade.

Rose spent a lot of time with her mother. They would bead and quill together in winter and walk the prairie during spring, summer and autumn, looking for native plants. When Rose was little, the mother had often told her eldest daughter some of the stories she had heard from her mother. She told her about the Fort Laramie treaty of 1868 and the way life used to be in the tribal village and about some of the things that had happened to her as a small girl growing up in the last part of the nineteenth century. Years later, Rose would always say the most influential person in her life had been her mother, Edith Bull Bear.

By fifteen, the daughter was already a strong-willed, independent young woman. Intense, driven, determined, Rose had her own ideas about how things should be done and she wasn't shy about voicing them. She worked hard and expected others to do the same. If they didn't, she had a short fuse that often gave way to stern admonishments. She had learned the value of native medicine from her mother and she enjoyed caring for others, finding comfort in the long prairie walks. From an early age, she liked to be in charge of things, to be in control.

All his life, Guy Dull Knife had been slow and easy-going, even-tempered and mild-mannered. In his family, he had been the practical joker, laughing, teasing, poking fun and playing tricks on others. He was terrible with money. If he found any in his pockets, he frequently gave it to the kids in the camp, telling them to go to the store and buy themselves a soda or some candy. His mother eventually made him give her the money for safe-keeping.

After a while, Guy Dull Knife finally got the courage, and he and Rose Bull Bear joined the others in the Rabbit Dance and they later said they both knew it would happen after that first night on No Flesh Creek. For the next three years, he courted her steadily, taking her to different dances, to the rodeos and fairs, to ceremonies and traditional powwows, to the Yellow Bear Camp to meet his parents. She brought him home to her house near American Horse Creek. They were married in Martin, South Dakota, by a justice of the peace in the spring of 1925. Afterward, the medicine man, George Poor Thunder, blessed them in the traditional Indian way.

The newlyweds had little money, no land and no stock, and for several years they lived at *Ti Hanska,* the long house of George and Mary Dull Knife in the Yellow Bear Camp. While her husband rode broncos and helped his father ranch, Rose became a midwife and, eventually, the unofficial camp doctor. She had acquired a good deal of knowledge about native medicines and she walked the Yellow Bear hills, looking for roots, herbs, leaves and flowers. She would gather the wild plants, then store them in her medicine bag until they were needed. For winter colds and influenza, she used wild sage, boiling the leaves, then brewing them into a tea. She burned a rope of braided sweetgrass for asthma, instructing sufferers to breathe the scented air. To induce hunger in children, the elderly or animals, she relied on the marijuana that grew along Yellow Bear Creek. In her medicine bag, she stored native cures for coughs, fevers, chills, toothaches, snakebites, infections, poison ivy, constipation and diarrhea. And there were other uses for some of the plants she found.

"I don't believe my wife ever used any shampoo as long as she lived," the old man said. "She would take the roots of the yucca plant and boil them until it became like a paste. That is what she used to shampoo her hair with all of her life. She cut her hair only once, when her father died. The rest of the time it was long and straight. My wife had beautiful hair."

Almost a century earlier, after traders and trappers first came to their lands, Lakota war parties had used mirrors to communicate, flashing signals from canyons and hilltops to monitor movements and coordinate attacks. In the Yellow Bear Camp of the 1920s, and for several decades after, the people lived without telephones and automobiles, often scattered at great distances across the canyons and hills. The families used hand-held mirrors to communicate, flashing signals to one another if they needed help, if they needed to go to town, if someone was about to give birth, if the elderly were out of wood and water, if someone was sick.

During the early years of their marriage, Rose Bull Bear traveled through the camp with her medicine bag. There were no doctors at Yellow Bear, and for several years, she delivered many of the babies and tended to the sick and injured. Gunshot wounds and broken bones were a common problem. For hunting mishaps, she used a heated tweezers to remove buckshot. Many roamed the camp on horseback, fracturing legs and arms in spills along the rough trails. She used moss and mud to pack the broken limbs, tree branches and rawhide to set the broken bones.

During their first few years of marriage, after his younger brothers were old enough to help with the ranching, Guy Dull Knife began spending more and more time at the fairs and rodeos. He had been on horses most of his life, and at six-feet-five and nearly three hundred pounds, he was a lot to remove, even for a spirited bronco. Competing against cowboys from throughout the country, he won his share and used the prize money to buy food for his family and farm equipment for his father. Often, he rode bareback.

"At one time or another, I probably broke about every bone in my body riding broncos," the old man said years later. "I never went to a doctor. Rose would take care of it. She didn't have any training for a nurse or anything like that, but she knew what she was doing. She could look at my arm or my wrist and tell how to set it right. She got pretty good at doctoring people up."

After a while, the word got around. The Yellow Bear families of the 1920s used their mirrors to signal and she would go because she enjoyed it and because there wasn't anybody else.

During the Depression years of the mid-1930s, Rose and Guy Dull Knife occasionally returned to the Yellow Bear Camp to see his parents. One time, an elderly woman from a remote part of the camp heard that Rose had come to visit. She had had a bad stomachache for several days and she sent word for Rose to come and see her. After arriving, Rose asked for a glass of water and dropped two tablets of Alka-Seltzer in the glass. When it started to fizz, the old people in the room became frightened. "They had never seen anything like it," Guy Dull Knife said. "They thought she was blessed with a great power. She could make cold water boil without putting it on the stove. They couldn't get over it and so, after that, she was in even greater demand whenever we came back to visit my parents."

Throughout America, a casual exuberance had spread across the land by the summer of 1927. On the coast and in speakeasies up and down the great river towns, jazz came to symbolize the new age. On Wall Street, ticker tape charted fortunes won and lost, and the city began a vertical expansion, the streets below choked with Model Ts from new Ford assembly plants. The Yankee right fielder set a standard for home runs that summer, and abroad, Picasso and Stravinsky had collapsed the boundaries of art and classical music, while a German physicist and an Austrian neurologist explored the limits of space and the human mind. Homesick in Paris, the twenty-eight-year-old Hemingway would soon move to the southernmost tip of the United States to work on a novel about love and loss in the Great War.

Late that summer, twenty-eight-year-old Guy Dull Knife and Rose Bull Bear moved to their new home on the Pine Ridge Reservation. Atop a small knoll overlooking Red Water Creek, ten miles east of Kyle, they pitched a tent and considered their good fortune. As part of the allotment process, she had received 80 acres. Together, they had accumulated forty head of cattle, two horses and a plow, and now they had their own land. They would live in the tent until spring, then build a new home near the creek, close to fresh water, close to firewood.

The winter of 1927 was harsh. They kept the tent in the shelter of trees, but deep snow, subzero temperatures and a frigid wind made the first months on their new land uncomfortable ones. Some of the cattle froze to death and they were always hungry. Rose's parents, Peter and Edith Bull Bear, lived in a log house on the other side of Red Water Creek. It wasn't far from the tent, and if it got too cold, they sometimes crossed over and stayed with the Bull Bears. He had met them many times before, and his wife often talked about her parents, but it wasn't until that winter that Guy Dull Knife got to know his mother-in-law.

Born on the adjacent Rosebud Reservation in 1887, Edith Bull Bear was three years old when Big Foot's people arrived at Wounded Knee Creek and she was an elderly woman of eighty-five when the American Indian Movement led an occupation of the village at Wounded Knee nine decades later. Her early years typified those of many full-blood Lakota women of her generation.

Edith's family lived in a remote section of the Rosebud, in a rural district just across the line from Pine Ridge. It was a long way to the nearest town and the closest school. Cut off from children her own age, she stayed at home and learned how to take care of the house. Reservation field matrons taught her to be quiet and hard-working. Using the traditional Christian wife as a model, the matrons told young Edith that Indian women should be seen and not heard. She accepted their advice and, for a long time, she was quiet and reserved, a young Christian woman who stayed at home, working domestic jobs and learning how to be a good wife. It was the custom then.

By the end of the nineteenth century, as caretakers of its native people, the federal government had come to believe that Indian society should reflect the social order found throughout America and Europe. Men should be dominant, women subordinate and passive. Government policies reflected that viewpoint and reservation schools became the primary instrument to carry it out. At school, the sexes were segregated. Boys were taught the manual skills of carpentry, blacksmithing, shoe-making, ranching, farming and dairy work. Girls were taught domestic skills: cooking, cleaning, washing, sewing and homemaking.

For a long time, these policies severely disrupted the social structure of the people living on the reservations, undermining the Lakota's traditional concept of a tribal village, where men and women had long shared mutual responsibilities and respect. The policies also reversed the long-established roles of men and women within the tribe. Lakota men, the traditional warriors and hunters, were to become farmers—the harvesters and gatherers. Lakota women were relegated to beading and quilling, using their decorative skills for household objects and learning how to become good wives. Unlike the pre-reservation days, they no longer had a say in any matters affecting the political, social or economic welfare of the tribe. By design, women were excluded from all dealings with the federal government. In matters of law, government regulations, work requirements and land rights, the government dealt only with Lakota men.

Lakota women, however, often fared better than men throughout the latter part of the nineteenth century and well into the twentieth. For many men, the leap from warrior-hunter to Christian farmer was too great. It could not be bridged in a few years, or a generation, and many gave up trying, the whiskey often helping to dull the transition. For many women, it was less of a leap from tribal village to government reservation. Lakota women had always centered life around their families. In good times and bad, they had been persevering and resourceful, supervising the domestic economy and familial well-being in careful detail. They had continued to do so, new policies or not.

Edith Bull Bear was not yet a teenager when she learned what had become of her father, Lone Bull, and it changed forever the way she and her daughter looked at government policies directed at their people.

Lone Bull had fought at the Little Bighorn, and fourteen years later, he, Short Bull and Kicking Bear were among the main Ghost Dance leaders on the Pine Ridge and Rosebud reservations. In December 1890, he had moved Edith and the rest of his family to a small camp just south of Wounded Knee, where he continued to help organize and lead the Ghost Dancers. During the fighting at Big Foot's camp, Seventh Cavalry troops shot the small girl's father in the knee and killed his horse. Afterward, Lone Bull was among twenty-seven troublemakers rounded up and shipped to Fort Sheridan, Illinois, outside of Chicago, on orders from General Miles.

In a photograph taken of the prisoners in early 1891, Lone Bull is standing behind Short Bull and Kicking Bear, wrapped in a heavy wool blanket, holding a beaded ceremonial bag and his pipe. He is dark-skinned and erect, three eagle feathers fastened in his shoulder-length hair. The prisoners expected to return home to their South Dakota reservations after spending six months at the fort. But shortly after they arrived, Buffalo Bill Cody began lobbying the government and military for permission to use the banished Ghost Dance leaders in his Wild West Show. Although they were federal prisoners and the Office of Indian Affairs had officially banned the use of Indians in such shows, Cody's influence was considerable and he eventually gained their release. On March 30, 1891, Lone Bull was among the prisoners who left Fort Sheridan in Cody's custody and joined the Wild West Show for a twelve-month European tour. That was the last his family heard of him.

"One evening, a buggy pulled up in front of my grandmother's house and a man got out," said Guy Dull Knife Jr. "He had short

Guy and Rose, in the early years of their marriage.

hair and he wore a white man's suit. His face and hands were almost white, not an Indian color. It wasn't until he was only a few feet away that they recognized him. It was my grandmother Edith's father, Lone Bull. He had been gone for more than seven years. They hadn't heard anything since he had been taken from the reservation to the fort, and for years they assumed he was dead. They had all buried him in their minds long ago. The night he came back, they thought they were seeing a ghost.

"My mother told me that Lone Bull had been lured away from the Wild West Show, more or less kidnapped, by white people from back East who promised him a good job. At that time, many Indians were hungry and desperate and they would jump at anything that could mean some money and food for their families. This is what Lone Bull did.

"But the job turned out to be in a circus sideshow, like a freak show. They eventually got him back East and they kept him in a cage that was a part of the circus. They wanted him to see all of the white people who lived in the East and they wanted all of the white people back there to see what a savage looked like. It wasn't that many years after the Little Bighorn and there was still a lot of resentment over what the Indians did to Custer. So they wanted to show these people what the savages who killed Custer really looked like.

"Lone Bull told my grandmother that they kept him in this cage with a ball and chain around his foot and they would throw him scraps of meat like you would feed a wild animal. Sometimes, he wouldn't be fed for several days and he thought he would die. When they got to a city or town, a man would usually try and excite the crowd by telling them what he had inside the cage. When he pulled back the cover, the people would rush the cage and throw dirt, sticks and rocks at him."

Lone Bull arrived home in the summer of 1898, and afterward, he was allotted land near Allen, on the nearby Pine Ridge Reservation, not far from the Yellow Bear Camp. He moved his family there, and his daughter, Edith, took care of him. Later, Edith's daughter, Rose Bull Bear, helped care for her elderly grandfather. A rock had blinded him in one eye and he walked with a limp, slowly and stooped over, and she helped him get around the house and the new land.

During the years after Lone Bull moved to Pine Ridge, the government increasingly believed that Lakota men were ill-suited to succeed as farmers and ranchers. It viewed Indian land as a valuable, underutilized resource and, more and more, the individual allotments were squeezed from many directions. Prohibited by government policy from using their land as collateral, the Lakota were unable to borrow money for farm equipment, stock and seed. Many were forced to sell or lease their land to neighboring whites to survive. With access to private capital, white farmers could then invest in lands they had bought or leased from the Indian. Occasionally, Lakota men ended up working for subsistence wages on land they had leased to whites, land that they owned.

In 1924, Congress granted citizenship to U.S. women and American Indians. On Pine Ridge, as elsewhere, agents and government officials soon began administering the new citizenship oaths, often in the form of mass swearing-in ceremonies. When an official called out a name, each prospective citizen arose and recited a pledge of allegiance that had been scripted in advance. For a Lakota woman, the government representative first asked her to stand up, then presented her with a work bag and purse. After she accepted these, the official began the citizenship oath:

"This means that you have chosen the life of the white woman— and the white woman loves her home. The family and the home are the foundation of our civilization. Upon the character and industry of the the mother and the home maker largely depends the future of your Nation. The purse will always say to you that the money you gain from your labor must be wisely kept. The wise woman saves her money, so that when the sun does not smile and the grass does not grow, she and her children will not starve.

"I give into your hands the flag of your country. This is the only flag you have ever had or will ever have. It is the flag of freedom, the flag of free men, a hundred million free men and women of whom you are now one. That flag has a request to make of you, (white name), that you take it into your hands and repeat these words:

'For as much as the President has said that I am worthy to be a citizen of the United States, I now promise to this flag that I will give my hands, my head, and my heart to the doing that will make me a true American citizen.'

"And now beneath this flag I place upon your breast the emblem of your citizenship. Wear this badge of honor always; and may the eagle that is on it never see you do aught of which the flag will not be proud."

After the government's grant of citizenship, Indian women were allowed to own land for the first time. It was often a complicated process, but Lakota women eventually began to receive allotments on the Pine Ridge Reservation. Rose Bull Bear was among the first to do so, and shortly after she got her allotment, she and her husband moved to their 80 acres along Red Water Creek.

They had survived the winter and most of their cattle were still alive. The spring of 1928 looked promising.

In early spring, they moved their tent to a nearby timber reserve. By day, Guy Dull Knife chopped ponderosa pine, cut the trees into logs

and stacked them in neat piles. Rose helped load them in the back of
a horse-drawn wagon, and when it was full, they drove it to the top
of the small knoll. It was beautiful land. Wild plum and chokecherry
lined the creek bank. From the knoll, the shortgrass prairie unfolded
as far as the eye could see, rolling swells of ranchland covered in
wildflowers and pine. They slept in the tent at night and hauled logs
twice each day, once in the morning and once in the evening.

Working together, they laid a foundation of red bricks, cut and
fit the logs and chinked the gaps between them with mortar. By mid-
summer, they had finished the home where they would live for the
next forty-five years. It had two rooms, one to eat in and one to sleep.
The roof was blue shingles and the floors were wood. A woodstove
heated the kitchen, and their wooden furniture — tables, chairs,
shelves and a bed — had all been built by hand. When the house was
finished, Guy Dull Knife cut down sixteen willow saplings and dug a
firepit outside. He got several rawhide thongs, some red trade cloth,
stones, a few blankets and a roll of canvas and, in the front yard, he
built a sweat lodge.

Their cattle herd eventually grew to three hundred head. Guy
Dull Knife put in a branding corral down by the creek, watched over
the cattle and began to raise horses on their land. As was his custom,
he continued to get away as often as he could to ride broncos at the
local fairs and rodeos. Rose planted large gardens of corn, squash,
cucumbers, radishes, onions, beets, tomatoes, potatoes, cantaloupe
and watermelon. For a while, she hauled water in wooden buckets
up from the creek for her gardens. After the tribe drilled a well and
installed a hand pump, it cut her watering trips in half. In summers,
she walked down to the creek and picked the wild plums, chokecherries and blackberries. Her husband had dug two good-sized root cellars near the house, and in the fall, she canned fruits and vegetables
and stored them with the potatoes in the cellars. They added a large
chicken coop behind the house; for many years after, they had fresh
eggs and poultry. Winters, Rose stayed inside and beaded. Her parents and their neighbor, Dewey Beard, were frequent guests and a
fresh pot of coffee was often on the stove. With the first snows came

the usual round of colds and flu, so she kept her leather medicine bag well-stocked.

When the Depression arrived, Guy Dull Knife and Rose Bull Bear were a little better off than many of the Oglala Sioux on the Pine Ridge Reservation.

The Depression hit hard everywhere, perhaps the reservations hardest of all. People already stretched thin during good times were stretched even more during the 1930s. As it did nationwide, the government's Works Progress Administration and Civilian Conservation Corps created jobs throughout the Pine Ridge Reservation, and for much of the decade Guy Dull Knife worked on a series of WPA and CCC projects for fifteen cents an hour. In addition to maintaining their farms and ranches, he and other Lakota men fanned out across Pine Ridge, living in the federal work camps that had been mobilized to build new roads, schools, bridges and dams. Many of the reservation's lakes were stocked with bass during the Depression years.

Rose often accompanied her husband to the work sites. They packed their tent, food, a few belongings and her medicine bag and drove to the distant camps in a buckboard. Some of the other wives came, too, and while the men worked, women built campfires and cooked the evening meals. They slept in tents at night and when the job was finished, they broke camp and moved on to the next project. Occasionally, someone came down with a snakebite, toothache, a cold or the flu and Rose would take care of it. She often said she could walk a quarter mile in any direction and find everything she needed. When her supply of native plants began to dwindle, she left the camp and returned with a full bag.

If she had been in camp awhile, the word got out and there would be requests from sick or injured Indians at the surrounding work sites. During a good part of the decade, while her husband helped with the new construction projects, Rose took her medicine bag and drove the buckboard to different camps, brewing wild sage into a tea, burning the sweetgrass, packing mud around a broken arm. Sometimes, one of the women would give birth in the camps and she would help deliver the baby.

During the late 1930s, after she began spending more time at home, the newly created government on Pine Ridge appointed her as a tribal guardian. Tribal elders remember the decade as the toughest of their lives. Severe droughts had wiped out most of the crops, and some families were down to slaughtering their starving horses and dogs to survive. Mental illness, a rare disease in the old days, began to affect many Sioux; alcoholism became a chronic problem. Throughout the Depression, poverty and disease took their toll, leaving Lakota children in a vulnerable state. If parents disappeared, died in a car wreck or were jailed for drunkenness, their homeless children needed help. The tribe set up a network of guardians who could take the children into stable homes until other arrangements were made. Rose sometimes heard a knock in the middle of the night, and there would be an infant who needed a bottle of milk, diapers changed, clean clothes, someone to rock it back to sleep, to hold and care for it.

The children were usually returned home after several weeks or months. A few were abandoned, orphaned, and they had nowhere else to go. When the tribe once found a six-week-old infant abandoned in a trash can, she was taken to the Dull Knifes and they raised her as a daughter. For years, Rose was a frequent visitor at reservation rummage sales, to make sure she had plenty of toys and clothes on hand.

By the 1930s, many adult Lakota had become cultural orphans. The prolonged effort to bleach all Indianness from the reservations had largely succeeded. Banned since the early 1880s, the Lakota language was spoken by fewer and fewer Sioux. The Sun Dance had been officially outlawed, driven underground for six decades, and many Lakota youngsters no longer knew what it was or what it had meant to their people. Traditional ceremonies and social dancing began to fade away as many parents were increasingly ashamed to be Lakota. They did not want their children to know the language, the traditional dances and rituals, or the old ways. On Pine Ridge, more and more adults read the Bible, brought their children to church and kept them in government schools. They insisted the children learn

English, while they tried to earn a living as cowboys and ranchers. After a time, some of the Lakota children began making fun of the Indian kids with long hair who still spoke the language and knew the traditional ceremonies.

In the log house on the hill above Red Water Creek, the ceremonies were usually held at night, in the dark. The *Yuwipi,* "they wrap him up," was one of their oldest, an ancient ceremony in which someone requests help from the spirits to cure an illness or solve a problem. From the beginning, it had angered missionaries, who considered it the height of devil worship. It was an elaborate ritual requiring the presence of a powerful medicine man, a *Yuwipi* man.

During the 1930s, George Poor Thunder often came to the house of Guy Dull Knife and Rose Bull Bear to conduct the *Yuwipi* ceremony. By custom, it began when a patient or family member presented a sacred pipe to the medicine man, requesting his help in contacting the spirits. Those asking for the ritual agreed to host a thanksgiving dinner within a year of the ceremony if it proved successful. After Poor Thunder accepted the invitation to act as an intermediary, the *Yuwipi* began at sundown with the customary purification rites.

While Poor Thunder conducted the sweat lodge ceremony outside, invited guests prepared the Dull Knife home for the *Yuwipi.* One room was cleared of all furniture. Doors and windows were covered with heavy tarps, nailed to the walls to ensure no light could come in or out. At the center of the empty room, a sacred altar was constructed. Four coffee cans filled with earth were placed on the floor at the corners of a square. In each can were colored strips of cloth signifying the different directions: white for north, red for east, yellow for south and black for west. The four cans were connected by cotton strings wrapped in tobacco ties—one-inch squares of colored cloth filled with a pinch of tobacco. Each string contained four hundred ties, representing the number of spirit helpers Poor Thunder would use during the ceremony. Near the altar, the helpers laid a bed of sage where the medicine man placed his sacred objects—an eagle-bone whistle, his pipe and pipe bag, stones, rattles and tobacco offerings. The one who had asked for a cure from the spirits sat near the altar, near the singer and his drum. Everyone else sat in a circle around the square.

The room prepared, Poor Thunder's assistants gave each participant a sprig of sage to wear behind the right ear so the "spirits may know them." The medicine man was then led into the center of the square. His helpers first tied each of his fingers together, then put his arms behind his back and bound them with rawhide thongs. Next, a star quilt was draped over his head and body. The helpers then wound a long leather rope around his neck and body, securely binding the quilt with a series of knots. After they had finished tying him up, they laid Poor Thunder face down on the bed of sage and extinguished the kerosene lamp. The old medicine man had taught Guy Dull Knife the sacred songs when he was a young boy in the Yellow Bear Camp, and now in the darkened room, he began to sing the songs of the *Yuwipi.*

The ceremony sometimes lasted all night. Throughout, Poor Thunder used his sacred objects and powers to contact the spirits of birds, animals and humans, inviting them into the room to tell him how he might cure the sickness. Those who attended said they could hear the spirits leaving and entering the darkened space. They heard objects flying across the room and saw flashes of light. Sometimes, the floors and windows would shake. When the last song had been sung and the lamp turned back on, Poor Thunder sat alone in the center of the altar, the bindings gone, his hands and arms free.

During the years when the medicine man journeyed to Red Water Creek, a series of unusual developments began to unfold far from the Pine Ridge Reservation, in the corridors and backrooms of the nation's capital. A one-time New York City social worker, dispirited by problems plaguing the industrial East, had sought refuge in the American West. He got as far as Arizona, where he became enchanted with the traditional religion and culture of the Pueblo. His name was John Collier and, in 1932, he became President Franklin Roosevelt's new commissioner of Indian affairs.

In December 1933, Commissioner Collier arrived for a goodwill tour of South Dakota's Sioux reservations. He wanted to see and meet the Lakota people, to hear firsthand their complaints and problems, and he wanted them to know about his plans for an Indian New Deal. On Pine Ridge, Collier addressed a banquet of 350 employees and Oglala leaders. Dramatic changes were underway, he told them, changes that would give the Lakota far greater control over their political and economic welfare. Preserving the Indian way of life, their culture and traditions, he said, had become a high government priority. Expressing sentiments that few Lakota had ever heard from a white official, Collier told the Oglala:

"We believe that the government should eliminate the old policy on the Indian's heritage. We believe that your Indian heritage is just as practicable and good, and just as much needed by America as is the Anglo-Saxon heritage or the German heritage or the Scotch or Irish or Norwegian heritage. . . . Hundreds of different tribes of Indians built up the old Indian traditions through ages of toil and prayer and struggle with nature and with man, and that which was worked out in those olden days was an achievement of the human spirit just as bravely as that which was worked out in England, Italy, or by the Jewish race. . . ."

On the Rosebud Reservation, he vigorously condemned the long practice of suppressing Indian dance, custom and religion. "It was illegal, unconstitutional and wrong, and it is not going to be done anymore," said Collier. As to their political independence, he told the Rosebud Sioux that "the present administration is not merely willing for you to govern yourselves. We are determined that you shall and must do it. . . ."

After his speech, the astonished Lakota presented Collier with a beaded pipe bag. The new commissioner grew somewhat mystical.

"When I heard the old men singing when I came in this morning, it gave me the best feeling I have had for three months. . . . And who is there in the State of South Dakota—what white person—who can make anything as beautiful as this? . . . Five hundred years from now in the future, when there won't be any more railroad trains, and probably there won't be any more automobiles or any more sky-scrapers, and when they will have forgotten about most of the things happening in our time, five hundred years from now, people all over the world will go and look at things like this and say they are beauti-ful and great, the work of a great people. This is the old Indian life."

From the beginning, Collier had envisioned a sweeping overhaul of federal policy and government-Indian relations. Back in Washington, he proposed scrapping the allotment process altogether and prohibiting the leasing of reservation land to non-Indians. All surplus land, he suggested, should be returned to tribal ownership. To help restore the diminished native land base, he urged Congress to set aside $2 million annually for the purchase of any land needed to stimulate reservation economies. Under Collier's guidelines, Indian lands would become exempt from state and federal taxes and each tribe could operate business enterprises within reservation boundaries.

As part of his education reforms, Collier ordered Lakota children transferred from missionary boarding schools to government day schools. By 1934, the church-run schools were dependent on public tax dollars and Collier issued an order prohibiting compulsory reli-gious worship or instruction in any school receiving federal or tribal money. From now on, Indian schools should emphasize the value of Indian culture and tradition, he said.

In January 1934, Collier reversed the government's long-held position on native worship and made Indian religious freedom a mat-ter of federal policy. His directive to all reservation and missionary personnel stated: "No interference with Indian religious life or cere-monial expression will hereafter be tolerated." For half a century, the power to arbitrate civil disputes on Pine Ridge had resided within the federal Office of Indian Affairs. The new commissioner proposed creating tribal courts to resolve all legal disputes affecting Indian tribes.

Of his many proposals, it was Collier's vision of Indian self-government that became the most significant. Under his plan, the Lakota and other Indian nations could control their own lives through tribal governments. In theory, the tribes would submit constitutions and by-laws—blueprints for governing the reservations—to the federal government. After receiving approval, they would then have the power to hold elections, create taxing districts, fund colleges, resolve civil disputes and administer land transactions. Eventually, the relationship between reservation and federal government would mirror the relationship between city and state.

Throughout, Collier had envisioned hitching traditional tribal government to a modern, democratic vehicle modeled after the United States. In so doing, it would allow American Indians an opportunity to shape their own economic, legal, cultural, religious and political fate—a reversal from their long years as largely impotent wards of the Great Father. He wanted proposals that would preserve Indian customs and values, not wash them out by force. In the end, his approach stood at the opposite end of assimilation, the government's long-standing belief that turning red into white would solve the Indian Problem.

Collier's radical overhaul of Indian-government relations landed on the desks of U.S. Congressmen in mid-February 1934. Called the Indian Reorganization Act, the massive bill contained more than fifty pages grouped into four sections. On page after page, it detailed the extent of the administration's revolutionary proposals, and it wasn't long before Collier was engulfed by a swarm of detractors.

Some church and missionary leaders viewed the concept of Indian religious freedom as a throwback to the days of savagery and barbarism, undermining a century of Christian progress. Allowing Indians to determine hiring and promotion policies within the Bureau of Indian Affairs threatened many of the bureau's career employees. Private businessmen saw little advantage in a bill that froze them out of reservation holdings, denying access to potentially valuable land and resources. A number of congressmen, meanwhile, came to regard any attempt to fashion Indian sovereignty along tra-

Guy in the 1930s.

ditional tribal lines as a communist enterprise. Indians themselves, although generally supportive of the bill's philosophical contents, also had problems with some of the proposals.

On Pine Ridge, the Oglala Lakota had already written and adopted a series of tribal constitutions, the first in 1921, twelve years before Collier arrived with his proposals for a new form of Indian self-government. The early tribal constitutions on Pine Ridge showed that the Oglala had a firm grasp of democratic government and they also provided the Lakota with a greater degree of autonomy than what Collier proposed. But, politically, the Pine Ridge Reservation had become a fractious community, and its early constitutions were constantly amended to reflect the multitude of divergent viewpoints. None of the early attempts at self-government had taken hold by the time Collier arrived.

Of greater concern after Collier's arrival was the division of the people of Pine Ridge into two distinct camps: the traditional full-bloods who maintained their lands and old ways, and the mixed-bloods who had sold their allotments and moved to Pine Ridge village. In the old days, after the first wave of treaties began to change their lives, some Sioux had started hanging around the various forts, looking for government handouts. The Lakota referred to these people as *Wagluhe*, "Loafers." The *Wagluhe* came to be one of several distinct bands within the Oglala Sioux Tribe and many in this band, the hangers-around-the-fort, were mixed-bloods.

Eighty years later, the growing number of landless mixed-bloods hanging around the agency worried the traditional Lakota full-bloods in the outlying districts. They were concerned that mixed-bloods would come to dominate tribal government and eventually control the land, reservation jobs, schools, churches and the police. On Pine Ridge, as elsewhere, there was a bitter and rancorous debate over Collier's master plan.

After months of heated discussion, Congress passed the Indian Reorganization Act in June 1934. Gutted at random and stripped by compromise, the final bill reflected the concerns of its many detractors and bore little resemblance to Collier's initial vision. Each of the four original sections was demolished, reworked into a mishmash of unrelated provisions. The Court of Indian Affairs was scrapped altogether. A proposal to create new reservations was ignored, and federal appropriations earmarked for existing reservations were eventually slashed to minimal levels.

Nevertheless, the watered-down version managed to incorporate one salient feature: It ultimately led to the creation of tribal government upon many of the nation's reservations. On Pine Ridge, the Oglala narrowly approved the IRA in September 1934 by a vote of 1,169 to 1,095. On January 15, 1936, the first tribal government, adopted under the guidelines of the Indian Reorganization Act, came into being on the Pine Ridge Reservation.

Although it had passed congressional and Oglala muster, Collier's landmark legislation continued to be the source of much debate throughout the remainder of the 1930s and for decades beyond.

In 1940, the old man reluctantly gave up riding broncos. He discovered, at age forty-one, that it was a younger man's sport. A year later, he also discovered he was too old to go abroad and fight the Germans again.

His efforts to volunteer rejected, Guy Dull Knife stayed home in the months after Pearl Harbor and tended his cattle along Red Water Creek. For a while, Rose Bull Bear stayed with him, quilling and beading during the winter, planting two large gardens in the spring of 1942. By summer, the U.S. war effort had mobilized throughout the nation and across Pine Ridge. Rose volunteered to work in a factory that mass-produced shatterproof windows for American fighter planes. That summer, she left for Rapid City and moved in with her sister, Lizzie, who lived near the factory. By the end of the year, the old man was one of the few Dull Knifes and Bull Bears not actively engaged in World War II.

His younger brother, Jeffrey, enlisted in the army, ending up in Gen. George S. Patton's Third Armored Division. Before leaving,

*Guy's brother, Jeffrey,
World War II.*

Guy Dull Knife gave his brother the sacred medicine bundle he had worn twenty-five years earlier in World War I. Jeffrey Dull Knife returned safely, but was badly shell-shocked. He would spend the rest of his life in and out of a Veterans Administration Hospital in Hot Springs, South Dakota.

Shortly before Rose left for the factory, her brother Stephen received his army draft notice. Stephen's Lakota name was *Tatanka Isnala,* Lone Bull. Before he departed for basic training, Edith Bull Bear summoned him to the family home along Red Water Creek. She told her son he must go and fight with courage and bravery, that he must do it to honor his grandfather's name. Assigned to the U.S. Army's Eighth Infantry Division, Stephen Bull Bear landed on Omaha Beach on June 6, 1944.

His cousin, Morris Bull Bear, was also a part of the D-Day invasion. Attached to Lt. Col. William C. Westmoreland's Ninth Division, Morris was among the first Allied troops to hit the beach. After the war ended, when he stepped off the train in Rushville, Nebraska, wearing his uniform and medals, a local café refused to serve him. After returning to Pine Ridge, he became an Episcopalian minister.

Two of Rose's cousins also served in the war. Lawrence Bull

Bear was an air force tail-gunner on a B-17, "The Flying Fortress," and Moses Bull Bear fought with an army infantry unit.

Not long after the war ended, the life Guy Dull Knife and Rose Bull Bear had known for two decades changed quickly. In 1946, the traditional full-blood Lakota living in the backcountry became a councilman for the Oglala Sioux Tribe, elected to represent the people of the Medicine Root District. Rose had been interested in politics all her life and she encouraged her husband to run for office. They had often attended the district meetings together, dropping in and seeing what they were like. Everyone knew him, and they knew he and his wife had long stood for many of the traditional Lakota ways. He did not campaign or go door to door or make any speeches. He entered his name on the ballot and the people voted him into office. At the time that he was first elected, many of the tribe's best jobs—its hiring and supervisory positions—had gone to the mixed-bloods who could read, write and speak English.

From the beginning, Rose and her mother, Edith, took an active interest in Guy Dull Knife's political career. They were familiar with most of the district issues and they talked with many of the people who lived there. In the evenings, the three of them often sat around the kerosene lamp in the kitchen, talking politics late into the night. They had been entrusted with a measure of political control and it was novel and exciting. At a time when few Pine Ridge women had the time, energy or motivation for politics, Rose and Edith were different. They had not forgotten what happened to Lone Bull and they viewed the new form of government spreading across Pine Ridge as a way of preventing it from occurring again. When tribal meetings were held, Rose was often present. She knew the topics scheduled for debate and she occasionally wrote her husband's speeches. Sometimes, before a vote, she sat in the back, nodding her head one way if he should vote yes, shaking it another way if it should be no. At home and in the meetings, she liked to be in control.

She had always loved children, had delivered them in the camps and raised them in her home, but Rose had never had any of her own. Throughout their marriage, her husband had always longed for children, mostly a son, but she had been uncertain about bringing a child into the world she saw around her. She didn't know if it was the right thing to do. The war now over, the new tribal government offering a promise of better days to come, Rose Bull Bear gradually changed her mind.

Twenty-two years after they were married, she and her husband became the parents of a baby boy. They called him Guy Dull Knife Jr.

Chapter Nine

Walking the Red and White Road

His grandfather and great-grandfather had been born in tipis on the northern plains, his father on the dirt floor of a log house. On May 7, 1947, Guy Dull Knife Jr. became the first of his family born in a hospital.

The old house is still standing, sixty-six years after his parents built it by hand. No one lives on the hill above Red Water Creek anymore and he returns infrequently, scattering meadowlarks along the rutted road, driving slowly through a field of buffalo grass. This was the old neighborhood, the place he shared with family and friends. He went to the sweat lodge for the first time here and helped cover the floor with sage when the medicine man came. Grandmother Edith stepped on a baby bull in the front yard one summer and, in the fall, George and Mary Dull Knife came over the hills from the Yellow Bear Camp. Later, when the village at Wounded Knee was under siege, some of the AIM people found their way to his childhood home. Four or five times in the past few years, when he and the children were hungry, he almost sold the land where the old house sits. In his quiet, hard-to-hear voice, it is clear why he couldn't bring himself to do it.

As an only child, Guy Dull Knife Jr. was seldom without his parents. If his mother and father left the reservation to work, he went with them. If they went away on business, they brought him along. During the many family gatherings and ceremonies held at their house, he was always included. The small child was never left alone.

Among his earliest memories are the frequent trips he and his parents made to the village of Pine Ridge. Once a month, Guy Dull Knife Sr. and Rose Bull Bear would gather up their young son and drive sixty miles west for the tribal council meetings.

"We would always stay at the hotel there, and after the meetings, Mom and Dad would sit at a table in the room and discuss all the political issues of the day. Sometimes, they would really go at it, arguing and debating what was the best thing to do. Before long, Dad would be pretty exhausted and he'd just want to eat and go to bed. But Mom would keep going. She would sit at the desk and write his speeches until it was late at night. I was only about four or five at the time and I didn't understand anything they were talking about, so I would just sit on the bed and watch until I couldn't keep my eyes open anymore. I didn't know how to explain it at the time, but I was proud of my mother and father. I knew they were doing something they believed in, even if I didn't know what it was.

"During these trips, Mom would get really mad at Dad some-times. She'd slave over a speech of his and then he might get up the next day and completely ignore it. Or she would want him to vote one way on an issue and when he voted just the opposite, she'd be furious. Mom was probably a little like Nancy Reagan. She had a strong will and a strong sense of right and wrong and she always wanted a say in anything that was going to affect our lives. But Dad had his own ways and his own mind about things, too, and once he made it up, there was no changing it."

Throughout the 1950s and '60s, Guy Dull Knife Sr. ranched and represented the people of the Medicine Root District, many of them traditional Oglala full-bloods living in the backcountry. The kids were his favorite and he invited them into his home often enough that young boys and girls of the Kyle area came to regard him as a kind of camp counselor. Like he had done all his life, the old man loved to tease and joke. He was a character who didn't much mind which way a prank fell, as long as there was a laugh. After his truck ran out of gas one time, he lit a match to peer inside and a three-foot flame shot out of the open tank. The explosion blew his hat across the road and badly singed both eyebrows and lashes. In the end, no one laughed harder than the old man.

On family outings to the grocery store, he maintained a long-running scheme that Rose never caught on to. "When she wasn't looking," said the son, "he'd fill up the bottom of the grocery cart with sardines, then cover them up with the rest of the food. When we'd get to the checkout stand, there'd be a long line of people and it would be too late to unload them. So even though me and Mom couldn't stand the things, we'd usually have to go along with it. The whole time, Dad would just stand there looking kind of innocent. But when we got home, he'd usually have to eat them outside."

For a while, his father also continued another lifelong habit: giving away whatever money he had. The boy remembers him as the easiest touch in Kyle, digging into his pocket whenever a kid wanted a soda, a neighbor needed gas money, or an elderly acquaintance was hungry. Rose eventually took over the finances and ran the household on a strict budget. "If she hadn't," said her son, "we wouldn't have had any money."

Money was scarce throughout his childhood. During the 1950s, many traditional full-bloods still lived in crude log houses and dugouts scattered across the rural districts. A few made do with tipis and tents. Like the house his father had lived in a half century earlier, Guy Jr.'s boyhood home had no electricity, plumbing or running water. In the yard were hand pumps and an outhouse, and inside, kerosene lanterns and a woodstove provided light and heat. Hunger and poverty overwhelmed many of the Pine Ridge households, and few were the families who did not have relatives in a Rapid City hospital, sick with tuberculosis.

In his family, the boy's mother left little to chance. She made sure they had enough to get by, squeezing dollars and cents, making ends meet, supervising the domestic budget in careful detail.

Each autumn, the family drove south through the Nebraska Sandhills until they reached the Scottsbluff area. To bolster their income, his parents spent much of September picking sugar beets and potatoes at five cents a bushel. While his mother and father worked the fields, Guy Jr. sat beneath a shade tree, doing his homework or drawing in a notebook. They cooked around an open fire at night and slept in a tent, returning to the fields shortly after sunup. Before leaving, Rose made sure they were well stocked for winter. In Scottsbluff, she used some of the money they had earned from picking to buy 100-pound blocks of sugar and salt. Kerosene, too, was cheaper in bulk, and they loaded up on the fuel that would start their winter-morning fires and keep the lanterns burning. Usually, they'd also set aside five hundred pounds of potatoes. After all the commodities were loaded in the bed of an old Ford truck, they drove back through the Sandhills to Red Water Creek.

At home, the family boiled their garden corn in 50-gallon barrels, stripping the cobs with knives and laying the kernels out to dry on sheets of canvas. Rose sun-dried wild plums and berries she had gathered from the creek bank and canned the vegetables from her gardens. Potatoes they had picked in the fall and much of the food they had grown in summer ended up in the root cellars. While the weather was still good, the boy and his father drove a buckboard to the reservation's timber reserve. They chopped wood by day and slept in the tent at night. When the wagon was full, they returned home and cut the trees into logs for a winter wood supply. Three or four times each fall, the family loaded up some of their cattle and drove to a sale barn in nearby Gordon, Nebraska. Rose made sure the proceeds went in the bank, a safety net in case of emergencies. In the last warm days of autumn, they would butcher a cow, cure and dry the meat for the cold months ahead. When the snows came, the boy sometimes rode out to the fields with his father and uncle and helped them fill the hayracks so the cattle wouldn't starve. Most of the time, Guy Jr. hauled water and chopped wood. It was hard work and, as a small boy growing up on the Pine Ridge Reservation, winter was his least favorite season.

Summers were different. When the weather turned nice, he and his parents often drove to the Yellow Bear Camp to visit George and

Mary Dull Knife. One year, his grandfather built him a net of chicken wire and he and his cousins would race to the creek, jump in and drive the trout downstream, into the net. They'd take the fresh trout home and have a fish fry later that night. When it got dark, they crawled into a tent in the front yard of *Ti Hanska*, telling jokes and making up stories until they fell asleep. His father had had him riding almost as soon as he could walk and, at Yellow Bear, Guy Dull Knife Jr. could always find a horse. On hot afternoons, he and his friends rode down through the hills and out to the creek. It was shady and cool there and, at several spots, beaver dams had created deep pools, good places to fish and swim.

"I'm sure I didn't realize it at the time," the son said years later, "but Pine Ridge was like a big camp. Kids in the East still pay a lot of money for a week of swimming, camping, fishing and horseback riding. For those of us growing up on the reservation, it was a way of life."

Sometimes George and Mary Dull Knife returned the favor and rode across the hills in a buckboard to visit the boy and his parents. They would spend a few days or a few weeks, depending on the time of year, and he was always happy to see their wagon pull up in the yard. In the winter, he had sat on his grandfather's lap and laughed at the stories of Buffalo Bill Cody and the Wild West Show. They walked the fields together in the fall, returning home with the native plants that made his mother and grandmother happy. It was on one of their walks that he had first heard the story of the big guns firing along Wounded Knee Creek.

No matter which season they came to visit, the boy's father and grandfather went to the sweat lodge each evening around sundown. In the summer before he started school, they invited him to join them. He had often wondered what went on inside the dome struc-ture a hundred feet west of their home, and when they closed the flap across the doorway, he was surprised at how dark it got. Soon, his grandfather poured water on the bed of glowing rocks and he was a little scared of the heat. George Dull Knife had once taught his son, and on the hill above Red Water Creek, the grandfather and father began to teach the boy the sacred songs and prayers of the sweat lodge ceremony.

During the ceremony and at the Yellow Bear Camp and throughout his early childhood years, he only heard the language of his people. By the age of six, the boy spoke Lakota well, but he knew only a few words of English.

From the hill where they lived, Guy Dull Knife Jr. could see his neighbor's house, and whenever he saw the car pull in, it was his custom to race over as fast as he could.

Dewey Beard loved kids and there was usually a good supply of candy and soda inside his dugout about a mile down the road. When the boy first met him, Beard was ninety-three. Slim, tall and erect, he still rode bareback through the Kyle backcountry, usually on a withered brown mare that looked as old as him. In winter, he stalked deer and rabbit, sometimes through deep snow. In summer, the old man and his second wife, Alice, pitched a canvas tipi at Cedar Pass and posed for tourists in the Dakota Badlands. Their only son, Tommy, was sick with tuberculosis at the time and they worried constantly about his health. If they weren't in the Badlands, the old man could usually be found beneath a canopy of pine boughs, sitting in the shade of his front yard. Beard hated living in the dugout, preferring a tipi or the outdoors instead. In the early years of the 1950s, he still longed for the old days and the old way of life.

If his family went to one of the many reservation powwows in those years, they often saw Beard there. He used to show up wearing a cavalry jacket and gunbelt that fascinated the small boy. Guy Dull Knife Jr. had never met anyone like his neighbor, and when he got a little older, after the candy and soda had been passed around, he and his friends sometimes sat beneath the pine boughs, listening for hours to the old man's stories.

Born in 1857, Dewey Beard was eighteen the summer the Lakota and their allies gathered on the Little Bighorn River. In their language, they called it the Greasy Grass, and by late June of 1876, he told the boys, the Indian camp stretched for more than four miles along the riverbanks. All seven tribes of the Lakota Nation were there—no one could remember a larger gathering—and the tribes were arranged in separate camp circles, each a half mile across, each with its own leaders. In his camp, the Miniconjou, the leaders were Hump, Fast Bull and High Backbone. Crazy Horse was in charge of the Oglala. Two Moon, Lame White Man and Ice Bear led their good friends, the Northern Cheyenne. The different camps agreed that one man would act as head chief for everyone gathered in Montana that summer. This was the Hunkpapa holy man, Sitting Bull. He had the strongest power and the people knew he would not sell the Black Hills, that he would fight to the end for the old way of life.

Guy Jr. and his friends did not know anyone who had been in the battle they had often heard about, and the young boys asked the old man a lot of questions. He said he had first ridden with a war party two years before Custer, when he was sixteen. In those days, the Lakota made sure a young man had earned his membership in the elite warrior societies. Young boys were taught early how to fight, how to endure pain and hardship. They played many games to prepare them for the warrior life and they were told that to die in battle was a warrior's greatest honor. Sometimes, older boys would lead the younger ones to a spot on the edge of camp where a pit of coals had been dug. An older boy took one of the burning coals and placed it on the younger one's arm. Whoever could endure the longest without crying out in pain won the game. In spring, they often played a game called "throwing at each other with mud." They divided into teams, each member armed with short sticks and a pack of mud balls, some of them laced with burning coals. The two sides charged one another, using their sticks to fling the mud balls at one another. The swing-kicking game, he said, was the roughest. In this game, they formed two facing rows, each boy holding a robe in one arm to act as a shield. At a command from an older boy, the two sides charged, using whatever tactics were needed to get an opponent on the ground. Frequently, a hard, swinging kick behind the knee dropped him in his tracks. When he fell, the other side grabbed the boy by the hair and kicked him in the face. The game ended when one side, bloodied and exhausted, finally gave up.

He had played these games growing up, and at sixteen, he went on the raid with older warriors for the first time. Before the fighting began, the war party leader took a rawhide thong and tethered one of his ankles to the ground, to make sure he wouldn't panic and try to flee. If he survived, he would become a member of the warrior society. If he didn't, they would bury him with honors.

Along the Greasy Grass, the old man said, the Oglala were camped at the north end of the large village, the Hunkpapa on the south. After the shooting began, Sitting Bull's lieutenant, Chief Gall, led a large war party across the river at one end of the camp, eventually advancing from the south toward a hill where Custer and the soldiers of the Seventh Cavalry had taken refuge. Unseen by the soldiers, Crazy Horse and hundreds of his warriors swept up a deep ravine, coming in from the north. Beard had a young horse that wasn't broken in yet, and when the fighting started, the elders in the Miniconjou camp told him to stay away. He ignored their warnings and charged across the river, riding toward the hill where Crazy Horse and Gall had now closed in from both sides.

When he arrived, the battle was desperate. Both sides had dismounted, fighting hand-to-hand in thick clouds of dust that made it difficult to see. He heard screams and war cries coming from all directions then, and saw many Indians racing to count coup on the dead and dying soldiers. The sound the bullets made reminded him of a swarm of flies buzzing in his ear. Before he could dismount, the intense gunfire spooked his young horse and he was thrown to the ground, briefly losing consciousness. When he woke up, he saw a lieutenant from F Troop—not much older than himself—coming toward him through the dust. He grabbed a war axe from the ground and charged the soldier, clubbing him again and again until he lay still. He stripped off his jacket and took his gunbelt and began to look for his rifle, but the bullets kept coming, around his head and at his feet, kicking up too much dust to see, and he decided to leave.

All night, the sound of victory drums went up and down the river, mixed in with the high-pitched keening of women who had lost husbands, brothers and sons. The next day, the great encampment broke up into smaller bands and fled quickly in different directions. The scouts already reported more soldiers were coming and the people traveled as lightly as possible, leaving behind any objects that might slow them down. In his village, women left even the large rocks they had used for years to pound the dried meat into pemmican. After fording the river and moving across open land, they saw many bodies clustered on the flanks of the hill and along the ridges, and the dead horses were everywhere.

He liked to talk about the past, but he said little to the boys about Wounded Knee. In Lakota, he was called *Wasu Maza* – Iron Hail – and years after the massacre, Gen. Nelson Miles had invited him to Washington and introduced Beard to a number of military officials. Among those he met was Adm. George Dewey, naval hero of Manila Bay and the Spanish-American War. Later, he formed his own name by taking an old Sioux nickname and adding it to the admiral's surname. In the 1950s, Dewey Beard preferred telling Guy Jr. and his friends what his life had been like at their age. He showed them ornate boxes the Lakota had once used for storage, and he taught them a game that he and his friends had played in their villages on the northern plains. It involved tossing deer antlers into the air and catching them a certain way. Points were scored depending on the kind of toss and catch, and after a time, the boys began to play it among themselves, teaching their friends the new game. Sometimes Guy Jr. returned home after an afternoon beneath the pine boughs and took out his pencils and notebook and tried to draw a picture of his neighbor.

When the old man was ninety-seven, the tuberculosis took his son.

"We saw him sitting on the porch outside the wake and he had cut his hair and slashed his body in the traditional sign of mourning," Guy Jr. said. "There were deep cuts all over his arms and legs and he was sitting in a pool of blood. Dewey was beside himself. He sat there crying and wailing in his pain and grief and no one could get through to him. Finally, someone called an ambulance and they took him to the hospital. He lived through more than anyone I have ever known, but he did not live a long time after Tommy died."

On February 28, 1955, the boy's grandfather died at the age of eighty. George Dull Knife had known the old way of life on the high plains and the capitals of the Old World. He had ridden bareback and crossed an ocean, worshipped at the Sun Dance and sat in a church. In the end, he had lived long enough to see the bow and arrow give way to the atomic bomb.

The wake lasted three nights. There were no roads at Yellow Bear and people he had known from his days with the Wild West Show, as a tribal policeman, rancher and ceremonial singer, arrived on horseback and buckboards at the old Episcopal church. Some brought freshly slaughtered cows and venison. Others came with *waǰna*, the powdered meat mixed with chokecherry juice, and the Indian pudding, *wojapi*. There wasn't enough money for a coffin, so a few days before the funeral, Guy Jr. and his uncle drove to Martin, South Dakota, and bought some pine boards. Daniel Dull Knife, who had been named for the racehorse, Red Wing, returned home with the wood and built a coffin for his father.

The day of the funeral was bitterly cold. The family put George Dull Knife's body in the pine box and placed it in the back of a horse-drawn wagon. "Everyone walked behind the wagon for the trip from the church to the cemetery," said Guy Jr. "The cemetery is on a small hill overlooking the church. There was a couple inches of snow on the ground and the wind was blowing pretty good. When we got to the cemetery, my father and his brothers carried the coffin to the grave and they all prayed to *Wakan Tanka* before the preacher spoke."

Guy Dull Knife Jr. was seven years old when he started kindergarten at the Kyle Day School, the same school his mother had attended in the years before World War I. Among his new classmates, he soon discovered he spoke the poorest English, knowing how to say only "yes," "no" and "Can I go to bathroom?" He felt awkward and out of place. The boy was large for his age, wore long hair and talked in the language of his people. From the beginning, a pattern developed that would continue for many years. "All through grade school, I was the biggest and dumbest Indian in my class. It didn't take the other kids very long to pick up on that, and a lot of them, they really let me have it.

"In the cafeteria line, they'd say: 'What are you doing here? They're not serving dog meat today.' Sometimes, a group of them would surround me outside of class and say, 'Hey, Indian boy, you'd

George Dull Knife (right) and cousin Albert Poor Bear, Yellow Bear Camp, late 1930s/early 1940s.

better not try and use any of your *Yuwipi* black magic to get a good grade.' "

He did poorly in class, not knowing what was expected of him or how to cope with the other Indian kids, the teachers and school life in general. Feeling isolated and remote, he began to withdraw. After a while, the school's Bureau of Indian Affairs administrator sent him to a psychologist for evaluation. They thought he had a learning disability, or was possibly retarded.

By third grade, he had learned considerably more English, but he could neither read nor write. He felt ashamed of this and so, like his grandfather had done with Buffalo Bill Cody in the previous century, Guy Jr. tried to improve his reading with newspapers. "I would bring the school newspapers home with me, and at night, I would try and copy down paragraphs in English and then read them back to myself, out loud. It eventually helped my reading, but not too much with the writing. Nothing really did. To this day, I do not know how to write."

Throughout his early years at the Kyle Day School, Guy Dull Knife Jr. also remained one of its few non-Christian students. He knew little about the ways of the church, and his ignorance provoked a good deal of taunting from classmates and dismay from the teachers. "They used to tell me that when I died, there'd be no place to bury me. They said only Christians could be buried in the reservation cemeteries, and if I didn't come to my senses, they'd end up burying me in some ditch by the highway." Some of his own family began to echo similar sentiments. His uncle, Morris Bull Bear, who had served in the 101st Airborne during World War II, was now an Episcopal minister in Kyle. "He used to tell me that there was no such thing as an Indian anymore. That it was time for me to become a Christian like everybody else. He said I had to forget about the sweat lodge and the Sun Dance and our sacred songs. And he would tell me, over and over, that I had to stop listening to my father. That I shouldn't follow his ways because they were the work of the devil.

"I was only a small boy then and what he said really upset me. I had never heard anybody talk about my father like that. Finally, I went to my mother. I was crying real hard and I told her everything Uncle Morris had said. My mother told me to pay no attention. To just ignore it—let it go in one ear and out the other. She said, 'You're never going to have blond hair and blue eyes, so don't waste any time trying to be something you're not. You're an Oglala Sioux and that's what you'll always be. You can't change it and you shouldn't want to. Be proud of that, no matter what.' "

At the Kyle Day School, religious instruction was held every Monday afternoon. Students had to choose whether they wanted to go to the Episcopalian class or the Catholic class. In fourth grade, Guy Dull Knife Jr. told his teachers he didn't want to go to either. He said he wanted to be a Lakota, like his mother and father. "The first time I saw Poor Thunder do the Yuwipi ceremony in our house, I was scared and a little embarrassed. But I had to go along with it because it was my family. As I got older, I began to understand why it was important to keep our traditions from dying out." After a while, his teachers gave up. They made him sweep the classroom floors and hallways on Monday afternoons. Later, they put him in a room by himself with his paints and brushes. He did artwork for the school newspaper and the posters for school activities. During the winter holiday, he made Christmas cards and sold them to the teachers for some pocket money.

After school, if the weather was nice, the boy would often walk the road to Dewey Beard's house. He loved his stories about the old days and he wished he had lived back then. That life made sense to him, his did not. He saw no point in school, and the constant teasing made him depressed. On Fridays, exam day, he began going to the bathroom and bloodying his nose, pounding it with his fist, then telling his teachers he was too sick for the test. Finally, he stopped going altogether.

"I would get up real early, before anyone else was awake, and I'd make a sandwich and hide it down by Red Water Creek. The bus would come to pick me up on the road by our house, but I'd hide in the creek until it went by." He had a dog named Billie White, and a sharp low whistle sent the mutt scurrying to the underbrush. The boy and his dog would spend the rest of the day patrolling the creek bottom. When he saw the bus go by in the afternoon, he went back home.

After his grandfather died, his grandmother continued to live at the Yellow Bear Camp. All her life, Mary Dull Knife had been afraid of the cavalry jacket and rifle her family had taken at the Little Bighorn. She thought if the white people ever found out, they would arrest her and put her in jail. For more than half a century, she kept the sergeant's jacket and a .45/70 carbine buried in a trunk at *Ti Hanska*. When her grandson discovered the secret, he took an instant liking to the Custer souvenirs. He cut the sergeant's stripes off the cavalry uniform and sewed them on a sleeve of his denim jacket. Through trial and error, he found that .410 shells fit the old carbine. The boy also had a Nazi sword his Uncle Jeffrey had taken from the World War II battlefields and he had long known of the binoculars Buffalo Bill gave his grandfather. Sometimes, while his classmates studied the Bible, Guy Dull Knife Jr. walked the creek bottom in sergeant's stripes and binoculars, the Nazi sword around his waist. Billie White kicked up birds and rabbits and he would try and shoot them with the Little Bighorn carbine. He liked to pretend he was a Sioux warrior living in another century.

It didn't last very long. When the absences piled up, his teachers notified Rose and she gave the boy a good spanking. After that, he had to bring a note from school each day saying he had attended classes. His mother signed the paper and he returned it to his teachers the next morning.

He returned reluctantly, but all through grade school he could never adjust. Like his father before him, the boy learned one set of values at home, another in school. The two worlds seldom seemed in harmony. "I remember I had one teacher in fourth or fifth grade who flat out told us that we were a conquered nation, a conquered people, and the sooner we accepted that fact, the better off we'd all be. If we didn't give up our language and stop the devil worship, he said, none of us would ever amount to anything. Most of the BIA teachers were like him. They were basically there to intimidate, to train us not to be

Indians. That was their job and they were pretty good at it because many of the kids grew up feeling ashamed of who they were."

As a small boy growing up on the Pine Ridge Reservation, Guy Jr. had loved his grandfather's Wild West Show stories. When he was older, he would think back on some of the TV shows he had seen — *Gunsmoke, Have Gun Will Travel, Cheyenne, Bat Masterson* and *Davy Crockett* — and the games he and his friends used to play. "In the summer, when we were in fifth and sixth grade, we all had horses and sometimes we would play cowboys and Indians. We would usually choose up sides first and everyone would pick who they wanted to be. Some kids wanted to be Crazy Horse or Red Cloud or Sitting Bull, but a lot of the Indian kids always wanted to be John Wayne. When we went to the movies sometimes, the kids would cheer for the cavalry."

Of the many teachers he had in school, one stood out. His fifth-grade teacher saw how it was with Guy Jr. and she began to take him under her wing. She bought him a bike one time and gave him a new BB gun and, every now and then, she took him into town with her. She used to sit him down after school, alone in the classroom, and tell him not to give up, to fight for what he believed in. If he did, she said, things would change. They would eventually get better.

"Her name was Mrs. Hopkins and she was a black woman teacher from Alabama. She told me that I should look to her as an example. In her own hometown, she said, she could walk into a restaurant and not get served. She had gone to college to make herself better, but when she finished, she couldn't get any teaching jobs in Alabama. She said the only job she could get was on an Indian reservation and that is how she had ended up at Pine Ridge. Things were bad for her people, she said, but they were starting to get a little better because they had leaders who wouldn't give up and that is what I should do, too. Not to let it get to me and always fight for what I believed in.

"One time, she went to see the principal on account of me. His name was Norris Newkirk and he had forbidden any Lakota to be spoken at school or on the grounds outside. She told him she didn't think that was right and he said he was the principal and those were the rules.

"It was a very confusing time. One teacher was telling me to fight for what I believed in and another one was saying we were a conquered people and I should give up or my life would be a waste. I didn't really know where Alabama even was at the time, but I understood what Mrs. Hopkins said and I have never forgotten her."

When school ended, the reservation became a summer playground. They rode bareback all over, into the hills and over to Potato Creek, where an elderly couple ran a small general store. The owners were hard of hearing and couldn't see very well and Guy Jr. and his friends would ride up, pull some empty soda bottles from the back of the store and bring them around front, cashing in the empties for two cents each. A white rancher named Mays owned property adjacent to the Dull Knifes, and every summer he had a large watermelon patch. The boys would ride over after dark and crawl through the patch, thumping melons until they found some good ones. They'd slice them open and sit on their horses, eating the ripe melons in the moonlight, thinking they were great warriors.

Sometimes, the Sioux boys from Red Water Creek challenged the Potato Creek boys to a war. Several days before the appointed encounter, both groups scoured the countryside for old ball bearings and marbles. On the day of the fight, the two war parties met in an open field between the creeks, whooping and hollering and firing slingshots at one another, charging in and counting coup, arguing who had won the battle.

Between battles, the boys often went to the creeks and fields searching for toads. When they had captured five or six, they made miniature stick riders from chicken wire and held "toad rodeos" on a shady patch of dirt. Arrayed across a starting line, the toads were sent bucking and hopping by gentle prodding with sticks. The boys bet sodas on whose man could stay on his toad the longest. For a few summers, Log Cabin syrup containers were also valuable toys. They collected as many as they could, rinsing them out at the hand pumps and using them to fashion ranches, farms and forts. A properly used knife could carve plastic into barns, fences, homes, stockades and corrals.

Late one spring, the boy's father was out riding the fields when he found a baby bull whose mother had died. He took the baby and laid it across his saddle and rode home. The bull was only a few days old, so they kept it in a box by the stove, where Rose nursed it with a baby bottle. His father started calling it Elmer, and after several weeks, the bull had grown accustomed to the house and didn't want to go outside. They put it outside anyway, but it wouldn't leave the front yard.

"Elmer had a favorite sleeping spot on a path that cut through our yard," said Guy Jr., "and one day my grandmother Edith came walking up the path to visit. She didn't see Elmer and ended up stepping on him. When she did, Elmer jumped up with grandma on top of him. She fell off and then Grandma beat the hell out of Elmer with her wooden cane. Dad didn't stop laughing for a week."

By late summer, the fruit would be ripe and Rose sent her son and his friends down to the creek bottom with 5-gallon wooden buckets. From the wild plums, chokecherries and blueberries they gathered, she made jams, jellies and Indian pudding.

Guy Jr. also took care of the family chickens. With three hundred in the flock, there were plenty of eggs to gather each day, many of which he sold to neighbors and relatives. He made the morning rounds with empty coffee cans, then put the eggs on an old mattress and washed them with a sponge. After they were clean, he laid the fresh eggs on a roll of suspended chicken wire to dry. From the proceeds, he bought a new BB gun, and he and Billie White took off in the afternoons to hunt along the creek. It was usually in summer when he saw the snakes, plentiful on the reservation and creatures that terrified him.

One summer day, Frank Fools Crow came to visit the Dull Knifes. Guy Jr. was wearing a medal that Buffalo Bill had given his grandfather and his grandfather had given him. It was a medal commemorating the Paris Exposition of 1889 and it had an Indian head on one side and the Eiffel Tower on the other with the inscription "Wild West Show." Fools Crow saw the medal around the boy's neck and wanted it for his own. A few days later, he showed up with a new .22 rifle and a fresh box of shells. Guy Jr. thought it a fair trade and he exchanged his medal for the rifle. Years later, when he saw the old man wearing it at powwows, he wished he had never agreed to the swap.

Fools Crow was then sixty-eight. He had been a medicine man and an influential civic leader on Pine Ridge for years, eventually becoming a ceremonial chief of the Sioux. The summer he traded for the medal, Fools Crow had been on a long movie tour with the boy's uncle, Daniel Dull Knife. In 1959, after they finished shooting the film *War Bonnet*, the studio sent both men on a thirteen-city promotional tour. One of the cities they and two other Pine Ridge Lakota, Billy Fire Thunder and Norma Shields, visited that summer was Memphis. A few days before they arrived, the local newspaper ran a small item announcing their visit and it caught the eye of a local resident, whose mother was part Cherokee. He asked his people to get in touch with the movie group and they did.

On an early summer afternoon, Elvis Presley invited the Lakota to Graceland. They arrived at the gates and were taken inside, to a downstairs living area where Presley offered the four Sioux lemonade and cookies, then iced tea and sandwiches. Daniel Dull Knife had lived and worked for many years on the Northern Cheyenne Reservation in Montana. An artist who spoke little English, he was struck by the room's decor. Everything was white — the walls, curtains, rug, sofa, tables and chairs. Presley wanted to know about their music, and after everyone had eaten, he asked the Sioux to play for him. The boy's uncle moved to a drum set in one corner and began to sing the traditional Lakota songs Poor Thunder had taught him as a boy in the Yellow Bear Camp. While he played the drum and sang, Fools Crow, Fire Thunder and Shields danced Indian on the white rug.

When they finished, their host asked if he could play for them. Daniel Dull Knife had never heard of Presley and he said he would be honored. The four Sioux sat on a couch while Presley got his guitar and began to play, moving quickly across the rug, snapping his fingers and shaking his legs, singing "Jailhouse Rock." The boy's uncle didn't think the guitar work was too good, but he liked the singer's voice. Afterward, they tried to teach him a Lakota song and a little of the Rabbit Dance. When it was time to go, Presley gave each of them a large autographed poster and walked them to the door. He thanked them for coming and they thanked him for the invitation. When they got to the end of the driveway, the Sioux were surprised to see so many young girls and to hear the noise they made when the gates swung open. Daniel's wife, Bessie Dull Knife, kept the autographed poster in a trunk at her home in Rapid City, South Dakota, but a disastrous flood in 1972 destroyed the trunk and its contents. "My husband said he treated them very nice and took good care of them. He seemed to really like them and he had a good time listening to the music," she said.

"We liked the Beatles and the Rolling Stones. It drove my mother crazy, but that's about all we used to listen to. Rock and country-and-western. We got kind of obsessed with the music in those years, that and our hot rods."

As teenagers in the 1960s, the boys swapped their war ponies for cars, and toad-racing gave way to cruising. Guy Jr. got his first car in ninth grade, a '57 Ford his Uncle Jeffrey bought him. Reservation driving laws were lax and the wide open spaces of Pine Ridge offered ample opportunity for joy rides. When they got older, he and his friends would pile in the jalopy and drive off looking for summer jobs. Each time, they started out in Gordon, Nebraska, about forty miles south of Kyle, where a coin toss determined their next move. Tails, they drove east; heads, they went west. They hauled alfalfa and worked at a factory in Nebraska, ran a jackhammer for a construc-

Guy and Rose, in the late 1960s.

tion crew in Wyoming and toiled at the Homestake Gold Mine in South Dakota. "Mom would pack us all a lunch, but we'd usually have it eaten before we got to Gordon. There were no jobs on the reservation, so we'd just drive from town to town looking for any kind of work. We ran out of money in Grand Island, Nebraska, one time and had to sell our blood for gas money home."

On Pine Ridge, they spent much of the day working on their cars, then raced them along remote drag strips at night. Sometimes, they hit 100 mph on the rough reservation roads, "crazy, insane stuff that didn't seem so crazy when you were sixteen." When he was sixteen, Guy Jr. asked his parents if he could borrow the family car one evening for a quick trip to Kyle. He was gone all night, having taken a carload of boys and girls to the village of Pine Ridge and on to Hot Springs, South Dakota, about a hundred miles away. They had had a few beers when they got back to Kyle around sunrise, and were waiting for the stores to open so he could gas up the car.

"We were just kind of hanging around when I saw Mom and my Uncle Levi pull up in our old truck. Mom was staring at me in a certain way that she had and I said, 'Oh, oh.' She got out of the truck and started taking off her belt and I thought she was just bluffing. I was almost a man and I assumed she knew I was too old for this kind of stuff. She walked up to the car and told me to get out and then she started whacking me in front of all my friends, including a girl I had been trying to impress all night. After a while, my cousin, Adolph Bull Bear, who was also in the car, got out and tried to bail me out. 'Auntie Rose, we didn't mean no harm. We didn't mean to cause any trouble.' Before he could finish, Mom turned on him and began whacking the hell out of Adolph, too."

Rose's intolerance of disobedience and her scorn for alcohol were well known, and Adolph Bull Bear knew it as well as anyone.

Years earlier, he had returned to the reservation from Korea, where he had been with the army's 187th Regimental Combat Team. He had gone to Kyle one afternoon after the war, gotten drunk and was trying to pick a fight with anyone in his path. At six-foot-two and 225 pounds, he didn't have many takers, but he was still trying when Rose pulled up at the grocery store in her truck. She got out, took off her belt and put the leather to the back of Adolph's legs, telling him he had disgraced the family, then ordered him home until he sobered up. Adolph did as he was told.

On February 24, 1961, the boy's grandmother died at the age of eighty-one. She had lived in the Yellow Bear Camp all her life, in the same log house for sixty-five years. It had no electricity, plumbing or running water when she had given birth to her oldest son in February of 1899, and it had none in February of 1961. In his life, her husband had been to Paris, London and Rome, to New York and to many of the large cities on the East Coast. At her death, the farthest Mary Dull Knife had traveled from *Ti Hanska* was Gordon, Nebraska, forty miles south. After a simple ceremony, the family buried her beside her husband, in the cemetery on the hill at the top of Yellow Bear.

At the Oglala Community School, a Bureau of Indian Affairs

high school in the village of Pine Ridge, Guy Dull Knife Jr. kept up his artwork, but did poorly in everything else. Like many of his friends, he enrolled each semester in the school's auto mechanics class, spending several mornings a week learning how to fine-tune an engine, mount and align wheels, sand a car body and paint it properly. Boys and girls were segregated in dormitories where few drugs were available, but there was a good deal of alcohol and "huffing"— sniffing airplane glue. For a short time, the seventeen-year-old from Red Water Creek became a campus bootlegger. From money he had earned elsewhere, he'd buy gallon jugs of cheap wine, pour it into Dixie cups and sell them to students for a dollar a cup. When school officials eventually discovered his business, they kicked him out of the dorm. When Rose found out, she had a fit and straightened him out in a hurry.

She had hated the new music from the beginning and the alcohol for as long as anyone could remember. In his high school days, she saw the toll the years had taken on her son, his friends and their generation. Guy Jr., like many who had been raised in traditional homes, knew how to speak Lakota, but he seldom did. Mixed-bloods dominated the high school in Pine Ridge, and the teasing and taunting was relentless for those who persisted in the old ways. Most of his peers wanted to be white and their social system came to reflect the values of the dominant culture. In the dorm rooms at night, at small gatherings in workshops and classrooms, during their carefree meetings and social encounters, English had long ago become the only language spoken. On transistors and car radios, Indian music was seldom heard, replaced by rock and roll and country-and-western. Native dancing gave way to modern dancing, and traditional food to fast food. The '60s teenagers of Pine Ridge did not want to hear the elders talk about culture and customs. In those years, many were ashamed of their parents and grandparents.

"My cousin cried a lot of times during her teens because of her father. All of the traditions that Uncle Daniel believed in embarrassed her and she hated him because of it. She didn't want to bring friends to her house or have him around whenever anyone came over. She was ashamed of his Indian looks and his broken English and she said many times that she wished he would die."

Daniel Dull Knife spoke Lakota and Cheyenne fluently. For a long time, he lived on the Northern Cheyenne Reservation in Ashland, Montana, where his youngest daughter was a student and football cheerleader at the St. Labre Indian School. In Ashland, Daniel designed the molds for a factory that mass-produced Indian goods. Guy Jr. had watched his father's youngest brother tan hides as a boy, then fashion them into traditional clothing. When Uncle Daniel was sober, he had a way with beading and quilling that few men knew how to do. He had been caught driving one year with a jug of whiskey and no license and a judge sentenced him to ninety days in jail. Quiet and soft-spoken, he sat in the jail, beading and quilling. After finishing a piece, he got the jailer to sell his goods for a commission. Daniel had saved more than a thousand dollars when the judge learned of his enterprise, and with two weeks still to serve, he ordered the Indian released. A few years later, he stumbled out of a bar one night in Rapid City, South Dakota, and collapsed on the street. A fire truck backed over him, killing him on the spot.

They had their disagreements, but Guy Jr. often felt lucky that his parents were around for his high school years. His father believed what he believed and he minded his own business. If Uncle Morris and the others felt the Bible could solve their problems, he wouldn't interfere. Guy Sr., too, had long enjoyed the stories in the book, but they didn't affect him the way the other beliefs did. Guy Sr. ranched his land, represented his people at the tribal meetings and went to the sweat lodge each evening. Guy Jr.'s mother disliked rock, particularly the Rolling Stones, but she let him listen to it as long as he did not forget the older songs. They might all be gone someday, she said, and then the people would come to him for his knowledge. At family gatherings in their home, she made Guy Jr. sing traditional Indian during the Lakota ceremonies.

"Mom had waited a long time to have a child of her own and once she did, she was always there for me, even when I really messed up. All through high school, when my cousin and the others didn't want to bring their friends home, she kept telling me, 'You can't be what you can't be.' That was her favorite expression. She said it over and over and she gave me the confidence not to cave in."

One afternoon in eleventh grade, Guy Dull Knife Jr. and a descendant of Chief Red Cloud got into an exchange of words that led to an ugly fistfight in a hallway of the Oglala Community School. Like other traditional full-bloods on Pine Ridge, the Dull Knife and Bull Bear families had long disliked Red Cloud. The ambitious young warrior had killed Chief Bull Bear in 1841 and had ultimately signed the agreement that led to the loss of their Black Hills in 1877. Some Lakota also believed that Red Cloud's intense jealousy had indirectly led to the death of Crazy Horse. His hand in the killing of two chiefs and the confiscation of the sacred hills forever tainted Red Cloud's name in the eyes of many full-bloods. Guy Jr.'s classmate did not share the Dull Knife and Bull Bear opinion of his great-great-grandfather.

"It began when I said something between classes about Red Cloud killing old man Bull Bear and he kind of lost it. He said I was nothing but a stupid Cheyenne and that I should go back to Montana where I belonged. If it hadn't been for his grandfather, he said, I wouldn't even be here. That in the old days, his grandfather had saved my grandfather's ass and I had better not forget it. Looking back, it was real childish stuff, but we really went at it. We were beating the hell out of each other and covered with blood by the time our friends jumped in and broke it up."

Guy Jr.'s closest friend throughout high school was Byron DeSersa, great-grandson of the Oglala holy man, Black Elk. During much of the '60s, Guy Jr. and Byron DeSersa were inseparable. After school was out, they used to jump in one of their cars and drive to the Black Hills. They put their elaborate costumes—turkey-feather bustles, moccasins and ankle bells—in the trunk and spent much of the summer dancing Indian at different powwows through-out the Black Hills area. On summer nights, when they were sixteen, seventeen and eighteen, the two friends often showed up in Keystone, a bustling tourist town near Mt. Rushmore. They staked

out a busy intersection, put on their costumes and performed traditional Lakota dances for visitors to the hills. Tourists deposited dollar bills in a bowl on the pavement and there were times when they
made sixty dollars for an evening of dancing. For the two friends, it
was good money, spent in part on school supplies, and they hated to
see the summer end.

When they returned home, the two teenagers were often struck
by the poverty they saw on the Pine Ridge Reservation, a bleakness
temporarily obscured by a summer of dancing in the free-spending
tourist resorts of the Black Hills. During much of the 1960s, there
were few modern homes on the reservation, and many traditional
Oglala continued to live on their own land, scattered across great
distances, in log houses without electricity, telephones, running
water or plumbing. By 1967, Guy Jr. had never been in a home with
a toilet. The only plumbing he had seen on Pine Ridge was in the
schools. At the Yellow Bear Camp, he knew of several families still
living in tipis. Tract housing would arrive in a few years and it would
all begin to change, but in those years, many full-bloods still had
their land, their traditions and ceremonies, and they still had the Sun
Dance. Banned in 1881, it had been performed underground for
more than seventy years. Beginning in the early 1950s, the government had eased some of the restrictions, allowing the dance to go
public, but prohibiting the traditional flesh offering and any piercing
of the chest. As bleak as things were, believed many of the traditionals, there was still hope as long as they had the Sun Dance.

To Guy Jr. and his friend, the reservation sometimes seemed like
a kind of concentration camp. Poverty and alcohol wiped out the
young and the old, blunting hope on every road. Many of the people
they knew seemed permanently stuck, unable to move forward or
backward, trapped in lives that ended each day the way they began,
lives that sometimes ended in a speeding car buried in a reservation
ditch. The two boys were looking for something different, something
better.

At the end of eleventh grade, Guy Jr. dropped out of the Oglala
Community School. Restless and bored, he wanted to learn a trade

so he could earn some money, and in the summer of 1967, he applied to the Job Corps. All along, he assumed he would be going to their training site in the nearby Black Hills, where many of the Sioux boys from Pine Ridge had been sent. A letter he received a few weeks later informed him that he would be going to St. Louis instead.

When he arrived at the St. Louis Job Corps training site in August 1967, he was surprised at the size of the facility and the number of boys there. He had never been this far from home and he felt a little intimidated. There were fifteen hundred boys from throughout the United States, and he was the lone American Indian among them. Guy Jr. had decided he wanted to be a cook, and so each morning, he attended classes, learning how to make omelettes, hash browns, salads, casseroles, meat dishes, cakes and puddings. In the large kitchen where he worked, the radio was usually on and he remembered hearing *Sgt. Pepper's Lonely Hearts Club Band* a lot of mornings that summer. Late afternoons and evenings were reserved for rec time and fighting. Most of the boys were black, white and Hispanic and most had joined different gangs, fighting all the time.

"An hour didn't go by that there wasn't some kind of racial taunt and a fight would break out. It seemed like it happened every day I was there, but no one ever bothered me. A gang fight could be going on and I could walk right through it with nobody saying anything to me. One day, the supervisor called me into his office and said, 'Well, chief, where do you stand?' I said I didn't stand anywhere. I told him it was none of my business and I tried to stay out of it.

"The whole time I was there, it was like I was invisible, like I didn't really exist."

After a year in St. Louis, he returned to the Pine Ridge Reservation, and within a month, a letter arrived at the home on Red Water Creek. On August 28, 1968, Guy Dull Knife Jr. maintained his family's record of having fought in every American war this century.

Chapter Ten

A Lakota in the
Que Son Valley

At the family trailer home in Loveland, Colorado, it is a warm after-noon in early June and Cora Yellow Elk sits quietly at the kitchen table, beading bracelets she hopes to sell at a powwow later in the month. Guy Dull Knife III has flipped over his 10-speed in the yard outside, and during these first few days of summer vacation, he and a friend are busy tinkering with the gears. Sprawled across an easy chair in a living room corner, daughter Nellie nods her head to the music inside the Sony Walkman she is seldom without. Little Torrie, the three-year-old granddaughter, races up and down the carpeted hallway in a pair of orange shorts and yellow flip-flops, past the pen-and-ink drawing of Chief Dull Knife, the red and white flag of the Oglala Sioux Tribe and the black trunk from the Wild West Show days, until she is close enough to toss her pacifier on Cora's bead pile. She whirls around and takes off down the hallway, shrieking and laughing all the way to the bedroom.

At the end of a bookshelf above Nellie's head rests a dull, cam-ouflage-green helmet with a single gold star set in red on the front. On the right side, above the ear-line, a splotch of faded red is still vis-ible. Across the left side of the helmet is an inscription written in black capital letters: KILLED BY DULL KNIFE—APRIL 8, 1969—ROCKPILE, VIETNAM.

It has been twenty-three years since Guy Dull Knife Jr. returned from the war. Like many others who went to the jungles of Southeast Asia in the late 1960s and early '70s, he came back home and struggled to get on with his life and forget a lot of what happened there, but even now, in the midst of drinking a cup of coffee, or showering before the others are awake some mornings, or driving to the store for bread and milk, clips and fragments from the past arrive unexpectedly and it will be a while before he can shake them. "I guess you could say I was pretty much of a gross human being back then. But back then was back then. You had to do what you had to do to survive. It wasn't always what you wanted to do, but I didn't know any other way at the time."

Classified 1-A after his stint with the Job Corps, he got his draft notice and took a bus to Sioux Falls, South Dakota, passing his army physical there on August 28, 1968. A few days later, he and the other new recruits flew to Fort Lewis, Washington, for eight weeks of basic training, then eight weeks of infantry training. He got a ten-day leave shortly after Christmas and returned to the Pine Ridge Reservation. Back home, he wore his new army uniform wherever he went and saw the old crowd of friends. Some of the boys would soon be going away, too, and a few had already returned. They asked him how it was and slapped him on the back and wished him luck. Byron DeSersa came to the house one afternoon and it got a little awkward at the end. They finally put their arms around one another and said good-bye.

It was early January and there had been a little snow; he spent a few days helping his father feed their livestock. He took a long walk along Red Water Creek one afternoon, and two days before it was time to go, Chief Fools Crow came to the house and performed the *Yuwipi.* He asked the spirits to watch over him while he was away, to guide him safely to the other world if anything happened. When the ceremony ended, Fools Crow gave him two eagle feathers to wear, as the Lakota had always done, and he gave him the sacred medicine bundle. A little smaller than a golf ball, it had been to World War II and Korea, and two others had already returned safely from Vietnam with the bundle. He didn't know what was in it. No one did. Only the medicine man knew and he was the only one who could open it.

The next morning, he fastened the leather thongs around his neck and tucked the small bundle beneath the collar of his new army uniform.

On the night before he left, his mother said she would like to talk to him. He was starting to get afraid and he knew that she knew, so she had lit the gas lantern and asked him to join her at the wooden table in the kitchen. The army had tried to teach him many things, but he still didn't know what it would be like if he had to kill someone, what it would do to him then and after, and he also knew what his death would do to his parents. He had intentionally blocked it all out until this night, and when he felt the first welling in his eyes, he had hurried outside to the yard, but not quickly enough. That night, Rose Bull Bear told her only child that it was normal to be afraid, to feel sad inside. If he were ever in a position to take someone's life, if it were kill or be killed, he should do it and not let it destroy him. His grandfathers and great-grandfathers had all fought for their land and way of life and they had killed, too. He had no brothers and sisters, no wife and children, she said, and his parents were both elderly and would probably not live much longer. " 'So don't cry, son,' she said. 'If you die, we will be right behind you and we will all see each other soon in the Spirit World. While you're away, do everything you can to stay alive and try not to take everything too seriously. Try to find at least one thing every day to laugh about and never forget how much we love you.' That is what she told me and I always tried to remember it."

The next morning, he flew to the southern Gulf Coast, to Fort Polk, Louisiana, for four weeks of advanced jungle training. Sweltering, steamy and swampy, the Louisiana bayou country was like the place he was going; for three weeks, he and the other young army grunts sat in a military classroom, learning survival techniques designed to give them equal footing in jungles controlled by veteran North Vietnamese Army regulars and the Viet Cong. They learned what to eat and what not to eat, how to treat wounds, guard against dehydration and infections, and how to identify the deadly snakes of

Southeast Asia. To see how much they had absorbed, the army recruits were turned loose in the Louisiana swamps for their final week of training.

He had never been in a bayou, and for seven days he and his fellow recruits marched through swamps infested with insects, snakes and alligators, bivouacking on small islands and spits of land at night. They used a compass to navigate, built concealed campfires and slept on the ground. After a few days, they stumbled upon a small farm, and he and a few others slipped away and stole some chickens, killing and eating them later that night. In the southern swamps, it got quiet after dark, and the occasional splash, the swarm of insects, the rustling of the brush, made them jumpy. They sometimes sat around the fire at night, talking quietly, wondering what it would be like and what would happen to them when they finally got to the other place.

"The Indian has always had a deep attachment to his home and his land," he said years later. "That is why Chief Dull Knife tried to walk back to Montana. He could not think of dying in a place so far from where his own mother and father were buried. After a while, the Indian knew he could never go back to the old days and the old way of life, so he decided that the best thing was to try and go along with the system. That is what happened to my father and it's what happened to me.

"When I got my draft notice, I had no idea where Vietnam was. I had to look it up on a map. I had never seen or heard of a Vietnamese before and I had no idea what the war was all about. My mother had wanted me to stay out of it and I could have, because I was the sole surviving son in my family and my parents were old. But I didn't want to stay out of it. I wanted to go. I wanted to get away from the reservation and I wanted to see what it was like to be in battle. I had heard the stories all my life — from my father and my uncles and cousins and from Dewey. By the time the jungle training ended, most of the others believed they were going to Vietnam to fight communism. I never really believed that. When it was time to go, I had talked myself into believing that I would go into the jungle as a Sioux warrior. That is how I planned to survive, as my people had always done. Not as an American GI, but as a Lakota."

Chief Dull Knife's great-grandson left for Vietnam on the evening of February 3, 1969.

He had never seen anything like Cam Ranh Bay, the massive U.S. military complex constructed along the Vietnamese coast, where he arrived after the long flight from Fort Lewis. Located on the South China Sea northeast of Saigon, Cam Ranh Bay was a principal point of entry for thousands of young American soldiers, average age nineteen, who were coming to fight in the war, and the departure point for those who had already served and were returning home. The sprawling logistical installation measured fifteen miles by five miles, housing and employing 20,000 U.S. servicemen, and as American involvement neared a peak in early 1969, its waterways churned with warships, and fighter planes cluttered the maze of runways. C-130 Hercules and C-141 Starlifters arrived at all hours with shipments of food, medicine, supplies, ammunition and equipment, and fresh troops flew in around the clock. By the beginning of the year, 536,100 Americans were "in-country."

Guy Dull Knife Jr. felt overwhelmed. He saw that many of the new recruits were young and poor, drawn mostly from the inner cities and the rural backcountry, and he felt that many were as disoriented as he was. As privates, they slept in tents and spent most of their first few days filling sandbags and pulling KP duty. Each morning, they walked to the Replacement Center where a large bulletin board listed the names and combat assignments for new recruits. A large map of Vietnam was posted beside the bulletin board, and red pins identified the location of American military units. He was surprised at how much red was on the map, especially the tight clusters bunched throughout the north. On his fourth morning at Cam Ranh Bay, a young Navajo came up and said he had seen his name on the bulletin board. He said the Lakota was going a long way north. Guy Dull Knife ran scared to the center building and quickly scanned the bulletin board. It was true. He was going north, to a place called Chu Lai.

Located north of Cam Ranh Bay, fifty-five miles from the vital American air base at Da Nang, Chu Lai was one of several coastal cities making up a key line of defense for the South Vietnamese Army and its American allies. He arrived in Chu Lai by military transport and spent the next ten days in a refresher course for men headed to combat zones in the battlefields north and west of the Vietnamese coast. The training course allowed them to acclimate to the intense heat and humidity while they learned how to fire enemy weapons, the Chinese-made AK-47 rifles, and they were taught how to identify the many different kinds of hand grenades and booby traps they would encounter on patrol and in firefights with the North Vietnamese Army and the Viet Cong. The preparation also included pep talks from senior army staff, which stressed the military psychology the infantrymen were to employ when they reached the jungles.

"They told us over and over that we should not regard the Vietnamese as human. They said we would never know the names of the people we were fighting, who they were or where they came from, and when we were out on patrol, we should look at it the same like we were going hunting back home. You were not really killing people, you were killing an enemy and the enemy in this war was not a human."

When the ten-day course ended, each man received his assignment. Guy Dull Knife was told to report to the U.S. Army's Bravo Company, Second Battalion, First Infantry Regiment, 196th Light Infantry Brigade, the same regiment his father had been in half a century earlier. At the 196th's equipment center in Chu Lai, he got a helmet, two hand grenades, an entrenching tool, C-rations, a rucksack and belt, seven canteens, a poncho and poncho liner, a bayonet and an M-16 and ammunition. He and 150 others were in what the army called a front-line unit. They were going to the jungle to conduct search-and-destroy missions, to find the enemy, to kill or be killed.

President Nixon had been in office a few weeks when their helicopters landed at the 196th's base in the Que Son Valley, in an area of Vietnam the military called I Corps. The broad valley ran east and west through the north country, where rugged mountains and thick jungles required penetration by foot. It ended near the Laotian border, not far from the Ho Chi Minh Trail. About a year earlier, on the evening of January 30, 1968, seventy thousand Communist soldiers had come down the trail and staged a carefully planned series of offensive strikes throughout the South, including the capital of Saigon. The bold raids had swept into more than a hundred cities and towns, some of which had been thought impregnable, and both their scope and ferocity caught the South Vietnamese and American troops off guard. Launched during Tet, the Vietnamese lunar New Year and a mutually agreed-upon truce period, the punishing attacks were carried out by Viet Cong units in the south and North Vietnamese Army regulars in the north. The Tet Offensive had been designed to spur uprisings throughout the south, an objective never achieved, but it changed for good American public opinion about the war. Television cameras captured the furious fighting in the ancient coastal city of Hue and inland battles at Dakto and Pleiku — and the images of American soldiers shipped home in body bags flickered across television screens throughout the homeland. At Khe Sanh, a massive Communist force besieged the American Marine base, and in the White House, President Lyndon Johnson tried to follow the battle on a sand table built in the war room. Two months after Tet, Johnson announced he would not seek a second term as president.

Guy Dull Knife was shocked at how grotesque everyone looked. He saw shaggy beards and ragged clothes, filthy bodies and dirty uniforms. Some had wild tattoos across their backs and chests, and there were ugly welts and raw red sores up and down their arms and legs. Their eyes didn't look right, and in the snatches of conversation that first afternoon, numbers consumed his unit, the men all counting backward from 365 until they arrived at a precise figure signaling their return to "The World." For now, many would return to Chu Lai, coptered in for three days of R and R. They had been in the field for ninety days, walking the jungle trails, fighting the NVA, search-and-destroy, trying to stay alive. In the year before he arrived, the

company had a 65 percent casualty rate and the survivors were looking forward to the whorehouses, to three days of eating and drinking
as much beer and steak as they could before rotating back to the
field. He heard their transistors beating with hard rock and sometimes smelled the smoke from the plant his mother had used to
induce hunger, and when he looked out from the top of LZ Baldy,
the dark, green jungle rolled west in an unbroken line toward Laos.

Nothing like it had ever been along Red Water Creek, or even at
Fort Lewis and Fort Polk, and he felt right away there was something in the air at the army base in the Que Son Valley that his training and preparation might not resolve. The CO was glad to see him.
After the new recruits had unpacked and gotten a tour of the field
base, the commanding officer pulled Guy Dull Knife aside and
started to grin. "Well, chief, I think I've just found my new point
man," he said.

Walking point was among the most hazardous assignments of
the Vietnam war. On jungle patrol, search-and-destroy missions and
routine reconnaissance, the point man walked ahead of the main soldier body. The trails were laced with trip wires, covered with booby
traps and land mines, and contained the camouflaged "pungi pits,"
deep holes filled with sharpened bamboo stakes embedded upright
on the bottom, stakes that were often coated with the urine of water
buffalo to induce infection. Dense foliage on either side of the trail
offered numerous ambush possibilities, and it was often the eyes and
ears of the point man, and an innate sense of danger, that determined
whether those who followed arrived home in a black, zippered body
bag, a wheelchair or walking on their own.

"They thought because I was Indian, I could see the bushes and
the trees moving in the jungle better than the white soldiers and the
black soldiers, so they made me walk point right from the beginning.
But it turned out O.K., because if I walked point, it meant I didn't
have to go out on any of the night ambushes. And for all I know, they
may have been right. During the whole time I walked point for my
company, we only lost eighteen men."

That first night, and every night for the next few weeks, Guy

Dull Knife was taught how to walk point by a middle-aged Vietnamese man. The former Communist had fought the French in the '50s and the Americans throughout much of the '60s. After the North Vietnamese Army had wiped out a South Vietnamese village, killing a number of his relatives, he had flipped sides and volunteered to work for the U.S. military. The army had assigned him to the 196th Light Infantry and he became what was known as a "Kit Carson scout" during the Vietnam war.

"He spoke pretty decent English, and as we were getting ready to go out that first night, he asked me what my name was. I told him and he looked kind of puzzled, so I said I was an American Indian. He looked at me for a while and then he started to smile. He put his hand to his mouth and made a few war whoops. 'Like in a John Wayne movie, huh?' I laughed and said, 'Yeah, just like in a John Wayne movie.' " They finished packing and moved out of LZ Baldy, heading for the jungle.

During their weeks together, the middle-age man taught the young soldier how to read the jungle floor for booby traps and showed him the best places to camp. His nickname was *Papa-san,* and in broken English, he explained the military tactics of the NVA, how they fought and how they thought, their battle habits, strategy and techniques. And he told him when and why an ambush was most likely.

"He was small and wiry and tough and I remember he could walk forever without complaining. He always carried a rucksack with him, stocked with the kind of foods he liked. Every once in a while, he would throw a couple of chickens in the sack before we started out. If he thought it was safe, he'd pull out a chicken and kill it."

Sometimes, the Lakota from Pine Ridge and the Kit Carson scout from Vietnam would squat on their haunches, roasting fresh chicken together in a small clearing in the Asian jungle.

"I got along with the Vietnamese real well the whole time I was there. We kind of looked alike in some ways and it seemed to make a difference. To me and them."

By late February 1969, *Papa-san* had taught him all he knew and Guy Dull Knife Jr. was on his own, walking point for Company B, Second Battalion, of the 196th Light Infantry.

The heat and humidity was far worse than Louisiana and his life-long fear of snakes left him paralyzed. Back in "The World," they had told him it was a bamboo viper. In Vietnam, the soldiers called it a "two-stepper." "If it got you, you dropped after two steps, went into a coma and never came out." When he first started walking point, he often felt more terrified of the snakes than of an enemy ambush.

The first few months were the worst. Everything they needed was in rucksacks on their backs. His rucksack weighed more than sixty pounds and he often felt like a pack animal, trudging through the mountains and the thick bush. They walked and patrolled until dark, then slept on the ground, watching for snakes at night. He sometimes fastened the two eagle feathers to his helmet back in camp, but not on patrol. There was no point flashing white in the dark green, it could get you killed, so he kept them in his rucksack. Point was lonely. He was often ten to twenty yards ahead of the company. Each step, you could be taken out half-a-dozen ways. A sudden squawk of birds and monkeys up ahead, then the stillness and he would freeze. It could be a predator, mating calls, or the NVA. You never knew. He was on a swinging bridge that one time, maybe twenty-five yards ahead of the others. The bridge kept swinging with each step, each shift of his weight, and he had to grab the sides with both hands to keep from tumbling over. Four or five steps from the end, a couple of VC opened fire and he could hear the first bullet pass in front of his face. The platoon leader screamed for him to get down, but he'd never been shot at, and in the panic he stood up and tried to race back across the bridge, running and falling, the bullets splintering the wood at his feet, until his men opened fire in the bush below and the shooting stopped.

On patrol, the jungle became a fearsome enemy. It was hard to see anything, and they walked with the heavy packs, sweating, often sick with dysentery, bugs and snakes above and below, nerves raw.

There were firefights almost every week. Many times, they went no more than a hundred yards before an ambush left someone bleeding to death on the jungle floor. A lieutenant in his unit stepped on a land mine and was blown to pieces. A buddy hit a mine and lost both legs. An early morning ambush killed three more. Two or three times when he was on patrol, the NVA let him pass. He was fifteen or more yards down the trail when the main body arrived at the ambush point and he could hear all the shooting behind him. Cut off and alone, he had to stay put. *Papa-san* had warned him never to go back until the shooting stopped. In the confusion, charging back in the bush, he could be shot by his own men as well as the enemy. It was the worst part of walking point.

As they sloshed through rice paddies, their boots filled with water and they would go days without taking them off. Their feet developed a fungus that spread through the webbing of the toes and the itching would be unbearable. In the fields, razor-sharp elephant grass sliced their skin, and in the intense heat and humidity, bacteria got into the open cuts; many came down with jungle rot, sores swollen with pus that could be drained and treated after they made it back to camp. There were two kinds of malaria and they were given a large orange pill once a week for the bad kind and a smaller white pill each day for the other kind. Many of the grunts tossed the pills in the bush, hoping they would get the disease. If they were lucky, they would be pulled from patrol, laid up in a hospital for weeks or months at a time. In the dense, dark foliage, incendiary shells were sometimes used as marker rounds to help pinpoint bombing targets or to illuminate the terrain. The grunts called them "Willie Petes," "Whiskey Papas," "Wilson Picketts," or just "WPs." The military called them "white phosphorous" shells. Launched by 105mm howitzers or jets flying overhead, the metal canisters exploded on impact, igniting with oxygen and burning everything they touched. The phosphorous occasionally got on their hands and arms by accident and began to burn through their skin, and then they had to pack mud around the wounds to cut off the oxygen and keep the skin from burning to the bone. He and many of the others in Bravo Company had arms covered with thick red welts.

Sometimes, they fought all day to capture a hill or clearing, and would abandon it the next day. Of the original one hundred men in his unit, more than fifty had been killed or wounded by the end.

After a while, the stubble on his face thickened and he didn't care too much about his uniform or his body and he could feel that his eyes had started to look like the others he had seen when he had first arrived in the Que Son Valley. His nerves started to go bad and he didn't sleep too well. He thought that many of the men in his unit were no longer in their right mind and he wasn't too sure about himself, either. What was a Sioux boy from Pine Ridge doing here? he often thought. It was like a game and there were no rules anymore. He sometimes felt as if he were at the edge of the Dakota Badlands, moving quietly through the pines, deer-hunting with his father and his uncles. The only thing that mattered now was staying alive. Most of the others felt the same way.

"The search-and-destroy missions were about as horrible as it got. Our objective then was to move in and wipe out, to eliminate as much as possible, all living things. When we were finished, we could sometimes see young children absentmindedly walking over the bodies of their parents.

"Some of the people in my infantry unit used to sight their rifles on peasants working quietly in the fields and let them have it, just for target practice. Someone's mother or father would have their brains laid out in a rice paddy just for target practice."

On patrol one night, he saw a figure in the moonlight, squatting on the trail ahead, digging a hole. He raised his rifle and fired and the figure slumped over. It was his first kill. He walked to the body and found a bag of C-4 plastic explosives lying on the ground. When he carefully rolled the body over, he saw that it was a young girl, maybe fourteen or fifteen. She had long black hair and looked like a lot of the teenage girls from his home. He leaned over and vomited and stayed sick the rest of the night.

"After I had been there awhile, I often wondered if what we were doing to the Vietnamese wasn't the same as what the army had done to us. We were kicking them out of their homes, killing all their animals, herding them from one place to another and trying to force a government and a way of life on them that they didn't really want."

Fighting the NVA was different. It was a regular army, well-trained and well-equipped, and many of the men had spent much of their lives fighting the French, the Americans and the South Vietnamese. Like most American troops, the 196th had a good deal of respect for the NVA. They were good soldiers.

Guy Jr. (right) in Vietnam.

"Every morning, every morning when you were out on jungle patrol, you would wake up to the sound of NVA soldiers exercising with these bamboo sticks. It was always very early and you would lie there on the ground listening to the clicking sound of those sticks going up and down the valley. When the sound stopped, it got real quiet and then you knew that the enemy had finished their breakfast and exercise routine and they had started coming through the jungle looking for you. Even today, when I hear the sound of those bamboo chimes blowing in the wind, it makes the hair on my neck stand up."

After a while, Guy Dull Knife stopped thinking about where he was and why and what he was doing. "Too much thinking could get you killed," he believed. He wanted to survive, to get back home. He wanted to see his mother and father, see his friends again and walk along Red Water Creek, and he began counting backward. Walking point, he pretended he was a Sioux warrior in another place and time. In the spring of 1969, they had gone farther north, up toward the DMZ, and he was ahead of his unit, about to step into an open clearing in the jungle. "He was squatting in the clearing wrapping a wounded comrade's arm. Neither one heard me and so I stepped back into the trees and brought the rifle up slowly. I didn't want either of them to have a chance and they didn't. I fired my M-16 twice and they both dropped in their tracks."

He could tell from the gold star set in red that the one doing the bandaging was a high-ranking NVA officer. Sometimes the bodies were booby-trapped and he carefully pulled a knife from his belt and sliced the right ear off each man. He took the colonel's rucksack and his helmet and gave them to a buddy to keep for him. He put the ears in his own rucksack. "After a battle, you are always supposed to bring back proof to your chief that you have been a good warrior. It has always been that way and that is what I did in Vietnam."

After Korea, his cousin, Adolph Bull Bear, had returned home with eight scalps. Another cousin, Webster Poor Bear, was with the 173rd Airborne Brigade in Vietnam. His CO threatened to have him court-martialed if he didn't stop scalping NVA soldiers. Guy Dull Knife heard that another Indian, a Winnebago in a nearby unit, had also risked a court-martial for his method of counting coup on the enemy. A point man in his unit, the Winnebago would sneak up on an NVA sentry, tap him on the shoulder and give his war cry before slitting the sentry's throat. "He was a good point man, but it drove the platoon commander crazy. Everyone else was walking quietly through the jungle and the point man was yelling out his war cry. The CO told him to stop or he'd have him court-martialed, at least that's the story I heard."

In Vietnam, there were days when each side wanted to live more than fight, when both the Americans and the NVA seemed too weary, disgusted and dispirited to risk dying that morning or afternoon or evening. The two units would unexpectedly encounter each other in the jungle and each would let the other pass by. Every now and then, his company spent several days setting up an ambush. When the time came to open fire, no one moved. It didn't seem worth it.

"One afternoon, we were supposed to be guarding a bridge and everyone was in the river bathing or swimming instead. While we were in the water, an NVA unit came marching over the bridge. The platoon leader looked up and gave them the peace sign. They kept walking and we kept swimming. No one fired a shot.

"There was one guy from Denver who ended up spending most of his tour of duty with the enemy. Shortly after he got to Vietnam, he sold his M-16, his ammunition and all of his army equipment on the black market in Saigon. He bought some civilian clothes and just kind of wandered off into the countryside. He eventually made it to Cambodia and took up with a whore there and traveled all over, drinking and going to parties and raising hell. When his tour of duty was almost up, he wandered back in and told everyone that he had been a POW and had somehow managed to escape. He said he had spent most of the time in North Vietnam and that he had ended up liking the North Vietnamese and didn't want to fight them."

He had been in the valley about three months when a soldier approached him in camp one day and said another Indian had just arrived in the company. The soldier motioned toward a distant hill where the new arrival was unpacking beneath a tree. Guy Dull Knife started walking toward the hill and when he got closer, he saw the hair and coloring and bone structure and he started to get excited.

"Ni Lakota he?"

Francis Whitebird turned around, grinning "from ear to ear." He was a Brulé Sioux from the Rosebud Reservation, just across the Pine Ridge line, and it wasn't long before the two men were sitting beneath the tree, talking in the language from back home. Whitebird had grown up in Wanblee, on the eastern edge of Pine Ridge, and they soon discovered they knew some of the same people and had been to many of the same places as kids. He had an undergraduate degree in agriculture from South Dakota State University and would earn a master's from Harvard after the war, but in the early spring of 1969, Whitebird was an army medic assigned to Company B of the 196th.

Down the hill a ways, a chaplain was celebrating Mass for the

Catholic soldiers in the company while the two Lakota got caught up on news from the reservations. It seemed like Guy Dull Knife had been away for years and he pumped the new arrival for details from Indian Country and the United States. In midtalk, the dust began to fly at their feet and the sharp cracking sound of an AK-47 drove them behind the tree. The chaplain and his soldier flock dropped to the ground and the two Lakota low-crawled down the backside of the hill to a protective gully below. In a few minutes, the sniper fire stopped. "Welcome to Vietnam," Guy Dull Knife said.

He had been horribly homesick from the beginning and it was good to have another Sioux in the company. The two became friends, the way it happens to soldiers in combat, out on patrol, back in camp, talking in their language about what they would do when they got home. In the old days of their people, warriors received an eagle feather for each coup counted on an enemy. If they did it enough, their bravery could be displayed in a full headdress of eagle feathers. In Vietnam, he and Francis Whitebird counted coup on the enemy for each other, hoping that if one made it back alive he would have enough for a war bonnet.

During the first few months, when Guy Dull Knife returned to camp after days of patrol, he would see the other soldiers tear open the letters from home and read them over and over. Like his father at the Haskell Institute, in the years before World War I, he could barely write, and the sight of the others reading their letters made him feel sad and empty, desperate for something from his family. After a while, he bought a tape recorder in Chu Lai and he started sending long tapes back to the Pine Ridge Reservation. Rose had gotten sick with diabetes, but she could tell from his voice and so she started recording over his tapes and sending them back with news from home until he was getting almost one a week. Every now and then, he would come out of the jungle and find a package with a South Dakota postmark and he would eagerly tear it open. Inside, his mother had sent bags of *wasna,* the powdery dried meat war parties had taken with them in another century, and he would eat it around the campfire in the Que Son Valley. It got to be a standing joke with some of the men in the company. They would look at the strange texture and say, "What are you doing, chief—eating that sawdust again?"

They had been told not to eat any of the Vietnamese food, but he and Francis Whitebird paid no attention to the directive. The rural villages of the Vietnamese were scattered up and down the territory they patrolled, and after three or four days in the jungle, they would come back in and eat whatever was for sale in the dusty village center. They often didn't know what it was and they didn't ask. It tasted good and they ate it.

One of the things he had missed most throughout much of his early military life were the children. They had always been in his home growing up and were everywhere on every reservation he had ever been, and then he had gone weeks without seeing any, only men about his age, during basic training, at Cam Ranh Bay, in Chu Lai, walking the jungle day after day, back in camp, back in the jungle. In the rural villages along the Laotian border, he began to see them again and they made him feel connected to something he didn't want to lose. When he went into the jungle, he could feel it starting to slip away and it had scared him for a long time. He believed some of the others felt the same way, but no one ever talked about it, so he wasn't sure.

After a while, his company got to know some of the rural villagers living their traditional way of life, and he looked forward to coming in after patrol and seeing all their children. They were fascinated by the large American servicemen, the uniforms and equipment, their different colors, their language and their money. The older boys would offer to carry their things for a few dong. When they saw them coming down the dirt roads, young teenage girls would run toward the men, wanting to sell them sex or bottles of soda. Behind the soda girls trailed dogs and the younger kids, small and lean, barefoot, black hair and dark skin, staring sheepishly at the big men in uniform walking toward their village.

He and Francis Whitebird began to spend more and more time with the kids in one village they frequently returned to after patrol. They tried to teach them some Lakota words and a few Lakota songs, and after a while, they rounded up about a dozen of the smaller ones and began to teach them the Rabbit Dance. The kids loved it. They watched the two big men jumping around in the dirt and then they tried it, hopping first on one foot, then the other, over and over, laughing and giggling. After a time, the sergeant or the platoon leader would arrive and they would grab their M-16s and leave, walking back down the road, heading for the jungle.

An old man in the village sold cheap rice whiskey, and they used to buy it and put it in their canteens before they left. If it was a slow night, they would occasionally get pretty lit, then find a safe place to crouch for a few hours. They were amazed at how beautiful the tracers looked, arcing above the treetops in the black jungle night.

In the jungle, one of his buddies had a monkey as a pet. He kept it back in camp, occasionally bringing it along on patrol. One morning, while everyone slept, the monkey pulled the trigger on a M-60 machine gun, spraying rounds across the camp. Everyone jumped and dove for cover. "When the shooting stopped and we saw what happened, one of the men calmly stood up and blew the monkey's head off."

Ten or twelve of them were resting along a trail one afternoon. A black private jumped up and screamed, pointing to the tree overhead. One of the men opened fire and a huge snake dropped to the ground. It was a python, about eighteen feet long and ten inches around.

He found himself sitting alone with part of his squad one night, sitting in a burned-out Buddhist temple near the edge of the tree line. There had been a firefight the day before and they were waiting until dawn to rejoin the rest of the unit. In the burned-out temple, the clock still worked and it kept clicking back and forth. After an hour or so, he jumped up and sprayed it with his M-16.

On a clear evening in late July 1969, on a night patrol near the

Laotian border, he and six men from Bravo Company were hacking their way through the jungle. Their machetes flashed in the moonlight, and as they hacked, each man heard the message coming from the radioman's portable unit at the same moment. A voice from the base said an American was walking on the moon. The seven men from Bravo Company stopped and stared up at the sky. No one spoke for a while and then the point man started hacking again and they moved along in silence, deeper into the jungle.

They came out a few days later and rejoined the rest of the company, usually about a hundred men altogether. The monsoon season had arrived. During this time, it rained all day for weeks and then it would rain harder. There was no place to go, no shelter, and the rain and mud, the humidity and insects, made their nerves worse than usual. You could get careless during the monsoons and a lot of the men made sure their backward-counting math was accurate to the day. They were glad to be off patrol, heading back to the village to eat and rest and drink a little before another round in the mud and rain with the NVA.

He and Francis Whitebird were walking in the middle of the pack, down the road to the village, and they could see the first of the soda girls running out to meet them. A few dogs scooted down the edge of the road on both sides as some of the men at the head of Bravo Company began drifting into the village. In the distance, behind the soda girls and the dogs, they could see the heads of some of the younger kids bobbing up and down, heading toward them, and it wasn't until they got closer that they could see what the children were doing. They were doing the Rabbit Dance.

He and Francis Whitebird looked at each other at the same time and they looked away at about the same time. Then they both started running through the puddles until they reached the kids and they each put one on their shoulders and kept walking down the road. When they reached the village, some of the kids behind them were still trying to hop, first on one foot, then the other.

Later that day, they told the soda girls in the village near Laos that some of their countrymen had been up walking around on the moon. The soda girls laughed and looked at them like they were all crazy.

He had been counting backward for a long time now, and by the middle of December 1969, the number was down to less than fifty out of the original 365. About a week before Christmas, they were out on routine patrol when incoming rockets sent everyone scrambling for cover. Before he could make it to safety, he felt a thud in his back and he could feel the blood pouring into his uniform. He staggered forward and wondered why he wasn't losing consciousness. His back was soaked and his shoulders were numb. When he got down in the cover, he reached around and took off his rucksack and saw that the shrapnel had shattered his canteen. He opened his rucksack and removed the two eagle feathers, smoothed them out and put them away. He knew that he had been lucky and his nerves got worse each day as the numbers went down and each time he had to go back out on patrol.

That Christmas, he and some of the others from the 196th were flown to Qui Nhon, a city east of Pleiku on the South Vietnamese coast. He couldn't believe how hot it was, but he enjoyed the huge holiday show the military staged for the troops that year. He saw Bob Hope and the Dallas Cowboys football cheerleaders—a lot of the grunts got pretty worked up. It was the largest crowd he had ever seen.

After a few days of R and R, they flew out of Qui Nhon and returned to their army base, back on patrol, back to the jungle. Many times during the previous year, he did not think he would be around to see 1970, but nothing bad happened throughout the first month of the new year.

On February 1, 1970, Guy Dull Knife boarded a TWA jet at Cam Ranh Bay and flew back to the United States, his tour of duty completed.

They came out the door in their uniforms, walked down the

steps, and when they reached the last one, many of the men dropped to their knees and kissed the ground. After they stood up, they saw that a lot of people were clustered behind a chain-link fence along one edge of the tarmac. They were shouting and waving signs, and after a while, some of them started throwing eggs and tomatoes at the red-eyed group of soldiers walking toward the terminal. Some of the men did not get it. They hadn't seen a newspaper, magazine or TV in months and they were surprised and confused at what they saw in their first few hours back home. The kids were mostly white, mostly their age, and they had lived in a different world for the last twelve months. Many of the people he had fought beside probably didn't know what a college deferment was. It hadn't come up in their conversations. He had heard Francis Whitebird talk about it once, but it was a word Guy Dull Knife couldn't spell. They didn't really have a choice, he thought. They got drafted, went overseas, did their job and now they were back.

He didn't want any trouble. He just wanted to go home. In the airport, Guy Dull Knife went into a restroom and took off his uniform, changing into civilian clothes. Then he went to a counter at the Seattle-Tacoma International Airport and made arrangements for a commercial flight to Rapid City, South Dakota. He didn't call his parents. He wanted to surprise them.

When he got to Customs, they wanted to know about the thing around his neck. He said it was his sacred medicine bundle. They laughed and told him to open it. One of the inspectors thought it probably contained narcotics, that he was trying to smuggle good Asian heroin back into the States. He told them that he couldn't open it, that no one could, only the medicine man. They told him again that he had better open the bundle or airport security would arrive to open it for him. The people were piling up behind them and they were not in a good mood and neither was Guy Dull Knife. He asked if he could call his home in South Dakota and have someone explain to them that he was telling the truth, that he was forbidden to open the bundle and so were they.

One of the inspectors accompanied him to a pay phone and he

called a neighbor, asking her to tell his mother to call him at the number of the airport telephone. About twenty minutes later, the phone rang and he explained the problem to his mother in Lakota, asking her if she could drive over to Chief Fools Crow's house and have him call the airport pay phone in Seattle. After about half an hour, the phone rang again and Fools Crow talked to the customs inspector, telling him about the history of the medicine bundle and that he had prepared this one almost thirty years ago and, in the custom of the Lakota, it was forbidden for anyone but himself to open it. The inspector believed what the old man had told him. He apologized to Guy Dull Knife and they both had a good laugh, and then Guy flew to South Dakota. At the airport in Rapid City, he took off the civilian clothes and changed back into his uniform and waited for his mother and a cousin to pick him up for the drive back to the Pine Ridge Reservation.

For days afterward, there were feasts and parties at his home on the hill above Red Water Creek. Rose would start crying for no reason and his father couldn't tell enough of his friends and neighbors and relatives and tribal councilmen that his son was back home from the war. The old crowd of friends stopped by and he took a long walk along the creek one afternoon. He drove to the home of Chief Fools Crow another afternoon, gave him eight right ears taken from NVA soldiers, and they had a long talk before he left.

For weeks afterward, he wore his uniform all the time, to visit relatives, to see old friends, for grocery runs to Kyle, on trips to the village of Pine Ridge. "I was a hero to my people. They didn't have much to give, but wherever I went, they would stop me on the street and slap me on the back and stuff dollar bills in my pockets. A lot of them were strangers. They really respect the uniform on the reservation and they were proud of me and all the Lakota who had served in Vietnam."

Among the 12,000 Oglala Sioux on the Pine Ridge Reservation then, 175 served in the Vietnam war. Nine died. The name of each Vietnam vet is listed on facing slabs of granite erected in a weedy corner lot in the village of Pine Ridge. The names include Guy Dull

Knife Jr. and his first cousin, Peter Bull Bear, a Green Beret and Golden Eagles Parachute Club member, the first Oglala Sioux to serve with the U.S. Army Special Forces. Cousin Ray Bull Bear was with the 173rd Airborne Brigade and another cousin, Peter Mesteth, served as an army combat engineer. A shell tore off the top of his skull and Mesteth returned home to the village of Kyle with a steel plate in his head. East of Kyle, in the village of Wanblee, the Pumpkin Seed family had five sons, four of whom went to Vietnam. Descendants of Chief Big Foot, each of the four returned safely from the war. In the years after they returned, three of the four Pumpkin Seed boys who had served in Vietnam died of diabetes.

On the outskirts of Wanblee, on a small, grassy knoll across the street from Crazy Horse High School, stands a large wall monument erected to Sioux veterans who have fought in all the wars. The names are listed alphabetically below an inscription:

> *To those who served in the Armed Forces of the United States of America against nations which ruthlessly sought to destroy the sacred principles of democracy, liberty, justice and equality.*

After a time, the people living in the Medicine Root District, the people that his father represented at the tribal council meetings, made it official: They welcomed him back with a traditional honoring ceremony. On an evening in the winter of 1970, Guy Dull Knife Jr. was the guest of honor at festivities held at the Little Wound School gymnasium in Kyle. They killed a buffalo from the tribal herd and roasted it like in the old days, and some of the guests brought fresh beef from their cattle herds. All the Dull Knifes were there and a lot of the Bull Bears and many of his boyhood friends and high school buddies came, too. He wore his army uniform and toward the end of the ceremony, they made him stand and lead everyone in the social dance that they had done for generations when courting and to express their joy and happiness. He was a little embarrassed when he took the floor, but they were all laughing and cheering, and so he started hopping first on one foot, then the other, and soon he was at the head of the line, leading everyone around the gym in the traditional Rabbit Dance of the Lakota.

It had all happened so fast and he wasn't sure about his footing sometimes. He had lost more than twenty pounds and his arms still burned. His legs and back were covered with sores and he didn't think his eyes were quite right, yet. But he was happy. It was good to be home.

Chapter Eleven

The Badlands

He couldn't sleep and he couldn't go outside. He didn't want to be left alone and he didn't want to be with anybody. In little more than a week, Guy Dull Knife Jr. had gone from walking point in the Que Son Valley to walking the banks of Red Water Creek. For weeks and months afterward, he could not make the two worlds fit. Along the creek, he imagined there were VC in the bushes and he would run back to the house. Driving the reservation roads, he believed they were mined and he turned the car around. In Vietnam, no one was allowed to go anywhere alone, and after a few moments inside the outhouse, he thought he could hear incoming rockets and he would open the door and run. He began asking others to walk him to the bathroom. At night, when he lay down on the mattress, the sores on his back and legs covered the sheets with pus. His arms still stung from the phosphorous and he could not get comfortable. When he collapsed from exhaustion, the nightmares began and he often awoke in a sweat. Then he would get up and walk until the comfort of sunlight let him relax.

It was late in the winter of 1970 when he drove to the home of Chief Fools Crow. The old man chief was almost eighty and he lived in a small log house near Kyle, out in the backcountry where many of the traditional full-bloods kept their homes and land and culture. Fools Crow listened to the young soldier, and afterward he began taking him to the sweat lodge in the evenings. After a time, he performed a *Yuwipi*, asking the spirits to calm the young man's nerves, to

keep him strong, to help him regain his footing. During the ceremony, Guy Dull Knife Jr. returned the sacred medicine bundle he
had worn in the other world.

By early summer, he began to feel better and he took a job working at a moccasin factory in the village of Pine Ridge, the bustling
community in the reservation's southwest corner where the tribal
offices and the federal Bureau of Indian Affairs were located. Rose's
diabetes had worsened and now there were heart problems, too. At
seventy-one, his father had the land and livestock to tend and he continued to represent the people of the rural Medicine Root District at
the tribal council meetings. While the old man maintained the ranch,
his son did the cooking and cleaning. In the evenings, they both took
care of Rose.

Guy Jr. worked at the factory for almost three years. He liked
the job. In the beginning, it gave his days a rhythm and purpose, an
8-to-5 stability that was soothing. The money helped his family and
the work occupied his mind. Each morning, he drove west from Kyle
to Sharps Corner, then south through the hamlets of Porcupine and
Wounded Knee. The drive took him across the old buffalo country,
across rolling prairie studded with ponderosa pine and Colorado
spruce, past creek bottoms scrabbled in oak, ash and elm and towering stands of cottonwood. South of Wounded Knee, he picked up
U.S. 18 for the last sixteen miles into Pine Ridge. During the long
daily commute, he noticed more and more that there was a great deal
of difference between the people who lived on the lands through
which he drove and the ones who lived in the village where he
worked. By early 1972, the differences came out in the open and
gradually swept across the whole of the Pine Ridge Reservation.
After a time, he could no longer take his customary route from home
to the factory.

"That was the first time in my life that I ever heard the words
'goon' and 'AIM,' " he said years later.

It had been building for a long time, since 1851, when the first
peace treaty had been signed between the United States and the
westernmost division of the Great Sioux Nation. The treaty allowed

settlers and fur traders to pass safely through Lakota lands in exchange for regular shipments of food, domestic animals and farm tools. The annuities were dispensed at Fort Laramie, Wyoming Territory, where some Lakota began hanging around the fort, waiting for the rations promised in the treaty. The hangers-around-the-fort seldom had to venture far for whiskey and molasses, and during the next three decades, as starvation and land loss crippled the old ways, more and more Lakota came into the agencies near the forts.

Their resistance broken, some of the older chiefs were anxious to retain positions of power and influence and they were easily flattered and manipulated. Make-believe chiefs were created and propped up and the government increasingly began pitting Indian against Indian. It is how new treaties came into being and the Black Hills were lost. The divide-and-conquer strategy eventually broke the Lakota into two camps: "hostiles" and "friendlies." The hostiles were traditional. They fought for the land and the old ways, and if they were prominent, they were usually destroyed, sometimes with the help of their own people. When a bayonet sliced through his kidney, Crazy Horse's arms were pinned from behind by his childhood friend and former lieutenant, Little Big Man. Indian police shot Sitting Bull in the doorway of his home. When Lakota Ghost Dancers brought the army to Pine Ridge, Northern Cheyenne troops were marched south to help subdue their old friends and relatives. Half-breed scouts were the first to find Big Foot and his people.

For a hundred and twenty-five years, it was often the friend-lies—those Lakota who acceded to the wishes of the military, the government, the police, the missionaries and the reservation agent—who survived and occasionally prospered and it was the traditionals who often died, who felt the full brunt of sickness, alcoholism, corruption, isolation and despair.

One evening in February 1972, two white brothers savagely beat a middle-age Oglala man in Gordon, Nebraska, stripped him from the waist down and stuffed him in the trunk of their car. They bought two cases of beer and a quart of wine and drove around town. A half-hour later, they stopped at a local American Legion hall and shoved the severely injured man through a rear door, trying to push him toward the crowded dance floor. Several legion members asked the Indian if they could help him home, but the half-naked man shook his head and walked away. The Oglala, a local ranch hand who came from the Pine Ridge village of Porcupine, stumbled to the Gordon jail. He told the jailer he wasn't feeling very well and asked to spend the night. The next morning, he walked to the local used-car lot where he lived. Raymond Yellow Thunder, fifty-one, collapsed on the front seat of a pickup truck and died of a brain hemorrhage.

About a week later, another Oglala heard the story of Yellow Thunder's death from a friend of the family. Russell Means had also grown up in Porcupine before moving to California and then to Ohio. In 1970, while he was in charge of Cleveland's Indian Center, Means attended a conference of the American Indian Movement in Minneapolis. Founded by urban Indians in 1968, AIM wanted to consolidate a disparate group of national Indian organizations. High on its list of objectives were an end to police harassment, a restoration of treaty rights and a push toward Indian sovereignty. AIM leaders wanted American Indians to get away from a century of federal guardianship, to try and reclaim a measure of their own language, culture and heritage. They wanted the right to be Indian and live with traditional Indian values, and they envisioned using political force and publicity to achieve their goals. When Means returned from the Minneapolis conference, he opened an American Indian Movement office in Cleveland, and shortly after hearing the story of Yellow Thunder's death, he went to Nebraska. AIM leaders were meeting with other Indian groups in Omaha at the time, and several Oglala said the family wanted someone to help them investigate the beating death in Gordon. They asked AIM to come to the Pine Ridge Reservation.

Among many Oglala traditionals, apathy and despair had become an accepted way of life by the winter of 1972. That spring, Richard "Dickie" Wilson, a mixed-blood, won the tribal presidency in a bruising election against a traditional full-blood. Gerald One Feather had taken most of the rural votes while Wilson claimed almost all of the Pine Ridge village votes. A plumber by trade, Wilson was a heavy drinker who had narrowly missed being indicted in 1969 on charges of misusing $6,000 in federal funds. On the job-starved reservation, the new president soon began packing the tribal payroll with relatives and cronies and firing those who had not supported him. It was what the traditionals had feared forty years earlier, when John Collier had first come to Pine Ridge offering the Oglala Sioux a new form of government.

Dickie Wilson loathed the American Indian Movement. He hated its leaders, its sympathizers and everything the organization stood for. He and his supporters, dependent on the U.S. government and tribal jobs for their livelihood, feared AIM's potential effect on the traditionals and, after a time, he began using federal funds to arm a private police force. Drawn heavily from unemployed, mixed-blood supporters, the private force roamed the reservation, often drunk, looking for troublemakers, harassing, arresting and beating those with darker skin and longer hair. They called themselves the Guardians of the Oglala Nation. The people in the backcountry began referring to them as the "goon squad."

Shortly after arriving on Pine Ridge, Russell Means and other AIM members organized a demonstration to protest the beating death of Raymond Yellow Thunder. Soon, a caravan of a hundred and fifty cars and six hundred Indians streamed across the South Dakota border into Gordon, where they encountered a large force of sheriff's deputies, state troopers, local police and a few FBI agents. A number of reporters and a *Life* magazine correspondent were on hand to cover the event, and it remained tense for two days while Indian leaders demanded justice and an airing out of the community's treatment of Indians.

In years past, Leslie and Melvin Hare had sometimes bragged of catching Indians and hot-wiring their testicles to car batteries. They had been known to buy broken-down horses for ten dollars apiece and tie them to fence posts, betting a six-pack on which man could fell his animal first with an axe handle. The county attorney eventually charged them with Yellow Thunder's death. Both men were later convicted of manslaughter and false imprisonment and sent to prison. Melvin Hare ended up serving ten months of a two-year sentence at the Nebraska State Penitentiary, while his older brother, Leslie, served two years of a six-year sentence.

Before leaving Gordon that winter, AIM had succeeded in getting two Indian prisoners released from jail, a local cop suspended and a pledge from city officials to create a human rights commission. When the caravan crossed back into South Dakota on March 9, life on the Pine Ridge Reservation had been fundamentally altered.

Many traditional Lakota, for years the object of scorn among mixed-bloods, neighboring ranchers and in the white border towns, had long felt powerless to do little more than grind out an existence in the backcountry. In the traditional village of Porcupine, relatives of Raymond Yellow Thunder had gotten nowhere when they asked the federal Bureau of Indian Affairs, the tribal government and a few private attorneys for help. As a last resort, they had turned to AIM. Like many others, the traditional Lakota were at first wary of urban Indians and their organizations. If they had wanted to help, believed many, why were they living in cities and not on the lands of their ancestors? Almost overnight, AIM's commitment and sudden involvement in Gordon earned the city Indians' credibility and respect within the traditional communities. AIM's presence galvanized the elders, the youth, the chiefs and medicine men, providing hope where little had existed. Among many, it awakened a long-dormant sense of self-respect and pride, feelings that also began to emerge in the urban Indians. After years away from the land and their people, some started hearing the language again, going to the sweat lodge, following the medicine men and listening to the elders.

The Gordon incident had led to the first significant alliance between urban and rural Indians, and before long, Oglala traditionals asked AIM to help investigate their treaty and land rights, complaints of police brutality and the wisdom of extending reservation mining leases. It is what Dickie Wilson, the BIA, the FBI and the Nixon administration had feared all along.

Richard Nixon was widely admired by many of the Indian people. As president, he restored the Menominee to tribal status and had returned Mount Adams to the Yakima, another sixty thousand acres to the Warm Springs tribes of Oregon and a large tract of land, including their sacred Blue Lake, to the Taos Pueblo. Nixon had also ignored the "termination" practices prevalent in the 1950s—federal policies designed to dissolve tribal constitutions, dismantle the reservations and relocate their inhabitants in American cities, thus opening up Indian land for the government and private corporations. Instead, Nixon initially embraced the concept of self-determination.

By early 1972, however, his administration was overwhelmed. National Guard troops had shot and killed four white students at Kent State and tens of thousands of antiwar demonstrators continued to organize and march in opposition to the Vietnam war. In the security-conscious White House, the president's men became obsessed with student activists, urban terrorists, Black Panthers, communists and Democratic opponents, with any individuals or groups that posed a real or imagined threat to national security. Soon, Watergate would consume Nixon and his staff.

Throughout the 1970s, the U.S. government also had a renewed interest in marshaling its domestic resources. Weary of depending on foreign oil, the government wanted to shore up its own energy reserves to ensure that the country's economic welfare could not be threatened by hostile nations abroad. Indian lands offered vast quantities of valuable natural resources. They contained large timber reserves, mining operations and mineral deposits. A number of reservations held substantial oil and gas reserves and extensive coal deposits, easily accessible to strip-mining, and many tribes had leased their lands at rates exceedingly favorable to the government and multinational corporations. In government parlance, these lands were sometimes called "national sacrifice areas."

Working together, private corporations and the government

envisioned a massive power-grid of coal-firing plants and thermal-generation stations sweeping out of the west, delivering cheap energy and large corporate profits. By 1972, billions of dollars were at stake in the mineral-rich Indian lands of the western United States.

Twenty years earlier, uranium had also been discovered at the southern edge of the Black Hills. In the Cold War era of nuclear stockpiling, uranium became a prized commodity, one the military desperately needed to remain competitive with the Soviets. By the late '60s, a newfound domestic market for nuclear energy created a dramatic rise in the price of uranium. With uranium prices soaring, multinational corporations began an intense exploration of the entire Black Hills region. In the spring of 1972, Oglala traditionals were asking the American Indian Movement to help them enforce the Fort Laramie Treaty of 1868, the treaty that had once set aside all of the Black Hills for the Lakota people.

Edith Bull Bear was eighty-five in the fall of 1972. Early on the morning of November 3, a four-mile caravan of Indian activists arrived in Washington, D.C. The caravan, inspired by Martin Luther King's March on Washington in 1963, had been conceived at a Rosebud Sun Dance that summer, refined in Denver and polished in St. Paul, Minnesota. It began on the West Coast in October, then crossed through the Great Plains and headed east, picking up hundreds of Indians—young and old, traditional and nontraditional, from cities and reservations—along the way. Known as the Trail of Broken Treaties, the caravan and its leaders hoped to illuminate the inequities of American Indian life, much as the massive civil rights demonstration had done for blacks almost a decade earlier. The leaders arrived with a twenty-point proposal, and near the top of the list was the proposition that American Indians should be governed by their original treaties. For the Lakota, the Treaty of 1868 was paramount.

When the caravan entered the nation's capital on election eve

1972, Edith Bull Bear was believed to be the oldest AIM member who had journeyed to Washington in the name of Indian civil rights.

"Before she left, she got all of us together and she told us it was O.K. to give your life for something you believe in," said her grandson, Guy Dull Knife Jr. "Mom was too sick to go then, but Grandma was still active and so she went. She had never hesitated to speak her mind and she was a political force at an age when most of the others had long since given up. After that, we started calling her 'Grandma Militant.' "

Chief Fools Crow and Charlie Red Cloud, grandson of the famed Oglala, had joined the caravan, too. When the elders arrived at the church where they were supposed to stay, it was full of rats. Among the caravan leaders were Russell Means and Dennis Banks, a Minnesota Ojibwa and co-founder of AIM. Leonard Peltier, a young Ojibwa-Sioux from North Dakota, was chosen to help coordinate security. The leaders refused to let their chiefs and elderly stay in the church. Instead, they decided to go to the federal Bureau of Indian Affairs.

When they arrived at the BIA building, events soon got out of hand. Leaders had asked for a meeting with high-ranking Nixon officials and they wanted decent housing for the elderly. Neither was granted, and about 6 p.m., when a riot squad arrived to evict them, a melee ensued. Doors and windows were shattered and some of the younger Indians went on a rampage, doing considerable damage to the building's interior. While federal police ringed the BIA headquarters, the Indian activists barricaded themselves inside.

"Grandma said it was scary and spooky inside the building," Guy Dull Knife Jr. said. "She said no one knew what to do and they thought they would all be shot. She said she sometimes gave the younger people pep talks. She told them the story of her father and she said they couldn't let something like that happen again. She told them that to die for something you believed in was a good thing. From what she had always heard and believed in, she told them, it wasn't so bad on the other side, in the Spirit World."

After five days, the standoff ended. The government provided

$66,000 to pay for the Indians' transportation out of town, and the caravan left Washington in a wave of bad publicity. Two months later, the government essentially rejected the group's twenty-point proposal and the FBI classified AIM as a radical organization. Its leaders were placed high on the bureau's list of "key extremists."

Edith Bull Bear and the Oglala delegation returned to Pine Ridge, where AIM's role in the occupation of the BIA had enraged the tribal president. Dickie Wilson got a resolution banning all AIM activities on the reservation and he asked U.S. marshals to help secure the local BIA building. Earlier that year, AIM had returned from the Gordon protest and held a celebration on Pine Ridge, and Wilson assured his supporters there would be no repeat this time. "If Russell Means sets foot on this reservation, I, Dick Wilson, will personally cut his braids off," the president said.

After years of living in California and Ohio, Russell Means, an enrolled tribal member, had decided to return to the traditional community of Porcupine. He wanted to study traditional Lakota ways and establish a food co-op. It was common knowledge throughout the reservation that he would also run for president of the Oglala Sioux Tribe. Late in 1972, while he was trying to tell residents in the village of Oglala about the Trail of Broken Treaties, Means was arrested by BIA police and taken to the local jail.

Guy Dull Knife Jr. was eating breakfast at a café in the village of Pine Ridge one morning when the tribal president walked over and asked him what he was driving. Guy Jr. nodded toward a battered Ford Mustang parked outside and Dickie Wilson said that was too bad. He said he could be driving a new car. A BIA police car. Guy Jr. didn't answer. He finished his breakfast and walked out.

"He wanted to get guys who had been to Vietnam. He was afraid of their knowledge of weapons and their training, what they could do, and he wanted them on his side. He tried to recruit them as soon as they returned, while they were still walking around in a kind of daze. He asked Byron, too, but Byron gave him the same answer I did."

Byron DeSersa had also done a tour in Vietnam, as a grunt with the Fourth U.S. Infantry. After he returned, the two old friends spent a lot of time together. Byron more or less moved in with the Dull Knife family on Red Water Creek and they often talked about the war and the conditions on the reservation. They were worried about what they saw.

"You could go to the jail in Pine Ridge every Monday morning and when they released the drunk tank, there would only be full-bloods," Guy Jr. said. "No half-breeds. The half-breeds were all cops and they never hassled their own. Only the full-bloods. At that time, if you were a full-blood, you could expect no justice on or off the reservation. It got to the point where the only justice you could count on was if you had a gun."

On the evening of January 21, 1973, Wesley Bad Heart Bull, an Oglala full-blood, was fatally stabbed by a white man outside a bar in Buffalo Gap, South Dakota, a small town west of the Pine Ridge Reservation. After Darold Schmitz was charged with second-degree manslaughter, the state's minimum homicide charge, the victim's mother asked AIM for help. AIM leaders wanted the charge upgraded to murder and they wanted to protest what they felt was a dual system of justice in the state.

On February 6, more than two hundred Indians marched into the Black Hills, to the courthouse in Custer, South Dakota, for an open meeting with tense state officials. When local whites heard of AIM's plans, they got their guns and unsuccessfully tried to blockade all roads into the hills. Heavily armed police were called in and they eventually told the angry group that only Russell Means, Dennis Banks and two others would be allowed inside. When the victim's mother tried to enter, police grabbed her, saying she had cursed them, and a riot swept the town. An abandoned chamber of commerce building burned to the ground, a section of the courthouse went up in smoke and two police cruisers were overturned and set on fire. There was an hour-long rampage of tear gas, fighting and confusion.

When it ended, thirty Indians were jailed on charges of rioting,

arson, burglary and malicious damage. Of the thirty, nineteen were
later indicted, including Sarah Bad Heart Bull. Her son's killer, free
on five-thousand-dollar bond, was never jailed and received a two-
month suspended sentence. Mrs. Bad Heart Bull, a forty-four-year-
old mother of four, was eventually convicted and sentenced to one to
five years in state prison. Back on the reservation, Dickie Wilson
issued a formal press release suggesting state officials kill all AIM
members, and he offered his private police force to assist. Shortly
after the riot ended, the U.S. Attorney General sent sixty-five federal
marshals to Pine Ridge.

Guy Dull Knife Sr. had represented the rural people of the Medicine
Root District for more than twenty years and had called the Pine
Ridge Reservation home all his life. A week after his seventy-fourth
birthday, he joined the chiefs and medicine men, the elders and many
of the traditional Oglala, for a series of meetings in a community log
house called Calico Hall, just west of Pine Ridge village. Wilson had
fired the tribe's elected vice-president for supporting AIM and had
recently canceled a scheduled hearing on his own impeachment.
When the traditionals went to the BIA a week earlier, to protest the
illegally canceled hearing and cheap land rentals for outside ranchers, they were turned away from their building by heavily armed
U.S. Marshals, fortified with sandbags and machine guns. All open
meetings had been banned and FBI agents continued to arrive in
increasing numbers. The goon squad roamed and terrorized at will,
and the traditionals no longer felt safe in the lands that had been set
aside for them more than a century ago.

It was up to the chiefs and the people, as it had always been, and
on the evening of February 27, the headmen of the tribe decided to
make a stand. About six hundred people crowded into Calico Hall
that night. Guy Dull Knife Sr. arrived with Rose's brother, Stephen
Bull Bear. With the backing of the people, Chief Fools Crow
announced they had decided upon a symbolic confrontation. And
they had decided, once again, to ask AIM for help. Ellen Moves

Camp, a tribal health worker and Wanblee mother of six, had lost her job for supporting AIM. She was at the meeting when the decision was made.

"We decided that we did need the American Indian Movement in here because our men were scared, they hung to the back. It was mostly the women that went forward and spoke out. . . . And when we kept talking about it, then the chiefs said, 'Go ahead and do it, go to Wounded Knee. You can't get in the BIA office and the tribal office, so take your brothers from the American Indian Movement and go to Wounded Knee and make your stand there. . . .' "

Late that night, Guy Dull Knife Sr. and Stephen Bull Bear joined a caravan of three hundred Lakota that drove in the dark to the small village of Wounded Knee. The two elders watched from their car as the white-owned trading post was stripped of food, clothing, a few guns and ammunition. As police began to move in, the two old men avoided a pair of roadblocks, drove back to Red Water Creek and told their families what had happened.

By the morning of February 28, the village of Wounded Knee was surrounded by a force of U.S. Marshals, FBI agents, BIA police and Wilson's private army. Access roads were barricaded and the area sealed off. Within a few days, the federal government moved in seventeen armored personnel carriers, truckloads of .30-, .50- and .60-caliber machine guns and crates of fully automatic rifles. Stored in the BIA building were boxes of armor-piercing, .357-Magnum shells, AR-15 rifles, 41,000 rounds for the M-1s and 133,000 rounds of M-16 ammunition. They were bolstered by 24,000 flares, a dozen M-79 grenade launchers, 600 cases of C-S gas, 100 rounds of M-40 high explosives and a fleet of helicopters. For a while, there was talk of bringing in the Eighty-second Airborne, the army's elite paratrooper division.

Inside the village, the three hundred Indian men, women and children huddled with their leaders: Russell Means, Dennis Banks and an Oglala named Pedro Bissonette. The people decided they would not leave until the government agreed to evaluate the many complaints of police abuse, investigate the BIA and reexamine their rights under the Treaty of 1868. Unlike in Washington, they agreed not to give up until they had a firm commitment. They had not planned on a long occupation, only a few days to dramatize the conditions on the reservation. Before the week ended, the Crow and Northern Cheyenne canceled mining leases on their reservations, potentially jeopardizing the excavation of coal, oil and uranium in Montana. When the South Dakota Sioux leaders proclaimed an Independent Oglala Nation on Pine Ridge, the tribal president labeled AIM a communist conspiracy led by renegade terrorists. Soon, there was little food left in the village, and police roadblocks were allowing none into Wounded Knee.

Off and on for the next few months, Guy Dull Knife Jr. was one of many men and women who traveled the reservation at night, coming over the hills of the backcountry and slipping into the village with packs of food, medicine, weapons, ammunition and winter clothing. They knew the land, had lived there all their lives, and they were able to get around the roadblocks and run supplies into the besieged village.

"When Grandma Edith first heard about what happened, she threw a fit. 'You should be down there in that village helping your people instead of sitting around up here on your butts. Now get going,' she told us."

Both sides had constructed bunkers, and on nights when he traveled the backcountry alone, running supplies, Guy Dull Knife Jr. could hear the distant gunfire and smell the gas and he could see the red flares burning the land. This was his home, he thought, and the government had sent him to Vietnam to fight for it. And when he returned, they had propped up a corrupt dictator and armed his goons and come after his people for demanding democracy on the reservation. "Pine Ridge was more dangerous for me than Chu Lai," he said. "We had become the VC in our own homeland."

As the siege made front-page news, Indian people began to arrive from throughout the country. They had no place to stay and makeshift camps sprang up across the reservation. At the Dull Knife home, they came from Minnesota, New York, Illinois and California.

Sniper fire made staying near the roads too dangerous, so the old man let them camp on Red Water Creek. A young Micmac from Nova Scotia, Anna Mae Aquash, helped cook the meals some nights and they often made bonfires and danced in the traditional way. Alcohol and drugs were forbidden, and in the evenings, Guy Dull Knife Sr. led the sweat lodge ceremonies.

The stalemate ended on May 8, 1973, after the government agreed to send a White House delegation to discuss the Treaty of 1868 with the traditional Oglala. After seventy-one days, it had cost $7 million and was the longest armed conflict in the United States since the Civil War. Two Indians died from gunfire and a federal marshal was partially paralyzed. Ten weeks and tens of thousands of rounds had left the small village in ruin. Alone among the structures not damaged was the memorial on the hill above Wounded Knee Creek, the mass grave containing the remains of Big Foot and his people.

Not long after the roadblocks went up during the occupation, he quit his job at the moccasin factory. It was too dangerous and he had taken to driving an ambulance for a while. By the summer of 1973, Guy Dull Knife Jr.'s nerves had gone bad again and he began to drink; his mind was not on the job or the condition of his people. Rose was very sick—diabetes and her heart. They had taken her to the hospital in Gordon and the doctors said he and his father shouldn't be too far away. For most of three days, he sat by the bed and held her hand. She told him to stop drinking and take good care of his father, that he probably wouldn't live much longer. After a time, she couldn't talk anymore and she seemed to be asleep. On the evening of July 22, she opened her eyes and looked around and found the eyes of her son. He squeezed her hand and she closed her eyes.

More than two hundred people came to the log house on Red Water Creek to pay their respects. After the wake, the family bought an expensive leather satchel and filled it with the things she would need for the journey to the other side. The son put her finest clothes inside and his father brought a bag of fresh *waʃna*. They put her sacred pipe in the bag and an eagle feather and forty silver dollars. At the grave, Edith Bull Bear placed Rose's medicine bag in her daughter's hands and she was laid to rest.

Edith took it hard. The strong old woman had outlived her daughter and the grief overwhelmed her. By early 1975, her health had deteriorated badly. She died on February 2, Rose's birthday. In the Episcopal cemetery a mile south of Kyle, where Chief Little Wound and his black adopted son, *Ha Sapa,* and Lone Bull are buried, the mother and daughter lie side by side.

The old man could not adjust, could not live in the house anymore, and a few months after Rose died, he and his son moved to Wanblee, a traditional community about forty miles northeast of Kyle, at the edge of the Dakota Badlands. They kept their land, but they no longer ranched. Guy Dull Knife Jr. got married in Wanblee and he and his first wife, Pearl, eventually had four small children to care for. They all lived in the same house and the young grandchildren helped the old man think about something besides Rose. To support his growing family, Guy Jr. took a job with the Community Action Program while his father continued to serve on the tribal council, working with other traditionals to bring democracy back to Pine Ridge.

In the aftermath of Wounded Knee, neither complaints of BIA corruption nor a reevaluation of the 1868 treaty were seriously considered and no attempts were made to prosecute Dickie Wilson or members of his private police force. Instead, the government arrested 530 people, indicting 185 on charges of conspiracy, larceny, arson, theft and assault for their roles in the occupation. Three of its principal leaders—Banks, Means and Bissonette—were grouped together for a separate trial in St. Paul, where a judge and jury eventually acquitted Banks and Means of all charges. The trial judge, a one-time Assistant U.S. Attorney in South Dakota, was displeased with both the FBI's and the government's handling of witnesses and evidence in the case. "It's hard for me to believe," U.S. Judge Alfred Nichol said, "that the FBI, which I have revered for so long, has stooped so low."

Of the government, Nichol said, "I am forced to conclude that the prosecution acted in bad faith at various times throughout the course of the trial and was seeking convictions at the expense of justice. . . . The waters of justice have been polluted, and dismissal, I believe, is the appropriate cure for the pollution in this case."

Charges against the third leader, Bissonette, had been dismissed earlier on the grounds of gross government misconduct. On October 17, 1973, BIA police fatally shot the Oglala leader, claiming he had reached for a gun when they tried to arrest him. The gun was never produced and the case never investigated. During the next three years, more than sixty unsolved murders would occur on the Pine Ridge Reservation.

With the occupation over and many of its participants tied up in lengthy trials, the goon squad went on a rampage. The names of traditionals who had supported AIM were kept on a list and the homes of known and suspected sympathizers became frequent targets of vigilante shootings. Beatings and arrests were commonplace. Chief Fools Crow's home was fire-bombed and burned to the ground. The homes of Eddie White Dress and Severt Young Bear were riddled with bullets. Nine-year-old Mary Ann Little Bear lost an eye in a drive-by shooting.

"The reservation back then was run like the Mafia. People were kept in line by intimidation and violence," Guy Dull Knife Jr. said. "If you did anything to try and buck the system, you ended up face down in a ditch."

He and Byron DeSersa began to spend more and more time together. After Vietnam, DeSersa became a tribal attorney, got married and eventually joined AIM and moved to Rapid City. He traveled a lot, and when he came to the reservation, he often went to the Dull Knife home in Wanblee, staying for weeks at a time. One morning in late June 1975, he and his wife were en route to Pine Ridge from Hot Springs, South Dakota. It was a warm day and when the radiator on their car overheated, they drove onto the property of friends, the Jumping Bulls, near the traditional village of Oglala.

While he and a few others were trying to repair the broken radiator, they heard gunfire from across the hills, not far away. The shooting continued off and on for some time and then there was a good deal of confusion. DeSersa and his wife ran down a hill, through a thick grove of trees, until they reached White Clay Creek. Soon, swarms of FBI, BIA police, state troopers, Wilson's private force and local ranchers had surrounded the property. Later that day, DeSersa and his wife began walking the backcountry, eventually arriving at his home village of Manderson about twelve miles east of the Jumping Bull property.

It wasn't long before they learned that two FBI agents and an Indian had been killed in the shootout, prompting the largest manhunt in FBI history. Eventually, four AIM members were arrested and indicted on first-degree murder charges in the deaths of the two agents. Three were ultimately acquitted. The fourth, Leonard Peltier, was convicted and sentenced to consecutive life terms in a disputed case that has spawned years of controversy.

By early 1976, a new sense of hope began to spread slowly across the Pine Ridge Reservation. Al Trimble, a respected, hard-working mixed-blood from Wanblee, had overwhelmingly defeated Wilson in the tribal elections. Wilson would remain in office until April, when Trimble was scheduled to be sworn in as the new president of the Oglala Sioux.

On the afternoon of January 30, 1976, Guy Dull Knife Jr. and Byron DeSersa drove to Interior, South Dakota, a small town about thirty-five miles northwest of Wanblee, to buy groceries. When they returned a few hours later, two friends ran up the driveway as they were unloading the food. They were scared and out of breath. A caravan of goons had rolled into Wanblee, they said, and they had been unloading weapons and ammunition in a house across the street. The BIA police were with them. They told Guy and Byron to be careful.

Inside the family home, his father and father-in-law were watching over the small grandchildren. Guy Jr. and Byron stood by the car, nervous, not sure what to do. After a bit, Guy Jr. reached beneath the driver's seat and pulled out a fully automatic M-1 rifle with a 30-round banana clip. Byron reached down and grabbed a 12-gauge. When he stood up, a bullet ricocheted off the car roof and Guy Jr. opened fire, spraying the house across the street until Byron made it safely inside, where they both dove on the floor.

A hail of bullets poured into the side of the house, and Guy Jr. screamed for his father and father-in-law to get the children in the basement. He and Byron low-crawled across the living room, returning fire until the shell casings piled up on the floor and they ran out of ammunition. When the firing stopped, the goon squad, armed with AR-15s and government-issue bulletproof vests, surrounded the house.

"They were bitter about losing the election," said Guy Jr., "and they wanted to retaliate while they were still in power. My father and all of the people of Wanblee had campaigned hard for Trimble and my name had been on their hit list for a long time. So they came looking for us and some of the others in Wanblee."

BIA police soon arrived and kicked in the front door. The children started screaming and the old man ran up the basement steps. The cops told Guy Jr. they were taking him to jail for possession of an unregistered automatic weapon, assault and battery, and resisting arrest. Three weeks shy of his seventy-seventh birthday, the old man confronted the cops in the front yard. "Dad told them, 'If you're going to take my son away, then take them, too.'" He was pointing to the goon squad. The cops ignored him and handcuffed Guy Jr., shoving him into the back of a squad car.

Guy Dull Knife Jr. did not think he would make it to the Pine Ridge village jail. Neither did Byron. There was a hundred miles of open road between Wanblee and the jail. The remote and rugged Badlands was only a few miles away. In Lakota, Byron told his friend he would follow behind as far as Kyle. From Kyle, he would arrange for others to escort the police car to the Pine Ridge village jail. When they reached Kyle, the arrangements were made and

Byron and a few passengers turned around and quickly headed back to check on the old man and other friends in Wanblee. About a mile from town, a four-wheel-drive truck overtook Byron's car and the goon squad opened fire, shredding the door on the driver's side.

Three .44-Magnum shells tore into his leg and DeSersa lost control of the car. When the truck pulled up behind them, he told the other passengers to run. They took off into the trees with the goons behind them. His leg nearly severed, DeSersa dragged himself across the front seat of the car and out the door, but he could not make it up the steep embankment. Black Elk's great-grandson bled to death in a ditch along Highway 44 outside of Wanblee.

They put Guy Jr. in a cell by himself at the rear of the jail. He thought they might beat him unconscious and then hang him, making it appear a suicide. He said it had happened to others. Instead, a trustee told him later that he had just heard a radio dispatcher directing an ambulance to Wanblee. The trustee said there had been a shootout and Byron was dead. Alone in his cell that night, Guy Jr. wept for the first time in years.

In the morning, the police let him go. He figured they wanted to get him alone on the road back to Wanblee. His father-in-law was waiting for him outside the jail and they made it back home without any trouble. The old man was badly shaken, but he calmed down when he saw his son. He told Guy Jr. the goons had returned the night before and shot up the town, but the people had banded together and driven them back to Pine Ridge.

After a few days, word got back that the goons had put a bounty on him. His friends put him in a car and drove to Rapid City, about a hundred miles west of Wanblee. In the Lakota Homes section of town, Guy Dull Knife Jr. stayed with Auntie Bessie. It was a bad time for him, one of the worst. Cut off and alone, he could not attend the wake and funeral of his best friend. After a while, some of the AIM people brought money and helped move him out of state.

On February 24, not long after Guy Jr. left South Dakota, a rancher discovered the body of a woman in a pocket of the Badlands not far from Wanblee. She had died from a .38-caliber slug fired into the back of her head. The victim was Anna Mae Aquash, the woman who had sometimes helped prepare meals at the Dull Knife camp during the occupation. She had worked long and hard for the traditional people and was loved by many on Pine Ridge. Her killers were never found. Four men were eventually charged with the murder of Byron DeSersa. Two were acquitted and the two others served two years each for the killing.

Guy Dull Knife Jr. ended up in Sheridan, Wyoming. He was there for three months, wanting to go back home, waiting for someone to tell him it was safe. He was worried sick about his family and his elderly father and the promises he had made to his mother. He didn't know anyone in Sheridan and he got lonely and depressed. His nerves got the better of him and he started with the bottle again, heavily, waiting for someone to tell him he could go home and not have to worry about ending up in the Badlands.

In April 1976, a large celebration occurred in Wanblee after Al Trimble was sworn in as the new president of the Oglala Sioux Tribe. Guy Dull Knife Jr. left Wyoming and came back home. For the Pine Ridge traditionals, many of whom had grown accustomed to taking shotguns for the short drive to school and back, it was the first time in years they could sit in their homes, visit friends, ride the reservation roads with their children and not have to worry so much. The first time in years they had something to celebrate.

The traditional Lakota had always loved their land and culture. For many, these were one and the same and they had fought for both, had not wanted to see either overwhelmed and destroyed by those who did not feel the same, Indian or white. They had suffered and endured a long reign of terror during much of the 1970s, and when it ended, they began to see some changes they hoped would improve the lives of their people.

After Trimble became president, the goon squad faded away and the lawless state ended. Traditionals who had joined and supported AIM were elected to the tribal council and many found decent jobs in tribal government. The BIA police system was dismantled in 1977, replaced by a tribal police force composed of officers elected by people from the rural districts they served.

The reservation poverty did not go away. Beginning in the late 1960s and early '70s, cluster housing had come to Pine Ridge, pulling people off their land and packing them into homes concentrated in small areas. The cluster housing created Indian ghettos throughout the reservation, and almost overnight, it increased the already substantial problems associated with alcohol. Poor sewage, plumbing and roads followed the move from rural life to tract housing, and government statistics eventually determined that the Oglala Sioux were the poorest people in America.

But in the aftermath of Wounded Knee, something else also occurred on the reservation that never found its way into the batch of statistics traditionally used to measure community wealth. The education of Lakota children on Pine Ridge fundamentally changed. Its principal schools had always been called day schools, the names reflecting their location or a government-issued number. Beginning in the late 1970s, all the names were changed. The Kyle Day School became the Little Wound School, and day schools in Allen and Pine Ridge were renamed in honor of chiefs American Horse and Red Cloud. In Wanblee, teenage students now went to Crazy Horse High School.

Inside, teachers no longer told Lakota children they were a conquered people. History books began to reflect their own culture as well as the dominant one. Sections on the Civil War included information on what Indian people were doing then and how government policy affected them. They were told how their tribal government originated and how it worked, knowledge previously reserved only for the state and federal government. The schools helped provide Lakota children with a sense of who they were and where they came from that had been missing for three generations.

There were changes outside the classroom, too. Christian names increasingly gave way to ancestral names. In Kyle, the Oglala Lakota College added numerous language, history and traditional culture courses; a new radio station on Porcupine Butte eventually began broadcasting native music, powwow dates, songs dedicated to deceased loved ones, a wide range of public service announcements and interviews with tribal elders. An Indian-owned and operated newspaper — *The Lakota Times* — started covering all aspects of Pine Ridge life, and in time, a rich cultural identity began to emerge among a new generation of Oglala.

Outlawed for the most part throughout the Wilson years, the Sun Dance also returned to Pine Ridge. During the Moon of Red Cherries, parents began going into the hills once again and their children started to learn the traditional songs and understand what they had meant to the Lakota people.

In the summer of 1976, during the nation's bicentennial celebration, Guy Dull Knife Jr. made a vow to participate in the ritual that tribes of the northern plains had observed for hundreds of years. The traditional Sun Dance was near Wanblee that year, and though he was young and healthy, he was still a little afraid. Those who pledged would pray and dance around the sacred cottonwood tree, facing the sun for four days without food or water. The dancers would sacrifice their bodies and offer their suffering for the good of everyone, as they had always done, and the people would thank them for their bravery and courage, for making them stronger.

That summer, the medicine man entered the sacred dance circle on the afternoon of the third day, pouring cups of water on the ground in front of them. Their lips were severely chapped and swollen under the boiling sun. Guy Dull Knife Jr. felt light-headed and he thought he might pass out when the cold water hit his feet. The old man was among the singers and drummers gathered in a circle behind them, and their chanting and drumming helped keep his son and the other dancers strong until the medicine man left.

On the afternoon of the fourth day, he lay on his back on a buffalo robe near the cottonwood tree and the medicine man pinched his breast and cut a hole through the folds of his flesh with a knife. Guy Jr. had an eagle-bone whistle clenched in his teeth and when the knife went in, the whistle snapped in half. The medicine man skewered a cherry stick through the hole and helped him up and the Sun Dance leaders brought out a rope with one end attached to the cottonwood tree and they fastened the other end to the stick in his breast. He began to dance and pray, leaning backward, his arms at his side, straining against the rope until it grew taut, trying to use the weight of his body to pull the stick from his chest. He kept leaning backward, pulling harder and harder, until the stick finally came through the flesh and he was free.

In the Sun Dance of the Lakota, the dancers often dedicate their sacrifice to the spirit of loved ones, to help ease their passage to the other world. In the summer of 1976, Guy Dull Knife Jr. dedicated his to Byron DeSersa.

For a long time, he enjoyed his new job as director of the tribe's Community Action Program. In Wanblee, he wanted to try something different, to create programs that would help both the elders still living on their land and the young kids packed in cluster housing. Guy Jr. was looking for programs that could cut through the red tape and fulfill practical, day-to-day needs. Many of the rural elderly still relied on stoves for winter heat, so he initiated a wood-cutting service. Using tribal money, he hired eight men who spent three days a week chopping and gathering wood and two days delivering it. They stockpiled the wood near the old people's homes, and the elders used it for heating and cooking fuel. He also created a Hot Meals on Wheels program that was among the first on Pine Ridge offering free food deliveries to the elders.

For the kids, he tried to start a summer basketball league and made sure there were nets on the outdoor baskets at Crazy Horse High School. The CAP office also attempted to organize a summer baseball league, chalking out a ball diamond, getting equipment, hiring coaches, compiling rosters and creating schedules. But there were problems with parents and getting the coaches and equipment, and the program never really got off the ground.

After a time, Guy Jr. found it difficult to keep his mind off the art he had enjoyed as a boy in the old Kyle Day School. He had begun to paint again and he was surprised at how soothing it felt, how much he enjoyed it and how much it meant to him. As CAP director, he was in frequent contact with many of the Oglala elders on the eastern edge of the reservation and he often asked them about the old ways and customs, the clothing and rituals and how it used to be. Painting, he knew, was only two-dimensional and he wanted to try something different. He had an idea and so he talked to the old people every chance he got. He often wished his mother and grand-mother were still alive. They had known the history of his people as well as anyone and he had a lot of questions now that had not occurred to him when he was younger.

A few months before her death, Edith Bull Bear had made one last journey away from home. In December 1974, she and four dozen Lakota traveled five hundred miles to a federal courthouse in Lincoln, Nebraska, where sixty-five defendants were on trial on various criminal charges stemming from the occupation at Wounded Knee. The defendants had asked the judge to dismiss the charges, claiming the U.S. government had no jurisdiction to prosecute them under the Treaty of 1868, a treaty they said the government had violated by illegally seizing the Black Hills. Throughout the occupation, the treaty had been the key issue and the trial judge wanted to hear the Lakota perspective, their oral history of the treaty, so he had invited some of the traditionals to his courtroom.

Edith was eighty-seven years old and in poor health. She did not know the English language and she sat quietly in the jury box with the other forty-eight defense witnesses. When her name was called, she arose slowly and told the court she preferred to be sworn in on the sacred pipe instead of a Bible.

Through an interpreter, the old woman stood before U.S. District Judge Warren K. Urbom and recounted what became of her father, Lone Bull, in the years after Wounded Knee. In the direct and simple language she had used all her life, she told him, too, what she knew about the treaty and the ways of her people:

"My grandmother told me about the 1868 treaty. She always talked about the treaty. From what she said, I learned that the government made a lot of promises it kept for only two years. After that, a lot of the promises were broken. . . .

"The land was never given to us. That belonged to us already. White people weren't supposed to come into our country but even with that in the treaty they still came in anyway. . . .

"Before the coming of the white men to our country, whenever we made a promise or made a deal with someone, we respected and honored the word of that promise. . . .

"I was born in Rosebud territory, but I am a Sioux Indian, a Lakota. There is no difference between us—the Rosebud Sioux and the Pine Ridge Oglala. We are Lakota, and whenever we see each other, we shake hands. We are happy to see each other. We traded our best horses with each other. That's our way of life."

The old woman returned to her seat and sat down.

Five years after her death, the United States Supreme Court ruled that the government had illegally confiscated the Black Hills from the Lakota. According to the terms of the Fort Laramie Treaty of 1868, no subsequent changes or land cessions of any kind could be made unless they were approved—in writing—by three fourths of the adult Sioux males. Eight years later, in 1876, a special government commission prevailed in getting the Sioux to relinquish their rights to the sacred Black Hills. The agreement, signed by only 10 percent of the adult Sioux males, was accepted by Congress and passed as the Sioux Act of 1877 a year later. The June 1980 Supreme Court decree upheld an earlier federal claims court decision that "a more ripe and rank case of dishonorable dealings will never, in all probability, be found in our history. . . ." In its effort to open the Black Hills to gold mining, the nation's high court said, a duplicitous government threatened the desperate Sioux with starvation and forced a small group of friendly chiefs and headmen to sign the prewritten agreement—an "abrogation" of the 1868 treaty.

The courts awarded the Lakota $17.5 million in damages, plus interest dating from 1877, a sum amounting to $122 million. When a government commission had first arrived wanting to buy the Black Hills, Crazy Horse had refused even to consider the offer. It was wrong, he said, to sell the land on which the people walked.

More than a century later, the Lakota rejected the $122 million judgment and went back to court. They said they didn't want the money. They wanted the land.

Chapter Twelve

A Century after
Wounded Knee

He used to love driving the backcountry in his beat-up car. In the years after Vietnam and the goon squad, he would get in the old Ford and drive across the land, at all hours of the day and night, different seasons and different landscapes providing stability and calm and the time to think things through. It had changed little over thousands of years, and some days he would drive for an hour and come across a distant rise and see a half-dozen antelope motionless in the vast field, their rumps white in the high, hard heat of late summer, standing quietly in the shortgrass prairie that rolled west toward the darkening hills. The Black Hills were where his people had always believed they came from, the place where the holy woman gave the starving people their sacred pipe and the seven sacred ceremonies, and it is where the winter herds had found shelter before moving out to the open plains in the Moon of Red Grass Appearing. The Lakota had followed them, first on foot and then on horseback, and, alone in his car, he sometimes tried to imagine what it must have been like a little more than a century ago, to come upon the same rise and see the buffalo from hill to horizon, moving slowly through the native grass, occupying all of the space where the half-dozen antelope now grazed.

There was always plenty of time to think on these drives, that was often the point, and he frequently didn't know what thoughts might occur until he was far from the cluster housing and tribal bureaucracy. That, too, was the point. He thought himself a simple man, with simple needs, and whenever it got too complicated, he got in his car and drove the land, and maybe in the middle of a hay meadow, he found himself thinking about Chief Dull Knife and it sometimes made him sad, but most of the time, he felt something else whenever he thought of the journey home from the fort on the White River in the winter of 1879.

He could be in the Badlands in a matter of minutes, his car sweeping dust clouds across the green valley floor, past massive rock formations that looked like prehistoric animals, towering sentinels of sandstone, shale and volcanic ash standing guard along the twisting flanks of a narrow dirt road. If he took the shortcut, he passed Wolf Table and below Devil's Pass, then across a section where irrigation and fertilizer had turned the land into lush green rows of corn. In an hour, the route snaked back into the silent Badlands, ending abruptly at the Stronghold. He would turn off the car and walk between the sheer walls, wondering what was going through the minds of Short Bull, Kicking Bear and Lone Bull, what the Ghost Dancers were thinking when the news arrived from *Cankpe Opi Wakpala.*

Far to the south, the white buttes ringing Manderson are topped in dark green forests of ponderosa pine, powdered in snow during winter, clean and fresh by late spring. Black Elk is buried in Manderson and so is Byron, and he often used to drive the area, sometimes arriving there without knowing it at first, thinking how the pines always smelled in the Moon When the Ponies Shed. It is said that the elderly parents wrapped their son in a red woolen blanket and put him on a travois and traveled north from Nebraska in the early fall of 1877. After three days and nights, they stopped and removed the body, hiding the remains of Crazy Horse somewhere in the hills above Wounded Knee Creek, perhaps in the buttes near Manderson. There are a lot of stories and no one knows for sure. No one ever will.

He had gotten the idea on one of the long drives over the land and he couldn't shake it. Through the canyons and coulees, across the rivers and ravines, in the valleys and forests and prairie, he kept thinking about the old man chief and George Dull Knife and Dewey Beard, about Frank White Buffalo Man, Amos Lone Hill and Vernon Sitting Bear. He often thought of Rose and Edith and he remembered Byron all the time. He wasn't really sure if he could pull it off and he sometimes thought all the driving was a way to buy time, to bolster his courage as much as anything.

"I was kind of at a crossroads back then. When I looked around me, nothing seemed to make a lot of sense. I was really surprised at first how good it felt to be painting again, to be using my hands and my mind at something I had always enjoyed and hadn't done for so long. The old people kind of saved me in a way. They got me interested in the old ways that I had gotten away from and I wanted to do something with that feeling I had, but it was beyond anything I could do with oil and canvas. It was the right time to take a few chances, I thought, and just see what happened. I figured I didn't really have a whole lot to lose."

Guy Dull Knife Jr. wanted to try to sculpt three-dimensional figures, statues that would reflect the history, culture and traditions of the Lakota. He had felt a kind of terror when he first realized how much had been lost, and so he had spent several years talking to the elders, asking questions, studying the old ways, gathering the threads of his people's past. He envisioned a series of statues that would tie it all together, preserve the old way of life for his children and their children, for all the Lakota. The statues would depict many of the different dances that had once been important to his people, dances that said much about their way of life and that few knew how to do or even remembered anymore. They would be sculpted in precise detail, cast in bronze and handpainted and he would dedicate each to a different loved one.

He had no formal training as an artist, had never been to school to study painting or sculpting, but it was an idea he believed in. He had taught himself to paint and he figured he could do the same with sculpting. The lack of experience didn't scare him as much as the thought that all the foundries were in the city, hundreds of miles from his home.

Guy Dull Knife Jr. didn't know if he could leave Pine Ridge, if he could live away from the land and the people. He had been to the St. Louis Job Corps, gone to Fort Lewis, Fort Polk and Vietnam, but it wasn't the same. Each trip away had been for a specific duration and he knew he would return when it ended. For many full-bloods born and raised on the reservation, leaving home was often as daunting now as it had been in the years of Carlisle, Hampton and Haskell a century earlier.

The reservation was an insular world. It had its own customs, language, habits, rhythm and rules. Most everyone had lived there all their lives and they knew and understood what was expected and how to survive within the reservation boundaries. Crossing the border was different. The world of the dominant culture had terrified many full-bloods for generations. Within a few minutes, a few miles, the rules and rhythms changed and expectations were dramatically altered. In the old days, when the Lakota chiefs and headmen first arrived at the soldier forts to talk treaties, they were often amused at what they saw. White officers would sit in a chair for a few moments, glance at their watch, get up and pace, sit back down, look at their watch and start pacing again. The people never understood how a timepiece could prompt such behavior and many still didn't, Guy Jr. among them.

In his youth, he, like many Pine Ridge Lakota, had ventured no farther than the border towns, and the early impressions had never left. He remembered the dirty looks, the waiting for whites to enter first, the standing in line, others cutting in front of them, the occasional cursing, clerks tailing him up and down the aisles and the signs that said NO DOGS OR INDIANS ALLOWED. He often felt afraid and intimidated and he didn't really relax until they crossed back to their own land and people. They were two vastly different worlds and few on Pine Ridge had acquired the necessary skills and courage to compete in the culture that surrounded their homeland.

"When I was a small boy and I had started drawing a little bit, my grandfather always used to encourage me. He would watch me try and draw a horse, the animal that he loved above all others, and he would tell me how good it was and then he would tell me all about the horse and the many different ways we used to use them. Some for hunting just the buffalo, some for pulling the travois, some for courting and some for fighting. He said that when the Lakota first got guns, the noise had spooked the horses. That could be dangerous if they were out hunting buffalo or in a battle, so the warriors would take pine tar and boil it into a kind of gum or putty and then use it to plug the horses' ears. I would listen to all of his stories and then I would try and draw them.

"Later, when I told Dad about what I was thinking of doing, he encouraged me, too. He said if you really wanted to do something and if you worked hard at it and didn't give up, all the hard work and effort was bound to pay off somewhere down the road."

In May 1984, Guy Dull Knife Jr. loaded up the car and crossed the border, taking the road over the shortgrass prairie of South Dakota, through the high plains of eastern Wyoming, then south along the front range of the Colorado Rockies.

Before leaving, he and his first wife had decided to go separate ways. There had been a boy born in 1979 and a girl in 1982. They named the daughter Nellie and they called the first-born son Guy Dull Knife III. The three older children would stay in Wanblee with their mother; the two younger children would go to Denver with their father. Guy Jr. could not leave the old man behind. When Guy Sr. had retired from the tribal council in 1980, they had given him a large flag of the Oglala Sioux Tribe to commemorate his thirty years of service to the people, and the flag was among the items Guy Jr. had carefully packed and put in the trunk of the old car. Heading south on Interstate 25, Nellie and Guy Dull Knife Jr. rode in the front seat. In the back were eighty-five-year-old Guy Dull Knife Sr. and five-year-old Guy Dull Knife III.

He arrived in Lakewood, Colorado, a west Denver suburb, in late spring with the two young children, his elderly father and six dollars. For a while, they moved into the suburban home of a cousin, Barbara Iron Crow, Uncle Daniel's daughter. They had never lived in a place with sidewalks, paved streets, a garage, a fenced-in yard and neighborhood parks, with good plumbing, central heat, air-conditioning and polished wood floors. The old man slipped on the floor in his stockinged feet one day and broke his hip and was laid up for the first few months they were there.

Guy Jr. began looking for work each morning, checking the local papers and employment offices, looking for anything to bring in some money. At a job service center one day, he saw an ad for a body collector. He filled out the application and listed his cousin's phone number, and when the Denver county coroner's office called a few days later, he went in for an interview.

"When I showed up to apply for the job, they explained to me that the work could be pretty gruesome and they asked me upfront if I thought I could handle it. I explained to them that I really needed the job and that I had spent time in Vietnam and had driven an ambulance back on the reservation and so I didn't really think it would be a problem."

One of his first assignments was on a call near Lakewood, not far from where they were living. After the parents of a college-age girl had died suddenly in an auto accident, their daughter had inherited quite a lot of money and she had moved into a spacious, suburban Denver home with twenty-two cats. Police investigators later discovered a diary in the house. The entries showed that she had been overwhelmed by the loss of her parents and had gradually gone from being a normal college student to a severely depressed young woman with serious mental illnesses. In the end, she had starved herself to death. When Guy Jr. and a co-worker arrived, they found hundreds of newspapers piled up inside, leaving only narrow corridors throughout the house. They were told to gather the owner's belongings, and while they were pulling her luggage from a basement storage rack, a piece of the woman's arm fell to the floor. The cats had eaten her and dragged her bones to different parts of the house.

Working long hours for the coroner's office, he eventually saved enough so the family could move into their own rented home, where everyone pitched in with the chores. Guy Dull Knife III helped entertain his younger sister, and the old man often took care of the two grandchildren, telling them stories about his days in the rodeo and his first Sun Dance, about life in the Yellow Bear Camp when he was their age and how it had been for their people in the days when his father was a boy. Guy Jr. did the cooking and cleaning and he mended their clothes. "I don't know exactly how, but I think my mother knew I might end up a bachelor, so she taught me how to cook and sew and it came in handy. We got by O.K."

That fall, on Veterans Day 1984, he and Francis Whitebird went to Washington, D.C., joining thousands of others for the dedication of a memorial to those who had served in the Vietnam war. The memorial depicted three soldiers: one white, one black and the third a composite of Hispanic, Indian and other minorities who had fought in Vietnam. Guy Jr. was taken by the statue. It was rich in detail, cast in bronze at a Long Island foundry, and the expressions of the men captured what it had been like in another place and time.

When he returned to Lakewood, he bought a good stock of paper and several ink pens and he began to sketch some of the faces from his past and a few of the dances that had once defined the Lakota way of life. He knew there were two good foundries in Loveland, fifty miles north of Denver, and he tried to sketch when-ever he could find the time. The job was grueling and he never knew when the phone might ring and he would need to put away his pen and paper and go out on a body call. Some days, when his father wasn't feeling well, Guy Jr. would have to drop off Nellie at his cousin's and take his young son with him.

He got a call one time to remove a dead woman from her home, and when he and his son walked in, they were overwhelmed by the smell. From the foyer, they could see the body lying on a waterbed. He pulled out a handkerchief and covered his nose and told the boy to wait on the porch. Guy Dull Knife III went outside for a while, then came back in and followed his father to the bedroom. Four or five feet from the bed, they saw the woman's hair and skin begin to move and they both jumped back. When the father stepped closer, he saw the maggots covering her body and he told his son to go out in the yard and stay there.

"A lot of times, I couldn't eat for days after removing one of those bodies. I dropped fifty pounds in less than a year. The pay was good, and I needed it, but in the end, I couldn't take it anymore. I don't think any normal person could."

He quit the job after eighteen months and went on food stamps for a while, looking for another line of work in the mornings, drawing at the kitchen table after the old man and the children were asleep. Pine Ridge was 350 miles to the north, and on weekends, holidays and summers, they returned home as often as they could. The children played with their cousins, rode horses and explored the creek bottoms, and the old man could hear the language again and the music and he saw the old crowd of friends he had known all his life.

In Wanblee, Guy Jr. began seeing Cora Yellow Elk. Her great-grandfather, the medicine man Chips, had interpreted the vision of the young Crazy Horse, had given the Oglala war chief his great power, and Cora began telling Guy Jr. the stories of her family. She was quiet and reserved, loved children and had a good sense of humor. He admired her quill and beadwork and thought it the equal of Rose and Edith's. She was taken by his cooking and sewing, his kindness and his artwork. They soon found out they had a lot in common and they began to see each other as often as they could.

In 1989, Guy Jr. and Cora and the two children and his father all moved to Loveland, Colorado. They rented a two-bedroom trailer on the north end of town and decorated it with familiar surroundings. On a wall of the living room, they put the large red and white flag of the Oglala Sioux Tribe, the one presented to the old man after he retired, and on another, they hung a pen-and-ink portrait of Chief Dull Knife. They cleared wall space in the small dining area and put up neat rows of black and white postcards of the old leaders—Little Hawk, Red Horse, Low Dog, Rain-in-the-Face, Gall and Sitting Bull—and they found places for the braided ropes of sweetgrass and holy sage. At the end of the couch was the black humpback trunk George Dull Knife had brought from Paris in the 1890s. Inside, they kept the photographs, souvenirs, keepsakes and mementoes from five generations of Dull Knifes.

Guy Jr. and Cora soon got the kids in a public elementary school, not far from their new home in the north Loveland trailer park. It was the first public school any Dull Knife had ever gone to. He wanted Nellie and Guy Dull Knife III to study hard and get off on the right foot, to learn to read and write and get a better education than he had. He didn't know what they might do as adults, but he knew they would need skills far greater than either he or his father had acquired, and so school was high on the list of priorities. The two children walked to the bus stop each morning and walked home in the afternoon, returning with assignments in math, geography, social studies, health and American history.

Neither Guy Sr. nor Guy Jr. knew how to write, but Cora did. She had attended the Oglala Lakota College in Kyle for a while and she helped the children with their studies. In the evenings, after the homework was finished, the father and grandfather often told the children stories of Lakota history, stories that had been passed down from one generation to the next.

Late one winter afternoon, about a month after they moved to Loveland, the family was getting ready to eat dinner when there was a knock on the door. Guy Dull Knife Jr. got up from the table to answer it. He was surprised to see a Larimer County Sheriff's deputy standing on the front porch of their trailer.

"He wanted to know who I was and what I was doing for a living and why I had chosen to live in Loveland. I didn't really know what to say at first. Finally, I just said that I was a sculptor and that I had moved from the Pine Ridge Reservation to Loveland to be closer to the foundries and my work. I said I hadn't caused any trouble and I wasn't planning on causing any, but from that day on, the city police or the county sheriffs would pull me over two or three times a week and ask me the same questions over and over. Who was I and what was I doing and why had I come to Loveland.

"I almost gave my life for this country four different times and

Grandnephew Sean Brin, Desert Storm.

they acted like I had committed a crime moving from South Dakota to Colorado."

Each time he got pulled over and questioned, they all got nervous. No one knew what to make of it. After two or three months, the questions stopped and he and Cora and the children and his father went about their business.

The old man was now more than ninety years old and he needed to be in a place where there was twenty-four-hour medical care. Guy Jr. began looking for a good nursing home not far from their trailer, and after visiting several, they settled on Sierra Vista, about three miles away. Guy Sr. did not want to go, did not want to leave the family home, but Guy Jr. told his father they would visit often and bring him home on weekends, and the arrangements were made.

Not long after he arrived, the family learned that Uncle Daniel's grandson, Sean Brin, was going to the Middle East. He was with the U.S. Army, his unit among the first scheduled to leave for Saudia Arabia as part of a massive American buildup that would culminate in the Gulf War. Guy Dull Knife Sr. was the family elder, and before his brother's grandson left, he helped prepare the young Lakota soldier for battle. The old man gave Sean an Indian name, *Hupahu Luta*, Red Wing, in honor of the horse his father had loved at the beginning of the century, and he gave him a small flag of the Oglala Sioux Tribe to take to Desert Storm.

During his first few months at Sierra Vista, the old man felt cut off and alone, homesick the way he had been as a teenager at the Haskell Institute and as a young soldier along the western front. Above his bed, Guy Dull Knife Sr. carefully arranged a row of photos of his son, his grandchildren and great-grandchildren, his friends and one of Rose, and he put some sage and sweetgrass on the wall above them. At night, he prayed for Sean and Rose, for the spirits of all the loved ones who had gone to the other side, and he read the old Bible in Lakota most evenings before falling asleep. In the morning, he ate and counted down the hours until he would see Nellie and Guy Dull Knife III after school, and he waited patiently for the weekend, waiting to go back to their home.

Their small metal home on the edge of a trailer park at the foot of the Rocky Mountains housed a diverse range of activities. The family had no telephone, and friends and relatives from Pine Ridge frequently arrived at all hours of the day and night, bringing the latest births and deaths, ailments and illnesses, marriages and divorces, updates on tribal politics, new housing plans, road closings, basketball scores, jokes, gossip, hunting trip results and upcoming pow-wow dates.

Early one evening, a cousin, Webster Poor Bear, pulled in the parking lot, and he and Guy Jr. soon retired to the living room couch, where they sat beneath the portrait of Chief Dull Knife and relived a night they had spent in the Vietnam jungle. Ten feet away, the old man sat quietly in his wheelchair, oblivious to the war stories, watching *Dances with Wolves* on the VCR, staring at the familiar faces, not needing to look at the subtitles. In a large black beanbag chair in the corner, his grandson pulled on a purple and gold Los Angeles Lakers T-shirt and laced up a pair of black Nike hightops, temporarily lost in his Sony Walkman and a Guns 'N Roses tape. Back at the dining room table, Nellie worked out the last of her long-division problems due the next morning. Cora sat across the table, making pipestone earrings. The pipestone, red catlinite quarried in

Minnesota, had been cut in the shape of small peace pipes, and transforming them into earrings was a delicate task. The small pipes were notched at one end and she patiently threaded the hole with sinew and then strung four red and white beads—the Lakota's sacred number and the colors of the Oglala Sioux flag—to the sinew before fastening it to a quill which was tied to a small silver hook that goes through the ear.

Behind the dining room table, at the far end of the trailer, the kitchen sometimes served as both a food processing center and a makeshift studio. A fresh pot of coffee was brewing amid a half-dozen mugs, some clean and dry, some stuffed with paintbrushes. Across the countertop, the dishes, silverware and glasses mixed in with a few paint-stained rags and palettes, a loaf of bread and crackers, a deerhide bag, several piles of colored beads, cans of soup and hamburger patties, a stack of pen-and-ink sketches, a chisel, several lumps of clay and a box of macaroni. On the floor were a baby's high-chair and a thirty-pound block of alabaster.

Guy Dull Knife Jr. eventually carved a small workspace from one of the kitchen corners where, propped against a back wall of the trailer, behind a white bedsheet rigged up to enclose his studio, half a dozen paintings stood in various stages of production. On a small table in front of them were six clay figures, richly detailed, each wearing an elaborate costume that captured a different traditional dance of the Lakota. Each clay model had taken between seventy-five and a hundred hours to complete.

"For the first time in my life," he said, "I found something to do that I really, really loved. Nothing else really seemed to matter. Only the statues."

Guy Jr. taught himself how to sculpt in the Loveland trailer home. When he first began, he would sit at the small table in the kitchen corner working late into the night, using whatever makeshift tools he could find around the house—spoons, knives, chisels, screwdrivers—shaping the mounds of clay over and over, until they gradually began to resemble what he was looking for. Later, after months of feeling his way along, he rented a cheap room in a Loveland motel.

Using coathangers from the room and a pocketknife, he spent the night fashioning a clay model of an Oglala war chief. In the morning, he was surprised at how well it had turned out.

As he improved, he gained confidence and he became more ambitious. He had been saving the block of alabaster until he felt he had acquired the necessary skills, and after a while, he bought an old drill and began to shape the heavy white stone. It was early November then, a raw chill coming down from the mountains, and the dust from the alabaster spread from the kitchen corner through the rest of the trailer. Cora insisted he hang a bedsheet around the cramped workspace, but it did little to stop the dust, and he was told to set up shop in the front yard. He found two old sawhorses and a sheet of half-rotted plywood and set up a worktable. He ran an extension cord out of a trailer window, got his drill and bits, a pack of dust masks and a pair of plastic goggles from Sears, and went to work in the front yard.

He had known from the beginning that he wanted to sculpt a white buffalo emerging from a snow bank out of the alabaster block, but he wasn't certain of the animal's exact proportions, how high the hump arched up behind its head, the length of the legs in relation to the thick body. He got the *Dances with Wolves* tape, stuck it in the VCR, selected a good shot from the chase scene and put the tape on Pause, carefully studying the animal, sketching it a few times with pencil and paper. Then he went back in the yard and began chiseling, bringing the stone in each evening and returning to the yard the next day. The white buffalo now sits in the living room of a well-to-do Des Moines art collector.

In the fall of 1992, the first of the desktop clay models he had made in the kitchen of the trailer home finally emerged from the Loveland Sculpture Works as a sixteen-inch, fifteen-pound bronze statue. More than a dozen years had passed between the idea and execution, and Guy Dull Knife Jr. entitled it "To the Great Spirit." Dedicated to the Lakota medicine men and elders, present and past, the statue depicted a holy man offering the sacred buffalo calf pipe to *Wakan Tanka*. For generations, the Lakota have used the pipe to offer their prayers to the Great Spirit, to the Four Winds and the Four Directions, and to *Maka Ina,* Mother Earth, believing it will help them remember that they and the animals, the birds and fish and the plants, all living things, are meant to look out for one another.

In the bronze statue, the holy man wears eagle feathers, symbolic of exceptional deeds, and the beadwork on his clothes is of an old design, one that Edith and Rose had used all their lives. The beads are black, red, yellow and white, the colors of the four directions.

Guy Jr. had taken Polaroids of the six clay statues in his trailer home and he had shown them to some of the many collectors, dealers and gallery owners in Loveland and nearby Estes Park. He explained what he was trying to do, that he wanted to tell the history of his people through a set of bronze statues, a history he had learned from his parents and grandparents and from the elders of the Pine Ridge Reservation. Several art dealers were intrigued by the photos and his effort to preserve Lakota culture.

An Estes Park dealer, a fellow Vietnam veteran, offered to help. "When he first saw the drawings of the statues, he couldn't speak for a while. He knew, he knew right away—in the way a lot of us who came back from Vietnam know these things—what the statues meant to me and why I had worked so hard on them." The art dealer loaned him the money to get started and made some introductions and, after a time, Guy Jr. got his own workbench and access to modern tools, equipment and expertise at the Loveland Sculpture Works. He and Cora started taking the children to school, then driving to his studio, where he spent the day converting pen-and-ink drawings to clay models to plaster molds to melted wax shells and then to bronze statues.

All along, his dream had been to do eighteen dancers, cast in three sets of six dancers each. Money and time were a constant problem. As they had since leaving Pine Ridge, they were living day to day, scraping by, selling a painting, a sculpture, beadwork, some earrings, to pay the rent, keep food on the table and the kids in clothes, help pay for his father's medications and still have enough time to keep working on the statues. There were significant foundry bills, too. For months, Guy Jr. was caught in a bind. Before releasing any statues, the foundry needed money to cover its costs. But he couldn't pay them unless the statues were released from the foundry and sold to collectors. Finally, several patrons and benefactors came up with the money to continue his work.

By early November 1993, the first set of six was finished. After the statue dedicated to the Great Spirit, the next to emerge was of a traditional Lakota dancer. In the old days, his people had come together to eat, play games, race their horses, to sing and dance. At these gatherings, the older men of the tribe would often dance in traditional ways. In the statue, Guy Jr. has the dancer wearing an eagle feather head roach originally made of braided hair from the porcupine and the white-tailed deer. The dancer's cape was of buffalo hide and the breastplate fashioned from buffalo bones tied together with sinew. In one hand is a fan made from the right wing of the spotted eagle. His bustle is of eagle feathers, its beadwork the colors of the four directions. In the other hand, he carries a beaded pipe bag, signifying that he has often journeyed to a distant hill, praying and fasting for four days and nights in the *humbleciya* ceremony, the vision quest. The pipe carrier learned the sacred songs of their ceremonies, and through his wisdom and knowledge, the people came to regard him with honor and respect.

Guy Jr. dedicated the statue of the Traditional Dancer to his uncle, Amos Lone Hill, a pipe carrier and respected elder, a fullblood from the backcountry who had lived his life according to the old ways of the Oglala Sioux.

A third statue was of the Hoop Dancer, a modern, difficult dance using a traditional theme. To the Lakota, the hoop is a circle representing the unbroken cycle of life, a life that comes from the earth and returns to the earth. The circle is divided into four parts, symbolic of the four phases of the moon and the four seasons. The dance begins with the dancer spinning four hoops around his body, and as it progresses, the dancer adds four hoops at a time until there are sixteen or more spinning at once.

Vernon Sitting Bear was from Kyle, a good friend of Guy Jr.'s who used to sing and dance with his Uncle Daniel. On the Pine Ridge Reservation, he was one of the originators of the Hoop Dance and Guy Jr. dedicated the statue to him.

The people had long revered the eagle, and in the old days, there was a special dance to celebrate its place among the Lakota. The dancers used eagle-bone whistles, hoping their sound would be heard and the eagle would know of their gratitude and see the dancers far below. Frank White Buffalo Man was one of the last Lakota who knew how to do the Eagle Dance. "I watched every move he did as a young boy and there was no one like him. Later, when I was in high school, I would go with him into the Black Hills every summer and he would dance and I would sing. I made the statue for him. There's almost no one around anymore who knows how to do this dance, and if a statue could somehow help bring it back, help revive it, that would be the greatest tribute to him."

Two other statues were among the six he finished at the foundry in the fall of 1993. The War Dancer displayed the intricate details of a warrior's life. Guy Jr. sculpted eight eagle feathers, awarded for bravery and acts of kindness, atop a wolfskin headdress, symbolic of the animal's cunning and loyalty and its fierce fighting skill. He used red paint on the warrior's face to reflect a bloody battle, and black paint for the mourning of dead and wounded. Five white dots clustered between the red and black represent close friends and relatives killed or wounded. In the right hand is a raised coup stick used to strike an enemy in battle, the ultimate act of bravery. In his left hand, two scalps hang from a war shield painted with the warrior's personal battle symbols, rain and hail. On his breechcloth and moccasins, a beaded tipi design tells the number of successful raids he has made on Crow and Pawnee camps. The dancer wears a gunbelt and jacket taken off a Seventh Cavalry lieutenant from F Troop and it is dedicated to Dewey Beard.

The last statue depicts the Fancy Dancer, a recent dance that emerged after modern powwows began holding contests. The dancer wears two feathers inserted into hollow bone rockers that are tied to

Three statues by Guy Jr.:
War Dancer, Fancy Dancer, Eagle Dance.
(DAVID PENNEY)

a head roach. Two feather bustles are decorated with dyed plumes matching the beadwork and angora around his ankles. It is one of the Lakota's most colorful, and, throughout, the dancer must keep pace with a rapid, escalating drumbeat, making it one of the most difficult and demanding. "When I first showed his mother a color photograph of the statue, she was really touched by the likeness," Guy Jr. said. He dedicated the Fancy Dancer to Byron.

A friend in Des Moines had arranged for the six statues to be exhibited at a local gallery in early November. Guy Jr. and Cora got a relative to watch the kids, then they carefully packed the statues and took Interstate 80 to Des Moines, seven hundred miles east. On the evening of November 9, 1993, about two hundred and fifty patrons arrived for the exhibit. In a separate room at one end of the gallery, the statues were neatly arranged on dark wood pedestals, each with a card explaining the tradition of the dances. While a Rabbit Dance played from the tape deck and a small braid of sweetgrass burned in one corner, Guy Dull Knife Jr. and Cora Yellow Elk stood quietly behind a table, watching the guests looking at the statues and reading the cards, answering questions about himself, about his life and his people, about the history and origins of his work. They were tired and a little nervous, and when the night ended, the gallery owner said he thought there might be several orders for the full set of eighteen statues. It was the best news they'd had in a long while, and afterward, Guy and Cora, a few friends and the gallery owner all went to a local restaurant to celebrate.

They headed west to Loveland the next day and talked about spending the rest of the winter and early spring at his workshop in the foundry, working on statues of the Horse Dance, the Sun Dance, the Rabbit Dance and nine others that would complete the full set.

Guy Jr. started sculpting clay models for the remaining statues after they got back, and when the kids got their two-week Christmas break from school, the family went to Pine Ridge for the holidays. In early January, they returned to Loveland and when they got to the trailer home, they noticed that someone had busted out the large living room window. The inside had been ransacked, but not much of any value had been taken, so they straightened up the mess and went back to their daily routines.

About two weeks later, Guy Jr. arrived home from the foundry one afternoon and found a small plastic bag hanging on the doorknob. He went inside and opened it and found a Ku Klux Klan pamphlet and several handwritten sheets of paper with swastikas around the top and sides. The handwriting on the Xeroxed papers said Loveland had been a good community before the Indians and Hispanics started moving in and if they had any sense, they would leave town. He read the papers and glanced at the pamphlet and decided to ignore them.

About ten days later, another bag arrived on the doorstep, the messages more personal, directed specifically at the family. It said they were Indians and Indians belonged on reservations, not in Loveland. If they knew what was good for them, they wouldn't try to make a living in a place where they were not wanted. This was not their country. The country belonged to whites, the message said. It was signed "Your Local Klan."

"It was the first time I had ever come across anything quite like that and I couldn't really ignore it. If it had been only me, I wouldn't have paid any attention to it. I figured if I could survive the NVA and the goon squad, I could survive the Klan, or whoever was behind it.

"But Cora was eight months pregnant then and the kids always walked home from the bus stop. We would have Dad with us on the weekends a lot of times and I didn't want anybody to wake up and find a cross burning on the lawn, or worse."

In early February 1994, Guy Dull Knife Jr. decided to leave and moved his family from Loveland to Hot Springs, South Dakota, about forty miles northwest of the Pine Ridge Reservation. The old man's arthritis was acting up in the severe cold and he was confused on the long drive north. Cora was due any day with the baby, and the day after they arrived in Hot Springs, Guy Jr. took his wife and his father to the hospital. Afterward, he started looking for a rental home and quickly made a deposit on a small, two-bedroom bungalow close to the hospital and not far from the school where he enrolled Nellie and Guy Dull Knife III. When relatives from Pine Ridge arrived to look after Cora, the children and his father, Guy Jr. returned to Loveland, making two seven-hundred-mile round-trip drives to gather their clothes, furnishings and belongings.

He arrived back in Hot Springs on the morning of February 12, and that afternoon, Cora went into labor. Thirty-three hours later, they were the parents of a baby girl.

Nellie and Guy Dull Knife III couldn't believe how small their sister was, how much hair she had and how thick and black it was. Their father had picked them up after school on Valentine's Day and brought them to the hospital and everyone stood around the bed while Cora nursed the baby. After a while, Guy Jr. left, saying he would be back in a moment. He walked down the long corridor, toward the opposite end of the hospital. Guy Sr. was sitting up in bed when his son arrived. He helped the old man into his wheelchair and pushed him back the way he had come.

Guy Sr. did not know what had happened until he got inside the room. He had been born in February 1899, and when he saw the little girl born in February 1994, the old smile came back and he rolled his chair to the edge of the bed, staring at the small bundle nursing at its mother's breast. Cora gently lifted the baby and gave her to Guy Jr. and he walked around the end of the bed. The old man held out his arms and cradled the baby in his lap, staring down at her, unable to speak.

After a time, he looked up, looking at the faces in the room, looking at his son.

"*Owang waste.*"

The mother and father both agreed she was beautiful. Guy Jr. told his father that he and Cora had decided on a name during the night. They would call the girl Mary, in honor of the old man's mother, Mary Red Rabbit. The old man looked up at them, and when he started to cry a little, the son put his arm around his father's shoulder.

An old woman shuffles silently along the edge of a dirt path. She carries an empty plastic jug and follows the deep ruts of dirt, downhill and across an open field, toward a red water pump poking up through the weeds at the edge of Wanblee. A young man hobbles toward her, coming out of the field and up the hill, an empty pantleg quietly flapping in the afternoon breeze. At the trailhead, the neighborhood children gather around a foot-deep crater hewn from the roadbank, splashing in the rainwater, shoving and pushing and laughing, sitting all the way down when it gets too hot. Their voices hang in the thick air like dust from the road. "It's my turn . . . go get your squirtgun, Jenny. . . . I'm going to tell your mom. . . . Stop splashing me in my face. . . . When Sherri's mom is drunk, she gets to spend the night at my house. . . ." Neighborhood dogs come and

Four generations of Dull Knifes. Left to right: Tonette, Guy III,
Torrie, Guy Sr. (seated), Nellie, Cora Yellow Elk, Guy Jr.
(BOB FADER)

go, darting near the kids, in and around the passing junkers, hob-
bling down the road that disappears into the barren yards and crum-
bling fences and tarpaper sheds of the cluster housing. Far beyond,
past the old woman and the young man, the kids and the dogs and
the houses, lie the rich green fields, fading into the shortgrass prairie.

In 1994, for the fourth consecutive year, government statistics
defined Shannon County, South Dakota, home of the the Oglala
Sioux, as the poorest county in the United States. The percent of the
people living in poverty was more than four times the national average—63 percent versus 14 percent. Their babies were twenty times
more likely to be born with fetal alcohol syndrome, and the infant

mortality rate was six times the national average. Pine Ridge teenagers killed themselves three times more often than other American teens and, a century after Wounded Knee, an Oglala man was expected to live no more than forty-six years.

Guy Dull Knife Jr. has come to Wanblee to pick up the kids. It is early June, the Moon of the Blooming Turnip. Out of school for the summer, they have been visiting their mother and he wants to pick them up and drive the land, relax, take a vacation, camp out a little, visit some new places and maybe a few old ones. He is relieved now that his father is in a good nursing home in nearby Martin, South Dakota, not far from the old Yellow Bear Camp. "He got a physical before going in—his '100,000-mile checkup'—and the doctors said he's in great shape. He might live forever," said the son. A niece is an administrator at the nursing home, and many of its residents are Pine Ridge elders. When Guy Jr. last saw him, the old man was sitting in the courtyard, in the sun, talking and laughing with eighty-nine-year-old Winnie Good Voice Elk, the widow of his best friend from childhood, the one he had ridden bareback to Martin with, thinking they had gotten drunk on root beer in the early years of the century.

The fort is a good hundred and fifty miles away, and there's no rush. Guy Jr. wants the kids to see and feel what he does and they start out driving the backcountry, past a couple of black and red signs, diamond-shaped, planted in a ditch between Martin and Wanblee, the end of the road for two crash victims. When a male and female bobcat and six cubs dart across the loose gravel a few hundred yards past the signs, he stops the car. Guy Dull Knife III bolts from his seat, scrambles across a ditch and stares at a tree across the barbed wire. The six babies are aligned on a branch, staring back.

"Should I catch one, Dad?"

"No."

"Why not?"

"You see that mother and father in the next tree? That's why."

As a boy, he'd had a bobcat as a pet. Rose nursed it with milk in an eyedropper, then a baby bottle, and they kept it in a box. For a long time, it was like a dog, staying around the house on Red Water Creek, waiting for food, scaring away some of the coyotes. It disappeared into the creek bottom one day and never came back. He didn't think the neighbors in Hot Springs would take kindly to a bobcat.

He can't find the cut-off to *Ti Hanska*, it's been a while, but the kids don't mind. They've never been to the end of the road before, and when they reach it, he points the car toward the faded clapboard church that has stood alone at the top of Yellow Bear for 113 years. The boy and his sister can't wait to explore it; they burst inside and walk by a grizzled potbelly stove at the rear, past a row of chipped wooden pews where a weather-beaten Bible lies open near the front, past the rusty ceiling hooks where kerosene lanterns once hung and up to the loft, home to families of swallows and pigeons and an occasional owl.

Guy Dull Knife Jr. stands outside, looking toward the hill a quarter mile west where the wagon ruts end. He has forgotten the power of the sky and the land from the top of the old camp. It's been so long.

"My grandfather taught me so much, so much that I didn't understand until I was much older. He used to look at my drawings when I was a very small boy—five or six—and he would say, 'Always trust yourself. Don't trust anything or anybody but yourself. If you can remember that, you will be all right.'

"Many times when we were out walking the land, he would tell me how important it is to respect everything that's alive. Even a little dog or cat, he would say. 'If you see a cat that's hungry or a stray dog, call it over and feed it—it's the same as you.'

"What he probably taught me most, even though I didn't know it then, was how to be Indian, to think and act like an Indian. It's completely different. When you leave the reservation, it's always 'Time to go to the bathroom now. Time to sit down and work at the desk now. Time to play with the kids. Time to eat. Time to go to sleep.' Everything in between is lost in the shuffle. We're not like that and that's one reason why I think it's been so difficult to adjust. We've spent a lot of time, maybe too much, trying to hold onto all the things in between."

He starts walking west, along the tracks through the buffalo grass, and soon the children scramble up, keeping a few paces behind.

"We don't look at wealth the same way. We don't measure a man's wealth by how much he has accumulated. In the old days, the man who had almost nothing—who had given everything away—was often thought to be the wealthiest man in the village.

"There isn't a day that goes by now that I don't long for the old days and the old way of life and I think I got a lot of that from my grandfather."

The boy and his sister have heard the stories and seen the photographs and they follow their father along the dirt ruts as they climb the small knoll where George Dull Knife and Mary Red Rabbit are buried. The children stand quietly at the top for a few minutes, then move away, leaving their father in front of the iron crosses that poke through the grass three feet apart.

He takes the old route from Kyle, the one he used to drive to the moccasin factory, heading west toward Sharps Corner. Riding through Porcupine, he tells the children the Pine Ridge Reservation is unique in many ways. It is the second largest reservation in the country—larger than Rhode Island, Delaware or Connecticut. The Oglala were once the largest and most powerful band of all the Lakota, and their leaders—Crazy Horse, Red Cloud and Black Elk—are well known throughout the world. On the reservation, he says, there are many different markers and memorials to their people. There are memorials to the Lakota who fought and died for the U.S. Army, and memorials to Lakota who fought and died against the U.S. Army.

At the top of the hill, a chain-link fence encircles the mass grave, and on an early afternoon in June, dozens of colored cloth strips—red, white, black and yellow—flutter from the top of the fence. Nellie and Guy Dull Knife III ask about all the colored strips of cloth and he tells them they are left each year by Lakota Sun Dancers who dedicate their sacrifice to the spirits of the Wounded Knee dead. To the east, well past the ravine where the people fled, he motions to a series of hills, one of which, he says, is the hill to which their great-grandfather rode after the blizzard a little more than a century ago.

A memorial built in 1903 still stands at one end of the grave, and the children and their father stand in silence, reading the inscription:

This monument is erected by surviving relatives and other Ogalalla and Cheyenne River Sioux Indians in memory of the Chief Big Foot Massacre Dec. 29, 1890. Col. Forsyth in command of U.S. troops. Big Foot was a great chief of the Sioux Indians. He often said, "I will stand in peace till my last day comes." He did many good and brave deeds for the white man and the red man. Many innocent women and children who knew no wrong died here.

Southwest of Wounded Knee, the road into Pine Ridge village passes the new hospital, a gleaming, 117,000-square-foot building designed and decorated in Indian themes. Outside, the flag of the United States and the flag of the Oglala Sioux Tribe flap on adjacent poles. The family wants to check up on a relative who may lose her foot from diabetes, and they pull into a spacious parking lot half a mile down the road from the church where Big Foot's people were laid out on a bed of straw. Inside, they are told the relative has not yet arrived, so they walk through one of the new wings, looking at the furnishings in the two-month-old hospital. There are million-dollar computers, state-of-the-art monitoring equipment, a new respiratory therapy program, an intensive care unit, CAT scans, outpatient wards and birthing rooms. Down one hallway, a room is also set aside for the medicine men.

The relative has still not arrived when the tour ends, and Guy Jr. gets back in the car and drives south toward the Nebraska border. In Rushville, he crosses the railroad tracks and tells the children that this is the place where their grandfather left for Kansas, for the Haskell Indian school in the fall of 1915. They ask why he went so far away to school and he says the old man's father thought it was the best thing to do back then. On the far side of the tracks, U.S. Highway 20 comes across the four-hundred-mile length of northern Nebraska, from the fertile Missouri River bottomlands in the east, through the vast cattle country of the central Sandhills, gradually giving way to the Panhandle, to the White River and the Pine Ridge country of the west.

He has been here before and it has never been easy. For the last twenty-five miles, Cora has been driving and Guy Jr. is content to stare out the window, taking in the startling confluence of freshwater streams cutting through green valley floors surrounded by a succession of plunging sandstone buttes covered in pine. The children have been riding a long time and are anxious to get out and explore the grounds of the old fort. Cora pulls into the park entrance, and the kids are almost out of the car before she stops in a stall across the street from the visitor's center.

Fort Robinson looks much like it did more than a century ago. The adobe homes where the officers lived are neatly aligned on one side of a horseshoe-shaped parade ground. Across the way, on the near side of Soldier Creek, stand the old cavalry stables, the blacksmith and harness shops, and the military hospital. On a summer Saturday afternoon, there are many tourists milling about, a few speaking in the foreign languages of their homelands. Guy Jr. and Cora and the kids get out of the car and walk toward a two-story white clapboard building on the far side of a grassy quadrangle.

Halfway across, a large stone marker rises up from the grass. They stand behind a group of tourists reading the bronze plaque:

Chief Crazy Horse—Oglala War Chief of the Sioux Nation—Killed Near This Spot September 5, 1877.
   A great chief of heroic character. He fought to the last to hold his native land for the Indian people.

The two-story wooden building trimmed in green, once the post headquarters, has been converted to a branch of the Nebraska State

Historical Society. It is now a museum housing artifacts of the fort's military past, from wars between the army and Indians to wars between the army and Germans. There are photo exhibits, an audio-visual center, interpretive displays, a library, a souvenir shop and several rooms filled with the history of the American West. Guy Jr. has been working on a sketch of a cavalry officer and he and his son go to a room housing several uniforms, where he carefully inspects them to make sure he has the number of buttons, the cut and color of the uniform and the insignia exactly right. In November 1890, the Buffalo Soldiers, the all-black Ninth Cavalry, left Fort Robinson under the command of Maj. Guy V. Henry, heading for Pine Ridge and the Ghost Dancers. Cora is in the next room, looking at the fort's display of Wounded Knee.

In a rear room on the second floor, twelve-year-old Nellie Dull Knife comes through the door and stops when she sees the photo hanging on a back wall of the room. It is a large blowup of a photograph taken at the White House in November 1873, the same one that has hung in her family's living room since she was a baby. In the photo, Little Wolf is standing to the left and Chief Dull Knife is seated beside him, staring impassively at the camera. He wears a fringed buckskin jacket, leggings, a bone choker and beaded moc-casins. In his left hand is the long-stem, traditional pipe of the chief. Nellie walks slowly through the crowded room, stopping a few feet in front of the photograph. "That's my great-great-grandfather," she says. A few of the visitors turn around, and she smiles a little awk-wardly.

Guy Dull Knife Jr. cannot take crowds for too long, and after forty-five minutes he wants to get back in the car and drive farther into the state park. They take a road that loops behind the old adobe officers' quarters and begin to climb into the backcountry. To the east, the walls of the Red Cloud Buttes shine white in the late after-noon sun, and they keep driving until they are alone, coming upon a hillside dusted thickly in the colors of early summer, in yellow yucca and lavender lupine, in snowberry, chokecherry and skunkbush sumac. He wants to walk the land a little and he asks the children to come with him, and after they cross the ditch and start climbing the hillside, he begins to tell them what the Lakota called the various plants and flowers in their language and how they were once used by their people.

Crossing to the southern slope of the hill, Guy Dull Knife Jr. finds the plant he has been looking for. He kneels down and carefully parts the grass around a dull green plant with a faint purple bloom. He asks his son to go to the car and get the tire iron out of the back, and when the boy returns, he begins digging with the sharpest edge, and tugging, then digging some more until there is a large mound of fresh dirt and the plant slips easily out of the earth. He tells the children that their ancestors did more than hunt the buffalo. In early June, they would go to the prairie and hunt the wild turnip, too. They ate them raw and dried them in braids and used them to flavor their meats and soups and stews.

Guy and Nellie want to taste the turnip, so he pulls a pocketknife from his jeans and removes the outer layer, cutting the fresh white meat into slices and handing them to his children. They like the taste and they ask their father if they can walk the hillside and look for some more on their own. He says it is all right.

From the southern slope of the hill, the fort looks like a toy model, like something a child had constructed and set up in his bedroom, the quarters laid out in military precision, the wide open space of the parade ground anchoring the buildings, the flagpoles and cannons and hitching posts placed in just the right spots. At the lower end of the fort, facing the old parade ground, two buildings stand alone—the guardhouse that Crazy Horse refused to enter and the adjutant's office where he died. Next to the adjutant's office, four blue poles mark the outline of the barracks that Chief Dull Knife and his people broke out of, fleeing for the buttes above the White River 115 winters ago.

"I went to Montana to see his grave one time and it was kind of overrun and covered with weeds. I've been thinking a lot lately of making some kind of monument to him, maybe a bronze sculpture of some kind that could be placed near the grave. He was a good man, a great chief, and I really want to do something to honor him."

The trip to the fort always gets him thinking and he stands on the top of the hill, watching the heads of his children bobbing in the grass far below, talking about the things he would like to do, about the dream he has. Now that his father is in a good nursing home and Cora and the baby are fine and the older children are getting an education, he wants to start working on the bronze sculptures again. He wants to finish the last dozen statues of the dancers, complete the full set of eighteen. In his dream, he would sell enough of the sets to build a home on the hill above Red Water Creek. There would be enough room for the family and it would be on the land that he cannot leave, and he and his children would be able to walk the prairie during the seasons, gathering the different plants and herbs, and maybe there would be a couple of horses. In the back of the house would be a small studio where he could work, and where he and Cora could teach the Oglala children of Pine Ridge how to bead and quill in the old way, how to paint and sculpt and learn some of the things that might get them away from the drugs and alcohol. A place, maybe, where they could nurture some of the young talent, provide a sense of Lakota history and tradition, a place to help keep his children and their generation from becoming like wind on the buffalo grass.

"If we are to make it as a people, our children must know about computers and the Eagle Dance. They must know the value of earning a living and about our traditional relationship with the earth. They need to know how to read and write and balance a checkbook, but they must also know who they are and where they came from. It is our job to teach them these things, just like our fathers before us. Then it will be up to them to help their children learn the ways of both the white world and the Indian world."

He says he doesn't know if he can make the dream work, but he wants to try.

From far below, halfway down the broad sloping hillside, Nellie

Dull Knife pops up from the grass, shouting and waving her arms. "Dad, Dad! Over here. Over here, Dad!"

It takes a few minutes for him to arrive, and when he does, he can see the large mound of fresh dirt in front of Guy Dull Knife III. The boy doesn't say anything, but he doesn't have to. The father can see how happy they are with the wild turnip they have found on their own.

For the sake of consistency and reader clarity, I have made a few some-what arbitrary decisions in the writing of this book. Throughout the text, the words "Sioux" and "Lakota" are frequently used interchangeably, as synonyms. I also chose to use "Lakota" and "Northern Cheyenne" (no "s") as the plural form of each word. And although Camp Robinson, the soldier outpost on the White River, did not officially become a fort until December 30, 1878, it is frequently referred to as Fort Robinson prior to that date. All Lakota words and phrases which appear in the text were reviewed for correct spelling and accurate translations by Francis Whitebird, an enrolled mem-ber of the Rosebud Sioux Tribe, who is a fluent Lakota speaker and teaches a Lakota language course. To avoid confusion, all diacritical and accent marks were omitted from the Lakota words and phrases. Depending on the specific ceremony and the circumstances, there can be variations on which colors represent the four directions. The colors and the directions they repre-sent that are used in this book are the same as the ones identified by the Oglala holy man, Black Elk, in Black Elk Speaks (p. 2). Finally, the text was generously reviewed—in whole or in part—by a good many indi-viduals, both Indian and non-Indian. Guy Dull Knife Jr. and Cora Yellow Elk read each chapter three or four times and any errors, in fact or omis-sion, clearly reside with the author.

Afterword

The old man had desperately wanted to live in three different centuries.

At age ninety-six, in the waning years of the twentieth century, it seemed a reasonable and realistic goal. After all, he'd just gone in for what his son wryly termed a "100,000-mile checkup," and all the vitals had checked out fine: strong heart, clear lungs, solid appetite, good liver and kidney functions.

One evening in mid-August 1995, four months after he'd proudly shown scores of friends and relatives a recently published book about his family, the old man was sitting alone in the far corner of a nursing home in Martin, South Dakota. He was reading in the dim light, a cheap blanket covering his still-powerful shoulders.

It seems ironic that after all Guy Dull Knife Sr. had been through—the poverty and numbing winters, the trenches and mustard gas of World War I, bronco riding, the Great Depression, sending his only child to Vietnam, a civil war in his own homeland, long years as a revered councilman and tribal elder, almost a century outwitting the vagaries of life in America's poorest county—that it should all have come to an end with the burning tip of an unfiltered Pall Mall striking the blanket.

"Dad struggled for three days. He wouldn't give up," said his son, Guy Dull Knife Jr. "But, in the end, the burns were too deep. I think he just decided to let go and begin his journey to the Spirit World, where my mother and his friends were waiting."

Often that is the way it has been for his family, the Dull Knifes of Pine Ridge, and his people, the Oglala Sioux: a struggle to survive, to overcome, to try to balance the old and the new, to blend the traditions of one century with the modern concepts of another. A struggle to find a secure home amid the crushing detritus of beer cans, unemployment, poverty, and boredom. A daily struggle to find a purpose and meaning, to hope on a reservation where hope is often taunting, elusive, ephemeral.

In many ways, the last six years of hope and hopelessness, triumph and tragedy since the death of Guy Dull Knife Sr. mirror the long history of both the Dull Knife family and the roughly twenty thousand Oglala Sioux who live on the nation's second-largest reservation.

Since this book's initial publication, South Dakota's Pine Ridge Reservation has been rocked with several high-profile, unresolved murders—murders of Oglala men that involve a rancorous, longstanding dispute over liquor sales in White Clay, Nebraska. The unincorporated border town of twenty-two boasts annual beer sales of about $3 million, mostly to residents of the dry reservation two miles away. The 1999 murders have sparked numerous demonstrations, arrests, court cases, law enforcement crackdowns, and an active FBI investigation. They have also sparked a renewed vigor to attack one of the reservation's most pernicious problems: alcoholism.

Events that occurred before and after the murders offered the Oglala a fleeting hope of both spiritual and economic rebirth. In May 1996 a sacred white buffalo calf was born on the five-thousand-square-mile reservation, the first such calf born on Indian lands in more than a century. Pine Ridge spiritual leaders widely hailed the birth as a sign of better days to come. Three years later, President William J. Clinton visited Pine Ridge, the first American president to visit an American Indian reservation in fifty-five years. Clinton pledged federal help in creating "Empowerment Zones" as a means of stimulating the moribund reservation economy.

For Guy Dull Knife Jr., the Vietnam veteran and artist, the six years since his father's death have also been a complicated time. After living for a while in Hot Springs, South Dakota, he and his wife, Cora Yellow Elk, and their five children returned in 1996 to the home on Red Water Creek that his father and mother had built by hand in 1928. While he and Cora care for their younger children, the older ones are taking care of themselves. Eldest daughter Tonya is an emergency medical technician with the Oglala Sioux Tribal Health Department. Daughter Nellie is married and the mother of a baby girl. Eldest son Guy Dull Knife III finished a Job Corps training program in Utah and plans to follow his grandfather and father by enlisting in the army.

For several years Guy Jr. served as the tribe's director of arts and crafts, a good job well-suited to his interests and talents. But the long hours spent standing on a concrete floor exacerbated a heart condition, and he had to resign. Soon he intends to hollow a dugout in a nearby hill and use it as an art studio, a place to resume his work on a series of statues commemorating the many different traditional dances of his people. But there are other concerns that occupy most of his time.

In December 2000, Cora gave birth to their sixth child, a son, born about three months prematurely. Baby Jeffrey Dull Knife's fingers were fused and his skull had only partially formed when he was born. His lungs were weak, and for two months he was on oxygen and in critical condition in an intensive care unit. A team of specialists at a Denver hospital performed a series of operations on him, and, although still weak and facing several more operations, the boy is surviving.

The father has no doubt that the highly trained medical specialists helped save his young son's life. And he has no doubt that other forces were at work too. Throughout the summer, a number of sun dancers on the Pine Ridge Reservation prayed for Jeffrey, dedicating the pain and suffering of their four-day ordeal to the boy. Earlier, one winter evening, when the boy was hovering between life and death, the Dull Knifes' good friend Richard Moves Camp, a revered medicine man among the Oglala, performed a ceremony for Jeffrey. "When it ended," Guy Jr. said, "Dickie told me not to worry. He said the boy would live."

And so he has.

It is something the old man had always marveled at. No matter how harsh the winter—the heavy snows, the numbing temperatures, the punishing winds—when spring returned, so too did life on the Pine Ridge Reservation.

Joe Starita
October 2001

Bibliography

1 . BOOKS

Albers, Patricia, and Beatrice Medicine. *The Hidden Half: Studies of Plains Indian Women.* Lanham, Maryland, 1983.

Ambrose, Stephen E. *Crazy Horse and Custer: The Parallel Lives of Two American Warriors.* New York, 1975.

American Indian Publishers. *Biographical Dictionary of Indians of the Americas,* vol. 1. Newport Beach, California, 1991.

Anderson, Robert, Joanna Brown, Jonny Lerner and Barbara Lou Shafer, eds. *Voices from Wounded Knee.* Rooseveltown, New York, 1974.

Andrist, Ralph K. *The Long Death: The Last Days of the Plains Indian.* New York, 1993.

Berkhofer, Robert F., Jr. *The White Man's Indian.* New York, 1978.

Berthrong, Donald J. *The Cheyenne and Arapaho Ordeal.* Norman, Oklahoma, 1976.

Biolsi, Thomas. *Organizing the Lakota.* Tucson, Arizona, 1992.

Bourke, John G. *Mackenzie's Last Fight with the Cheyennes.* New York, 1890.

———. *On the Border with Crook.* Lincoln, Nebraska, 1971.

Brininstool, E. A. *Dull Knife (A Cheyenne Napoleon).* Hollywood, 1935.

Bronson, Edgar Beecher. *Reminiscences of a Ranchman.* New York, 1908.

Brown, Dee. *Bury My Heart at Wounded Knee.* New York, 1970.

Clark, Robert A., ed. *The Killing of Chief Crazy Horse.* Glendale, California, 1976.

Connell, Evan S. *Son of the Morning Star: Custer and the Little Bighorn.* New York, 1984.

Cook, John R. *The Border and the Buffalo.* Chicago, 1938.

Crow Dog, Mary, and Richard Erdoes. *Lakota Woman.* New York, 1990.

Cruttwell, C.R.M.F. *A History of the Great War: 1914–1918.* Chicago, 1991.

Deloria, Ella Cara. *Waterlily.* Lincoln (Nebraska) and London, 1988.

Deloria, Vine, Jr. *Custer Died for Your Sins: An Indian Manifesto.* New York, 1970.

———. *Behind the Trail of Broken Treaties: An Indian Declaration of Independence.* Austin, Texas, 1985.

DeMallie, Raymond J., ed. *The Sixth Grandfather: Black Elk's Teachings Given to John G. Neihardt.* Lincoln, Nebraska, 1984.

Densmore, Frances. *Teton Sioux Music and Culture.* Lincoln, Nebraska, 1992.

Dockstader, Frederick J., ed. *Great North American Indians: Profiles in Life and Leadership.* New York, 1977.

Driving Hawk Sneve, Virginia. *They Led a Nation: The Sioux Chiefs.* Sioux Falls, South Dakota, 1975.

Eastman, Charles A. *Indian Heroes and Chieftains.* Lincoln, Nebraska, 1991.

Esper, George, and the Associated Press. *The Eyewitness History of the Vietnam War, 1961–1975.* New York, 1983.

Frazier, Ian. *Great Plains.* New York, 1989.

Freedman, Russell. *Indian Chiefs.* New York, 1987.

Giago, Tim. *Notes from Indian Country,* vol. I. Pierre, South Dakota, 1984.

Grinnell, George Bird. *The Fighting Cheyennes.* Norman, Oklahoma, 1989.

Halberstam, David. *The Best and the Brightest.* New York, 1969.

Hassrick, Royal B. *The Sioux: Life and Customs of a Warrior Society.* Norman, Oklahoma, 1964.

Highwater, Jamake. *The Primal Mind: Vision and Reality in Indian America.* New York, 1981.

Hoig, Stan. *The Peace Chiefs of the Cheyennes.* Norman, Oklahoma, 1980.

Hyde, George. *Red Cloud's Folk: A History of the Oglala Sioux Indians.* Norman, Oklahoma, 1937.

Jackson, Helen Hunt. *A Century of Dishonor.* New York, 1993.

Jensen, Richard E., R. Eli Paul and John E. Carter, eds. *Eyewitness at Wounded Knee.* Lincoln, Nebraska, 1991.

Karnow, Stanley. *Vietnam: A History.* New York, 1983.

Kehoe, Alice B. *North American Indians: A Comprehensive Account.* Englewood Cliffs, New Jersey, 1981.

McGillycuddy, Julia B. *Blood on the Moon: Valentine McGillycuddy and the Sioux.* Lincoln, Nebraska, 1990.

McGregor, James H. *The Wounded Knee Massacre: From the Viewpoint of the Sioux.* Minneapolis, 1940.

McLuhan, T. C., ed. *Touch the Earth: A Self-Portrait of Indian Existence.* New York, 1971.

Mails, Thomas E. *Fools Crow.* Lincoln, Nebraska, 1979.

Martin, Calvin, ed. *The American Indian and the Problem of History.* New York, 1987.

Matthiessen, Peter. *In the Spirit of Crazy Horse.* New York, 1983.

Miller, David Humphreys. *Custer's Fall: The Native American Side of the Story.* New York, 1992.

Nabokov, Peter, ed. *Native American Testimony.* New York, 1991.

Neihardt, John G. *Black Elk Speaks.* New York, 1932.

Olson, James C. *Red Cloud and the Sioux Problem.* Lincoln, Nebraska, 1975.

Ortiz, Roxanne Dunbar. *The Great Sioux Nation: Sitting in Judgment on America.* New York, 1977.

Powell, Peter J. *People of the Sacred Mountain.* San Francisco, 1981.

Powers, Marla N. *Oglala Women: Myth, Ritual, and Reality.* Chicago, 1986.

Powers, William K. *Oglala Religion.* Lincoln, Nebraska, 1975.

Prucha, Francis Paul. *The Great Father: The United States Government and the American Indians.* Lincoln, Nebraska, 1984.

Rosa, Joseph G., and Robin May. *Buffalo Bill and His Wild West: A Pictorial Biography.* Lawrence, Kansas, 1989.

Russell, Don. *The Lives and Legends of Buffalo Bill.* Norman, Oklahoma, 1960.

Sandoz, Mari. *Cheyenne Autumn.* New York, 1953.

Smith, Rex Alan. *Moon of the Popping Trees.* New York, 1975.

Smythe, Donald. *Guerrilla Warrior: The Early Life of John J. Pershing.* New York, 1973.

Standing Bear, Luther. *My People the Sioux.* New York, 1928.

———. *Land of the Spotted Eagle.* Lincoln, Nebraska, 1978.

Thornsohn, Stig, and Jens og Annette Damm. *The Dream of America.* Denmark, 1986.

Urdang, Lawrence, ed. *The Timetables of American History.* New York, 1981.

Utley, Robert M. *The Last Days of the Sioux Nation.* New Haven and London, 1963.

Vecsey, Christopher, ed. *Handbook of American Indian Religious Freedom.* New York, 1991.

Waldman, Carl. *Who Was Who in Native American History.* New York, 1990.

Walker, James R., and Elaine A. Jahner, eds. *Lakota Myth.* Lincoln, Nebraska, 1983.

Walker, James R., and Raymond J. DeMallie, eds. *Lakota Society.* Lincoln, Nebraska, 1982.

Walker, James R., Raymond J. DeMallie and Elaine A. Jahner, eds. *Lakota Belief and Ritual.* Lincoln, Nebraska, 1980.

Washburn, Wilcomb E., and Harold M. Hyman, eds. *The Assault on Indian Tribalism: The General Allotment Law (Dawes Act) of 1887.* Philadelphia, 1975.

Weatherford, Jack. *Native Roots: How the Indians Enriched America.* New York, 1991.

Wetmore, Helen Cody. *Buffalo Bill: Last of the Great Scouts.* Duluth, Minnesota, 1899.

Wilkinson, Charles F., and Christine L. Milkas. *Indian Tribes as Sovereign Governments.* Oakland, California, 1988.

2 . ARTICLES AND PERIODICALS

Akwesasne Notes. "Prosecution of Banks and Means Rests" (July 1974), 14–15.

———. "The Custer Trials Go On" (July 1974), 16–17.

———. "Ken Tilsen, WKLDOC Lawyer, Speaks on the Trials" (July 1974), 13.

Appleton, Caroline Dawes. "The American Indian in the War," *Outlook* (21 May 1919), 110–112.

Barsh, Russel Lawrence. "American Indians in the Great War," *Ethnohistory* (Summer 1991), 277–303.

Black Elk, Henry. "The Present Day Oglala Sioux," *University of South Dakota W. H. Over Museum News* (May 1952), 1–5.

Buecker, Thomas R. "A History of Camp Robinson, Nebraska," Chadron State College master's thesis (April 1992), 1–72.

———, and R. Eli Paul. "Cheyenne Outbreak Firearms," *The Museum of the Fur Trade Quarterly* (Summer 1993), 2–12.

Clow, Richmond L. "The Indian Reorganization Act and the Loss of Tribal Sovereignty: Constitutions on the Rosebud and Pine Ridge Reservations," *Great Plains Quarterly* (Spring 1987), 125–134.

Danker, Donald F., ed. "The Wounded Knee Interviews of Eli S. Ricker," *Nebraska History* (Summer 1981), 151–243.

Epp, Todd D. "The State of Kansas v. Wild Hog, et al.," *Kansas History* (Summer 1982), 139–146.

Grange, Roger T., Jr. "Treating the Wounded at Fort Robinson," *Nebraska History* (Sept. 1964), 273–294.

Great Plains Quarterly (Winter 1991).

Great Plains Quarterly (Winter 1994).

Green, Jerry. "The Medals of Wounded Knee," *Nebraska History* (Summer 1994), 200–208.

Guttman, Jon. "For Little Wolf and Dull Knife, Home Was a Thousand Heartbreaking Miles Away," *Wild West* (Oct. 1989), 55–56.

Hinman, Eleanor H., ed. "Oglala Sources on the Life of Crazy Horse," *Nebraska History* (Spring 1976), 1–49.

Keith, A. N. "Dull Knife's Cheyenne Raid of 1878," *Nebraska History* (Oct./Dec. 1924), 116–119.

The Literary Digest. "Lo, the Rich Indian Is Eager to Fight the Savage Hun" (1 June 1918), 56–62.

The Literary Digest. "American Indians True to Tradition in the War" (8 Feb. 1919), 54–57.

McDonald, J. Douglas, A. L. McDonald, Bill Tallbull and Ted Risingsun. "The Cheyenne Outbreak Revisited: The Employment of Archaeological Methodology in the Substantiation of Oral History," *Plains Anthropologist* (August 1989), 34–125.

Marley, Everett Leslie. "History of Pine Ridge Indian Reservation," University of Nebraska master's thesis (25 July 1935), 1–135.

Mason, W. Dale. "You Can Only Kick So Long . . . American Indian Movement Leadership in Nebraska, 1972–1979," *Journal of the West*, Vol. 23/No. 3, 21–31.

Meinhardt, Nick, and Diane Payne. "Reviewing U.S. Treaty Commitments to the Lakota Nation," *American Indian Journal* (Jan. 1978), 2–12.

Miller, David Humphreys. "Echoes of the Little Bighorn," *American Heritage* (June 1971), 28–39.

Miller, Yvonne. "Tribes That Slumber," *True West* (May/June 1980), 38–41.

The Morning Star People. "Ancestors Come Home," St. Labre Indian School (Feb. 1994), 4.

Moses, L. G. "Wild West Shows, Reformers, and the Image of the American Indian, 1887–1914," *South Dakota History* (Fall 1984), 194–221.

Nebraska History. "Wounded Knee Special Edition" (Fall 1990), 170–212.

Nebraskaland Magazine. "Fort Robinson Illustrated" (Jan/Feb. 1986), 3–114.

Roberts, Gary L. "The Shame of Little Wolf," *Montana: The Magazine of Western History* (July 1978), 37–47.

Smythe, Donald. "John J. Pershing: Frontier Calvaryman," *New Mexico Historical Review* (July 1963), 220–243.

Spindler, Will H. "Tragedy Strikes at Wounded Knee," *Gordon Journal Publishing Company* (1955), 30–37.

Tate, Michael L. "From Scout to Doughboy: The National Debate over Integrating Indians into the Military, 1891–1918," *The Western Historical Quarterly* (Oct. 1986), 417–436.

Twiss, Gayla. "A Short History of Pine Ridge," *The Indian Historian* (Winter 1978), 36–39.

University of Nebraska School of Journalism Depth Report No. 7. "As Long as the Grass Shall Grow" (7 June 1971), 1–39.

Wounded Knee Legal Defense/Offense Committee. "Wounded Knee 1890–1973" (Nov. 1973), 1–30.

3. GOVERNMENT PUBLICATIONS

Commissioner of Indian Affairs. *Annual Reports* (1877–1880).

———. *Annual Reports* (1868–1898).

Congressional Record, 90th Cong., 2d sess. "Medal of Honor 1863–1968" (1968).

Dept. of Interior, U.S. Census. *Pine Ridge Indian Reservation 1886–1907.* Nebraska State Historical Society.

Dept. of Interior, Office of Indian Affairs. *Constitution and By-Laws of the Oglala Sioux Tribe of the Pine Ridge Indian Reservation of South Dakota* (Jan. 1936).

———. *The American Indian in the World War.* Bulletin 15 (1927).

———. *Treaty of Fort Laramie with Sioux, etc., 1851* (17 Sept. 1851). *Treaty with the Sioux-Oglala Band, 1865* (Oct. 28, 1865). *Treaty with the Sioux-Brule, Oglala, Miniconjou, Yanktonai, Hunkpapa, Blackfeet, Cuthead, Two Kettle, Sansarcs, and Santee—and Arapaho, 1868* (29 April 1868).

———. *Indian Schools and Education* (1 Sept. 1939), 1–13.

———. *Letter from Ivan Drift to Mr. John Collier, U.S. Commissioner of Indian Affairs.* Nebraska State Historical Society Archives (29 Dec. 1933), 1–5.

———. *Correspondence and Reports Between Agents Administering the Red Cloud/Pine Ridge Agency and Their Predecessors, Aug. 11, 1875–June 30, 1914.* National Archives Bureau of Indian Affairs Record Group 75.

Dept. of Interior, United States Indian Service. *Student File of Guy Dull Knife, Sept. 1915–June 1918.* Haskell Institute. Lawrence, Kansas.

————. *Letter from Pine Ridge Agent Charles G. Penney granting permission for Messrs. Cody and Salsbury to employ 125 Indians* (April 11, 1895).

House of Representatives Executive Documents for the 52nd Cong., 1891–1892. *Report of the Secretary of War,* vol. 1–5.

Senate Report, 46th Cong., 2d sess. *Select Committee to Examine into the Circumstances Connected with the Removal of the Northern Cheyennes from the Sioux Reservations to the Indian Territory* (June 1880), 1–327.

————. *Correspondence between Secretary of War and Post Commanders during Cheyenne Outbreak.* Nebraska State Historical Archives (Feb. 1879), 1–49.

South Dakota Bar Association Report. *Rules of the Court of Indian Offenses, Pine Ridge Reservation (1909).* University of South Dakota Library (21 Jan. 1909), 115–119.

U.S. Army. Camp Robinson, Nebraska. *Field Reports, Sept. 15, 1878–Sept. 27, 1879.* Nebraska State Historical Society Archives microfilm.

U.S. Army. *Proceedings of a Board of Officers, Jan. 1879.* An investigation of the Cheyenne Outbreak (Jan. 1879), 1–217.

U.S. Census Bureau. *Economic, Infant Mortality, Life Expectancy, Suicide Rate, and Alcoholism Statistics for Pine Ridge Indian Reservation.* 1990 Census.

U.S. Supreme Court. *United States, petitioner v Sioux Nation of Indians et al.,* Supreme Court *Reporter* 448 U.S. 371, 65L.Ed. 2d 844 (30 June 1980), 2716–2752.

————. *Summary of October 1979 Term: Indians.* Ibid. (Oct. 1979), 414–416.

4 . N E W S P A P E R S

Beaver City (NE) *Times-Tribune*
Chadron (NE) *Democrat*
Chicago *Tribune*
Denver *Post*
Gordon (NE) *Journal*
Indian Country Today
Kansas City *Daily Times*
Lincoln (NE) *Journal*
Lincoln *Star*
The New York Times
New York *Herald*
Omaha (NE) *Bee*
Omaha *World-Herald*
Rocky Mountain News
Sidney (NE) *Telegraph*
USA Today
The Washington Post

5 . A R C H I V E S

Camp, Walter. "Notes on the Flight of the Cheyennes and the Surrender of Dull Knife." Nebraska State Historical Society Archives, Box 3-5, envp. 71.

Sandoz, Mari. "Notes on the Dull Knife Outbreak for book *Cheyenne Autumn*." Nebraska State Historical Society Archives, MS565, Box 1.

Notes

4   *"His people, the Oglala":*   For a description of Sioux tribal organization and migration patterns, see Driving Hawk Sneve, *They Led a Nation,* pp. 1–3.

6   *"Some anthropologists believe":*   The origin of Native Americans is discussed in Kehoe, *North American Indians,* pp. 2–10.

8   *"More than a hundred thirty years":*   For background on the life and death of Crazy Horse from the Lakota perspective, see *Nebraska History,* "Oglala Sources on the Life of Crazy Horse," by journalist Eleanor Hinman, who conducted interviews in the 1930s with Oglala elders who knew Crazy Horse. A poignant retelling of the death of Crazy Horse can also be found in Frazier, *Great Plains,* pp. 94–119.

14   *"By the fall of 1841":*   Events leading to the death of Chief Bull Bear are discussed in Hyde, *Red Cloud's Folk,* pp. 50–55.

30   *"That fall, General":*   John Bourke, General Crook's aide-de-camp, was an eyewitness to the attack on Dull Knife's winter village, and he meticulously documents the army force and the number of friendly Indian scouts used in the raid in *Mackenzie's Last Fight with the Cheyennes,* pp. 1–44.

31   *"Wounded seven times,":*   For additional accounts of the raid on Dull Knife's village, see Grinnell, *The Fighting Cheyennes,* pp. 362–369; and Brown, *Bury My Heart at Wounded Knee,* pp. 290–293, one of several historians who state that Little Wolf was wounded seven times in the battle. See also Hoig, *The Peace Chiefs of the Cheyennes,* pp. 130–132.

33   *" 'Of the three . . .' ":*   Col. George A. Woodward is quoted in Hoig, p. 137.

33   *"Now, on this early spring morning":*   See Peter J. Powell's superb reconstruction of the Northern Cheyenne surrender at Camp Robinson in *People of the Sacred Mountain,* pp. 1141–1149.

33   *"Dull Knife and Little Wolf":*   That Dull Knife and Little Wolf neither understood nor agreed to the government's later contention that the Fort

Laramie Treaty of 1868 required them to move to the southern reservation in the Indian Territory is mentioned in Powell, pp. 827–830, and
Hoig, pp. 127–131.

35   *"Finally, government authorities"*:   That government officials told the
Northern Cheyenne they could return to their northern homeland if they
were unhappy in the south is found in Powell, p. 1149, and Hoig, p. 131.

37   *"The white hide hunters ..."*:   Sheridan's position on wiping out the buffalo as
an instrument of government policy and as an expedient means of crippling Indian resistance is quoted in Cook, *The Border and the Buffalo*, pp.
194–195.

38   *"It is not singular . . ."*:   Indian agent John D. Miles is quoted in the
Commissioner of Indian Affairs, *Annual Reports*, 1877, p. 85.

38   *"In addition to his duties"*:   For an account of Miles's dual business interests
at Darlington, see Berthrong, *The Cheyenne and Arapaho Ordeal*, p. 32.
Another view of the corruption practiced by Darlington agents is
reflected in a statement by Wild Hog given to a reporter for the New
York *Herald* (14 Feb. 1879), p. 126. That reservations were notorious for
their graft and corruption is evidenced also in an oft-quoted remark
made by General Sherman, who once defined reservations as "a parcel of
land inhabited by Indians and surrounded by thieves." See Matthiessen,
In the Spirit of Crazy Horse, p. 17.

39   *". . . and although we see . . ."*:   Miles is quoted in CIA, *Annual Reports*, 1877,
p. 85.

40   *"They gave us corn . . ."*:   Wild Hog describes the deprivations suffered by
the Cheyenne in the New York *Herald* (14 Feb. 1879), p. 126.

40   *"I have been sick . . ."*:   Testimony by Little Chief was given to the Senate
and contained in its *Select Committee* report (June 1880), an investigation
into the removal of the Northern Cheyenne from their homeland to
Indian Territory, p. 11.

40   *"We could not forget . . ."*:   Ibid., p. 19, for Wild Hog's feelings.

41   *"We are sickly . . ."*:   The statement of the chiefs to their people is in Hoig,
p. 132.

42   *"On September 15,"*:   Amos Chapman's statement that the Northern
Cheyenne escaped because of hunger is found in a military telegram
from Lt. Col. W. H. Lewis at Fort Dodge, Kansas, to army headquarters
in Fort Leavenworth, Kansas, Sept. 15, 1878. Found in U.S. Army,
Camp Robinson *Field Reports*, Nebraska State Historical Society
Archives.

42   *"[Miles] denies in toto . . ."*:   Hayt is quoted in CIA, *Annual Reports*, 1878, p.
23.

42   *"The truth is . . ."*:   Ibid., p. 24, for rest of Hayt's remarks on the Dull Knife
band.

42 *"worse than they went out":* Miles is quoted in Senate *Select Committee* report, p. 26.

43 *"Gen. John Pope":* For General Pope's telegraph, see Brininstool, *Dull Knife,* p. 12.

43 *"Sheridan's orders":* Sheridan's orders to Gen. George Crook are in Berthrong, p. 34.

44 *"We have come to ask . . .":* Little Wolf is quoted in *The Morning Star People,* "Ancestors Come Home" (Feb. 1994), p. 4.

44 *"The Arapahoe told . . .":* Old Crow's testimony is in Senate *Select Committee* report, p. 20.

47 *"We tried to avoid . . .":* Little Wolf's statement on avoiding settlements is in Grinnell, p. 413.

48 *"A. N. Keith,":* Keith's account is from *Nebraska History* (Oct. 1924), p. 3.

49 *"Tangle Hair, the Dog Soldier":* Tangle Hair on Little Wolf is from Powell, p. 1170.

50 *"A few days later,":* Chicago *Tribune* (30 Sept. 1878), p. 1.

50 *"Every available man . . .":* Telegram from Pope to Col. W. D. Whipple, Asst. Adjutant General at Chicago, Illinois Headquarters, Dept. of the Missouri, Oct. 10, 1878. Found in U.S. Army, Camp Robinson *Field Reports,* Nebraska State Historical Society Archives.

50 *"A dispatch from":* The Fort Wallace dispatch is in *New York Times* (5 Oct. 1878).

52 *"You can go that way . . .":* Little Wolf's statement to Dull Knife is from Powell, p. 1175.

54 *"Major Carlton explained":* Telegram from Major C. H. Carlton to Omaha Barracks, Neb. Headquarters Dept. of the Platte, Oct., 27, 1878. Found in Senate Report, *Correspondence* (Feb. 1879), p. 12.

55 *"General Crook commended":* General Crook's commendation is in his annual report to superiors at Headquarters, Dept. of the Missouri, Sept. 27, 1879. From U.S. Army, Camp Robinson *Field Reports.*

56 *"For a good while . . .":* Wild Hog's statement is in Senate *Select Committee* report on the removal of the Northern Cheyenne, p. 11.

56 *"They were very contented . . .":* Wessells's testimony comes from U.S. Army, *Proceedings of a Board of Officers,* p. 63.

56 *"The decision had been made":* That the Northern Cheyenne attempt to leave the southern reservation and return to their northern homeland was viewed as a serious threat to the settlement of the West can be found in a telegram from Lt. Gen. P. H. Sheridan, dated Sept. 19, 1878, to Gen. E. D. Townsend in Washington, D.C. In it, Sheridan says, "There is strong hope that the troops will be able to meet with them and capture or destroy them. . . . It is important for the peace of the plains and the success of the reservation system that these Indians be captured, and every

effort will be made to accomplish that purpose." Found in Senate Report, *Correspondence*, p. 41.

56   *"The orders, General Crook":* Crook's ambivalence toward the orders is found in his annual report to superiors, U.S. Army, Camp Robinson *Field Reports*, p. 3.

56   *"Among these Cheyenne . . .":* Ibid., pp. 3–4, for Crook's belief that the Northern Cheyenne would kill themselves before agreeing to return to the Indian Territory.

57   *"At this time, . . .":* Ibid., p. 4, for the weather conditions at Fort Robinson.

57   *"It would be inhuman . . .":* Crook's belief that it would be inhuman to try and remove Dull Knife's people in midwinter is in Senate *Select Committee* report, p. 4, Letter from the Secretary of War to the Chairman of the Committee of Indian Affairs regarding the escape of Cheyenne Indians from Fort Robinson.

57   *"I am here . . .":* Chief Dull Knife's statement that he was on his own ground and would never go back is found in Grinnell, p. 418.

58   *"I said, 'Look at us . . .' ":* Testimony of Wild Hog is from Senate *Select Committee* report, p. 11.

58   *"You can starve us . . .":* Dull Knife's statement that they would starve before going south is from Grinnell, p. 419.

58   *"They always told me . . .":* Captain Lawton is quoted in U.S. Army, *Proceedings*, p. 114.

59   *"I asked them if . . .":* Ibid., p. 64, for Captain Wessells's comment on removal of subchiefs.

60   *"It is true that . . .":* That the people refused to die shut up like dogs is from the testimony of Old Crow from Senate *Select Committee* report, p. 23.

60   *"A rear guard seemed . . .":* Private Janzchin's comments about the rear guard are in U.S. Army, *Proceedings*, p. 154.

61   *"They were the first . . .":* Ibid., p. 161, for the account of the Dog Soldiers as the first ones out.

61   *"The next day, January 10,":* For an account of the unloading of the dead, see Powell, p. 1211, and Grinnell, p. 423.

62   *"Now, will you go . . .":* Wessells's asking if they were now ready to go south is in Powell, p. 1211.

62   *"I found trails of two . . .":* Lawton is quoted in U.S. Army, *Proceedings*, p. 116.

63   *"I was afraid . . .":* Ibid., p. 118, for Lawton's comments on burning the horse.

63   *"The Indians were as well armed . . .":* Crook's report that the Indians were well armed is in Senate *Select Committee* report, p. 5.

64   *"I saw a little girl . . .":* Lawton's remarks on helping the little girl out of the pit are found in U.S. Army, *Proceedings*, p. 122.

64   *"I saw them search . . .":* Ibid., p. 112, for Lieutenant Simpson's comments on stripping the bodies.

64 *"From the appearances . . .":* Ibid., pp. 168–170, for Lieutenant Cummings's statement on scalping the bodies.

65 *"after she was wounded . . .":* Ibid., p. 151, for statement that one woman had her fingers shot off.

65 *"I found six stab wounds . . .":* Ibid., p. 175, for Lieutenant Cummings's examination of Big Antelope.

65 *"On February 4, Wild Hog":* For the account of Wild Hog's attempted suicide while in handcuffs, see Powell, p. 1241.

66 *"I did not feel . . .":* Old Crow's statement is from his testimony as quoted in Senate *Select Committee* report, p. 26.

66 *"A sergeant asked . . .":* Henry Clifford's comments that Dull Knife was not among the dead are contained in U.S. Army, *Proceedings,* p. 162.

CHAPTER 3

74 *"They think young George":* For an account of the Northern Cheyenne allowed to leave the Indian Territory for Pine Ridge, see Berthrong, *The Cheyenne and Arapaho Ordeal,* pp. 35–47.

78 *"My original convictions . . .":* President Jackson's comments on the American Indian are found in Thornsohn, *The Dream of America,* p. 80.

79 *"What white man can say . . .":* Sitting Bull's quote is in McLuhan, *Touch the Earth,* p. 77.

80 *"When he arrived,":* For McGillycuddy's comments on the death of Crazy Horse, see Hinman, "Oglala Sources on the Life of Crazy Horse," pp. 45–46, and McGillycuddy's *Blood on the Moon,* pp. 82–87.

81 *"For as long as any":* For an account of the Akicitas' role in Lakota society, see Hassick, *The Sioux,* pp. 17–29.

81 *"Agent McGillycuddy, however,":* McGillycuddy's remarks on the police force are from Commissioner of Indian Affairs, *Annual Reports,* 1880, pp. 11–12.

82 *"Admit that the Indian . . .":* CIA, *Annual Reports,* 1881, p. 45.

82 *"Locality and love of home . . .":* CIA, *Annual Reports,* 1879, p. 37.

83 *"The housing of these people . . .":* Ibid., p. 40.

83 *"If we wish to continue . . .":* Ibid., p. 38.

83 *"It is a mere waste . . .":* CIA, *Annual Reports,* 1880, pp. 40–41.

83 *"With the American Indian, . . .":* CIA, *Annual Reports,* 1884, p. 40.

83 *"The Indians generally . . .":* CIA, *Annual Reports,* 1882, p. 39.

83 *"They are rapidly adopting . . .":* CIA, *Annual Reports,* 1881, p. 45.

84 *"These were part of . . .":* CIA, *Annual Reports,* 1880, p. 39.

84 *"The departure of the Cheyenne,":* CIA, *Annual Reports,* 1879, pp. 38–39, for McGillycuddy's comment on how far the Oglala have advanced in the past year.

85 *"I do not wish . . .":* Sitting Bull's comment on reservation Indians appears in Nabokov, *Native American Testimony,* p. 192.

86 *"They have also made . . .":* McGillycuddy's remark that the Indians have abandoned many old customs, including the Sun Dance, is found in CIA, *Annual Reports,* 1884, p. 37.

86 *"In 1884, McGillycuddy":* The Court of Indian Offenses, its rules and guidelines, appears in the 1909 South Dakota Bar Association Report, pp. 115–119.

87 *"Father, we have served . . .":* Standing Soldier's remarks on the Indian police force are in CIA, *Annual Reports,* 1884, p. 41.

88 *"Five of these . . .":* The agent's report of five men lost to Cody's Wild West Show is from CIA, *Annual Reports,* 1890, pp. 50–51.

89 *"White men, well trained . . .":* McGillycuddy's disillusioned remarks appear in CIA, *Annual Reports,* 1881, pp. 46–47.

91 *"There is no selfishness . . .":* Senator Dawes's remarks appear in Washburn, *The Assault on Indian Tribalism,* p. 17.

92 *"They made us many . . .":* Red Cloud's oft-quoted comment is found in numerous Native American books and Western history anthologies.

93 *"My people looked . . .":* For Black Elk's comments upon returning to Pine Ridge, see Neihardt, *Black Elk Speaks,* p. 195.

93 *"It is hard to overstate . . .":* Commissioner T. J. Morgan is quoted in CIA, *Annual Reports,* 1891, pp. 132–133.

CHAPTER 4

98 *"When you get home, . . .":* Wovoka's letter to the Sioux delegation is cited in McGregor, *The Wounded Knee Massacre,* pp. 41–42.

100 *"Hope becomes a faith . . .":* For Mooney's observations on the Ghost Dance, see Utley, *The Last Days of the Sioux Nation,* p. 71.

104 *"At one point, Royer":* Royer's fleeting attempt to have a relative teach the Lakota the American game of baseball was told to the author by descendants of the baseball-playing relative.

104 *"Indians are dancing . . .":* Royer's November 18 telegraph message is found in Commissioner of Indian Affairs, *Annual Reports,* 1891, p. 128.

105 *"The pitiful little gardens . . .":* Elaine Goodale is quoted in Utley, p. 77.

105 *"From the best . . .":* See Chadron *Democrat* (27 Nov. 1890).

107 *"I don't want to . . .":* Sitting Bull's remark is quoted in Ambrose, *Crazy Horse and Custer,* p. 17.

109 *"Your white missionaries . . .":* Dr. Valentine McGillycuddy quotes Little Wound in *The New York Times* (3 March 1901).

111 *"Sitting Bull is . . .":* Agent McLaughlin discusses his views of Sitting Bull and the Ghost Dance in the CIA, *Annual Reports,* 1891, pp. 125–126.

113 *"convinced that Big Foot . . ."*:   Lt. Colonel Sumner offers his thoughts on Big Foot in a detailed report dated Feb. 3, 1891. See House of Representatives Executive Documents 1891–92, pp. 223–228.

113 *"If he succeeded in"*:   Red Cloud's offer of one hundred ponies if Big Foot could patch up a dispute on Pine Ridge is in Danker, "The Wounded Knee Interviews of Eli S. Ricker," p. 180.

116 *"If he fights, . . ."*:   The army dispatch to field commanders is in Utley, p. 193.

122 *"The struggle for the gun . . ."*:   Dewey Beard is quoted in Danker, pp. 180–200.

127 *"This is to certify . . ."*:   For Beard's army commendation, see McGregor, p. 107.

128 *"All of this . . ."*:   Dr. Eastman's observations appear in Utley, p. 3.

128 *"We tried to run . . ."*:   Statements of the Wounded Knee survivors can be found in McGregor, pp. 103–139.

130 *"It was a thing to melt . . ."*:   The remark from an observer at the mass burial is in Utley, p. 4.

131 *"Wholesale massacre occurred . . ."*:   The letter from Miles is quoted in Green, "The Medals of Wounded Knee," p. 201.

132 *"There is nothing to conceal . . ."*:   The army report written by General Scott is quoted in *University of Nebraska*, "As Long as the Grass Shall Grow," p. 9.

133 *"I kept going in . . ."*:   For Corporal Weinert's comment on rolling his cannon down the hill, see Jensen et al., *Eyewitness at Wounded Knee*, p. 128.

CHAPTER 5

145 *"One year, when 125 Indians"*:   The breakdown of Indians traveling with Cody and their monthly salaries are contained in a letter dated April 11, 1895, from Capt. Charles Penney, acting Pine Ridge agent, to the Commissioner of Indian Affairs found in the Nebraska State Historical Society, RG 508, pp. 261–264.

148 *"The meat was cut . . ."*:   Standing Bear, *My People the Sioux*, p. 251.

152 *"The effect of traveling . . ."*:   For Commissioner Oberley's comment, see Rosa, *Buffalo Bill and His Wild West*, p. 147.

153 *"The effect of the ghost dances . . ."*:   Minister Williamson's comment appears in Commissioner of Indian Affairs, *Annual Reports*, 1892, p. 459.

159 *"The allotments of their lands . . ."*:   Agent Penney's remark on allotments is from the CIA, *Annual Reports*, 1894, p. 289.

159 *"The Indians fear "that if . . ."*:   Acting agent Clapp is quoted from CIA, *Annual Reports*, 1898, p. 276.

160 *"The general outlook . . ."*:   Agent Penney's statement that the outlook for winter is not cheerful is found in CIA, *Annual Reports*, 1893, p. 289.

161   *"The besetting sin . . .":*   Penney's remarks on the besetting sin of Indians is from CIA, *Annual Reports,* 1894, p. 288.

162   *"He can see something . . .":*   Inspector Dew is quoted in CIA, *Annual Reports,* 1898, p. 280.

CHAPTER 6

171   *" 'My friend,' he told":*   Crazy Horse's reaction to being photographed is found in McLuhan, *Touch the Earth,* p. 67.

176   *"They [the Indians] look . . .":*   Marshall's comments are contained in the landmark 1831 ruling *Cherokee Nation v Georgia,* in which Marshall wrote the majority opinion. See Wilkinson, *Indian Tribes as Sovereign Governments,* p. 106.

178   *" 'Such a race,' he said":*   The comments of Commissioner Jones are found in Prucha, *The Great Father,* pp. 764–766.

186   *"My sun is set . . .":*   Red Cloud's farewell address is quoted in Walker and DeMallie, *Lakota Belief and Ritual,* pp. 137–140.

CHAPTER 7

192   *"Founded by Army Capt.":*   For information on Captain Pratt and the Carlisle Indian School, see Berkhofer, *The White Man's Indian,* p. 171, and Prucha, *The Great Father,* pp. 694–700.

192   *"A Lakota from the":*   The plight of Plenty Horses is described in Utley, *The Last Days of the Sioux Nation,* pp. 257–58 and 265–66.

193   *"The Haskell Institute opened":*   Background information on the Haskell Institute, its opening, its early problems and the cemetery for those who died there, is found in Miller, "Tribes that Slumber," pp. 38–41.

194   *"Guy Dull Knife arrived":*   All information regarding dates and correspondence while Guy Dull Knife Sr. attended Haskell come from his personal file, supplied to the author by the school.

202   *"The idea that an American . . .":*   General Scott is quoted in Tate, "From Scout to Doughboy," p. 424.

204   *"I have been almost amazed . . .":*   Commissioner Sells is quoted in *The Literary Digest,* p. 62.

205   *"Stand by the flag, . . .":*   The editorial encouraging Indians to stand by the flag appears in Barsh, "American Indians in the Great War," p. 288.

205   *"The men wanted to go; . . .":*   Joseph Cloud, quoted in ibid., p. 279, *Baltimore Star, New York Evening World,* President Wilson, quoted in ibid., p. 277.

209   *" 'War,' observed the":*   *New York Evening World,* quoted in ibid., p 289.

209   *"Yes, von Hind . . .":*   *New York Mail,* quoted in ibid., p. 291.

209   *"There was some question . . .":*   *Literary Digest,* quoted in ibid., p. 290.

211   *"Indian soldiers had suffered":*   For a detailed account of individual Indian heroism, see Tate, pp. 417–436, and Dept. of Interior, Office of Indian Affairs, *The American Indian.*

213   *"Perhaps the most enduring":*   Indian code talkers are discussed in Tate, p. 432.

214   *"war is a terrible thing, . . .":*   Louis Atkins is quoted in Barsh, p. 294.

214   *"One Cheyenne, typical, . . .":*   The Oklahoma Indian agent is quoted in Dept. of Interior, Office of Indian Affairs, *The American Indian.*

214   *"They were in practically all . . .":*   The 1919 Department of Interior releases are quoted in Barsh, p. 294.

214   *"On Pine Ridge,":*   For references to the economic and social conditions on the Pine Ridge Reservation, including its cattle herds during the war years, see V. Deloria, *Behind the Trail of Broken Treaties,* pp. 68–69. Additional background information for this chapter can be found in Cruttwell, *A History of the Great War: 1914–1918.*

CHAPTER 8

217   *"In a long-ago winter":*   The story of White Buffalo Calf Woman is a composite drawn from DeMallie, *The Sixth Grandfather,* pp. 283–285; Marla Powers, *Oglala Women,* pp. 42–52; and William Powers, *Oglala Religion,* pp. 81–83.

219   *"While women often dominated":*   For a detailed account of how the Lakota viewed women and the buffalo, and the relationship of men and women in traditional Oglala society, see M. Powers, *Oglala Women: Myth, Ritual, and Reality.*

235   *"A one-time New York City":*   For a description of Collier, see Deloria, *Behind the Trail of Broken Treaties,* pp. 192–198.

236   *"We believe that the . . .":*   Collier is quoted in Biolosi, *Organizing the Lakota,* pp. 63, xix and xx.

238   *"Collier's radical overhaul":*   Some of the background on Collier and the Indian Reorganization Act in this chapter is found in V. Deloria, pp. 187–206.

240   *"On Pine Ridge, the Oglala":*   For a thorough discussion of tribal politics among the Oglala of Pine Ridge before the IRA, see Clow, "The Indian Reorganization Act and the Loss of Tribal Sovereignty," pp. 125–134.

241   *"Nevertheless, the watered-down":*   For specific language of the government adopted in Jan. 1936 by the Oglala, see Dept. of the Interior, Office of Indian Affairs, *Constitution and By-Laws.*

CHAPTER 9

253   *"Among those he met"*: For Beard's meeting with Admiral Dewey and his name change, see Miller, "Echoes of the Little Bighorn," p. 39.

CHAPTER 10

275   *"Located on the South China Sea"*: A description of the massive U.S. military complex at Cam Ranh Bay can be found in Esper, *The Eyewitness History of the Vietnam War*, p. 92.

277   *"About a year earlier"*: Background on the Tet Offensive used in this chapter is contained in Karnow, *Vietnam: A History*, pp. 515–566.

CHAPTER 11

297   *"One evening in February"*: Detailed accounts of the beating death of Raymond Yellow Thunder, the investigation, and AIM's role in the aftermath are found in: The Gordon (NE) *Journal*, (23 Feb., 8, 15 and 29 March 1972) and the Lincoln (NE) *Star*, (5, 6, 8–11 March 1972).

298   *"Among many Oglala traditionals,"*: Information on Dick Wilson, his background and use of tribal funds, his attitude toward AIM and how he conducted his office, are found in Matthiessen's excellent account, *In the Spirit of Crazy Horse*, pp. 60–63, and in Anderson et al., *Voices from Wounded Knee*, pp. 17–19.

299   *"Shortly after arriving"*: See V. Deloria, *Behind the Trail of Broken Treaties*, pp. 70–73, for information used in this chapter on Wilson, Means, AIM and the demonstration in Gordon.

299   *"In years past, Leslie"*: Background information on Leslie and Melvin Hare was provided to the author from a personal friend who grew up in Gordon and knew the Hare family. Conviction and sentencing of the brothers is found in their criminal files at the Nebraska State Penitentiary.

300   *"In the traditional village"*: The Yellow Thunder family's attempts to get help before turning to AIM are found in Anderson et al., p. 13. The alliance between AIM and traditional Pine Ridge elders is recounted in Matthiessen, pp. 59–82.

301   *"Throughout the 1970s,"*: Background on the government's interest in maintaining control of Indian lands and its relationship with private corporations is found throughout Matthiessen's voluminous account, including pp. 104–106, 406–411 and 417–419.

303   *"After five days,"*: The Indians' departure from Washington, the government's rejection of their twenty-point proposal and the placement of its

leaders on the FBI's list of extremists are found in Matthiessen, pp. 54–56.

304   *"If Russell Means . . .":*   Wilson's remark regarding cutting off Means's braid, quoted in ibid., p. 61.

305   *"On the evening of January 21,":*   Information relating to the murder of Bad Heart Bull and details of the confrontation and ensuing riot in Custer can be found in Matthiessen, pp. 62–64, and V. Deloria, pp. 63–64.

305   *"When it ended, thirty":*   The number of Indians arrested and indicted as a result of the Custer protest and the disposition of the state's case against Sarah Bad Heart Bull are found in *Wounded Knee Legal Defense/Offense Committee,* "Wounded Knee 1890–1973," p. 15.

306   *"Back on the reservation,":*   Wilson's reaction to the riot in Custer, his press releases suggesting AIM members be killed and the arrival of sixty-five federal marshals on Pine Ridge are found in V. Deloria, pp. 70–71, and Anderson et al., p. 16.

306   *"It was up to the chiefs":*   See Matthiessen, pp. 63–64, for a description of events that led to the occupation of the village of Wounded Knee.

307   *"We decided that we did need . . .":*   Ellen Moves Camp is quoted in Anderson et al., p. 14.

307   *"Within a few days,":*   The list of government weapons brought into Wounded Knee are found in *Akwesasne Notes,* "Ken Tilsen, WKLDOC Lawyer, Speaks on the Trials," p. 13.

310   *"In the aftermath of Wounded Knee,":*   See Matthiessen, p. 82, for information regarding the lack of prosecution of Wilson and goon squad members, and the arrest figures of those involved in the occupation of Wounded Knee.

311   *"It's hard for me to believe . . .":*   Judge Nichol's remarks regarding FBI conduct and his comment on government prosecution in the case are found in Matthiessen, p. 98.

311   *"Charges against the third leader,":*   For sources on the murder of Bissonette and the lawless rampage against Pine Ridge traditionals, see *Wounded Knee Legal Defense/Offense Committee,* pp. 17–18, and Matthiessen, pp. 99–101.

313   *"Guy Dull Knife Jr. did not think":*   DeSersa's death is also described in Matthiessen, pp. 254–255.

316   *"But in the aftermath":*   Charlotte Black Elk, in conversations with the author, discussed at length some of the many changes that unfolded on Pine Ridge, changes that helped give Lakota children a stronger cultural identity than previous generations.

319   *"Edith was eighty-seven":*   Edith Bull Bear's appearance in federal court is found in Ortiz, *The Great Sioux Nation,* p. 43.

320   *"Five years after her death,":*   The U.S. Supreme Court decision regarding the Black Hills, the treaty of 1868 and the award of damages to the

Lakota is found in U.S. Supreme Court, *United States, petitioner v Sioux Nation*, pp. 2716–2752, and Supreme Court *Reporter*, "Summary of October 1979 Term: Indians" (Oct. 1979), pp. 414–416.

CHAPTER 12

343   *"In 1994, for the fourth":* Oglala Sioux and Pine Ridge Reservation health and poverty statistics are found in: Select Committee on Children, Youth, and Families, House of Representatives, 102nd Cong., 2nd Sess., Hearing, May 19, 1992, Washington, D.C., Fact Sheet, pp. 7–8; Indian Health Service statistics, 1991; Census Bureau data, 1992; *The New York Times*, 20 Sept. 1992, p. 1; *Washington Post*, 11 Nov. 1992, p. 3; *USA Today*, 30 Nov. 1992, p. 7; Omaha *World-Herald*, 23 June 1993, p. 8, and *USA Today*, 2 Sept. 1994, p. 5.

Index

Italics indicate illustrations